LLEWELLYN'S

1998
SUN SIGN
BOOK

FORECASTS BY GLORIA STAR

Editors: Roxanna Rejali and
Cynthia Ahlquist
Book Design: Roxanna Rejali
Cover Design: Anne Marie Garrison
Cover Art: Brian Jensen

Copyright © 1997
Llewellyn Publications
A Division of Llewellyn Worldwide, Ltd.
P.O. Box 64383
Dept. 932-6
St. Paul, MN 55164-0383

ISBN 1-56718-932-6

1997

JANUARY
S	M	T	W	T	F	S
			1	2	3	4
5	6	7	8	9	10	11
12	13	14	15	16	17	18
19	20	21	22	23	24	25
26	27	28	29	30	31	

FEBRUARY
S	M	T	W	T	F	S
						1
2	3	4	5	6	7	8
9	10	11	12	13	14	15
16	17	18	19	20	21	22
23	24	25	26	27	28	

MARCH
S	M	T	W	T	F	S
						1
2	3	4	5	6	7	8
9	10	11	12	13	14	15
16	17	18	19	20	21	22
23	24	25	26	27	28	29
30	31					

APRIL
S	M	T	W	T	F	S
		1	2	3	4	5
6	7	8	9	10	11	12
13	14	15	16	17	18	19
20	21	22	23	24	25	26
27	28	29	30			

MAY
S	M	T	W	T	F	S
				1	2	3
4	5	6	7	8	9	10
11	12	13	14	15	16	17
18	19	20	21	22	23	24
25	26	27	28	29	30	31

JUNE
S	M	T	W	T	F	S
1	2	3	4	5	6	7
8	9	10	11	12	13	14
15	16	17	18	19	20	21
22	23	24	25	26	27	28
29	30					

JULY
S	M	T	W	T	F	S
		1	2	3	4	5
6	7	8	9	10	11	12
13	14	15	16	17	18	19
20	21	22	23	24	25	26
27	28	29	30	31		

AUGUST
S	M	T	W	T	F	S
					1	2
3	4	5	6	7	8	9
10	11	12	13	14	15	16
17	18	19	20	21	22	23
24	25	26	27	28	29	30
31						

SEPTEMBER
S	M	T	W	T	F	S
	1	2	3	4	5	6
7	8	9	10	11	12	13
14	15	16	17	18	19	20
21	22	23	24	25	26	27
28	29	30				

OCTOBER
S	M	T	W	T	F	S
			1	2	3	4
5	6	7	8	9	10	11
12	13	14	15	16	17	18
19	20	21	22	23	24	25
26	27	28	29	30	31	

NOVEMBER
S	M	T	W	T	F	S
						1
2	3	4	5	6	7	8
9	10	11	12	13	14	15
16	17	18	19	20	21	22
23	24	25	26	27	28	29
30						

DECEMBER
S	M	T	W	T	F	S
	1	2	3	4	5	6
7	8	9	10	11	12	13
14	15	16	17	18	19	20
21	22	23	24	25	26	27
28	29	30	31			

1998

JANUARY
S	M	T	W	T	F	S
				1	2	3
4	5	6	7	8	9	10
11	12	13	14	15	16	17
18	19	20	21	22	23	24
25	26	27	28	29	30	31

FEBRUARY
S	M	T	W	T	F	S
1	2	3	4	5	6	7
8	9	10	11	12	13	14
15	16	17	18	19	20	21
22	23	24	25	26	27	28

MARCH
S	M	T	W	T	F	S
1	2	3	4	5	6	7
8	9	10	11	12	13	14
15	16	17	18	19	20	21
22	23	24	25	26	27	28
29	30	31				

APRIL
S	M	T	W	T	F	S
			1	2	3	4
5	6	7	8	9	10	11
12	13	14	15	16	17	18
19	20	21	22	23	24	25
26	27	28	29	30		

MAY
S	M	T	W	T	F	S
					1	2
3	4	5	6	7	8	9
10	11	12	13	14	15	16
17	18	19	20	21	22	23
24	25	26	27	28	29	30
31						

JUNE
S	M	T	W	T	F	S
	1	2	3	4	5	6
7	8	9	10	11	12	13
14	15	16	17	18	19	20
21	22	23	24	25	26	27
28	29	30				

JULY
S	M	T	W	T	F	S
			1	2	3	4
5	6	7	8	9	10	11
12	13	14	15	16	17	18
19	20	21	22	23	24	25
26	27	28	29	30	31	

AUGUST
S	M	T	W	T	F	S
						1
2	3	4	5	6	7	8
9	10	11	12	13	14	15
16	17	18	19	20	21	22
23	24	25	26	27	28	29
30	31					

SEPTEMBER
S	M	T	W	T	F	S
		1	2	3	4	5
6	7	8	9	10	11	12
13	14	15	16	17	18	19
20	21	22	23	24	25	26
27	28	29	30			

OCTOBER
S	M	T	W	T	F	S
				1	2	3
4	5	6	7	8	9	10
11	12	13	14	15	16	17
18	19	20	21	22	23	24
25	26	27	28	29	30	31

NOVEMBER
S	M	T	W	T	F	S
1	2	3	4	5	6	7
8	9	10	11	12	13	14
15	16	17	18	19	20	21
22	23	24	25	26	27	28
29	30					

DECEMBER
S	M	T	W	T	F	S
		1	2	3	4	5
6	7	8	9	10	11	12
13	14	15	16	17	18	19
20	21	22	23	24	25	26
27	28	29	30	31		

1999

JANUARY
S	M	T	W	T	F	S
					1	2
3	4	5	6	7	8	9
10	11	12	13	14	15	16
17	18	19	20	21	22	23
24	25	26	27	28	29	30
31						

FEBRUARY
S	M	T	W	T	F	S
	1	2	3	4	5	6
7	8	9	10	11	12	13
14	15	16	17	18	19	20
21	22	23	24	25	26	27
28						

MARCH
S	M	T	W	T	F	S
	1	2	3	4	5	6
7	8	9	10	11	12	13
14	15	16	17	18	19	20
21	22	23	24	25	26	27
28	29	30	31			

APRIL
S	M	T	W	T	F	S
				1	2	3
4	5	6	7	8	9	10
11	12	13	14	15	16	17
18	19	20	21	22	23	24
25	26	27	28	29	30	

MAY
S	M	T	W	T	F	S
						1
2	3	4	5	6	7	8
9	10	11	12	13	14	15
16	17	18	19	20	21	22
23	24	25	26	27	28	29
30	31					

JUNE
S	M	T	W	T	F	S
		1	2	3	4	5
6	7	8	9	10	11	12
13	14	15	16	17	18	19
20	21	22	23	24	25	26
27	28	29	30			

JULY
S	M	T	W	T	F	S
				1	2	3
4	5	6	7	8	9	10
11	12	13	14	15	16	17
18	19	20	21	22	23	24
25	26	27	28	29	30	31

AUGUST
S	M	T	W	T	F	S
1	2	3	4	5	6	7
8	9	10	11	12	13	14
15	16	17	18	19	20	21
22	23	24	25	26	27	28
29	30	31				

SEPTEMBER
S	M	T	W	T	F	S
			1	2	3	4
5	6	7	8	9	10	11
12	13	14	15	16	17	18
19	20	21	22	23	24	25
26	27	28	29	30		

OCTOBER
S	M	T	W	T	F	S
					1	2
3	4	5	6	7	8	9
10	11	12	13	14	15	16
17	18	19	20	21	22	23
24	25	26	27	28	29	30
31						

NOVEMBER
S	M	T	W	T	F	S
	1	2	3	4	5	6
7	8	9	10	11	12	13
14	15	16	17	18	19	20
21	22	23	24	25	26	27
28	29	30				

DECEMBER
S	M	T	W	T	F	S
			1	2	3	4
5	6	7	8	9	10	11
12	13	14	15	16	17	18
19	20	21	22	23	24	25
26	27	28	29	30	31	

TABLE OF CONTENTS

Meet Gloria Star. 5
New Concepts for Signs of the Zodiac 6
Signs of the Zodiac 8
Understanding the Basics of Astrology. 9
Using This Book 11
The Year 1998 at a Glance. 13
Ascendant Table 14
Astrological Dictionary 16
Meanings of the Planets. 22

1998 Sun Sign Forecasts

Aries 28
Taurus 51
Gemini 74
Cancer 97
Leo 120
Virgo. 143
Libra. 166
Scorpio. 189
Sagittarius. 212
Capricorn 235
Aquarius 258
Pisces 281
The Twelve Houses of the Zodiac. 304

1998 Sun Sign Articles

About Our Contributors 306

On the Path to Prosperity: A Journey through the Signs
    By Alice A. DeVille 307

All in the Family: Your Birth Order and Your Horoscope
    By Donna Cunningham 329

Why Am I Here? The Sun and Career Choices
    By Kim Rogers-Gallagher 340

Navigate the Starry Path of Love
    By Jeraldine Saunders 372

The Age of Aquarius
    By Estelle Daniels 379

Mayan Astrology
    By Ken Johnson 389

The Financial Forecast for 1998
    By Barbara Koval 392

Your Travel Outlook for 1998
    By Gloria Star 406

The Wonders of Vedic Astrology
    By Ronnie Dreyer 415

Psychic and Spiritual Planets in Astrology
    By Estelle Daniels 424

It's Time to Wind the Prediction Clock
    By Noel Tyl 438

Planetary Associations 446

Directory of Products and Services 447

MEET GLORIA STAR

All horoscopes and sign descriptions for this book were written by Gloria Star. An internationally renowned astrologer, author, and teacher, Gloria has been a professional astrologer for more than twenty years. She has written the *Llewellyn's Sun Sign Book* forecasts since 1990, and has been a contributing writer for the *Llewellyn's Moon Sign Book* since 1995. Most recently, she has been editor and contributing writer of a new anthology, *Astrology for Women: Roles and Relationships* (Llewellyn, 1997). She is also the author of *Optimum Child: Developing Your Child's Fullest Potential through Astrology* (Llewellyn, 1988), and has contributed to two anthologies—*Houses: Power Places in the Horoscope* (Llewellyn, 1990), and *How to Manage the Astrology of Crisis* (Llewellyn, 1993).

Gloria is listed in *Who's Who of American Women,* and is active in the astrological community. She has served on the faculty of the United Astrology Congress (UAC) since its inception in 1986, and has lectured for groups and conferences in the U.S.A. and abroad. She is a member of the advisory board for the National Council for Geocosmic Research (NCGR), has served on the steering committee for the Association for Astrological Networking (AFAN) and edited the AFAN newsletter from 1992–1997. She also writes a column for *The Mountain Astrologer* magazine.

NEW CONCEPTS FOR SIGNS OF THE ZODIAC

The signs of the zodiac represent characteristics and traits that indicate how energy operates within our lives. The signs tell the story of human evolution and development, and are all necessary to form the continuum of whole life experience. In fact, all twelve signs are represented within your astrological chart!

Although the traditional metaphors for the twelve signs (such as Aries, the Ram) are always functional, these alternative concepts for each of the twelve signs describe the gradual unfolding of the human spirit.

ARIES: The Initiator is the first sign of the zodiac and encompasses the primary concept of getting things started. This fiery ignition and bright beginning can prove to be the thrust necessary for new life, but the Initiator also can appear before a situation is ready for change and create disruption.

TAURUS: The Maintainer sustains what Aries has begun and brings stability and focus into the picture, yet there also can be a tendency to try to maintain something in its current state without allowing for new growth.

GEMINI: The Questioner seeks to determine if alternatives are possible and offers diversity to the processes Taurus has brought into stability. Yet questioning can also lead to distraction, subsequently scattering energy and diffusing focus.

CANCER: The Nurturer provides the qualities necessary for growth and security and encourages a deepening awareness of the emotional needs. Yet this same nurturance can stifle individuation if it becomes smothering.

LEO: The Loyalist directs and centralizes the experiences Cancer feeds. This quality is powerfully targeted toward self-awareness, but can be short-sighted. Hence, the Loyalist can hold steadfastly to viewpoints or feelings that inhibit new experiences.

VIRGO: The Modifier analyzes the situations Leo brings to light and determines possibilities for change. Even though this change may be in the name of improvement, it can lead to dissatisfaction with the self if not directed in harmony with higher needs.

LIBRA: The Judge is constantly comparing everything to be sure that a certain level of rightness and perfection is presented. However, the Judge can present possibilities that are harsh and seem to be cold or without feeling.

SCORPIO: The Catalyst steps into the play of life to provide the quality of alchemical transformation. The Catalyst can stir the brew just enough to create a healing potion, or may get things going to such a powerful extent that they boil out of control.

SAGITTARIUS: The Adventurer moves away from Scorpio's dimension to seek what lies beyond the horizon. The adventurer continually looks for possibilities that answer the ultimate questions, but may forget the pathway back home.

CAPRICORN: The Pragmatist attempts to put everything into its rightful place and find ways to make life work out right. The Pragmatist can teach lessons of practicality and determination, but can become highly self-righteous when short-sighted.

AQUARIUS: The Reformer looks for ways to take what Capricorn has built and bring it up to date. Yet there is also a tendency to scrap the original in favor of a new plan that may not have the stable foundation necessary to operate effectively.

PISCES: The Visionary brings mysticism and imagination, and challenges the soul to move into the realm beyond the physical plane, into what might be. The Visionary can pierce the veil, returning enlightened to the physical world. The challenge is to avoid getting lost within the illusion of an alternate reality.

SIGNS OF THE ZODIAC

Aries	♈	The Initiator
Taurus	♉	The Maintainer
Gemini	♊	The Questioner
Cancer	♋	The Nurturer
Leo	♌	The Loyalist
Virgo	♍	The Modifier
Libra	♎	The Judge
Scorpio	♏	The Catalyst
Sagittarius	♐	The Adventurer
Capricorn	♑	The Pragmatist
Aquarius	♒	The Reformer
Pisces	♓	The Visionary

UNDERSTANDING THE BASICS OF ASTROLOGY

By Gloria Star

A strology is an ancient and continually evolving system that can clarify your identity and your needs. Your astrological chart—which is calculated using the date, time, and place of your birth—contains many factors that symbolically represent needs, expression, and experiences that make up the whole *you*. A professional astrologer interprets this symbolic picture, offering you an accurate portrait of your personality.

The chart itself, your horoscope, is a symbol of the individual as a complete person. Generally, a natal (or birth) horoscope is drawn on a circular wheel. The wheel is divided into twelve segments, called the houses. Each of the twelve houses represents a different facet of the individual, much like the facets of a brilliantly cut stone. Your houses indicate the different environments in which you live your life and express yourself (such as home, school, work, institutions), and also represent your relationships (such as parents, friends, lovers, children, partners). In each environment, you show a different facet of yourself. At home, you may represent yourself quite differently than you would on the job. Additionally, in each relationship you will project a different part of yourself. Parents rarely see the side we show to our intimate friends.

The symbols for the planets, Sun, and Moon are placed within the circle and inside the houses. Each of these represents energy. You experience and express the energy of the Sun, Moon, and planets in specific ways. Refer to the following table for quick reference.

9

SUN	☉	The Ego Self, Willpower
MOON	☽	The Subconscious Self, Habits
MERCURY	☿	Communication, The Intellect
VENUS	♀	Emotional Expression, Love, Appreciation, Artistry
MARS	♂	Physical Drive, Assertiveness, Anger
JUPITER	♃	Philosophy, Ethics, Generosity
SATURN	♄	Discipline, Focus, Responsibility
URANUS	♅	Individuality, Rebelliousness
NEPTUNE	♆	Imagination, Sensitivity, Compassion
PLUTO	♇	Transformation, Healing, Regeneration

The way you use each of these energies is up to you. The planets in your chart do not make you do anything!

The twelve signs of the zodiac indicate the characteristics and traits that further define your personality and needs. Each sign has positive and negative forms of expression. The basic meaning of each sign is explained in the corresponding sections ahead. One thing to keep in mind: you have all twelve signs somewhere in your chart! But those signs that are strongly emphasized by the planets have greater emphasis. The Sun, Moon, and planets are placed within a certain degree of a sign according to their position at the time of your birth. The qualities of a sign, combined with the energy of a planet, indicate how you might be most likely to use that energy and the best ways to develop that energy. The signs add color, emphasis, and dimension to the energy of your personality.

The signs are also placed at the cusps, or dividing lines, of each house. The influence of the signs on the houses is much the same as their influence on the Sun, Moon, and planets. The basic indicator of the house would be influenced or shaped by the quality of the sign on the cusp of that house. When you view the horoscope, you will notice that there appear to be four distinctive angles dividing the wheel of the chart. The line dividing the chart into a top and bottom half represents the horizon. In most cases, the left side of this horizon is called the Ascendant. The zodiac sign on the Ascendant is your rising sign. This point in the chart shows the mask of your personality, and indicates the way that others are likely to view you.

In a nutshell, the Sun, Moon, or planet indicate what the energy is, much like the actor in a drama. The sign shows how the energy works, like the role the actor plays in a drama. The house indicates where the energy operates, like the setting or scene of a play. On a psychological level, the Sun represents who you think you are, the Ascendant depicts who others think you are, and the Moon shows your inner self.

Astrologers also study the geometric relationships between the Sun, Moon, and planets. These geometric angles are called aspects. Aspects further define the strengths, weaknesses, and challenges within your physical, mental, emotional, and spiritual self. Sometimes, particular patterns also appear within an astrological chart. These patterns also have meaning.

To understand cycles for any given point in time, astrologers study several factors. One commonly used technique is called the transit, which refers to the position of a planet at a given time. Using the positions of the planets, Sun, and Moon for any given date, an astrologer compares that position to your birth horoscope. The transit indicates an activation of energy in a particular area of your chart. The *Sun Sign Book* is written using the technique of transits.

As you can see, your Sun sign is only one factor among many that describes who you are, but it is a powerful one! As the symbol of the ego self, the Sun in your chart shows your drive to be noticed as a significant human being. Most people can easily relate to the concepts associated with their Sun sign, since it is tied to the ego or sense of personal identity.

USING THIS BOOK

The horoscopes in the following section are based on the sign the Sun was in at the time of your birth. Although we can examine a number of your needs and life situations from this information, there are many other factors a professional astrologer would explore to help you guide your life. If you would like more information to accompany the guidelines in this book, you might appreciate the personalized, more detailed insights you'll receive from a competent professional astrologer.

I've described the year's major challenges and opportunities for every Sun sign in the "Year Ahead" section. The first part of the section applies to all individuals born under the influence of the sign. In addition, I've included information for specific birth dates that will help you understand the inner process of change you'll be experiencing during 1998. The cycles described in this section illustrate your fundamental themes for the year ahead. Consider these ideas as underlying principles that will be present throughout the entire year. These cycles comprise your major challenges and opportunities relating to your personal identity. Blend these ideas with the information you find in the monthly forecast section for your Sun sign and Ascendant.

To best use the information in the monthly forecasts, you'll want to determine your Ascendant, or rising sign. If you don't know your Ascendant, the Ascendant tables (on pages 14–15 of this book) can help you determine your rising sign. They are most accurate for those born in the Western Hemisphere between 60–130 degrees longitude (e.g., the continental United States). These tables are only an approximation, but can be used as a good rule of thumb. Your exact Ascendant may vary from the tables according to your time and place of birth.

Once you've approximated your ascending sign using the tables or determined your Ascendant by having your chart calculated, you'll know two significant factors in your astrological chart. Read the monthly forecast sections for both your Sun and Ascendant to gain the most useful information.

The "Rewarding and Challenging Days" sections within this book's monthly forecasts indicate times when you'll feel more centered ("Rewarding") or out of balance ("Challenging"). The rewarding days are not the only times you can perform well, but you're likely to feel better integrated! These days support your expression of individual identity. During the challenging days, take some extra time to center yourself by meditating or using other techniques that help you feel more objective.

These guidelines, although highly useful, cannot incorporate all the factors influencing your current life situation. However, you can use this information as a form of objective awareness about the way the current cycles are affecting you at an ego level.

THE YEAR 1998 AT A GLANCE

There are some positive and exciting changes symbolized by the planetary cycles for 1998. One of the outstanding features of this year involves a challenge to break through our illusions and discover the underlying truths. These challenges emerge in the collective, by examining and uncovering our icons and beliefs. Outdated icons indicate that it is time to create new heroes and heroines and to develop a new mythology to reflect our current state of consciousness.

In many respects, this is a year that will highlight the importance of the spiritual realm. Humanity is ready to be uplifted, and our creative and technological developments are likely to illustrate and reflect that need. Expect some truly fanciful experiences through movies, TV, and even more magical developments in the world of computers and technology. With Uranus and Neptune both transiting through the sign of Aquarius, things once thought impossible may be within our grasp. Expect to see exciting news from astronomy and space exploration.

On the national and global political fronts, our challenges involve the need to deal with environmental and economic matters in a very realistic manner. Be ready for some of our leaders to try some very strange illusory ideas in their attempts to mask a real solution to our dilemmas in these areas. Since Pluto is still transiting in Sagittarius, further permutations in the law are also continuing. Although the legal system may need reform, it can also be manipulated and abused. It is my hope that truth will ultimately triumph over personal power issues.

On a personal level, seek opportunities to further develop your faith in higher law. Allow time and space in your life for your spirituality. Make this a year to accelerate your inner growth and demonstrate to yourself the truth that you are, indeed, creating your own reality.

Enjoy a purely delightful year!

Ascendant Table

Your Time of Birth

Your Sun Sign	6–8 AM	8–10 AM	10 AM–Noon	Noon–2 PM	2–4 PM	4–6 PM
Aries	Taurus	Gemini	Cancer	Leo	Virgo	Libra
Taurus	Gemini	Cancer	Leo	Virgo	Libra	Scorpio
Gemini	Cancer	Leo	Virgo	Libra	Scorpio	Sagittarius
Cancer	Leo	Virgo	Libra	Scorpio	Sagittarius	Capricorn
Leo	Virgo	Libra	Scorpio	Sagittarius	Capricorn	Aquarius
Virgo	Libra	Scorpio	Sagittarius	Capricorn	Aquarius	Pisces
Libra	Scorpio	Sagittarius	Capricorn	Aquarius	Pisces	Aries
Scorpio	Sagittarius	Capricorn	Aquarius	Pisces	Aries	Taurus
Sagittarius	Capricorn	Aquarius	Pisces	Aries	Taurus	Gemini
Capricorn	Aquarius	Pisces	Aries	Taurus	Gemini	Cancer
Aquarius	Pisces	Aries	Taurus	Gemini	Cancer	Leo
Pisces	Aries	Taurus	Gemini	Cancer	Leo	Virgo

YOUR TIME OF BIRTH

YOUR SUN SIGN	6–8 PM	8–10 PM	10 PM–MIDNIGHT	MIDNIGHT–2 AM	2–4 AM	4–6 AM
ARIES	Scorpio	Sagittarius	Capricorn	Aquarius	Pisces	Aries
TAURUS	Sagittarius	Capricorn	Aquarius	Pisces	Aries	Taurus
GEMINI	Capricorn	Aquarius	Pisces	Aries	Taurus	Gemini
CANCER	Aquarius	Pisces	Aries	Taurus	Gemini	Cancer
LEO	Pisces	Aries	Taurus	Gemini	Cancer	Leo
VIRGO	Aries	Taurus	Gemini	Cancer	Leo	Virgo
LIBRA	Taurus	Gemini	Cancer	Leo	Virgo	Libra
SCORPIO	Gemini	Cancer	Leo	Virgo	Libra	Scorpio
SAGITTARIUS	Cancer	Leo	Virgo	Libra	Scorpio	Sagittarius
CAPRICORN	Leo	Virgo	Libra	Scorpio	Sagittarius	Capricorn
AQUARIUS	Virgo	Libra	Scorpio	Sagittarius	Capricorn	Aquarius
PISCES	Libra	Scorpio	Sagittarius	Capricorn	Aquarius	Pisces

HOW TO USE THIS TABLE: 1. Find your Sun sign in the left column.
2. Find your approximate birth time in a vertical column.
3. Line up your Sun sign and birth time to find your Ascendant.

This table will give you an *approximation* of your Ascendant. If you feel that the sign listed as your Ascendant is incorrect, try the one either before or after the listed sign. It is impossible to determine your exact Ascendant without a complete natal chart.

ASTROLOGICAL DICTIONARY

AIR
One of the four elements. The air signs are Gemini, Libra, and Aquarius.

ANGLES
The four points of the chart dividing it into quadrants. The angles are sensitive areas that lend emphasis to planets located near them. These points are located on the cusps of the First, Fourth, Seventh, and Tenth Houses in a chart.

ASCENDANT
Rising sign. The degree of the zodiac on the eastern horizon at the time and place for which the horoscope is calculated. It can indicate the image or physical appearance you project to the world. The cusp of the First House.

ASPECT
The angular relationship between planets, sensitive points, or house cusps in the horoscope. Lines drawn between the two points and the center of the chart, representing the Earth, form the angle of the aspect, which is equivalent to the number of degrees of arc between the two points. Some important aspects used in astrology are the conjunction (two points that are 0 degrees apart, or in the same place), the opposition (two points, 180 degrees apart), the square (two points, 90 degrees apart), the sextile (two points, 60 degrees apart), and the trine (two points, 120 degrees apart). Aspects can indicate harmonious or challenging relationships between the two planets involved.

CARDINAL SIGN

Cardinal is one of the three qualities, or categories that describe how a sign expresses itself. Aries, Cancer, Libra, and Capricorn are the cardinal signs. Cardinal signs are believed to be those that initiate activity.

CHIRON

Chiron is a comet traveling in orbit between Saturn and Uranus. Although research on its effect on natal charts is not yet complete, it is believed to represent a key or doorway, healing, ecology, and a bridge between traditional methods and modern ones.

CONJUNCTION

An aspect or angle between two points in a chart where the two points are close enough so that the energies join. Can be considered either harmonious or challenging, depending on the planets involved and their placement.

CUSP

A dividing line between signs or houses in a chart.

DEGREE

Degree of Arc. One of 360 divisions of a circle. The circle of the zodiac is divided into twelve astrological signs of 30 degrees each. Each degree is made up of 60 minutes, and each minute is made up of 60 seconds of zodiacal longitude.

EARTH

One of the four elements. The earth signs are Taurus, Virgo, and Capricorn.

ECLIPSE

A solar eclipse is the full or partial covering (as viewed from Earth) of the Sun by the Moon, and a lunar eclipse is the full or partial covering (as viewed from Earth) of the Moon by the Sun. The points at which eclipses happen in the sky can indicate change if the point of the eclipse is prominent in a natal chart.

ECLIPTIC

The Sun's apparent path around the Earth, which is actually the Earth's orbit extended out into space. The ecliptic forms the center of the zodiac.

ELECTIONAL ASTROLOGY

A branch of astrology concerned with picking the most advantageous time to initiate an activity.

ELEMENTS

The signs of the zodiac are divided into four groups of three zodiacal signs, each symbolized by one of the four elements of the ancients: fire, earth, air, water. The element of a sign is said to express its essential nature.

EPHEMERIS

A listing of the Sun, Moon, and planets' positions and related information for astrological purposes.

EQUINOX

Equal night. The point in the Earth's orbit around the Sun at which the day and night are equal in length.

FEMININE SIGNS

Each of the twelve signs of the zodiac is considered to be either "masculine" or "feminine." The earth signs (Taurus, Virgo, and Capricorn) and the water signs (Cancer, Scorpio, and Pisces) are considered feminine.

FIRE

One of the four elements. The fire signs are Aries, Leo, and Sagittarius.

FIXED SIGNS

Fixed is one of the three qualities, or categories that describe how a sign expresses itself. The fixed signs are Taurus, Leo, Scorpio, and Aquarius. Fixed signs are said to be predisposed to existing patterns, and somewhat resistant to change.

HARD ASPECTS

Hard aspects are those aspects in a chart that astrologers believe to represent difficulty or challenges. Among the hard aspects are the square, the opposition, and the conjunction (depending on which planets are conjunct).

HORIZON

The word *horizon* is used in astrology in a manner similar to its common usage, except that only the eastern and western horizons are considered useful. The eastern horizon at the point of birth is the Ascendant, or First House cusp of a natal chart, and the western horizon at the point of birth is the Descendant, or Seventh House cusp.

Houses

Division of the horoscope into twelve segments, beginning with the Ascendant. The dividing line between the houses are called house cusps. Each house corresponds to certain aspects of daily living, and is ruled by the astrological sign that governs the cusp, or dividing line between the house and the one previous.

Ingress

The point of entry of a planet into a sign.

Lagna

A term used in Hindu or vedic astrology for Ascendant, the degree of the zodiac on the eastern horizon at the time of birth.

Masculine Signs

Each of the twelve signs of the zodiac is considered to be either "masculine" or "feminine." The fire signs (Aries, Leo, and Sagittarius) and the air signs (Gemini, Libra, and Aquarius) are considered to be masculine.

Midheaven

Highest point on the ecliptic, where it intersects the meridian that passes directly above the place for which the horoscope is cast. The southern point of the horoscope.

Midpoint

A point equally distant to two planets or house cusps. Midpoints are considered by some astrologers to be sensitive points in a person's chart.

Mundane Astrology

Mundane astrology is the branch of astrology generally concerned with political and economic events, and the nations involved in these events.

Mutable Signs

Mutable is one of the three qualities, or categories that describe how a sign expresses itself. Mutable signs are Gemini, Virgo,

Sagittarius, and Pisces. Mutable signs are said to be very adaptable, but sometimes changeable.

NATAL CHART

A person's birth chart. A natal chart is essentially a "snapshot" showing the placement of each of the planets at the exact time of a person's birth.

OPPOSITION

An aspect where two points in a chart are 180 degrees apart.

ORB

A small degree margin used when calculating aspects in a chart. For example, although 180 degrees form an exact opposition, an astrologer might consider an aspect within 3 or 4 degrees on either side of 180 degrees to be an opposition, as the impact of the aspect can still be felt within this range. The less orb on an aspect, the stronger the aspect is. Astrologers' opinions vary on how many degrees of orb to allow for each aspect.

OUTER PLANETS

Uranus, Neptune, and Pluto are considered to be outer planets. Because of their distance from the Sun, these planets take a long time to complete a single rotation. They are considered valuable in determining how an individual fits into his or her generation, as everyone born within a few years on either side of a given date will have similar placements of these planets.

PLANETS

The planets used in astrology are Mercury, Venus, Mars, Jupiter, Saturn, Uranus, Neptune, and Pluto. For astrological purposes, the Sun and Moon are also considered planets. A natal or birth chart lists the exact placement for each of these planets at that moment.

PLANETARY RULERSHIP

The sign in which a planet is most harmoniously placed. Examples are the Sun in Leo, and the Moon in Cancer.

RETROGRADE MOTION

Apparent backward motion of a planet in the reverse order of the signs, from Aries toward Pisces, etc. This is an illusion caused by the relative motion of the Earth and the other planets in their elliptical orbits.

QUALITIES

In addition to categorizing the signs by element, astrologers place the twelve signs of the zodiac into three additional categories, or qualities: cardinal, mutable, or fixed. Each sign is considered to be a combination of its element and quality. Where the element of a sign describes its basic nature, the quality describes its mode of expression.

SEXTILE

An aspect where two points in a chart are 60 degrees apart.

SOFT ASPECTS

Soft aspects are those aspects considered by astrologers to indicate good fortune or an easy relationship in the chart. Among the soft aspects are the trine, the sextile, and the conjunction (depending on which planets are conjunct).

SQUARE

An aspect where two points in a chart are 90 degrees apart.

SUN SIGN

The sign of the zodiac in which the Sun is located at any given time.

TRINE

An aspect where two points in a chart are 120 degrees.

VOID-OF-COURSE

A planet (particularly the Moon) is said to be void-of-course after it has made its last aspect within a sign, but before it has entered a new sign.

WATER

One of the four elements. Water signs are Cancer, Scorpio, and Pisces.

Meanings of the Planets

The Sun

The Sun indicates the psychological bias that will dominate your actions. What you see, and why, is told in the reading for your Sun. The Sun also shows the basic energy patterns of your body and psyche. In many ways, the Sun is the dominant force in your horoscope and your life. Other influences, especially that of the Moon, may modify the Sun's influence, but nothing will cause you to depart very far from the basic solar pattern. Always keep in mind the basic influence of the Sun and remember all other influences must be interpreted in terms of it, especially insofar as other influences play a visible role in your life. You may think, dream, imagine, and hope a thousand things, according to your Moon and your other planets, but the Sun is what you are. To be your best self in terms of your Sun is to cause your energies to work along the path in which they will have maximum help from planetary vibrations.

The Moon

The Moon tells the desire of your life. When you "know what you mean but can't say it," it is your Moon that knows it and your Sun that can't say it. The wordless ecstasy, the mute sorrow, the secret dream, the esoteric picture of yourself that you can't get across to the world, or that the world doesn't comprehend or value—these are the products of the Moon in your horoscope. When you are misunderstood, it is your Moon nature, expressed imperfectly through the Sun sign, that feels betrayed. Things you know without thought—intuitions, hunches, instincts—are the products of the Moon. Modes of expression that you feel truly reflect your deepest self belong to the Moon: art, letters, creative work of any kind; sometimes love; sometimes business. Whatever you feel is most deeply yourself, whether or not you are able to do anything about it in the outer world, is the product of your Moon and of the sign your Moon occupies at birth.

MERCURY

Mercury is the sense-impression antenna of your horoscope. Its position by sign indicates your reactions to sights, sounds, odors, tastes, and touch impressions, affording a key to the attitude you have toward the physical world around you. Mercury is the messenger through which your physical body and brain (ruled by the Sun) and your inner nature (ruled by the Moon) are kept in contact with the outer world, which will appear to you according to the index of Mercury's position by sign in the horoscope. Mercury rules your rational mind.

VENUS

Venus is the emotional antenna of your horoscope. Through Venus, impressions come to you from the outer world, to which you react emotionally. The position of Venus by sign at the time of your birth determines your attitude toward these experiences. As Mercury is the messenger linking sense impressions (sight, smell, etc.) to the basic nature of your Sun and Moon, so Venus is the messenger linking emotional impressions. If Venus is found in the same sign as the Sun, emotions gain importance in your life, having a direct bearing on your actions. If Venus is in the same sign as the Moon, emotions also gain importance, bearing directly on your inner nature, adding self-confidence, making you sensitive to emotional impressions, and frequently indicating you have more love in your heart than you are able to express. If Venus is in the same sign as Mercury, emotional impressions and sense impressions work together; you tend to idealize the world of the senses and sensualize the world of the emotions to interpret emotionally what you see and hear.

MARS

Mars is the energy principle in the horoscope. Its position by sign indicates the channels into which energy will most easily be directed. It is the planet through which the activities of the Sun and the desires of the Moon express themselves in action. In the same sign as the Sun, Mars gives abundant energy, sometimes misdirected in temper, temperament, and quarrels. In the same sign as the Moon, it gives a great capacity to make use of the innermost aims, and to make the inner desires articulate and practical. In the same sign as Venus, it quickens emotional reactions and causes you to act on them, makes for ardor and passion in love, and fosters an earthly awareness of emotional realities.

JUPITER

Jupiter is the feeler for opportunity that you have out in the world. It passes along chances of a lifetime for consideration according to the basic nature of your Sun and Moon. Jupiter's sign position indicates the places where you will look for opportunity, the uses to which you wish to put it, and the capacity you have to react and profit by it. Jupiter is ordinarily, and erroneously, called the Planet of Luck. It is "luck" insofar as it is the index of opportunity, but your luck depends less on what comes to you (Jupiter) than on what you do with what comes to you (the total personality). In the same sign as the Sun or Moon, Jupiter gives a direct, and generally effective, response to opportunity and is likely to show forth at its "luckiest." If Jupiter is in the same sign as Mercury, sense impressions are interpreted opportunistically. If Jupiter is in the same sign as Venus, you interpret emotions in such a way as to turn them to your advantage; your feelings work harmoniously with the chances for progress that the world has to offer. If Jupiter is in the same sign as Mars, you follow opportunity with energy, dash, enthusiasm, and courage, take long chances, and play your cards wide open.

SATURN

Saturn indicates the direction that will be taken in life by the self-preservative principle which, in its highest manifestation, ceases to be purely defensive and becomes ambitious and aspirational. Your defense or attack against the world is shown by the sign position of Saturn in the horoscope of birth. If Saturn is in the same sign as the Sun or Moon, defense predominates, and there is danger of introversion. The farther Saturn is from the Sun, Moon, and Ascendant, the better for objectivity and extroversion. If Saturn is in the same sign as Mercury, there is a profound and serious reaction to sense impressions; this position generally accompanies a deep and efficient mind. If Saturn is in the same sign as Venus, a defensive attitude toward emotional experience makes for apparent coolness in love and difficulty with the emotions and human relations. If Saturn is in the same sign as Mars, confusion between defensive and aggressive urges can make an indecisive person—or, if the Sun and Moon are strong and the total personality well developed, a balanced, peaceful, and calm individual of sober judgment and moderate actions may be indicated. If Saturn is in the same sign as Jupiter, the reaction to opportunity is sober and balanced.

URANUS

Uranus in a general way relates to the neuro-mentality, the creative originality, or individuality, and its position by sign in the horoscope tells the direction along which you will seek to express your most characteristic self in creative and original effort. In the same sign as Mercury or the Moon, Uranus suggests acute awareness, a quick reaction to sense impressions and experiences, or a hair-trigger mind. In the same sign as the Sun, it points to great nervous activity, a high-strung nature, an original, creative, or eccentric personality. In the same sign as Mars, Uranus indicates high-speed activity, love of swift motion, and perhaps of danger. In the same sign as Venus, it suggests an unusual reaction to emotional experience, highly idealistic and sensual, original ideas of love and human relations. In the same sign as Saturn, Uranus points to good sense; this can be a practical, creative position, but, more often than not, it sets up a destroying conflict between practicality and originality that can result in a stalemate. In the same sign as Jupiter, Uranus makes opportunity, creates wealth and the means of getting it, and is conducive to the inventive, daring, and executive.

Neptune

Neptune relates to the deepest wells of the subconscious, inherited mentality and spirituality, indicating what you take deeply for granted in life. Neptune in the same sign as the Sun or Moon indicates that intuitions and hunches—or delusions—dominate; there is a need for rigidly holding to reality. In the same sign as Mercury, sharp sense perceptions, a sensitive and perhaps creative mind, a quivering intensity of reaction to sense experience. In the same sign as Venus, idealistic and romantic (or sentimental) reaction to emotional experience; danger of sensationalism and love of strange pleasures. In the same sign as Mars, energy and intuition that work together to make mastery of life—one of the signs of having angels (or devils) on your side. In the same sign as Jupiter, intuitive response to opportunity generally along practical and money-making lines; one of the signs of security if not indeed of wealth. In the same sign as Saturn, intuitive defense and attack on the world, generally successful unless Saturn is polarized on the negative side; then, danger of delusions and unhappiness.

Pluto

Pluto is a planet of extremes—from the lowest criminal and violent level of our society to the heights people can attain when they realize their significance in the collectivity of humanity. Pluto also rules three important mysteries of life—sex, death, and rebirth—and links them to each other. One level of death symbolized by Pluto is the physical death of an individual, which occurs so that a person can be reborn into another body to further his or her spiritual development. On another level, individuals can experience a "death" of their old self when they realize the deeper significance of life; thus they become one of the "second born." In a natal horoscope, Pluto signifies our perspective on the world, our conscience and subconscious. Since so many of Pluto's qualities are centered on the deeper mysteries of life, the house position of Pluto, and aspects to it, can show you how to attain a deeper understanding of the importance of the spiritual in your life.

LLEWELLYN'S

1998
SUN SIGN
FORECASTS

BY GLORIA STAR

ARIES

The Ram
March 20–April 20

Element:	Fire
Quality:	Cardinal
Polarity:	Yang/Masculine
Planetary Ruler:	Mars
Meditation:	"I actively pursue fulfillment of my destiny."
Gemstone:	Diamond
Power Stones:	Bloodstone, Carnelian, Sapphire, Ruby
Key Phrase:	"I am"
Glyph:	Ram's Head ♈
Anatomy:	Head, Face
Colors:	Red, White
Animal:	Ram
Myths/Legends:	Jason and the Golden Fleece, Artemis
House Association:	First
Opposite Sign:	Libra
Flower:	Geranium
Key Word:	Initiative

Positive Expression:		Misuse of Energy:	
Assertive	Energetic	Reckless	Blunt
Innovative	Incisive	Combative	Childish
Daring	Courageous	Careless	Rash
Self-Reliant	Exciting	Abrasive	Impatient

28

ARIES

YOUR EGO'S STRENGTHS AND WEAKNESSES

Your free-spirited approach to life is evident in your desire to meet challenges head-on, with ample courage and determination to succeed in your aims. You are a true pioneer and enjoy the experience of reaching the heights on your own merits. When life seems to be at a standstill, you're the one who gets things moving again, playing the role of the "Initiator" of the zodiac.

Through the energy of Mars, your ruling planet, you assert the strength, readiness, and vitality necessary to tackle any obstacles in your path. Since your daring exuberance can feel abrasive to others, it's important to be aware of the effects of your actions and attitudes. Mentally alert and keenly aware, you keep your sights set on the path ahead, rarely looking back. Your leadership and courage can inspire others; and where there is apathy, your actions and interest in moving forward set you apart from the crowd. Sometimes, your impetuous and impatient nature can be your worst enemy, particularly if slowing down is necessary.

With a hunger for a life filled with passion, you sometimes forget to stop long enough to savor the sweetness of your creations and can forget the importance of taking time out to revitalize yourself before continuing onward. Your zest for life adds a youthful vitality and you are blessed with the ability to create a truly joyful life.

YOUR APPROACH TO ROMANCE

The games of love can be your specialty. From your flirtatious teasing to the victory of conquest, you can be an ardent and passionate lover. Since you probably lack the patience to wait for another to make the first move, you sometimes jump in before the other person is ready. If he or she is comfortable with your fiery nature and can allow you the room you need to feel free and alive, the relationship can work. Shy types wilt in your presence, and those who are too possessive will probably wonder why you moved on. You can sustain love, but only if you have room to move and grow.

The other fire signs—Aries, Leo, and Sagittarius—will easily accept your volatility and enjoy your sharp mentality. You can be extremely passionate with another Aries, but may need some time out to cool your flames if tempers flare. The lover in you is ignited by Leo's warm playfulness, but she or he will expect your loyalty. Sagittarius' fun-loving humor and come-hither antics can be quite invigorating.

Taurus' slow pace is a stark contrast to your lightning speed, but you may love the sensual moments you share. With Gemini, you discover that sexual chemistry begins with an outrageous exchange of ideas and you enjoy the diversity you share together. Cancer is protective and you love those warm hugs, but may feel put off if you're scolded for being late for dinner. Virgo has expectations, although you are enticed by the way she or he thinks.

It's almost impossible to forget the amazing attraction you feel for Libra, your zodiac opposite, but meeting those high standards can be exasperating. Scorpio provokes wild intensity until she or he starts playing control games, and then you're ready to get out of there! Capricorn's intrigue is that dry sense of humor and financial security, but your passion wanes beneath the weight of all those rules and commitments. You're at ease with Aquarius, and enjoy both friendship and the excitement arising from the free expression you share. You may feel strongly bonded once you drop your barriers with Pisces, but still may never know exactly where you stand.

YOUR CAREER DEVELOPMENT

You need challenges to achieve success, and may be most enthusiastic about a career providing both mental and physical stimulation. You're a natural in sales and promotion.

Occupations in beauty and hair design, auto design or mechanics, masonry, welding, metal-working, jewelry design, or the travel industry may hold your interest. You might prefer the physical challenge of athletics, coaching, police work, the military, dancing, occupational or physical therapy, or fire-fighting. If you want a mental challenge, then politics or medicine can be your forte. Whatever your choice, your job must provide ample room to exercise your leadership and independence and try new ideas.

YOUR USE OF POWER

The primary purpose of power in your life is to underscore your feelings of personal autonomy. You want to run your own life! The essence of power drives you when you've accepted the invitation to a challenge: whether it's a position of leadership, entering a race, or striking out into new territory. You are competitive and when you have positive, growth-oriented goals, you become more vigorous and alive. But if you are filled with anger, shame, guilt, or mistrust, you may choose targets that result in destruction, including yourself. The contrast between these experiences can be quite sharp, but you can make the best determination for your use of power when you're willing to take on the responsibilities resulting from your actions and choices.

Those apparently insurmountable obstacles can ignite your spirit, and you can create exceptional possibilities for yourself. When faced with inaction on the part of others, you can become frustrated, domineering, or selfish; but you'll accomplish more when you simply take the lead. You have chosen the spiritual path of self-knowledge, which arises from exploring both the outside world and the path to your true self residing deep in your soul. This is your ultimate challenge and it is here that your courage and honesty create a brilliant light in your path that illuminates possibilities for those who will follow.

FAMOUS ARIES

Timothy Dalton, Al Gore, Jennie Garth, Leeza Gibbons, Craig T. Nelson, Conan O'Brien, Paul Reiser, Dennis Quaid, Quentin Tarantino, Emma Thompson, F. Scott Turow, Peter Ustinov, Eudora Welty, Dianne Wiest.

THE YEAR
AHEAD
FOR ARIES

You can make significant progress this year, particularly if you maintain focus on your most significant aims. By applying creativity to your work, you not only gain greater enjoyment, but are also likely to receive recognition that can advance your reputation and opportunities. Your spiritual focus also expands this year through a stronger connection to your inner self. Challenges loom ahead, and your positive attitude toward dealing with them brings a powerful fire to your spirit.

Saturn completes its cycle in Aries this year, marking the end of a three-year period of stabilization and testing. Establishing your priorities is still important and if you have adopted an attitude of responsibility, honesty, and realistic expectation, then you can experience steady growth. During the last two years, you've also run into the areas in your life that show deficiencies and this is the time to fill them. Whether you need more experience or education or if you're simply proving your value through hard work, this is the year to fill in the gaps and establish a firm position. You're discovering the importance of self-discipline and making choices that are meaningful to you.

Jupiter moves into the sign of Pisces on February 4th, where it will remain throughout 1998. Influencing your need to develop a real trust of your inner self, this cycle of Jupiter allows you to amplify your awareness of the spiritual plane. Since Jupiter is traveling through the Twelfth House of your solar chart, you also gain greater awareness of your past and may spend more time reflecting on the events in your life that have led up to the present moment. But instead of getting stuck in "what was," you can take an objective look and are ready to release yourself from situations that were once important so that you can move on. This is the inner work necessary before you experience the outreach and broader exposure you will experience next year. The rule for success is to do the inner work now that will help you find and strengthen your sense of confidence by establishing a true spiritual base, then you'll be ready for the continued opportunities that arise next year.

The eclipses during 1998 bring your attention to spiritual and creative endeavors. Since this underscores the influences you're experiencing through the cycles of Jupiter, Saturn, and Uranus, you will feel most comfortable with your life when you have determined the best ways to incorporate spirituality into your everyday life. Trying to separate the experience of spiritual awareness from your "regular" life will seem futile, since your goal now is to know the feeling of integrating your inner awareness with your actions and efforts in the "outside" world. Your relationships are also part of this equation, and you may finally be able to allow a spiritual connection to those who share your heart. Giving love can be easier, since you are growing closer to the source of compassion, which can now flow readily through your own heart.

♈   ♈   ♈

If you were born from March 21st–25th, you're experiencing the positive stabilization that occurs from the influence of Saturn transiting in semisextile to your Sun. You're also feeling a significant enhancement of your creative sensibilities from Neptune's transit in sextile aspect to your Sun. With both of these influences occurring together, you will find it easier to manifest your dreams. Neptune's influence strengthens your imagination, while the energy of Saturn prompts you to build a solid foundation.

You'll also feel more confidence in choices that incorporate your needs for a career that's in harmony with your spiritual ideas and ethical values. You need to feel that your efforts are making a difference, and if you're in a relationship or job that does not support your personal growth, you may become quite disenchanted. That lack of interest is a sign that you need something more fulfilling in your life, but it will not happen magically by itself. You have to create it!

♈ ♈ ♈

If you were born from March 26th–30th, you're experiencing a renewed sense of vitality and a rejuvenation of spirit while Pluto transits in trine aspect to your Sun. The power and revitalization that can occur during this cycle can influence every part of your life, but may be most marked through the profound impact you experience as a result of restoring your faith in yourself. This process is aided by your awareness and use of spiritual truths that form the foundation for your morals, ethics, and ideals. Any situation that is out of step with your values will be practically useless now, and this is the time to walk away from those things that do not fit your needs and values, while stepping onto a more stable platform.

♈ ♈ ♈

You're feeling an amazing burst of energy that adds excitement and ingenuity **if you were born from March 27th–April 3rd.** Uranus is transiting in sextile aspect to your Sun, stimulating your desire to express your individuality. This energy can also awaken special talents that have been waiting for the right time to emerge. By seeking out situations that give you a chance to develop your independence and autonomy, you will not only feel greater satisfaction, but you'll also discover better ways to use your ingenuity. If you've been waiting for the right time to start a new job, enter a relationship, or make significant changes, it has arrived! The choices you make now can spur significant changes in your life path, opening doors to greater self-satisfaction.

♈ ♈ ♈

If you were born from March 31st–April 4th, you may be prompted to spend more time allowing your psychic and artistic sensibilities to emerge. Neptune's transit in quintile aspect to your Sun is the perfect time to blend your psychic awareness into your conscious life experience. Your spirituality can enhance every aspect of your life now, and the conscious effort you apply toward strengthening your inner awareness can add a powerful dimension to your life. Now's the perfect time to dust off your creative or artistic talents, or to take them into a more profound level.

This is your year to get everything in order and establish strong foundations **if you were born from April 3rd–21st.** Saturn's transit conjunct your Sun brings both testing and clarity. This cycle brings a well-defined awareness of the realities of your life. You're seeing the effects of your choices, attitudes, and actions, which allows you to align your priorities more clearly and carefully. You can now build a firm foundation for future growth.

The heaviness you're feeling may be the result of the responsibilities you're carrying. Taking responsibility for your own actions is absolutely imperative now, but you're also learning to avoid carrying burdens for others who can carry them on their own. (This includes making excuses for others!) You may be more ready for a commitment in your personal relationship, but if the relationship is not healthy, you'll need to re-evaluate your situation. Standing up for yourself is part of this process, but that does not mean that you can get away with trying to control everyone else.

This is a time of endings and completion and a year of consolidation and focus. Letting go of what you no longer need is part of this cycle, but to fully achieve this release, you must be honest about whether you're really finished or if you're just afraid to deal with your obligations. If you run away from something you need to deal with, you're absolutely assured of repeating the same situation until you finally become clear about your own issues.

♈   ♈   ♈

If you were born from April 10th–15th, this is a year of true grace in matters of developing and utilizing your special abilities. Uranus is transiting in quintile aspect to your Sun, an influence that is rather subtle, but an especially powerful one if you've been waiting for the right time to showcase your talents. This is also an excellent time to seek out gifted teachers whose support and insight help you raise your skills to a new level of mastery.

♈   ♈   ♈

It's important to be aware of the way you handle power and control issues this year **if you were born from April 11th–15th.** Pluto is transiting in sesquiquadrate aspect to your Sun, an influence similar to tacks hidden in your carpet. Just when you think you're walking in safe territory, you can be jabbed for no apparent reason. It's not those little "tacks" that are the problem—it's the way you handle them.

If someone in your life seems to be intent on challenging you or if there are situations that seem to come out of nowhere to test your power, you can actually strengthen your position if you respond with clarity, confidence, and insight. But if you lash out defensively, you may create an enemy or destroy your power base. If your own needs for power emerge in odd little ways, your awareness of others' responses to your actions and attitudes can help you make the adjustments allowing you to move forward instead of getting stuck in issues revolving around a hidden agenda.

♈ ♈ ♈

If you were born from April 19th–21st, you may be feeling a bit confused as a result of Neptune's transit in square aspect to your Sun. You were feeling the effects of this transit last year, too, and you're finally coming out of the fog a bit, thanks to Saturn's influence (see above). But you can still be tempted to try to escape the realities of life, and need to be especially careful when making decisions that can affect your long-term future. This is an excellent time to forgive and let go. Your spiritual needs require more time and energy and because you're spending time on the inner level, you may not be as attentive to the details required to manage your life effectively. Pay careful attention to your health now; avoid addictive behaviors and focus on clearing your energy. If you have health concerns, consult a health practitioner whose objectivity and expertise can help you.

TOOLS TO MAKE A DIFFERENCE

Since your needs to become more clearly connected to your inner self are powerful this year, you can derive exceptional benefit from meditation. There are many ways to meditate, but the goal is to achieve a sense of flow and harmony between your inner and outer lives. If you don't like the idea of sitting, try active meditation forms, which can include hatha yoga, tai chi, chi gong, or dancing.

Some time spent in contemplation can be invigorating and refreshing and you may welcome the new energy generated by these periods of release.

To strengthen and maintain your physical vitality, make an effort to incorporate consistent periods of physical activity into your life. You're prone to high stress thanks to Saturn's influence now, and the first step in releasing stress is to do something physical. Get involved in a community sports team, go out for a marathon, walk every day—commit to a lifestyle that keeps you active and alive. The flower essence remedies of impatiens, heather, Indian paintbrush, and scarlet monkeyflower may help you balance your energies and maintain a more even pace, emotionally and physically. There's an emotional component to vitality, too, and staying stressed out can sap your energy on other levels. When you're feeling down, wear those bright colors that make you feel alive. Bring something cheery into your work environment. Personalize your life more fully. Maybe it's time to get one of those "vanity" license plates for your car!

During your meditations, concentrate on building a sense of positive power and energy. After you've relaxed, close your eyes and imagine that you are surrounded by beautiful rays of light. These rays flow from the Source of All Life, and brightly glow all around you. Feel the warm energy as it hits your face, shoulders, back, chest, arms, hips, and legs. Feel the light penetrating every part of your body. Now, imagine that you are becoming crystal clear and surrounding you is a field of energy that is vibrant and alive. From within the center of your being, you see a brilliant diamond, reflecting all the light. This energy is always there, charging, protecting, and bringing balance into your life.

AFFIRMATION FOR THE YEAR

"My vision is clear, my hopes are pure, and my life is full of joy!"

ARIES/JANUARY

PRIMARY FOCUS
Associations within your community and among your peers can enhance your career. Clarifying the difference between friendly competition and hostile confrontation is crucial to a successful outcome.

HEALTH AND FITNESS
Physical vitality can be strong now, and this is an excellent time to step up your activity levels. Get involved in team sports or join a fitness class. Just watch your tendency to overdo it after the 21st.

ROMANCE AND RELATIONSHIPS
Flirtations can be fun and a very clear attraction feeds your imagination. But do a reality check before you jump into a new romance or get back together with an old love, since it's easy to let your passion get in the way of your better judgment during the Full Moon on the 12th. Listen to the advice of friends, whose objectivity may add a different perspective to the situation. A friendship may turn into a romance after the New Moon on the 28th.

CAREER AND FINANCE
Career satisfaction improves, especially if you're given an opportunity to advance or achieve recognition from the 11th–26th. Hard work and attention to detail pays off from the 1st–12th, but you're more easily distracted after the 15th. Pay special attention to your finances from the 7th–23rd and make sure you're staying on budget. Your sound judgment returns after the 23rd.

OPPORTUNITY OF THE MONTH
If you've done your homework, you'll be prepared to move into new territory from the 3rd–22nd, but be cautious of those who promise more than they can deliver.

AFFIRMATION FOR THE MONTH
"My actions now prepare me for a future filled with abundance."

Rewarding Days: 1, 4, 5, 13, 14, 23, 24, 31
Challenging Days: 7, 11, 12, 18, 19, 20, 25, 26

ARIES/FEBRUARY

PRIMARY FOCUS
New career developments can lead to better opportunities, and you may undergo a change of attitude once you evaluate your goals and set out on a different path. This is a good time to do the background work that will make it possible to launch your plans.

HEALTH AND FITNESS
An undercurrent of restlessness can keep you awake at night unless you're burning off your energy in positive ways during the day. Working out can actually help you sleep better!

ROMANCE AND RELATIONSHIPS
A secret affair may be intriguing but can get you into trouble if it goes too far. Try to clarify your underlying motivations. Maybe you really don't want to be that close now and if your lover is pressuring you for more than you're willing to give, you're likely to back away during the Full Moon on the 11th. Give yourself time to regain control over your life during the Sun's eclipse on the 26th. It's time to regroup.

CAREER AND FINANCE
Watch for those hidden agendas! It's frustrating to become caught up in the expectations of others, so clarify your agreements. Your unique ideas and solutions work to your advantage from the 2nd–19th, and you're in a great position to gather support from friends or professional alliances. Behind-the-scenes meetings can work to your advantage after the 20th, although it's best if your motives are pure, since schemes can backfire if their intention is harmful.

OPPORTUNITY OF THE MONTH
It's time to cut away from the things you no longer need—those old "props" from your past that are now in your way. But the way you do it determines whether or not it hurts.

AFFIRMATION FOR THE MONTH
"I am kind, gentle, and loving."

Rewarding Days: 1, 5, 9, 10, 19, 20, 24, 28
Challenging Days: 7, 8, 14, 15, 22, 23, 27

ARIES/MARCH

PRIMARY FOCUS

Your high levels of energy add to your effectiveness. Enlisting the support of friends or professional allies ensures greater success, although you'll probably prefer to take the lead. It's easy to be overbearing, so watch yourself!

HEALTH AND FITNESS

With Mars, Mercury, and Saturn in Aries now, you're running in overdrive. It's crucial to set a pace that allows you to move forward without driving yourself into physical and mental burnout.

ROMANCE AND RELATIONSHIPS

Your actions will be taken seriously, so be sure you know the consequences before you make any overtures. Your best insurance is to be yourself, so that deciding what you want or enjoy will be easier. If you need a second chance or if you're ready to open your heart to love, the New Moon in Aries on the 27th encourages you to try again.

CAREER AND FINANCE

You'll accomplish more now if you have a well-defined plan of action. Others may feel more confident trusting your abilities when they see the results of your efforts and your leadership can be highly inspiring from the 5th–17th. The lunar eclipse on the 12th emphasizes your need to work cooperatively with others and marks an excellent time to establish a more productive routine. Be careful with contracts after the 26th.

OPPORTUNITY OF THE MONTH

Whether you're leading the way or following what you've learned from someone you respect, your actions can have a definite impact after the 20th.

AFFIRMATION FOR THE MONTH
"I take full responsibility for my actions and attitudes."

Rewarding Days: 1, 9, 10, 19, 20, 27, 28, 31
Challenging Days: 6, 7, 8, 14, 15, 21, 22

ARIES/APRIL

PRIMARY FOCUS

This is a time of completion, when concentrating on finishing what you've started is very important. Shouldering your burdens with confidence strengthens your resolve and can lead to career advancement.

HEALTH AND FITNESS

Resting may be difficult, particularly if you're working long days to fulfill your list of obligations. If you take on extra work, then keep your priorities straight and let go of some of the small stuff. Schedule a massage on the 12th or 13th to help get rid of tension and stress.

ROMANCE AND RELATIONSHIPS

You're discovering some of your lover's secrets, and may feel ill at ease if what you discover destroys some of your illusions from the 10th–14th. During the Full Moon on the 11th, your partner may be more demanding and critical. Before you bolt and run, decide if you need to work out those issues. If it's time to end the relationship, let yourself really say good-bye so that you can move on. Spiritual values are the bonds that keep your heart open to love now.

CAREER AND FINANCE

During Mercury's retrograde in Aries through the 20th, you may feel like you're on the spot. There's no need to take the fall for somebody else, but you need to clarify your responsibilities. Avoid signing long-term contracts, and be careful with your expenditures. Avoid impulsive spending, particularly after the New Moon on the 26th. Honor your budget, and research large expenditures to get the best deal.

OPPORTUNITY OF THE MONTH

Your focus on solving problems works to your advantage from the 1st–9th. This experience may inspire you to set your sights on a new challenge in the near future.

AFFIRMATION FOR THE MONTH
"My mind is focused on the here and now."

Rewarding Days: 1, 5, 6, 15, 16, 20, 24, 25, 28
Challenging Days: 2, 3, 10, 11, 17, 1, 19, 30

ARIES/MAY

PRIMARY FOCUS
Attracting what you want is easy, if you're willing to pay the price! But this is one of those times when you will definitely not get something for nothing. You can also lose something you value if you fail to give the respect and gratitude necessary.

HEALTH AND FITNESS
Building your strength and endurance works to your benefit, but you need to take it gradually. You're still hanging onto tension this month, so remember to stretch throughout the day to stay flexibile.

ROMANCE AND RELATIONSHIPS
Venus is in Aries, increasing your attractive energy, so show your best attributes! A romantic interlude can be purely wonderful from the 3rd–18th, and you're ready to explore a deeper level of intimacy during the Full Moon on the 11th. Things can get serious after the 24th, when you may be challenged to take the next step. Halfway just does not work, and talking about your concerns sheds light on the issues during the New Moon on the 25th.

CAREER AND FINANCE
Careful attention to finances can make a big difference, and you may finally be willing to scale back on those unnecessary expenses just to catch up and feel more secure. Putting your time and material resources to work can turn your life around. Target the period after the 21st for networking, conferences, or interaction with others whose influence can help your career.

OPPORTUNITY OF THE MONTH
Venturing into new territory is easier when someone you know has made a few introductions. That scenario works to your advantage from the 21st–29th.

AFFIRMATION FOR THE MONTH
"I deserve honest, loving relationships."

Rewarding Days: 8, 9, 13, 14, 17, 18, 22, 23, 26
Challenging Days: 3, 4, 11, 12, 24, 25, 31

ARIES/JUNE

PRIMARY FOCUS

Increased travel, communications, and networking provide ample outlets for sharing your ideas while increasing your knowledge and skills. Keep a close watch on your finances, though, because you may have some large expenditures.

HEALTH AND FITNESS

A burst of energy keeps you going, but your endurance may be a bit low. Take time for rest and relaxation, and build up your reserves by gradually increasing activity levels. Get out in the open air and breathe!

ROMANCE AND RELATIONSHIPS

If you've felt deceived by someone you trust, regaining that trust may not be easy unless you can talk about your feelings and concerns. Direct and compassionate communication flows readily from the 1st–10th, and with the intensity of the Full Moon on the 9th, you're feeling clear about your own needs. Family concerns may take precedence following the New Moon on the 23rd, but you still have a little time for romance from the 24th–28th.

CAREER AND FINANCE

A realistic evaluation of your finances is part of establishing a strong sense of self-esteem. But it's difficult to be clear now, since you may miss important details if you rush in ill-prepared or uninformed. Consult an objective source before taking on any long-term obligations, since the friction between Saturn and Neptune is working to your disadvantage in matters of finance.

OPPORTUNITY OF THE MONTH

Enlist the support of those whose ideals and aims are similar to your own. Just make sure you're really on the same wavelength before obligating your own time or resources.

AFFIRMATION FOR THE MONTH
"I use my resources wisely."

Rewarding Days: 8, 9, 10, 13, 17, 18, 22, 26, 27
Challenging Days: 3, 4, 5, 11, 12, 24, 25

Aries/July

Primary Focus

Your mental creativity grows, and can be especially powerful when applied to speculative ventures or artistic projects. But friction or turmoil at home can distract you, and taking aim at those issues can make a difference in the quality of your life.

Health and Fitness

Find a good outlet for your competitive urges. Sports, recreation, and games can provide excellent benefits to your overall health. Achieving important fitness goals is most promising after the 23rd.

Romance and Relationships

Establishing a secure foundation requires dealing with the past, and old emotional issues can flare after the 6th. Trying to escape your responsibilities at home only leads to frustration, so take a careful look and get in touch with your deeper feelings during the Full Moon on the 9th. Open discussions provide creative solutions, helping you mend fences so that you can concentrate on those romantic yearnings that emerge during the New Moon on the 23rd.

Career and Finance

Schedule conferences, meetings, or presentations from the 1st–19th, when your ideas can stir enthusiastic support and action. You may feel a bit impatient with the slow wheels of progress from the 8th–22nd. Steady your own pace a bit to move things along. A chance to showcase your special talents emerges after the 23rd, when taking center stage may put you on the fast track toward success.

Opportunity of the Month

Launching your pet projects fares best from the 1st–8th, and then from the 23rd–30th. Those times in between are for regrouping, preparation, and fine detailing. Use them well.

Affirmation for the Month
"My words and actions spring from loving thoughts."

Rewarding Days: 6, 7, 10, 11, 15, 16, 19, 23, 24, 25
Challenging Days: 1, 2, 8, 9, 21, 22, 28, 29

ARIES/AUGUST

PRIMARY FOCUS
Mercury's retrograde and the eclipses are signals to be especially careful in the realm of speculative finance. Use this period to examine the products of your efforts. Think of this as a cosmic auditing period.

HEALTH AND FITNESS
Fitness needs to be fun if you're going to stay active now. Watch your diet, since it's tempting to give in to those sweet cravings too frequently. Setting limits can make a big difference.

ROMANCE AND RELATIONSHIPS
You're having second thoughts about a love relationship, especially if your needs are not being met. During the lunar eclipse on the 7th, take a look at your ability to receive love. Have you really wanted to be close, or were your insecurities prompting you to make choices that were more like a compromise than a promise? An unhealthy relationship ends now, but the vitality of love can bring true romance during the solar eclipse on the 21st—if you're ready!

CAREER AND FINANCE
Although you may be tempted, try to avoid signing new long-term contracts until after Mercury turns direct on the 23rd. This is the time to research details, and your own creative ideas may stimulate new directions mid-month anyway. So take your time, and figure out what you want—bottom line, no compromises. You'll be much happier with the results. A change in the financial climate on the 21st offers interesting possibilities.

OPPORTUNITY OF THE MONTH
Putting your talents to work is not only fun, but can garner attention from someone special after the 14th. This period begins a positive cycle for romance, too!

AFFIRMATION FOR THE MONTH
"My heart is open to love and joy!"

Rewarding Days: 2, 3, 7, 11, 12, 15, 16, 20, 21, 29, 30
Challenging Days: 1, 4, 5, 6, 17, 18, 24, 25, 26

ARIES/SEPTEMBER

PRIMARY FOCUS

Your talents give you a boost at work, and you may be willing to scale back the pressure for a while, allowing you to enjoy the experience much more! Improvements on the job are a top priority.

HEALTH AND FITNESS

Taking a physical inventory is a great idea. So think about scheduling your annual physical, evaluating your diet and exercise regimen, and making the adjustments to improve your wellness. Staying active with your favorite recreation can be inspirational.

ROMANCE AND RELATIONSHIPS

Your teasing nature is running in high gear, which can be quite endearing in a romantic setting. Just be sure you know what kind of signals you're sending, since your actions will prompt response from the 1st–8th. Marriage or partnerships require special attention after the 24th, although you may not feel like making any special changes just yet. If one of those changes is a commitment, get clear about what you mean by that before you start wearing a ring!

CAREER AND FINANCE

The lunar eclipse on the 6th (yes, there's another one!) stimulates your need to get in touch with your feelings about work. If you don't like it, why? What can you do to change the course of your professional life? Now's the time to determine the lifestyle you need by improving your skills or job situation. Consider changing your image on or after the New Moon on the 20th.

OPPORTUNITY OF THE MONTH

Cooperative ventures can be especially satisfying from the 7th–25th, but you may have to scale back your assertiveness if others are overwhelmed by your energy.

AFFIRMATION FOR THE MONTH
"My energy reflects the strength of love."

Rewarding Days: 3, 4, 7, 8, 11, 12, 16, 17, 25, 30
Challenging Days: 1, 2, 13, 14, 15, 21, 22, 28, 29

ARIES/OCTOBER

PRIMARY FOCUS

During this period of self-examination, you're taking a closer look at several aspects of your life. Others play an important role and you need associations that are equitable and mutually supportive.

HEALTH AND FITNESS

With Mars moving into your Sixth House, you're taking an active part in your health care. But you are also more prone to injury, so make sure you're participating in activities that are safe and for which you are adequately prepared.

ROMANCE AND RELATIONSHIPS

For a relationship to continue to grow, deeper levels of intimacy and understanding are necessary. Clarifying your roles within a relationship takes center stage during the Full Moon on the 5th, but you're also ready to talk about your needs, fears, and emotional ties after the 13th. The bonds you forge now can last a long time, and unless you feel that you have something truly special, your feelings are likely to change. It's time to grow or say good-bye.

CAREER AND FINANCE

Joint ventures can be quite profitable, especially if they support your creative aims and allow you to utilize your talents to their fullest. A partnership initiated following the New Moon on the 20th can be successful, but avoid vague role descriptions to avoid disagreements later. You're vulnerable to deception from the 23rd–31st, when jumping into unknown territory can be quite costly. Look before you leap!

OPPORTUNITY OF THE MONTH

New ideas and innovative technologies play an important role in your success from the 1st–10th. Look for avenues to simplify your job and free up more time for creativity.

AFFIRMATION FOR THE MONTH
"I gladly show gratitude toward others for their care and support."

Rewarding Days: 5, 6, 9, 13, 14, 23, 24, 28
Challenging Days: 11, 12, 18, 19, 25, 26

ARIES/NOVEMBER

PRIMARY FOCUS

Career growth and expansion comes from building your knowledge through travel, education, or thoughtful writing. You may feel quite confident about making plans to move ahead.

HEALTH AND FITNESS

Your psychological health is just as important as your physical well-being, and addressing your emotional needs, unresolved fears, or old issues can take a massive weight off your shoulders right now. Just imagine how much taller you'll feel!

ROMANCE AND RELATIONSHIPS

If you feel ready to experience transformation through loving, then now's the time to get beyond some major obstacles. Address your spiritual needs to allow your love to grow and you'll feel most comfortable dealing with these issues after the New Moon on the 18th. Meeting a new love through travel, educational, or cultural pursuits looks promising. An old flame could cross your path; are you ready?

CAREER AND FINANCE

Hard work pays off, and if you put forth the effort, you may even get that major project done. Money matters can be stressful during the Full Moon on the 4th, particularly where joint finances are concerned. But you also need to address your debt situation and make an effort to turn it around. Mercury begins its retrograde on the 21st, and after that time you may have more luck getting back in touch with established contacts. Address unresolved legal problems.

OPPORTUNITY OF THE MONTH

Contract negotiations, business conferences, and presentations can bring excellent results all month. But if you've not reached an agreement before the 21st, wait until next month to sign.

AFFIRMATION FOR THE MONTH
"In all matters I seek the Truth."

Rewarding Days: 1, 2, 5, 6, 9, 10, 19, 20, 28, 29
Challenging Days: 7, 8, 14, 15, 22, 23

ARIES/DECEMBER

PRIMARY FOCUS
Educational pursuits, travel, and cultural exchange open new horizons, personally and professionally. You also need healthy outlets for your competitive nature to avoid excessive conflicts. Listen to the needs of others before you jump to conclusions.

HEALTH AND FITNESS
Winter sports may be ideal, but you might also enjoy hiking or backpacking in a warmer climate. Getting into nature has many positive effects. A vacation can be a great rejuvenator this month.

ROMANCE AND RELATIONSHIPS
Stormy conflicts with your partner can be especially trying, and if you're not of the same mind, then those conflicts can be even more difficult during the Full Moon on the 3rd. You're more sensitive to criticism after the 12th, when you may also feel some pressure from your family. Communicate your feelings and needs while striving to reach an agreement. Keep your expectations clear and reasonable.

CAREER AND FINANCE
Although Mercury is in retrograde until the 11th, you can still make career progress. Financial prospects, business negotiations, and legal matters show promise, although you're likely to run into a few snags between the 12th and the New Moon on the 18th. Before you get set for a fight, decide how much you're willing to pay for what you think you want. Breaking free of situations that cost more than they're worth is the order of the day.

OPPORTUNITY OF THE MONTH
Your future looks brighter when opening your mind to new possibilities. Attend meetings, make presentations, or publish materials that illustrate what you have to offer.

AFFIRMATION FOR THE MONTH
"I am committed to standards that are ethically right."

Rewarding Days: 3, 7, 16, 17, 18, 21, 26, 27, 30
Challenging Days: 5, 6, 11, 12, 13, 19, 20

ARIES ♈ ACTION TABLE	These dates reflect the best (but not the only) times for success and ease in these activities, according to your sign.											
	Jan.	Feb.	Mar.	Apr.	May	June	July	Aug.	Sept.	Oct.	Nov.	Dec.
Change Residence						5–30						
Begin a Course of Study					25, 26							18
Join a Club	28, 29											
Ask for a Raise			28, 29									
Begin a Romance							23, 24	22				
Visit a Doctor		20–28	1–7						8–23			
Start a Diet	15–17	12, 13	11, 12	7, 8	4–6	1, 2, 28–30	26, 27	22, 23	18–20	15, 16	12, 13	9, 10
Seek Employment	12–31	1							7–30			
Take a Vacation	23–25	19–21	19, 20	15, 16	12, 13	8, 9	6, 7	2, 3, 29–31	26, 27	23, 24	19, 20	16–18
End a Relationship				11								
Change Your Wardrobe							1–31	1–31	1–7			
Seek Professional Advice	18, 19	14–16	14, 15	10, 11	7–9	3–5, 30	1, 2, 28, 29	24–26	21, 22	18, 19	14–16	11–13
Have a Make-Over			28, 29									
Obtain a Loan	20–22	17, 18	16–18	12–14	10, 11	6, 7	3–5, 30, 31	1, 27, 28	23–25	20–22	17, 18	14, 15

TAURUS

The Bull
April 20–May 21

Element:	Earth
Quality:	Fixed
Polarity:	Yin/Feminine
Planetary Ruler:	Venus
Meditation:	"I am the steward of my environment."
Gemstone:	Emerald
Power Stones:	Blue Lace Agate, Diamond, Rose Quartz
Key Phrase:	"I have"
Glyph:	Bull's Head ♉
Anatomy:	Neck, Throat
Color:	Green
Animal:	Cattle
Myths/Legends:	Isis and Osiris, Ceriddwen, Bull of Minos
House Association:	Second
Opposite Sign:	Scorpio
Flower:	Violet
Key Word:	Conservation

Positive Expressions:		Misuse of Energy:	
Loving	Affluent	Unyielding	Possessive
Substantial	Calm	Materialistic	Greedy
Enduring	Focused	Lethargic	Avaricious
Reliable		Obstinate	

 # TAURUS

YOUR EGO'S STRENGTHS AND WEAKNESSES

A quest for true love is the drive behind your life experiences—from relationships, to career options, to different places—and once your feelings of love are awakened, your devotion to the ideals, people, and expressions you hold dear can be unfaltering. Many forms of artistry attract your interest, and you may enjoy expressing your own creativity. Since your life is a continual building process, your role as "The Maintainer" of the zodiac plays an important role in attracting and accumulating resources.

You have an eye for quality and appreciate excellent workmanship, and just as importantly, desire to make the most of whatever resources you have at hand. Conservation of the Earth's resources may be an important quest, but you also have an interest in conserving the finest resources people have to offer and may be a dedicated patron of the arts. The energy of Venus, your planetary ruler, draws you to all that is loving, sweet, and beautiful, and attracts others to you who enjoy your stabilizing support.

Change is not easy for you, and you can become immovable and uncooperative if you feel threatened by change. Your stubborn attitudes and tenacious hold over your possessions can work against your own best interests some of the time. Learning to express steadfastness in an evolving world without falling into a rut requires you to develop a positive sense of personal worth that allows you to open to the never-ending flow of pure love.

YOUR APPROACH TO ROMANCE

To establish a love that grows, you seek adoration and love that feels total and complete, and hope for love that lasts a lifetime. You can express both strength and tenderness as a lover, and will be most expressive when you're involved in a trustworthy commitment. Any healthy relationship will go through changes, and if you are to avoid feelings of jealousy or possessiveness, you have to allow room for these natural tides to flow.

Although you may be most strongly drawn to the sensual passion you feel for your opposite sign, Scorpio, trusting one another can be difficult unless you're both open about your feelings. You're likely to feel most at home with the other earth signs—Taurus, Virgo, or Capricorn. Commitment, longevity, and trust seem natural with another Taurus. Virgo's practicality aids your desires for comfort, and you can enjoy a superbly sensual relationship. Complementary values strengthen your tie with Capricorn, and you'll find his or her drive toward financial stability quite appealing.

Aries is attractive, but just when you're getting comfortable, you may feel that she or he is pushing you to move. The challenge of Gemini's versatility can help you embrace new options, but you may feel somewhat out of breath trying to keep up with that darting about. Cancer is comfy, and the two of you can feel right at home creating a sense of family. Leo is fun, and that loyalty feels good until you run into conflicts over whose needs are most important.

Libra's refinement and beauty are enticing, but you can feel threatened by his or her indecision. You love Sagittarius' fun and generosity, but may loathe the time she or he is off on adventure. Aquarius simply does not give you enough personal attention. But with Pisces, you can float into fanciful romance while building a place to bring your dreams to life.

YOUR CAREER DEVELOPMENT

You'll be satisfied in your career when you have room for growth with a stable situation under your feet. Your head for business operates all the time, and you may perform best working in the world of finance, banking, investment, real estate, or retail sales. However, you also know good structure, and may want to apply this sensibility to the building industry, architectural design, furniture building, or handicrafts.

A career in the food industry can be rewarding, or you may prefer to offer "soul food" as a supportive and encouraging counselor or teacher. In the arts, you may be an accomplished singer or artisan, or you may funnel your creativity into clothing design, hairdressing, or the beauty industry. Work like gardening, farming, ranching, landscape design, floral arranging, or forestry allows you to stay connected to the Earth.

YOUR USE OF POWER

Just because you enjoy peace, don't think that you're not seeking some type of power! You know the power of holding on, waiting for the right time, and persevering through adversity; you can create power that builds a fortress of emotional strength and stability that can envelop everyone and everything your life touches.

You feel powerful when surrounded by ample material resources, loyal family, and good friends, although you may always struggle with the difference between "having" someone or something and knowing when to let go. When you're feeling vulnerable, the power of greed or possessiveness can overtake you. That's why endings, especially in relationships, are so devastating for you. You feel that you've lost your power, because you take in those relationships and the things you've accumulated through them as a part of your being.

Sharing your time and resources can actually increase your feeling of power, once you've gotten over the feeling of losing something when you give it away. The power you seek emerges when you learn the true meaning of abundance in all things. The timeless support you feel from Mother Earth stimulates you to guard and replenish her resources, and this use of your power can extend far into generations that are now only a whisper on the winds of time.

FAMOUS TAUREANS

Madeleine Albright, Irving Berlin, Johannes Brahms, Jane Brody, George Clooney, Queen Elizabeth II, Sugar Ray Leonard, Jack Nicholson, Al Pacino, Michelle Pfeiffer, Bronson Pinchot, George Takei, Randy Travis, Bob Woodward.

THE YEAR AHEAD FOR TAURUS

Keeping your balance this year can be a struggle, since you're challenged to maintain your focus while dealing with changes in the world around you. Sorting through the illusions perpetuated by a greedy society while staying connected to your deeper values can be a rather illuminating process for you during 1998. In that process, you may discover a new meaning in life.

The influence of Jupiter's transit in Pisces this year is centered on your need to create and manifest goals that lift your spirits while elevating your standard of living. You may even find that some of your goals have absolutely nothing to do with the material side of life, but that you are paying more attention instead to experiencing a quality of life that is connected to more profound goals that influence the world around you. This is a wonderful year to develop associations with friends and others whose interests mirror your own. You may also be prompted to work with your community or professional associates to create opportunities to benefit the collective in some way. (You're a part of that "collective society" yourself, too!) On the material level, the effects of Jupiter's transit can definitely improve your finances, although the rewards of increased confidence and optimism can actually be further-reaching than the limitations of the material plane.

Saturn moves into Taurus during the third quarter of 1998, giving you a preview of the tests you'll be experiencing through the year 2000. You'll be much happier with your life if you have a clear set of priorities when you step into the next millennium, and this is the time to clear away the debris and excess that could inhibit your ability to maintain those priorities. This energy can slow your progress a bit, but within that framework is a sure and steady pace. This is the cycle that allows you to build solid foundations and lasting commitments, but you must make choices that echo your deepest needs if you are to feel happy with the structures you build now. The period in which Saturn conjuncts your Sun will provide your most profound tests, and that is determined by your exact date of birth.

The eclipses of the Sun and Moon during 1998 emphasize your needs to balance the give-and-take experiences of life, and also provide a key to your feelings about what you require to feel truly secure and stabilized. Your creativity may also be enhanced, providing more opportunities to use your talents to enhance the quality of your life. Your awareness of the impact of your philosophical and spiritual leanings is becoming quite clear, and if you are to change anything that will fundamentally alter your sense of meaning and purpose, it will begin through developing your link to higher consciousness and unconditional acceptance of yourself and others. These changes can create a bridge between your previously held ideals and a more tolerant attitude toward the diversity that reflects the beauty of life.

If you were born from April 20th–24th, you're feeling the pressure of Saturn transiting in conjunction to your Sun. You may also be a little frustrated with the results of your efforts, since Neptune's transit in square aspect to your Sun may leave you feeling invisible or with a sense that your hard work goes unnoticed. Trying to force things to go your way can get you into trouble now, since in many ways, you're challenged to let go and relinquish control to your higher self. But this does not mean that you can dodge your responsibilities. Knowing which burdens are yours to carry and which you must release is the primary lesson of these cycles. In fact, the most difficult lessons may come from allowing someone else to suffer for their own mistakes.

Special attention to your physical health is another area that requires extra awareness. Your vitality can be easily undermined by chronic conditions when you're also dealing with new stresses and responsibilities. Taking a careful physical inventory, changing habits that are destructive or that deplete your vitality, and allowing ample time to rejuvenate and rest are all part of a healthy lifestyle. If you're feeling low or concerned, consult a professional to discover what's causing your distress. This can be the time when you experience a turnaround, but you first need to make yourself aware of the problems, and then take an active role in achieving optimum health.

The frustration of Pluto transiting in quincunx aspect to your Sun is very strong this year **if you were born from April 24th–30th.** Some things you've always counted on do not satisfy your needs now, and you may feel that your transitions from one life stage to another are more drastic than you had anticipated. This can be particularly true when you examine your emotional attachments and realize that you simply cannot hang on to everyone or everything. You're likely to experience changes that have a profound impact upon your sense of self. These can be positive changes, but the way you experience them can require major adjustments!

The greatest adjustments arise in your attitudes toward those things that you cannot control. Always remember that you can direct your own responses, even when something seems to come from out of the blue to alter your life. Your physical health can change significantly, too, particularly if you've been struggling to find the causes of any long-standing problems or complaints. This is a good period to discover root causes and deal with them directly. On a psychological level, you're ready to release some old issues and may finally be willing to let go of some of those old feelings of guilt or resentment that are impeding your progress. On the job, this is a great time to research, investigate, and renovate.

You're experiencing revolutionary changes **if you were born from April 25th–May 4th,** since Uranus is transiting in square aspect to your Sun. The effects of this cycle may be somewhat unpredictable, but you can count on a few surprises as the most predictable quality of this cycle! This is the time to create innovations in your life, but it's also time to let go of fears and inhibitions standing in the way of your personal growth.

Don't be surprised if you're feeling rebellious, because it's time for you to rebel! That rebellion is centered on your need to eliminate those things, situations, and attitudes from your life that limit your growth and inhibit your individuality. Since you're happier with changes you engineer, it's important to take a look at the things you really wish to alter and get to work on your part in changing them. Other people in your life may also be more unreliable, and you're quite likely to attract a number of unusual and unreliable individuals now. There are also likely to be some situations that you simply cannot control, which have the effect of modifying your life. The key thing to remember is that it's time to move into a more complete expression of yourself, leaving behind the things you no longer need and greeting the possibilities of a new and more rewarding future.

It's important to take steps that will help you build a strong foundation **if you were born from May 5th–20th**. Saturn's transit in semisextile aspect to your Sun provides an influence that draws your attention to the way you are taking responsibility for yourself and your actions. You're also experiencing a need to identify a sense of purpose in your life, since Chiron is traveling in opposition to your Sun this year. These two cycles together symbolize a type of identity crisis, but the identity issue is about finding a life path that makes your heart sing.

You're ready to feel self-assured, and if something is missing from that picture—like the right job or a workable relationship—then now is the time to do something about manifesting a more fulfilling life circumstance. Although you may have felt these needs last year, there is a greater sense of urgency now. You've heard the story about the straw that broke the camel's back? Well, you're also reaching the end of your tolerance for things you no longer need! Concentrate on strengthening the things in your life that are working, and then strive to eliminate those things that are producing negative results, or no results at all. Wasting your time and energy is no longer a viable option.

♈ ♈ ♈

If you were born from May 17th–20th, you're feeling the effects of Neptune transiting in trine aspect to your Sun, a cycle that began during 1997. This energy stimulates a profound quality of spirituality, imagination, and creative expression. If you're involved in the arts, you'll discover that your sensibilities are enhanced. This is a period of initiation into a heightened spiritual awareness, and you can experience a sense of merging your spiritual elements more completely into your life. Your psychic sense is also stronger now, and those impressions you receive can have a valid impact on your understanding and awareness.

However, because this cycle is rather internalized, you may discover that you do not have the drive to get out into the world and fight all those battles. You may crave peace, calm, and serenity and can even go out of your way to avoid conflict, confrontation, and dissension. This is a wonderful time to release and forgive, and can be a period of serenity; but it can also be a time of laziness and low motivation. If you want to use this energy to create change, you'll probably have to motivate yourself on a higher level, since the mundane may seem too ordinary or unappealing to bother.

TOOLS TO MAKE A DIFFERENCE

Finding the space within yourself that anchors the core of your being is one of your primary goals now, and you can use several tools to help you get there. Since Saturn will be transiting in your sign for the next three years, you also need some tools to help you build a more solid sense of security. As a beginning, think about your priorities. Which things are most important to you? What more do you want from your life? How can you get there? These questions can help you identify your goals and options, and those elements can form the anchor for your growth. You may encounter fear or guilt on the path toward achieving your goals. Confront those obstacles to determine how to go about realizing your dreams.

Conserve your resources now. That does not mean hoarding — it means knowing how to make the best use of what you have. Putting your resources to work for you includes positively using your talents and trusting your own abilities while evaluating the importance of others and their efforts, time, and resources more carefully. If you've not yet begun a serious program of recycling and reclamation, this is the perfect time to start.

Your physical health can be strengthened by taking action that boosts your overall vitality. Take inventory of your responses to stress, and make an effort to relieve stress through regular exercise coupled with reasonable periods of rest and recreation. Adopting a program that helps you stay in touch with your body, like tai chi or chi gong, can be highly rejuvenating. You might also enjoy receiving regular therapeutic massage, and learning massage techniques can be an excellent form of sharing with your partner, too! If you want to explore other forms of bodywork, deeper tissue work like Rolfing can be effective. To help the flow of your physical-emotional energy, you can also benefit from using the flower essence remedies of chestnut bud, chicory, iris, bleeding heart, and hound's-tongue. Surround yourself with colors that make you feel alive, and when you need a little extra boost, wear something in a shade of green that feels good to you. This is also a great time to clean out your closets, drawers, and attic spaces and get rid of the extra clutter in your life.

During your periods of meditation and contemplation, concentrate on letting your energy and beauty open to the world. Imagine that you are free, unfettered, and able to make choices that will allow you to grow. Think of yourself as a beautiful rose, ready to reach its full bloom. Before you can blossom, you have to break out of your bud stage. Opening those petals is not as easy as it looks, but you push through, breaking the barriers that have held your beauty until you were ready to blossom. There! You're free, and your fragrance fills the air as your color glows in the sun! Your life can reflect the same beauty and wonder as this rose, which returns season after season to bring pleasure and sweetness to the world.

AFFIRMATION FOR THE YEAR
"My life is filled with beauty and joy!"

TAURUS/JANUARY

PRIMARY FOCUS
It's easy to feel overly obligated, and unless your concentration is clearly centered on your priorities, you can undermine your effectiveness. Do not promise what you cannot deliver!

HEALTH AND FITNESS
You're more easily tempted to indulge in those delicious (but not so healthy) treats more frequently than usual this month. Allow some room for little indulgences here and there, but try to avoid making them a habit!

ROMANCE AND RELATIONSHIPS
Questioning your feelings in a close relationship can bring positive changes, and this is an excellent time to examine your needs and priorities more carefully. However, it's best to wait if you're thinking of starting a new romance, even though you may feel quite tempted during the Full Moon on the 12th. An old love may re-enter your life, but you're not interested in making the same mistakes.

CAREER AND FINANCE
Competitive work situations may actually lead to advancement, but you have to know your limits to avoid stepping on the wrong toes. Approach your expectations realistically, and make sure you're adequately prepared. Otherwise, you may experience an embarrassing outcome. Fresh possibilities emerge on the career front during the New Moon on the 28th, when you're in an excellent position to illustrate your expertise and abilities.

OPPORTUNITY OF THE MONTH
Mend fences by offering a gesture of apology or explanation for past deeds gone sour. Your actions are best received from the 24th–31st.

AFFIRMATION FOR THE MONTH
"My words reflect pure and loving thoughts."

Rewarding Days: 2, 3, 6, 7, 11, 12, 15, 16, 25, 26, 30
Challenging Days: 1, 13, 14, 20, 21, 22, 27, 28

TAURUS/FEBRUARY

PRIMARY FOCUS

The support of good friends and peers gives you confidence, encouraging you to move forward with career aims or personal goals. Take action to make your dreams a reality.

HEALTH AND FITNESS

You're feeling more physically centered and alive, and can take your fitness to a higher level by setting challenging goals. Team sports, fitness classes, or your favorite forms of recreation are excellent options for improving your vitality.

ROMANCE AND RELATIONSHIPS

Your confidence about your feelings is much stronger, and if you've been hoping for the right time to tell that special someone how you feel, here it is! You may also feel compelled to talk over family issues, and addressing your concerns may seem quite critical during the Full Moon on the 11th. Romance fares best after the 19th, and love can blossom following the solar eclipse on the 26th. If you're uncertain, talk about your feelings with a friend.

CAREER AND FINANCE

Networking with others in your field adds strength, particularly in matters affecting the overall climate at work. Set well-defined goals, and take actions to initiate broader options for your long-range future. Communication breakdowns or technological problems can be disruptive from the 1st–12th, but things are running smoothly after the 18th. Business travel, conferences, and workshops can enhance your reputation after the 21st.

OPPORTUNITY OF THE MONTH

Your efforts have a much bigger impact if others know what you've accomplished! Let your workmanship speak for you, but be sure someone is there to notice what you have to offer.

AFFIRMATION FOR THE MONTH
"My ethics and principles originate from absolute integrity."

Rewarding Days: 3, 4, 7, 12, 13, 22, 23, 26, 27
Challenging Days: 9, 10, 11, 17, 18, 24, 25

TAURUS/MARCH

PRIMARY FOCUS

Underlying tension arises from your need to gain recognition for your efforts at work, but you do have the power to change some causes of your frustration. The pressure of trying to keep up with innovative changes can add to your stress.

HEALTH AND FITNESS

You need extra time to rest, but may not find it easy to relax. Working off your tension through exercise can actually help you sleep better. Concentrate on letting go of what you cannot control. Your physical energy should improve almost immediately as a result.

ROMANCE AND RELATIONSHIPS

If you're fascinated by someone at work, just remember that you may only be seeing the public persona—not the complete person. Office politics can strain relationships at work and at home through the 19th, but you can get things in perspective during the lunar eclipse on the 12th if you take the time to listen to your deeper needs before taking action. You'll prefer to keep your personal life private after the 21st.

CAREER AND FINANCE

In order to keep up with changes at work, you may need to call in the support of those who share your interests or profession. There's also a lot happening behind the scenes, and careful preparation now can ensure positive results later. But watch for someone with a hidden agenda, since their manipulations can cause real trouble after the 21st. Try a different approach to communication problems at work after the New Moon on the 27th.

OPPORTUNITY OF THE MONTH

Even though Mercury retrogrades on the 27th, the last five days of the month can be very productive for establishing your position in the rank and file, even if you are sidestepping!

AFFIRMATION FOR THE MONTH
"I forgive myself for my past mistakes."

Rewarding Days: 2, 3, 11, 12, 21, 26, 29, 30
Challenging Days: 9, 10, 16, 17, 18, 23, 24

TAURUS/APRIL

PRIMARY FOCUS

Finishing old business is important to achieving your hopes and aims. If you try to start something new this month without first completing your current obligations, you can create major obstacles for yourself.

HEALTH AND FITNESS

Dealing with stress is absolutely necessary. Just pushing it away only increases your emotional and physical burdens. Pay attention to your physical limitations from the 1st–6th, and avoid high-risk situations after the 13th.

ROMANCE AND RELATIONSHIPS

Your friends are a major source of support, and if you're having troubles in your love life or just need extra comfort while dealing with the stress and strain of life, they're your best resource. You may feel confident about pursuing a romantic interest after the 14th, and can even begin an important relationship during the Taurus New Moon on the 26th. Friendship can blossom into passion, but keep your expectations clear to avoid disappointment.

CAREER AND FINANCE

Despite Mercury's retrograde through the 20th you can still achieve progress in your career. However, you must deal with conservative attitudes and frustrating delays. The way you handle these disruptions determines a lot, and if you pay attention to the details, use this time to clarify, research, complete, and improve, you'll be ready for a new project by the 26th. Watch for possible deception, loss, or costly inaccuracies from the 12th–21st.

OPPORTUNITY OF THE MONTH

After Mars moves into Taurus on the 12th, your energy is stronger. But don't expect a stark contrast at first, since you may feel more like a locomotive getting started than a rocket ship.

AFFIRMATION FOR THE MONTH
"I clearly define my goals."

Rewarding Days: 3, 7, 17, 18, 22, 26, 27, 30
Challenging Days: 5, 6, 12, 13, 14, 20, 21

TAURUS/MAY

PRIMARY FOCUS
You're prepared to stand up for yourself if necessary, and anyone trying to push you around will be unpleasantly surprised. You have the confidence, assertiveness, and strength of will necessary to forge ahead or to defend your position.

HEALTH AND FITNESS
Balancing your needs to rest and rejuvenate with the demands you're feeling from the world around you is not easy. The key may be to set a pace that allows you to conserve your energy while focusing your mental energy on relaxing your attitudes a little.

ROMANCE AND RELATIONSHIPS
An old love enters the picture. If you've not yet let go, there may be unresolved issues to address, particularly near the Full Moon on the 11th. If you're involved in another relationship, spending time fantasizing about the past does little good. It's time to deal with the here and now, and to release your old attachments. You're open to new possibilities, but cannot accomplish that if you're stuck in the past.

CAREER AND FINANCE
You're ready for the competition, and may have more drive and confidence when it comes to promoting your abilities and ideas. Attention to the details of a project brings excellent results after the 15th, so do your homework! Watch for potential misunderstandings or even outright deception from the 15th–18th, when you may fail to notice crucial facts. Take the time to revamp your budget following the New Moon on the 25th.

OPPORTUNITY OF THE MONTH
Opening to a powerful level of spiritual energy strengthens your creativity. It's time to release what you no longer need and open your heart to new possibilities.

AFFIRMATION FOR THE MONTH
"My heart is filled with pure love."

Rewarding Days: 4, 5, 6, 15, 19, 20, 23, 24, 27
Challenging Days: 2, 3, 10, 11, 17, 18, 29, 30, 31

Taurus/June

Primary Focus

Feeling romantic, your approach to life takes on an aura of realistic, yet hopeful expectation. Now's the time to get serious about what you want and need, although you may have to break out of some old attitudes to manifest those needs.

Health and Fitness

Ignoring physical complaints disrupts your peace of mind, so consult a health-care practitioner about your concerns. Finding enough energy to get through the day can be tough, since your stress levels are high. Taking time for fitness will make a huge difference.

Romance and Relationships

With Venus in Taurus through the 24th, you're feeling more ready for love and less inner resistance to opening your heart. But there are a few complications, particularly if you're attracted to someone who is unavailable. Communicating your needs during the Full Moon on the 9th results from pressing needs for intimacy. But you may also pull away, particularly if you're disillusioned with your current situation. Watch your expectations—they can be deadly!

Career and Finance

Be particularly attentive to financial matters, and if you cannot get the information you need, do not take the risk of investing your time or energy. Jumping into something of questionable value or integrity can be much too costly. After the New Moon on the 23rd, you'll have better information and may feel more confident about your options, so why rush into something? Network and communicate now, since your ideas set the stage for progress.

Opportunity of the Month

Get the facts before you make commitments after the 9th, since the promises will have a strong hold on your life for a long time.

Affirmation for the Month
"I clearly communicate my thoughts and needs."

Rewarding Days: 1, 2, 11, 12, 16, 19, 20, 24, 25, 28
Challenging Days: 6, 7, 8, 13, 14, 26, 27

TAURUS/JULY

PRIMARY FOCUS

Travel, communication, and interactive learning play a valuable role in your life now, but in order to take advantage of your options you must also take the initiative some of the time. This is not a time to wait around—it's a time to act, interact, and make your presence known.

HEALTH AND FITNESS

Short vacations and regular breaks in your routine provide the respite you need to maintain your energy. Watch your tendency to worry too much, and focus mental energy on things you can actually influence.

ROMANCE AND RELATIONSHIPS

Sharing your feelings is not always easy, but now you may at least be more comfortable talking about your needs and desires, especially if you share common ideals or philosophies with your sweetheart. Focusing on the spiritual essence of your relationships brings greater trust during the Full Moon on the 9th. Family issues become more urgent after the New Moon on the 23rd, when changes in your life may prompt criticism or misunderstandings.

CAREER AND FINANCE

Attending meetings or conferences or making presentations positively influences your career, and aligning yourself with those whose ethics reflect or agree with yours can place you in a more influential position. Make sure that you promise only what you can deliver after the 19th, since your reputation can suffer if you over-obligate your time or energy. However, you do have supportive friends in the ranks, so ask for help when you need it.

OPPORTUNITY OF THE MONTH

Although you may have questions about new situations that emerge from the 1st–8th, you'll be happier in the long run if you make an effort to accommodate these changes.

AFFIRMATION FOR THE MONTH
"I make decisions based upon a broad range of information."

Rewarding Days: 8, 9, 13, 17, 18, 21, 22, 26
Challenging Days: 3, 4, 5, 10, 11, 23, 24, 30, 31

TAURUS/AUGUST

PRIMARY FOCUS
Coping with Mercury's retrograde through the 23rd can be quite a hassle, especially if you're facing deadlines or waiting for final results. Concentrate on dealing with pressing priorities, and forget about exploring new options until you've finished what you've started.

HEALTH AND FITNESS
Staying active can be difficult, particularly if your schedule keeps getting interrupted. Allow some time for your fitness activities just to keep the tension at bay and to generate enough energy to get through each day—one day at a time!

ROMANCE AND RELATIONSHIPS
You may feel like you're in some kind of time tunnel, dealing with old family issues while trying to break into a new life. The lunar eclipse on the 7th draws your attention to the way you are pursuing your aim, and whom you are trying to impress in the process. Romance can be interrupted by family matters during the solar eclipse on the 21st, and pitting one against the other will only frustrate everyone.

CAREER AND FINANCE
Before agreeing to take on new responsibilities at work, clarify your obligations and the expectations of your superiors. Watch for potential disruptions and delays from the 14th–31st, and be on the alert for power struggles during this time period, too. Signing contracts and making new investments can lead to complications, so use this month to iron out details, and then consider signing those formal agreements after the 23rd.

OPPORTUNITY OF THE MONTH
Get back in touch with those who've supported you in the past if you need someone on your side from the 1st–14th. You may have to go it alone after that.

AFFIRMATION FOR THE MONTH
"My actions reflect my integrity, honesty, and caring."

Rewarding Days: 4, 5, 9, 10, 13, 14, 22, 23
Challenging Days: 1, 7, 8, 20, 21, 27, 28, 29

TAURUS/SEPTEMBER

PRIMARY FOCUS

Friction or turmoil at home can be the result of moving or busy projects, but you may also be dealing with emotional issues that need to be confronted. Clarify your main priorities, concentrate on creative solutions, and work toward resolving crises.

HEALTH AND FITNESS

Physical and emotional stress results from unexpected changes, but you can regain a sense of direction by letting go of the things (and people) you cannot control. Allow ample time for recreational activities, play, and creative enjoyment. Laughter is healing.

ROMANCE AND RELATIONSHIPS

Despite feeling a need to break away from those who seem to be holding you back, you still have to honor your responsibilities. Open your heart during the lunar eclipse on the 6th, when giving and receiving loving energy fills your heart. If someone in your family won't accept your lover, remind yourself whose life it is, after all. Renewed hope in love emerges during the New Moon on the 20th.

CAREER AND FINANCE

Your talents and artistry work to your benefit in career, and by cultivating your special gifts, you'll also feel more satisfied with your life. If you're feeling competitive, find out why, and watch your tendency to push a little too far from the 1st–7th—you don't want to alienate someone important! Finances stabilize after the 10th, when your investments also look quite promising. A lucrative situation is tantalizing, but be sure you get what you pay for.

OPPORTUNITY OF THE MONTH

Although you may be tempted to try one of those get-rich-quick schemes, avoid anything requiring you to invest too much. Set your limits and stick to them.

AFFIRMATION FOR THE MONTH
"My creativity flows from a loving heart."

Rewarding Days: 1, 2, 5, 6, 9, 10, 14, 18, 19, 28, 29
Challenging Days: 3, 4, 16, 17, 23, 24, 25, 30

TAURUS/OCTOBER

PRIMARY FOCUS
Ask for help, but you also need to extend your own support whenever possible. Taking advantage of the goodwill of others without showing your appreciation can undermine your reputation.

HEALTH AND FITNESS
Higher energy levels add to your confidence. However, there's a tendency to ignore your limitations, which can aggravate an old injury or weaken your vitality mid-month. Concentrate on building endurance, since you'll probably need it to meet your obligations.

ROMANCE AND RELATIONSHIPS
Getting closer to your sweetheart requires you to demonstrate your affection. You're in a very romantic mood after the 9th, and may finally be willing to take the risks of intimacy. Talk about your deeper feelings and become a good listener. This can be a time of positive reciprocity—when you each learn to give and receive. If you're not ready for a commitment and prefer to play the field, say so. Otherwise, you'll just get into trouble.

CAREER AND FINANCE
Work circumstances can improve, but they have to be inclusive or you'll feel caught in an uncomfortable compromise. Watch out for financial squabbles after the 10th, when the struggle to reach an agreement on joint property can get really sticky. If you feel someone is withholding information, confront them. Different situations or changes at work emerge after the New Moon on the 20th.

OPPORTUNITY OF THE MONTH
Speculative investments offer hopeful options from the 6th–15th. After that, anything new should be thoroughly investigated.

AFFIRMATION FOR THE MONTH
"I readily show my appreciation for the goodwill and
generosity of others."

Rewarding Days: 3, 7, 8, 11, 15, 16, 25, 26, 30
Challenging Days: 1, 2, 13, 14, 20, 21, 28, 29

TAURUS/NOVEMBER

PRIMARY FOCUS
Agreements with others must be carefully considered if they are to work to the benefit of all concerned. Although you may want to give someone the benefit of the doubt, make sure he or she really deserves your trust and support before you go out on a limb.

HEALTH AND FITNESS
Your physical vitality continues to improve and you'll be amazed at your progress if you concentrate on increasing your endurance. Remember to stretch, and develop some flexibility with that new strength!

ROMANCE AND RELATIONSHIPS
Partnerships can be rewarding, if you're in the right situation! Otherwise, you may find yourself pulling away. The Taurus Full Moon on the 4th marks a powerful period of emotional awareness, allowing you to take inventory of your deeper feelings. You'll succeed in bringing life back into an existing relationship or initiating something new if you make time for romantic interludes and relish the flow of love.

CAREER AND FINANCE
Speculative investments have a lot to offer, but you still have to limit your expenditures to avoid wasting valuable resources from the 1st–14th. During the New Moon on the 18th, a new source of funding may emerge, possibly from a business partnership or legal agreement. Negotiate during Mercury's retrograde from the 21st–30th, but don't show your hand. Avoid impulsively jumping to conclusions, since investigating uncovers a different set of options.

OPPORTUNITY OF THE MONTH
Sharing your creativity and showcasing your artistry works to your advantage from the 1st–17th. Others can be very helpful, particularly if they get something in return.

AFFIRMATION FOR THE MONTH
"I look beneath the surface to find the true value of my life."

Rewarding Days: 3, 4, 7, 8, 12, 22, 27
Challenging Days: 9, 10, 17, 18, 24, 25

TAURUS/DECEMBER

PRIMARY FOCUS
Those blocks in your path seem to be clearing now, but you still need to move carefully to avoid falling into the same old ruts. You make progress on the career front through education, travel, or publishing.

HEALTH AND FITNESS
Be careful during high activity levels, since you run the risk of injury if you're in high-risk or unfamiliar situations. If you're uncertain about whether or not to take that aerobics class, consult your physician. You do need to stay active, but at a level that is healthy for you.

ROMANCE AND RELATIONSHIPS
Getting rid of old emotional baggage is a key issue if your love is to survive. You're ready to take your relationship into a more spiritual level and a vacation retreat or time away from your regular schedule may offer just the chance you need to show your sweetheart how much you care. If you're seeking a new love, your best opportunities occur after the 12th, when you may meet someone while traveling. Reunions can also be quite wonderful after the 23rd.

CAREER AND FINANCE
The Full Moon on the 3rd marks an important time for evaluating your financial situation. Take a careful look at your debts and make plans to decrease your liabilities by getting rid of what you no longer need. The New Moon on the 18th is a good time to reorganize your finances or negotiate a long-term business agreement. Attend conferences or schedule meetings after the 12th, but watch out for competitors from the 12th–20th.

OPPORTUNITY OF THE MONTH
From the 20th–31st, you can take a much-needed break and still come out ahead. Blending business with pleasure is also an option at this time; just don't overdo the business part.

AFFIRMATION FOR THE MONTH
"I am whole, healthy, and happy!"

Rewarding Days: 1, 2, 5, 9, 10, 19, 20, 28, 29
Challenging Days: 7, 8, 14, 15, 21, 22, 23

TAURUS ♉ ACTION TABLE	Jan.	Feb.	Mar.	Apr.	May	June	July	Aug.	Sept.	Oct.	Nov.	Dec.
Change Residence							1–31	1–31	1–7			
Begin a Course of Study					24, 25							
Join a Club		26, 27										
Ask for a Raise				26, 27								
Begin a Romance									20			
Visit a Doctor			8–31	1–30	1–14				24–30	1–11		
Start a Diet	18, 19	14, 15	13–15	10, 11	7, 8	3–5	1, 2, 28, 29	24–26	21, 22	18, 19	14–16	11–13
Seek Employment		2–19							24–30	1–11		
Take a Vacation	25, 26	21–23	21, 22	17–19	14–16	1, 12	8, 9	4–6	1, 2, 28, 29	24, 25, 27	22, 23	19, 20
End a Relationship				10, 11								
Change Your Wardrobe									8–23			
Seek Professional Advice	20–22	17, 18	16–18	12–14	10, 11	6, 7	3–5, 30, 31	27, 28	23–25	20–22	17, 18	14, 15
Have a Make-Over				11								
Obtain a Loan	23, 24	19–21	19, 20	15, 16	12, 13	8–10	6, 7	2, 3, 29–31	26, 27	23, 24	19–21	16–18

These dates reflect the best (but not the only) times for success and ease in these activities, according to your sign.

GEMINI

The Twins
May 21–June 21

Element: Air
Quality: Mutable
Polarity: Masculine/Yang
Planetary Ruler: Mercury
Meditation: "My mind is linked to The Source."
Gemstone: Agate
Power Stones: Emerald, Alexandrite, Aquamarine
Glyph: Pillars of Duality ♊
Anatomy: Arms, Hands, Shoulders, Lungs, Nerves
Colors: Orange, Yellow
Animals: Monkeys, Talking Birds, Flying Insects
Myths/Legends: Peter Pan, Castor and Pollux
House Association: Third
Opposite Sign: Sagittarius
Flower: Lily of the Valley
Key Word: Versatility

Positive Expression:

Inquisitive   Flexible
Clever   Perceptive
Incisive   Articulate
Rational

Misuse of Energy:

Gossipy   Erratic
Frivolous   Unsettled
Unfocused   Prankish
Fickle

 # GEMINI

YOUR EGO'S STRENGTHS AND WEAKNESSES

Ever curious about the world, its people, and endless options, you are continually exploring new ideas. This keeps you young, and your ability to embrace diversity coupled with your adaptability to changing circumstances gives you a debonair personality. You have been "The Questioner" from childhood and you're still quizzical, and enjoy a wide variety of interests.

Your connection to the energy of Mercury stimulates your desire to be around others who are intelligent, and also adds to your thrill in other mental pursuits such as writing, travel, literature, and education. You may be a first-class negotiator, and have a knack for bringing the right people together and helping them find their common ground. Sometimes, though, you can be accused of playing both sides against one another in your attempts to avoid being stuck in one position. You can usually talk yourself out of those tight spots, though!

Your multifaceted personality and multifarious mind can be frustrating to those who want to know where you stand or who demand commitments before you're ready to give them. Juggling all those projects you have going can be exhausting. By integrating your natural intuitive abilities with factual understanding, you'll develop the trademark of ingenuity. Once your thirst for awareness has led you to surrender your mind to the Universal Mind, you may finally discover your true nature.

YOUR APPROACH TO ROMANCE

Since sharing ideas and making contact are high priorities, you are always relating. Your witty conversation can attract many different people, and you can entice others with your stories and tales like a modern-day Scheherazade. Although you may take a while to settle into a committed relationship, you can be an excellent partner, particularly if you have plenty of freedom to be yourself and your partner's intellectual gifts rival your own.

Your strong attraction to Sagittarius, your opposite sign, can be thrilling, although you may feel somewhat overpowered by this sign's wanderlust in the long term. You're most at ease with the other air signs—Gemini, Libra, and Aquarius—whose intellectual and social nature make you feel right at home.

Aries' assertive exuberance and independence are delightfully invigorating. Taurus is sensual and comfy until you want to go somewhere, when you may feel held back. Stimulated by another Gemini, you can also feel driven to distraction until you each set reasonable personal limitations. Cancer's emotional sensitivity is nurturing, but financial squabbles and struggles to feel free can result if he or she is too protective. Leo's dramatic warmth and flair for having fun can be truly heavenly. Sharing ideas with Virgo is thought-provoking, but sometimes tedious.

Libra's artistry and social graces are alluring. Engaged by Scorpio's intense emotionality, you can be frustrated by your different approaches to life. You can feel very connected to Capricorn, but be ready for a few power struggles. Aquarius feels like a breath of fresh air, and you'll enjoy exploring new options together. At least temporarily interested in Pisces, you enjoy those fantasy-filled nights but can get confused by what they want during the day.

YOUR CAREER DEVELOPMENT

Although you may not stick with the same career for your entire life, your choices will be centered on your need to use your mind, communicate, and build bridges that link ideas. You need a career offering the flexibility to change and try different things, and by developing your mental and communication skills, you can have a wide variety of choices.

Your fascination with the mind may lead you to a career in education or counseling. You can also be successful in politics, writing, public relations, speaking, advertising, or broadcasting. If you want to work with your hands, you might enjoy highly technical careers like dentistry, drafting, design, carving, secretarial areas, computer science, or musical pursuits. In the performing arts, you might want to express your wit and charm through comedy, clowning, story-telling, pantomime, juggling, or acting.

YOUR USE OF POWER

The strength of ideas and knowledge provide an honest sense of power to you. By attracting people from a wide variety of backgrounds, you can help develop programs that illustrate the true diversity of the human spirit. It is this patchwork of diversity that also represents power to you—the power of inclusion.

While your wit, contagious enthusiasm, and persuasive communication can be dazzling, you may fail to explore the depths of some situations. If you simply skim the surface, your projected air of superficiality can undermine your power and influence. Integrating your ideas with those of others and developing true understanding will strengthen your effectiveness.

You're well-versed for this high-tech world that is preparing to enter a new millennium, and you can be an integral part of the bridge connecting what has gone before and what is yet to come. You may be called on to link the divergent factions and cultures on the planet, and your ability to identify with the young may also make you a good candidate for empowering the generations who will take charge of humanity's future.

Learning to trust the wind beneath your wings will allow you to soar to the heights and open to your fullest potential, and in the process, the spirit of humanity can fly with you.

FAMOUS GEMINIS

King Albert II, Naomi Campbell, Clint Eastwood, Melissa Etheridge, Michael J. Fox, Kenny G., Steffi Graf, Lisa Kudrow, Alanis Morrisette, Mike Myers, Stevie Nicks, Frank Oz, Cole Porter, The Artist Formerly Known as Prince, Lea Thompson.

THE YEAR AHEAD FOR GEMINI

Although some of your old ideologies may be tested, the challenge to open to a more innovative understanding of life makes the experience quite worthwhile. The changes you encounter during the year stem from your need to release the things you've outgrown, although you may also find new avenues for self-expression that were previously unavailable to you. A long period of heightened awareness begins during 1998, and as a result of the inner connection you discover your life can become much more fascinating.

During Jupiter's transit in Pisces this year, your focus on expanding your career options is powerful. Opportunities that opened during the last year can be an excellent boost to your reputation, and you're also discovering that you expect more from yourself as a result. It's time to promote yourself and your abilities, and to let the world know you're there. But you also need to remember your limitations in the process, since just blowing your own horn without refining your talents can be a bit irritating to those who have to listen to the concert. The primary thing to remember with Jupiter influencing the Tenth House of your solar chart is that your reputation can grow, and whether that reputation is based on outstanding accomplishments or notorious blunders is up to you.

Saturn influences your solar Eleventh and Twelfth houses this year. Since you've probably been striving to clarify your long-range goals, your efforts center on putting those goals in place. By the summer, when Saturn moves into your solar Twelfth House, you may encounter obstacles you had not foreseen, although these are usually centered on your own internal resistance to some type of change. Granted, changes are usually easy for you once you have a good idea about how they work, but your deep psychological anxieties will test your ability to use your basic mutability in the most positive manner. Use this time to get a preview of your inner changes that will carry you into the new millennium. This year provides another chance to refine goals, eliminate those obstacles from your path, and manifest a stable platform for your personal and professional growth.

The outer planets—Uranus, Neptune, and Pluto—provide a strong stimulus that enhances your creativity and strengthens your sense of individuality. You're seeing real miracles in your life as a result of your ability to concentrate your awareness and mental ingenuity on the things that are in harmony with your higher needs. However, the solar and lunar eclipses will test your vision during 1998. Those tests arise from your old emotional programming and your desire to please those whose approval seems to endorse your personal worth. It's one thing to have support from those who understand your aims and endeavors, and another to alter your self-expression to gain that support. On other levels, you are also gaining a more profound awareness of the importance of discriminating between false value systems and embracing those traditions and values you've learned from your family that still form an important part of your identity. That's like the case of a zebra trying to change his stripes. Removing those things from your identity that are not appropriate or applicable to your personal growth is necessary, but trying to run away from who you are will be impossible.

♊ ♊ ♊

If you were born from May 21–24th, you're feeling an increased imaginative sensibility. With Neptune in trine aspect to your Sun, this can be an excellent year for any type of creative endeavor. This cycle is also exceptional for spiritual growth and heightened awareness, particularly if you devote time and energy to communing with your inner self. Additionally with Saturn's transit in semisextile to your Sun through summer and early autumn, your need to step into an increased focus and clarity concerning your responsibilities can prompt you to employ your talents more fully in the realm of your career or work. You can accomplish amazing feats by coupling your creative sensibilities with practical ideas and may feel inspired to take on projects that will have a positive effect in the world around you. If you are involved in work that has an impact on others, you may feel especially rewarded, particularly if you're in a situation allowing you to utilize your skills and abilities to their ultimate. But if your life circumstances are too inhibiting, you may want to reconsider your options and shift your focus to something that will fill your soul with joy.

♊   ♊   ♊

You need to make a careful assessment of your priorities **if you were born from May 25th–June 11th.** Saturn's transit in semi-square aspect to your Sun stimulates a need to devote your time to things that matter. All that unnecessary distraction in your life can be extremely frustrating, and you can become impatient with your own habit of taking on too many things at once. Simplify your life by eliminating the things that are not producing growth-oriented results. Learn to say "No" to the things that you really do not want to do, and give back some of the burdens you're carrying that really belong to someone else. Examine your body's reactions to your lifestyle and habits. If you need more energy, determine what you can do (or eliminate) to create it. In your career, concentrate on refining your skills, honoring your responsibilities, and listening to the expectations of others.

♊   ♊   ♊

You're feeling a powerful need to transform your sense of self **if you were born from May 26th–30th.** Pluto's opposition to your Sun marks a period of intense transformational changes. These changes can be both internal and external, and those that seem to be pummeling you from the outside can also serve as important signals for something you need to explore more carefully on an inner level. The core of this cycle centers on healing. That means you now have a chance to address and resolve old issues on physical, emotional, and spiritual levels. If you're in situations that are counterproductive to your growth, they are likely to end, either through your own efforts or through changing circumstances. You may also discover that some things just do not work out as you had planned, but you may uncover some very important options and opportunities in the process.

♊   ♊   ♊

If you were born from May 28th–June 5th, you're feeling an influx of inventive energy while Uranus transits in trine aspect to your Sun. But unless you do something to utilize this energy, you'll waste a valuable opportunity. Those things that emphasize your uniqueness are especially promising now, and by taking advantage of situations allowing you to showcase your talents and abilities you can move at the speed of light toward achieving your goals and realizing your hopes. If your work appeals to the collective (e.g. advertising, public service, or communications) you can have amazing success by stepping into the forefront with your unique contributions. This is also a rebellious cycle, and you're not likely to sit back while someone inhibits your chances or stands in the way of your growth. The rebellions you stage can be quite benign, and your ability to inspire the support of others surrounds you with those who share your ideals and hopes.

♊   ♊   ♊

You're experiencing a cycle of unusual choices **if you were born from June 5th–9th.** Neptune's transit in sesquiquadrate to your Sun can cloud your judgment when it comes to everyday matters. You can also be hornswoggled by unscrupulous characters and not even know it! Be particularly cautious in matters involving your money and resources, since what you think seems too good to be true probably is. However, this energy can be quite useful when applied to creative or artistic endeavors, especially if you need to break out of your routine and try something a little different just to gain a new perspective. This is a great time to rise above the ordinary into the realm of genius, even though you may not see it at the time!

♊   ♊   ♊

If you were born from June 12th–19th, you're feeling the disruptive influence of Uranus in sesquiquadrate aspect to your Sun this year. Jumping into new situations unprepared can leave you in quite a pickle. You may feel more like a daredevil, which is OK if you do your homework. But before you try bungee-jumping, make sure a team of experts checks your equipment. When applied to situations like romance, you can get yourself into trouble by becoming quite fascinated by someone who is emotionally unavailable, or you may send signals that you're interested when you don't even have time to wash the dishes! This cycle is a test of your ability to discriminate between those changes that will lead to growth and temptations that simply complicate your life.

Ⅱ   Ⅱ   Ⅱ

If you were born from June 19th–21st, you may feel a little confused while Neptune completes its transit in quincunx to your Sun. Although this cycle began last year, it is not yet over! You're still making adjustments between your dreams and the realities of your life. If you've been ignoring your inner promptings in favor of "pure" logic, you can run into ample opportunities to learn that your intuitive self was signaling you to follow the best direction. This is an excellent time to blend intuitive and rational processes, although the right mix between the two will vary with every situation, and leaning totally in one direction or the other will simply leave you exhausted and frustrated. Physically, take special care to avoid substances and environmental conditions that drain your energy, and if you're concerned about something that's bothering you, check it out with a professional. In relationships, learn to keep your emotional boundaries intact, or you will be left in a lurch more than once!

TOOLS TO MAKE A DIFFERENCE

Blending spiritual and philosophical ideals into your total life experience becomes a stronger impetus this year. Connecting to others who share your ideas can be quite inspiring, and your own ideas and beliefs can add a spark of hope to the lives of others, too. Allowing time for silence each day can be especially healing. Whether you do this through a period of meditation or contemplation, or if you just find a quiet place to allow yourself to feel calm and to release the impact of life around you, the effect can be one of strengthening your sense of wholeness. If you are continually bombarded by the energies of others, the stresses of your work and the cacophony of life can frazzle your nervous system.

This is an excellent year for learning and teaching, and whether you're attending weekend workshops or a full-scale course, you'll thrive on opening your mind to new ideas. Travel can also provide a broad range of benefits to your life this year. Journal writing can be an illuminating tool, and if your work involves writing, you might enjoy the contrast between reflective writing and logical reasoning. If your energy seems too scattered, you might benefit from using the flower essence remedies. Particularly useful for you are hornbeam, mimulus and white chestnut, and you'll also benefit from morning glory and blackberry essences. When you're feeling scattered, give yourself a moment to breathe deeply and fully, something you can do any time of the day. In the evenings, make sure you're really relaxing at the end of the day. If you need a little assistance, schedule regular massages, do hatha yoga or tai chi, and enjoy a relaxing cup of herbal tea.

During your periods of meditation and reflection, concentrate on letting yourself rise above the ordinary experiences of life. Imagine that you have wings and the capacity to fly into other dimensions. You can fly wherever you want to go, gliding through space and arriving at your destinations fully aware and safe. Explore many options. Allow yourself to return to places in your consciousness that are especially illuminating. At the end of your inner flying sessions, breathe deeply and remind yourself that you are centered within your own body and connected to the Earth in a positive sense. That connection allows you to share your ideas and commune with others, forever learning, and always open to the many possibilities of life.

AFFIRMATION FOR THE YEAR

"My mind is a vessel open to Truth."

Gemini/January

Primary Focus
This is an excellent time to learn more, as either student or teacher. Travel can also play an important role. The most important feature of this cycle is taking action to reach into a new realm of possibilities.

Health and Fitness
Getting back to nature can be invigorating now, and your favorite winter recreation may have the added benefit of lifting your spirits. A retreat or vacation can be enjoyable as long as you have plenty of freedom for spontaneity.

Romance and Relationships
It's time to take a careful look at the way you handle your close relationships. If your self-esteem is low, you may be too emotionally guarded, especially during the Full Moon on the 12th. Exploring your spiritual connection and establishing a bond that transcends the ordinary makes your relationships worthwhile. You may discover something exciting about your lover or meet someone absolutely fascinating during the New Moon on the 28th.

Career and Finance
Attending conferences, making presentations, and generating support for your ideas works to your advantage. Budgetary details are also important, and you must be very careful in matters of taxes, loans, inheritance, or joint finances since you may not be aware of significant details that affect the long-term outcome. If you need more time to review, take it, and distrust anyone who tries to push you before you're comfortable with your decision.

Opportunity of the Month
Publishing and teaching can be especially profitable now, but you also are in an excellent position to deal with courts and legal matters. Your opinions and ideas can sway others.

Affirmation for the Month
"My thoughts and actions open the door for a fulfilling future."

Rewarding Days: 4, 8, 9, 10, 18, 19, 27, 28
Challenging Days: 2, 3, 15, 16, 17, 23, 24, 29, 30

GEMINI/FEBRUARY

PRIMARY FOCUS
You're driven to establish yourself, and may go too far if you're only focused on your own agenda. Your success depends on your actions and efforts, but your reputation demands an attitude of confidence coupled with compassion.

HEALTH AND FITNESS
Although you need to remain active, try to set a few reasonable limits, since it's very easy to overdo it. Avoid high-risk situations from the 1st–14th, and watch your driving. Watch out for the other guy, too!

ROMANCE AND RELATIONSHIPS
You can be a bit short-tempered, and your words need careful consideration, since they can be inflammatory. Watch expectations of relationships, since you may feel frustrated when things are not going your way. The solar eclipse on the 26th draws your attention to family matters, and if power struggles are emerging due to family situations, take a careful look at your role, since you can diffuse the conflict by knowing when to step aside.

CAREER AND FINANCE
Watch your step in your drive to reach the top! You may run into major opposition from someone who feels threatened by your popularity, talents, or strengths. Your words and actions can inspire influential support during the Full Moon on the 11th, and the recognition you gain during this time can have a powerful impact. Steer clear of agreements requiring you to take on roles you don't like. Those affiliations only weaken your position.

OPPORTUNITY OF THE MONTH
The way you handle power struggles determines the cost of your success. Honor your ethics when faced with the challenge of taking a stand or stepping out of the way.

AFFIRMATION FOR THE MONTH
"My faith in Truth is my best defense."

Rewarding Days: 5, 6, 9, 14, 15, 16, 24, 25, 28
Challenging Days: 12, 13, 19, 20, 21, 26, 27

Gemini/March

Primary Focus
Promising progress on the career front requires you to adopt more advanced ways of thinking before you can fully manifest your hopes. Examine your motivations for success during the lunar eclipse on the 12th, and get ready to soar!

Health and Fitness
Both team and individual sports offer positive challenges to physical fitness, and you may also enjoy the energy generated by competitive situations. Staying active is your key to ultimate health now.

Romance and Relationships
Taking an energetic role in your friendships provides an excellent return. Love can carry you into an experience of pure bliss, and you may finally realize a long-held dream. Spiritual ideals open your heart and allow you to achieve union in a more mystical sense. It's easier to release your old attachments, which can bring an end to an outworn relationship, allowing you to experience true loving without the burden of old guilt or pain.

Career and Finance
Although you may face a struggle completing the obligations of a partnership or carrying out your social roles from the 1st–17th, you can accomplish your aims by taking the high ground. Aligning with others who share your ideals and interests opens the way for success, and you can also be instrumental in supporting someone whose talents benefit all concerned. Be very clear in your aims during the New Moon on the 27th, since you may get what you want.

Opportunity of the Month
Your innovative ideas and ability to deal with diversity put you in a position of leadership. Take advantage of it from the 15th–25th, when you can turn the tide.

Affirmation for the Month
"I have hope for my future and joy in this moment."

Rewarding Days: 4, 5, 9, 14, 15, 23, 24, 28, 31
Challenging Days: 11, 12, 19, 20, 25, 26

Gemini/April

Primary Focus
Concentrate on completing what you've already begun, and avoid the temptation to scatter your attention. Your integrity and reputation depend on your ability to follow through on those excellent ideas.

Health and Fitness
Work toward increasing your stamina while extending your flexibility, with a fitness approach like power yoga. Stave off overindulgence, and try to avoid those places with overstocked dessert carts.

Romance and Relationships
Although you may experience a separation from a friend, you can remain connected through continuing on in the spirit of your relationship. The Full Moon on the 11th can test a friendship, but also allows you to stabilize your close relationships by allowing for the natural flow of give-and-take. A misunderstanding with someone you love may result from different philosophical viewpoints, but before you say good-bye, make sure it's what you really want.

Career and Finance
With Mercury retrograde through the 27th, you may have a bit of trouble getting your ideas off the ground, although things that are already in motion can show progress—it's just a little slow. Avoid anything financially risky from the 7th–17th, and safeguard your valuables during this time, too. Plans for a new project or improved circumstances are readily formulated after the New Moon on the 26th, when your experience works to your benefit.

Opportunity of the Month
If you're aware that you could be the target of another's manipulation, that person has less power over you now. Keep your eyes open from the 5th–17th.

Affirmation for the Month
"I am mindful of my thoughts, actions, and feelings."

Rewarding Days: 1, 10, 11, 20, 21, 24, 28, 29
Challenging Days: 7, 8, 9, 15, 16, 22, 23, 26

Gemini/May

Primary Focus
Your path seems more certain and your aims and goals are focused, although you may be somewhat reluctant to take unnecessary risks. That's OK, since hazardous risk is not always required for progress.

Health and Fitness
You may need extra rest, and if you can't always add more hours of sleep to your schedule, at least promise yourself that you'll take more frequent breaks. Recharging throughout the day, including "power naps," helps you remain alert and energetic.

Romance and Relationships
Friends provide support, encouragement, and memorable moments. Even your romantic relationships grow through your mutual and unconditional love, and the commitments you make to those you love add clarity to your life. Strive to let go of the past, and make a promise to yourself to seek joy in everything. During the Gemini New Moon on the 25th you're feeling inspired to reach toward the future by acting on your ideas.

Career and Finance
Political action or efforts made on behalf of special interest groups stimulates progress and offers an opportunity for you to establish a positive edge to your identity. The Full Moon on the 11th draws your attention to your work environment, and marks a time of potential discord behind the scenes. After addressing the issues involved you can easily move ahead. Outline what you need from your job now, because you're ready to ask for adequate compensation on the 25th.

Opportunity of the Month
Get everything out of the way so you have plenty of time, room, and resources to take advantage of a special energy boost after the 24th.

Affirmation for the Month
"My true friends echo the message of my heart."

Rewarding Days: 2, 3, 7,8, 17, 18, 21, 22, 25, 26, 30
Challenging Days: 4, 5, 6, 12, 13, 19, 20

GEMINI/JUNE

PRIMARY FOCUS
Energized mentally and physically, you're in a great position to voice your ideas and generate an enthusiastic response. Avoid dogmatic postures, though, because they will stick with you, even if you temper your presentation later!

HEALTH AND FITNESS
Regular exercise is crucial, since if you don't burn off some of that energy, you'll feel like your nervous system is fried. Make sure you're getting adequate B-vitamins and minerals, and steady your pace whenever possible. All that rushing around is tiring!

ROMANCE AND RELATIONSHIPS
With the Full Moon on the 9th emphasizing partnerships, you're especially sensitive to partnership issues and serenity within relationships. Although it's tempting to push some of those issues, knowing when to step back and allow the dust to settle may allow for greater understanding, at least sometimes. But that's different from rolling over and letting someone assert their will over your own!

CAREER AND FINANCE
Contracts and agreements need special attention, but there's hope for a clear consensus. However, watch for competitive action from those who feel threatened by you from the 1st–6th; your own posture can make the difference between success and failure. Avoid emotionally driven expenditures, particularly near the New Moon on the 23rd, when you may think you just can't live without that new gadget. Research it carefully, and shop for a bargain.

OPPORTUNITY OF THE MONTH
You're almost unstoppable from the 1st–10th, but you can get into trouble if you fail to respond to the needs and reactions of others. Pay attention to those signals!

AFFIRMATION FOR THE MONTH
"I strive to achieve balance and harmony in all relationships."

Rewarding Days: 4, 5, 13, 14, 18, 22, 23
Challenging Days: 1, 2, 8, 9, 10, 28, 29

GEMINI/JULY

PRIMARY FOCUS

Watch your commitments—from time to money—since it's easy to have too much happening at once. To avoid feeling overwhelmed, sort through your priorities and concentrate on the top tier of obligations first. Don't sweat the small stuff!

HEALTH AND FITNESS

If you're feeling a little tired, it's probably because your endurance levels need to be strengthened. Gradually increase your stamina by making a commitment to fitness. Get into a class, walk, or do something you enjoy as recreation.

ROMANCE AND RELATIONSHIPS

With Venus in Gemini until the 20th, you're ready to experience greater fulfillment in your love relationships, and it's easier to show your most attractive features. Extend your appreciation to those you value and trust, and make an effort to connect with the people in your life whose support and understanding make a difference. You may actually open some new pathways by simply saying "hello" to the right person during the New Moon on the 23rd!

CAREER AND FINANCE

Money matters need extra attention during the Full Moon on the 9th, when joint finances require reconsideration, particularly if you've been dissatisfied with your end of the bargain. If you're appealing to others for their resources, you'll have the best response from the 1st–9th. It's easy to underestimate the costs of a large project mid-month, so remember that when you're planning your budget.

OPPORTUNITY OF THE MONTH

Your influence grows, thanks to your connections to others after the 23rd, so make important presentations, send correspondence, and attend meetings after that time.

AFFIRMATION FOR THE MONTH
"I use all my resources wisely."

Rewarding Days: 1, 2, 10, 11, 19, 20, 23, 24, 28, 29
Challenging Days: 6, 7, 8, 12, 13, 26, 27

Gemini/August

Primary Focus
Writing, communicating, and sharing your ideas is usually easy for you, and you can establish a powerful presence now, by extending yourself through your communicative abilities. Don't be afraid of offering something different, and take advantage of new technologies.

Health and Fitness
You could easily put your fitness needs aside in favor of all those commitments you have to juggle, but think again before trading your bike for that cushy chair. Getting outside in the open air can be invigorating after the 13th, so put it on your agenda!

Romance and Relationships
Your desire to experience a spiritual union during the lunar eclipse on the 7th is intense. Travel or vacation with your lover, and if you're looking for a new relationship, seek it in the places and activities that inspire your higher consciousness. To renew a tired relationship, plan a getaway or meet at your special rendez-vous during the solar eclipse on the 21st, when you're ready to share your innermost thoughts.

Career and Finance
Even though Mercury is retrograde through the 23rd you can still make important connections. However, you're in the best position to negotiate and clarify, and then to go forward with new plans after the 23rd. Impulsive expenditures are too costly, even if you do think you need to upgrade your system. Do the research and plan your purchases carefully. A conservative attitude works to your advantage in all dealings.

Opportunity of the Month
Legal matters, travel, and educational pursuits can be rewarding early in the month, although the final outcome may not emerge until October!

Affirmation for the Month
"I am a good listener."

Rewarding Days: 7, 8, 11, 12, 15, 16, 25
Challenging Days: 2, 3, 9, 10, 22, 23, 29, 30, 31

Gemini/September

Primary Focus

There's another lunar eclipse on the 6th, and it influences your need to balance career and family demands. Watch that tendency to sit on the fence until the last minute—lack of commitment can be costly!

Health and Fitness

Stress builds when you feel pressured by others early in the month. Find someone whose supportive nature encourages you to release that emotional backlog—see your therapist or astrologer!

Romance and Relationships

Family tension can increase, particularly if there are unresolved issues dancing just below the surface. Sort out your differences with siblings from the 1st–7th, and whenever possible, adjust your own attitude. Romance enters the picture after the 24th, but until then, you may feel like there's just no time to let down your emotional walls. Examine your deeper feelings, and trust your instincts to guide you. Pure logic may not suffice.

Career and Finance

Your career commitments take extra time and energy, but you can make the most of your efforts if you'll concentrate on developing a well-considered idea and sharing your plans with those whose influence will make a difference from the 1st–8th, and again after the 23rd. If you need to spend some extra time or money on projects around the house, schedule those from the 9th–23rd, and avoid the inclination to do everything yourself.

Opportunity of the Month

New ideas can be exciting from the 1st–4th, but do some research before you jump on the bandwagon. The New Moon on the 20th is a better time to take action.

Affirmation for the Month
"I consider the effects before I speak or take action."

Rewarding Days: 3, 4, 7, 11, 12, 16, 21, 22, 30
Challenging Days: 5, 6, 18, 19, 20, 26, 27

GEMINI/OCTOBER

PRIMARY FOCUS
Creative endeavors and romantic interests dominate your time, although you can be a little overwhelming in your actions or attitudes. If you're on the receiving end of power plays, think about your most effective options before you act.

HEALTH AND FITNESS
You're eager to participate in fun fitness activities, and may even make some recreational choices because of their social implications. That's OK; everyone has a hidden agenda sometime!

ROMANCE AND RELATIONSHIPS
With an open heart and flexible attitude, your approach to relationships allows a lot of room for pleasurable experimentation. During the Full Moon on the 5th you may have stars in your eyes, and you might want to check out your options with your best friend before you take action. A misunderstanding can lead to harsh disputes from the 11th–20th, so be clear about your intentions and actions, and try a fresh approach during the New Moon on the 20th.

CAREER AND FINANCE
Although your aims may be perfectly clear to you, someone else may view your actions as a call to arms, so be alert to the potential of conflicts in your career and competition from someone who feels threatened by you. Negotiations can break down mid-month, but by focusing on the spirit of your aims, you can make adjustments from the 18th–24th that lead to an agreement. Equipment failures can inhibit progress from the 6th–26th, so have a back-up plan.

OPPORTUNITY OF THE MONTH
Your creative ideas work to your best advantage from the 1st–10th, and during this time you'll also attract your best support from others.

AFFIRMATION FOR THE MONTH
"My heart is filled with love."

Rewarding Days: 1, 5, 6, 9, 10, 13, 18, 19, 28, 29
Challenging Days: 3, 4, 15, 16, 17, 23, 24, 30, 31

Gemini/November

Primary Focus
Interactions with others have a significant effect on your progress and effectiveness. However, cooperative efforts aren't as easy as you hope, particularly if you disagree over a division of labor or power.

Health and Fitness
Physical health concerns are high on your list, particularly if you're feeling overly tired due to the stress from work. Continue to allow ample time to stay active, and consider getting regular massages this month. Releasing tension is your best energy booster.

Romance and Relationships
Partnership issues emerge, and may center on your needs for increased autonomy. If you're feeling too penned-in, first determine how your own attitudes are playing a part; maybe you're holding yourself back. You're feeling less reluctant to talk about your concerns after the New Moon on the 18th, when you may also be more open to developing fresh solutions to your old issues. Romance is strongest after the 23rd.

Career and Finance
Conflicts or turmoil at work may simply be the result of changing circumstances that have everybody on edge. If there are issues that need resolution, they will emerge during the Full Moon on the 4th, when stubborn attitudes get in everybody's way. Mercury enters its retrograde cycle on the 21st, and legal agreements will need special consideration after that time. Negotiate, but wait to sign until you're sure of all the details. Something better may come up, anyway.

Opportunity of the Month
Breaking away from situations you've outgrown or that are working against your best interests is relatively easy now. Just try to keep damage control within reasonable limits.

Affirmation for the Month
"I handle conflicts with compassion and diplomacy."

Rewarding Days: 1, 2, 5, 6, 14, 15, 24, 25
Challenging Days: 12, 13, 19, 20, 21, 26, 27

Gemini/December

Primary Focus
Old issues emerge, and if you've left some things undone in the past, they seem to come back to haunt you now. Getting to the core is much easier, but you have to be honest with yourself about what you really want. If you're still holding a grudge, you won't get anywhere!

Health and Fitness
Getting or staying fit can be fun, and if you're looking for an excuse to get your partner involved, you may finally find it early in the month. Emotional stress is still high, so stay active to release the pressure.

Romance and Relationships
Before you assume anything about a relationship, talk about it first. Expectations can be a problem until after the Gemini Full Moon on the 3rd, and if you clarify your expectations, everything will run more smoothly. Do something romantically inspiring for your sweetheart, and you'll be amazed at your reward, particularly if you add a bit of fantasy to the picture from the 10th–13th. Try a different approach to your partnership during the New Moon on the 18th.

Career and Finance
Mercury's retrograde from the 1st–11th adds potential difficulties to contract negotiations, legal matters, and open disputes. Your words can be an effective tool, but you can also be manipulated by language with a hidden subtext, so read between the lines, and ask an expert if you want another opinion. Your investments fare very well after the 11th, when new technology also works to your advantage.

Opportunity of the Month
Showcase your talents and abilities by taking a few creative risks from the 12th–23rd. Just make sure your choices are appropriate for the audience and situation.

Affirmation for the Month
"My heart is open to the flow of pure love."

Rewarding Days: 3, 4, 7, 11, 12, 13, 21, 22, 30, 31
Challenging Days: 9, 10, 16, 17, 18, 24, 25

GEMINI ♊ ACTION TABLE

These dates reflect the best (but not the only) times for success and ease in these activities, according to your sign.

	Jan.	Feb.	Mar.	Apr.	May	June	July	Aug.	Sept.	Oct.	Nov.	Dec.
Change Residence									8–24			
Begin a Course of Study	28, 29						23, 24	22				
Join a Club			28, 29									
Ask for a Raise					25, 26							
Begin a Romance										20		
Visit a Doctor					15–31					12–31	1	
Start a Diet	20–22	17, 18	16, 17	12–14	10, 11	6, 7	3–5, 30, 31	1, 27, 28	23, 24	20–22	17, 18	14, 15
Seek Employment		20–28	1–7							12–31	1	
Take a Vacation	27, 28	24, 25	23, 24	20, 21	17, 18	13, 14	10, 11	7, 8	3, 4, 30	1, 2, 28, 29	24, 25	21, 22
End a Relationship					30, 31							
Change Your Wardrobe										5–30		
Seek Professional Advice	23, 24	19–21	19, 20	15, 16	12, 13	8–10	6, 7	2, 3, 29–31	26, 27	23, 24	19–21	16–18
Have a Make-Over					25, 26							
Obtain a Loan	24, 25	22, 23	21, 22	17, 18, 20	14–16	11, 12	8, 9	4–6	1, 2, 28, 29	25–27	22, 23	19, 20

CANCER

The Crab
June 21–July 22

Element:	Water
Quality:	Mutable
Polarity:	Feminine/Yin
Ruler:	Moon
Meditation:	"I am aware of my inner feelings."
Gemstone:	Pearl
Power Stones:	Moonstone, Chrysocolla
Key Phrase:	"I feel"
Glyph:	Breast or Crab Claws ♋
Anatomy:	Stomach, Breasts
Colors:	Silver, Pearl, White
Animals:	Crustaceans, Cows, Chickens
Myths/Legends:	Hecate, Asherah, Hercules and the Crab
House Association:	Fourth
Opposite Sign:	Capricorn
Flower:	Larkspur
Key Word:	Receptivity

Positive Expression:		**Misuse of Energy:**	
Protective	Intuitive	Defensive	Anxious
Maternal	Patriotic	Smothering	Isolationist
Concerned	Nurturing	Brooding	Crabby
Sympathetic	Tenacious	Suspicious	Manipulative

CANCER

YOUR EGO'S STRENGTHS AND WEAKNESSES

Your energy flows easily with the natural rhythms of the cycles of change. Your energy encourages growth as "The Nurturer" of the zodiac, and you can provide comfort, support, and understanding to those who share your life. The support of family is an integral part of who you are. Even those who may not be related to you may think of you as family, because you radiate concern.

Your awareness of the ebb and flow of life and special sensitivity to emotion stems from your easy affinity with the energy of the Moon. Your enjoyment of gardening, cooking, or crafts is an outpouring of this connection, and you may have a very special feeling for children. Since your environment is a natural extension of your energy, you create comfort zones at home and at work. Maintaining your emotional boundaries is sometimes difficult, since your psychic awareness and emotionality always seem to be working overtime. You can even become smothering in your attempts to protect those you love; cutting that emotional umbilical cord takes cooperation on your part!

Instead of over-insulating yourself from the impact of emotional vulnerability or becoming caught in the insecurity that emerges when you let go of the past, use your reverence for what has gone before as a platform for your growth. Allow your sensitivity to tell you when you've reached too deeply into another person's boundaries, and learn to balance gracefully backing away with a knowledge of when to open your inviting arms. Then, the natural rhythm that propels the dance of life will lift your heart as you sing your soul's song, "For everything there is a season."

Your Approach to Romance

For you, personal fulfillment includes creating a close relationship and building a family. Even though you can be extremely passionate when you're in love, you want to feel a commitment before opening your heart completely, and you can send mixed messages to those who are attracted to you because you're trying to stay safe while you're making your come-on. It's difficult for you to let go of old hurts, and these can work like a wall, just when you want to be close. Trust your intuitive sensibilities to help you know when to drop those barriers, and then let your natural cuddly self go to work! Once you're in the right situation, you have the capacity to enjoy a relationship that matures through mutual support, care, and understanding.

Your attraction to your zodiac opposite, Capricorn, can be exceedingly powerful, and if you share similar goals, you can unite your energies to build a secure future. You feel most at home with the other water signs—Cancer, Scorpio, and Pisces—whose emotional sensibilities complement your own. With another Cancer, you may share a devotion toward developing a strong family and home. Passion and sharing sensuality with Scorpio can leave you breathless, while Pisces' imagination and spiritual mysticism take you into the realm of ecstasy.

Strongly attracted to Aries, you may lose patience with his or her immaturity. Delighting in the strength and earthiness of Taurus, you may also build a foundation for a secure future together. You'll enjoy Gemini's wit and playfulness, but you must remember to give him or her plenty of personal space. Leo loves your attention, but you may not get the same in return.

Virgo's energy encourages a relationship built on understanding and cooperation. Libra's air of detachment can throw you off-balance. Sagittarius is fun, but this sign's unpredictability can leave you feeling nervous. With Aquarius, intimate surroundings can feel completely out of place, since he or she may be a more reliable confidante than lover.

Your Career Development

You attain the assets and possessions that help you develop the lifestyle you desire through your work in the world, and you need a career that offers a sense of emotional fulfillment. Since you know how to hold onto your assets, you may become quite influential and wealthy, and you're comfortable in positions of prominence. Patriotism may lead you into politics, and you can also enjoy teaching. Studies like anthropology, archaeology, or history can be fascinating, as can medical fields or counseling professions.

Businesses with a cyclical nature—such as real estate, investments, antiques, the hotel industry, restaurant or food industry or home furnishings—can be right up your alley. Personnel management or social work are good choices, and you can be persuasive in sales. Or you may decide to use your enviable green thumb in the floral or landscaping businesses.

YOUR USE OF POWER

When you know you're prepared for all contingencies, then you feel powerful. Through attaining a sense of safety and security in the world, your power emerges to its fullest, allowing you to grow and prosper in areas that also encourage growth in others. That feeling that emerges when you're bonded with those you love creates even more power in your life.

Since you have the capacity to see the link that defines the human family, you feel most worthwhile when you create a feeling of family with those who not only share your personal life, but who share common goals in the world of work. Once you've found a way to modify traditions from the past within the framework of current trends, you experience the power of building a bridge to the future. Strength emerges when you know that you and those you love are sheltered and safe. But to remain strong, you must maintain an open awareness of your needs and continue to find ways to stay connected to the Source that sustains you.

FAMOUS CANCERS

Roger Ailes, Pamela Anderson, Dan Aykroyd, John Bradshaw, Mario Cuomo, Princess Diana, Newt Gingrich, Tom Hanks, Sir Edmund Hillary, Larry McMurtry, Liam Neeson, George Steinbrenner, Faye Wattleton, Montel Williams, Pinchas Zukerman.

THE YEAR
AHEAD FOR
CANCER

Opportunities to broaden your horizons abound this year! Clarifying your goals while looking toward a brighter future allows you to reach for the stars from a stable platform. But you also have to concentrate on letting go of some of your old attachments, particularly those emotional ties that no longer support your growth. Changes in your work environment may also stimulate a need to make some adjustments that will allow you to move out of discordant or nonproductive circumstances and into situations that offer a chance to exercise your imagination and creativity.

With Jupiter transiting in Pisces during 1998, you're experiencing wonderful benefits from activities like travel, education, and cultural exchange. Political or legal situations can also play a marked role in your life this year. If you've been looking for a good time to expand your business or promote an idea that is personally meaningful, it has finally arrived. Jupiter is influencing your solar Ninth House, and the realms of publishing, higher education, philosophical and religious ideals, and international interchange can be featured elements of your life now. You may be drawn into more high-profile situations, and if you take advantage of your increased recognition in the most positive sense, you may be able to use your influence to stimulate positive changes. It's easy to enjoy life during this cycle, which increases your capacity for joy and strengthens your sense of personal confidence. Just be sure you don't become overly confident, particularly in situations that call for both confidence and hard work.

Saturn's transit begins its three-year influence in your solar Eleventh House, indicating that you need to take a careful look at your long-range goals and focus your aims on the things you really want and need from life. With both Neptune and Uranus influencing your solar Eighth House, you're also gaining insights into your deeper psychological motivations, and may become more interested in metaphysical subjects and the development of your psychic abilities.

The eclipses of the Sun and Moon draw your attention to several important issues. The solar eclipse on February 26th emphasizes your need to develop a link between your mentality and spirituality by opening your consciousness to the realm of the Higher Mind, and you'll gain some important insights into the way your mind operates. This is an excellent time to focus your mental energy on the changes you want to accomplish in your life, and to allow this realm of consciousness to work to your benefit. The lunar eclipse on March 12th can stimulate an important period of self-awareness, and is an excellent cycle for becoming aware of your inner voice. The Moon's eclipse on August 7th helps you become more aware of your emotional attachments, while the Sun's eclipse on the 21st pulls your concentration to your value systems. Yet another lunar eclipse on September 6th provides an exceptional time to pay attention to your emotional reactions to the changes you began during the February solar eclipse. All in all, these eclipse cycles challenge you to develop a more positive way of strengthening your personal worth.

If you were born from June 22nd–25th, you're experiencing a stabilizing influence from Saturn's transit in sextile aspect to your Sun. However, Neptune is also traveling in quincunx to your Sun this year, adding a dimension of over-idealism and dreaminess, which can undermine your stability if you take an unrealistic approach to life now. Fortunately, Saturn's influence can help you in this regard, and if you make an effort to use your creativity in practical ways, you can make significant progress, particularly in your career. You need a few escapes, and these can be accomplished in healthy ways. Feelings of withdrawal can accompany this period, too, although it's not a good idea to completely remove yourself from the public eye. In your career, concentrate on setting plans in motion to support your long-range hopes and goals, and make sure you're staying on top of your responsibilities. If you have physical health concerns, be sure to seek the advice of a professional whose skills can help you find the best way to deal with any health issues. Basically, you're a little more sensitive now, and it's a good idea to eliminate any habits that undermine your health or weaken your constitution.

You're feeling the frustration of Pluto's transit in quincunx to your Sun **if you were born from June 26th–July 2nd.** This cycle can be especially problematic if you have any chronic physical conditions or a recurring physical condition, because those old troubles come to the surface under this cycle. The good side is that you can get to the bottom of what's wrong and can finally treat the root causes, which offers the promise of true healing.

On the worldly side of things, this is an excellent cycle to make changes at work to strengthen your efficiency and effectiveness. If you've been the "fall guy," taking the brunt of the problems while somebody else takes the afternoon off, well, it's time for that to change. Make adjustments in your life that will allow you to utilize your power to its fullest, even if that means that you finally let go of those old co-dependent attitudes!

If you were born from June 29th–July 6th, you may experience several sudden changes while Uranus is transiting in quincunx aspect to your Sun this year. If you've finally had it with situations that are just not what you need, then this is the time to break away. If you're resisting changes you need to make, then the Universe may just engineer a few changes for you! The suddenness of the changes is more an observation than a reality, because when you get a close look at what's happening, you'll realize that you're finally allowing your individuality to emerge. It just takes a while for everyone else to get used to the new you (and you may even do a double-take when you glance in the mirror). It's time to let your uniqueness work to your best advantage, and to try something completely different.

Concentrate on developing your special talents this year **if you were born from July 4th–8th,** since Saturn's quintile to your Sun can be quite helpful. This is the perfect time to fine-tune your skills, to study with a master teacher, or to put your creativity to work. If you're in a position to teach or train others, you may also uncover their special talents and can become quite instrumental in shaping the lives of those who need support and guidance.

If you were born from July 9th–23rd, you're feeling the frustration of Saturn transiting in square aspect to your Sun. This cycle requires you to make a careful assessment of your responsibilities, and it also marks a superb time to get rid of those things that are cluttering your life. Old self-defeating attitudes can be the first thing to go, since now you're ready to focus on what you like, what works, and how you want to live.

You're likely to run into a few obstacles on your path toward success, but the key factor to remember is that those obstacles illustrate the areas in your life that need extra work or attention. In some respects, this cycle feels like a test; however you are the one testing yourself! Endings, separations, and losses generally occur in situations that you've outgrown. New opportunities arise in circumstances requiring you to be dependable, and you're likely to expect others to be reliable, too.

You get a special boost from Jupiter's fortunate influence in trine to your Sun **if you were born from July 10th–20th.** During the period from April through December, you're experiencing the supportive influence of Jupiter in trine aspect to your Sun, which marks a period of general good fortune. However, if you just sit around or decide to coast through life during this time, you'll be missing an excellent opportunity to advance in your personal and professional growth. This is also a period in which your generosity is stimulated, and you'll discover great happiness from simply sharing your time and energy with others. If your attitude during this cycle is one of greed or avarice, you'll be disappointed in the results. Your confidence is high now, and coupled with positive efforts, you can make great leaps toward achieving your goals and can even experience recognition along with advancement.

If you were born from July 13th–17th, you're feeling the disquieting influence of Pluto transiting in sesquiquadrate aspect to your Sun. It's important to make choices allowing you to make the most of your resources and personal power, but recognizing the right situations is not always easy under this influence. Simply reacting without thinking about implications can get you into trouble; careful consideration is necessary, and, as much as possible, you need to be clear about your intentions. If you're doing something just to please someone else, you are likely to lose respect for yourself. The key to working with the energy of this time is to be more aware of your needs and motivations, and to watch for the traps of a hidden agenda.

If you were born from July 21st–23rd, your creative and imaginative sensibilities are enhanced while Neptune transits in opposition to your Sun. This cycle began last year and finally completes its influence at the end of 1998. Although any artistic, creative, or spiritually focused endeavors are good outlets for this energy, the effects of this cycle can be very confusing. You are also more sensitive to the influence of others, and may have difficulty maintaining emotional boundaries.

Personal relationships need special attention, particularly if you're just beginning a new relationship, since it's easier to see only what you want to see. To avoid situations of deception (including self-deception), spend some time each day in reflection to stay in touch with your real feelings and needs. This is a period of spiritual initiation, and many of your old attachments and attitudes are fading away. Letting go of the past and opening to an expanded level of consciousness is the benefit of this cycle. But in earthly affairs, you can be deceived or misled, so use whatever tools and supports you have to gain objectivity.

Tools to Make a Difference

This is an important year to review and strengthen your physical health, and you may be ready to try more innovative and holistic approaches to caring for yourself. Of course, diet and exercise are important factors, but your psychological and spiritual changes are prompting some deep-level inner changes.

To release some of your old attachments, take the time to do some clearing—on every level. Set a schedule for cleaning out closets, desks, attics, and other areas that accumulate the clutter of time. You need room to open your consciousness and will feel more alive when there's less material "stuff" crowding you.

Flower essence remedies work on the etheric level to help create change, and you can benefit from using chicory, larch, honeysuckle, centaury, buttercup, and pomegranate. You might also feel a lift in your spirits when you wear colors like teal, turquoise, silvery hues, and pearl whites. When you're feeling low, give yourself time to do the things that fill your soul. Telling yourself you'll wait until you have free time accomplishes nothing!

During your meditations, concentrate on searching through your old emotions. Imagine that you are exploring an old, historic house. It seems familiar, as though you've been there before, yet somehow, it also feels quite distant. As you walk through the different rooms of the house, you see furnishings, portraits, and books that remind you of times past. Choose one room, and decide to explore it completely. Open the curtains and let the light shine in. As you touch and explore all these things, allow yourself to experience the feelings that emerge, and then move on to something different. Release feelings of pain or sadness, and focus on feelings of happiness. Feel yourself smiling, let yourself laugh. When you've completed your exploration of this room, you may decide to search another, but you may also decide to return to the here and now. Whatever your choice, hold in your heart the memory of what you've experienced, and remind yourself that all that has gone before has prepared you for a full life in the present moment.

Affirmation for the Year

"My consciousness is open to new possibilities.
I am filled with hope."

CANCER/JANUARY

PRIMARY FOCUS

Your feelings and needs concerning partnerships are a major issue, and this is a good time to examine the give-and-take in your relationships. You may be overly sensitive to criticism, but you can also be too critical yourself, so keep that in mind!

HEALTH AND FITNESS

Any chronic problems need to be addressed, and you may find some innovative approaches to dealing with these old difficulties. Avoid high-risk situations this month, since you're a bit accident-prone.

ROMANCE AND RELATIONSHIPS

If you've had a change of heart, it may be because your needs are changing. The Cancer Full Moon on the 12th stimulates an excellent period of inner awareness, and is a good time to talk about your needs, hopes, and desires with your partner. Old emotional wounds can be stirred up by what seems to be a repeating pattern, and this is a good time to experience a breakthrough. Concentrate on letting go of the past, and set a new course with the New Moon on the 28th.

CAREER AND FINANCE

Investments need careful consideration, and it's tempting to jump into something before you have all the facts. If someone is rushing you, take that as a clue that you need to investigate further. Taking a stand in joint financial matters, tax audits, insurance issues, or related financial concerns works to your benefit from the 16th–26th. If you're still not satisfied with the results, take your concerns to a higher level after the 28th.

OPPORTUNITY OF THE MONTH

Extracting yourself from joint ventures that have run their course, or that are no longer important or necessary, works to your benefit from the 1st–12th.

AFFIRMATION FOR THE MONTH
"I confidently release the things I no longer need."

Rewarding Days: 2, 3, 7, 11, 12, 16, 21, 22, 30
Challenging Days: 4, 5, 18, 19, 24, 25, 26

CANCER/FEBRUARY

PRIMARY FOCUS

You're looking toward the future, and now is an excellent time to broaden your horizons and expand your options. You may run into resistance from those who are overly dependent, but your self-assurance and confidence are strong enough for you to move ahead.

HEALTH AND FITNESS

Your physical vitality improves, and you may feel like taking a vacation or scheduling a retreat from your everyday obligations. It's easy to break free of your routine after the 11th.

ROMANCE AND RELATIONSHIPS

Through the Full Moon on the 11th, you're dealing with issues of emotional attachment and hidden anxieties. Your fears of intimacy may loom large until you find a common ground with your partner. That mutuality is best discovered in your shared ideals, which allow the spirituality of your relationship to grow. Traveling with your sweetheart during the solar eclipse on the 26th may be a good idea, unless you prefer to spend this time alone with your thoughts.

CAREER AND FINANCE

Make a careful assessment of your finances early in the month, and if you need assistance or support, be ready with your proposal from the 6th–9th. A financial power struggle can get nasty from the 1st–11th, but you can deal with it if you keep your emotions out of the way. Legal issues, educational pursuits, or travel can benefit your reputation or career after the 20th, and a proposal for a new venture is well-received after the 26th.

OPPORTUNITY OF THE MONTH

You're in an exceptional position to reach a settlement or agreement, or to generate enthusiasm for your plans after the 22nd.

AFFIRMATION FOR THE MONTH
"I respect the value and support of others."

Rewarding Days: 3, 7, 8, 12, 17, 18, 26, 27
Challenging Days: 1, 2, 14, 15, 16, 22, 23, 28

CANCER/MARCH

PRIMARY FOCUS

Your career takes top priority, and your drive to accomplish your aims can be quite strong. It's easy to adopt an excessively competitive attitude that can alienate some of your most stalwart supporters, so take care with your actions, since they have long-lasting effects.

HEALTH AND FITNESS

High tension at work can drain your physical vitality, and it's easy to allow it to build instead of releasing your stress. To avoid burnout, allow ample time-out periods, since those breaks in your schedule may help retain your effectiveness.

ROMANCE AND RELATIONSHIPS

Family turmoil can erupt, particularly if there are struggles for influence or dominating attitudes. Strive to accomplish understanding, but realize that your philosophical ideals may differ from those of others in your family. Clarify your values during the lunar eclipse on the 12th. You may also resist making changes after the 22nd, when you're likely to balk if the suggested alterations are not your own idea.

CAREER AND FINANCE

Although your ideas about getting ahead may seem OK on the surface, be honest with yourself about your underlying motives. Present your ideas, network at conferences, or send important communications from the 1st–8th. Watch for your own conservative attitudes to emerge after the New Moon on the 27th. On the financial front, joint resources show promise from the 5th–17th, and an associate from the past proves worthwhile after the 25th.

OPPORTUNITY OF THE MONTH

Make initial contacts of importance before Mercury enters its retrograde cycle on the 27th. Unless you can tie your actions or ideas to a practical base, your success will be limited.

AFFIRMATION FOR THE MONTH
"I am recognized for my integrity and honesty."

Rewarding Days: 2, 3, 6, 7, 8, 11, 16, 25, 26
Challenging Days: 1, 13, 14, 15, 21, 22, 27, 28

CANCER/APRIL

PRIMARY FOCUS

Your career may seem to be on hold, and the best progress may include maneuvering through the red tape. It's important to address the issues, and taking responsibility for personal satisfaction with your work can help you decide which path to follow.

HEALTH AND FITNESS

Mental stress drains your physical vitality early in the month, when regular stretching or massage can help revitalize you. Consider getting involved in a fitness class or team sports after the 15th, when the social interaction can lift your spirits while you stay fit.

ROMANCE AND RELATIONSHIPS

Tension with family or parents can be rather pressing through the Full Moon on the 11th, and if there are misunderstandings, you'll benefit by addressing them instead of ducking the issues. You may yearn for a relationship in which you share your most soulful needs, and after the 12th, you may meet a person whose ideals and spiritual yearnings echo your own. Unconditional love and acceptance are easier to manifest following the New Moon on the 26th.

CAREER AND FINANCE

Mercury's retrograde through the 20th is complicated by the disquieting energy of Mars and Saturn; you may run into a lot of resistance while trying to solve problems. There is hope for workable solutions after the 12th, but you may have to make technological adaptations first. Costly mistakes can set back your finances from the 9th–16th, when you're also more likely to misplace something valuable.

OPPORTUNITY OF THE MONTH

Professional allies and good friends make a difference in the quality of your life after the 26th. Before then, you may feel like you're on your own.

AFFIRMATION FOR THE MONTH
"I am confident in my own abilities."

Rewarding Days: 3, 7, 13, 22, 23, 26, 27, 30
Challenging Days: 4, 10, 11, 17, 18, 24, 25

CANCER/MAY

PRIMARY FOCUS
Political activities or involvement with friends and special interest groups can play an important role in your life now. You can make a difference when joined by others who share your ideals and interests.

HEALTH AND FITNESS
Remaining active keeps your energy strong. You might even enjoy an action-oriented vacation or a weekend in the country. Getting back to nature has remarkable benefit. If you don't want to go anywhere, how about doing that garden project this month?

ROMANCE AND RELATIONSHIPS
Making a commitment in your love relationship can turn the tide during the Full Moon on the 11th—and you'll expect the same depth of feeling from your partner. However, if you are not of the same heart and mind, you may decide to say good-bye. It's complicated, though, because there may still be old emotional hurts that play a part in your ability to be close. Take time to reflect and search your own heart for the truth after the New Moon on the 25th.

CAREER AND FINANCE
After a series of adjustments, situations at work are slowly improving. Attending conferences, meetings, or classes can benefit your career now, and forming an alliance with others in your field stabilizes your goals after the 15th. Review your finances, and if you are not being paid what you're worth, determine a path of action. Take steps to change your situation from the 8th–25th.

OPPORTUNITY OF THE MONTH
Friends and associates can be your best source of feedback, and talking over your ideas or concerns with a good friend can be highly illuminating during the Full Moon on the 11th.

AFFIRMATION FOR THE MONTH
"I have well-defined goals."

Rewarding Days: 1, 5, 10, 11, 19, 20, 27, 28
Challenging Days: 7, 8, 14, 15, 16, 21, 22

CANCER/JUNE

PRIMARY FOCUS

You're making progress slowly but surely, but there's a little behind-the-scenes work to be done before you're ready to make well-defined changes. This is the time to define your plans and gather your forces.

HEALTH AND FITNESS

With Mars transiting through your solar Twelfth House, you need extra time for rejuvenation. Overextending yourself physically, emotionally, or mentally is very easy, since your energy reserves may be low. Take ample breaks and consider a much-needed vacation.

ROMANCE AND RELATIONSHIPS

You may have secret fantasies about a friend or acquaintance, but before sharing your feelings, try to get a clear reading about their situation. You may simply be infatuated with the possibilities because you need an escape! An existing relationship can be stressful, but advice from a friend helps. Consider traveling with your sweetie after the 15th, or take the time for a romantic rendez-vous.

CAREER AND FINANCE

Undercurrents of frustration with your everyday work experience can percolate to the surface early in the month, giving you a chance to clear the air and eliminate some unreasonable situations. If you fail to address the problems, they can escalate during the Full Moon on the 9th. Communication improves after the 16th and you may even have a chance to launch a new project or idea after the 22nd. But first, you have to make sure it's what you want.

OPPORTUNITY OF THE MONTH

If you're ready to move on it, launch your pet project or showcase your talents during the New Moon in Cancer on the 23rd. The following week is also auspicious for prosperity and love.

AFFIRMATION FOR THE MONTH
"My heart is open to joy!"

Rewarding Days: 1, 2, 7, 15, 16, 24, 25, 28, 29
Challenging Days: 3, 4, 11, 12, 17, 18

CANCER/JULY

PRIMARY FOCUS
You're ready to meet your challenges head-on, and may even initiate new directions allowing you to move ahead with greater speed. You are also experiencing greater rewards for your efforts.

HEALTH AND FITNESS
Your physical energy is much stronger after the 6th, and by staying active throughout the day you can easily generate more vitality. Seek out enjoyable forms of recreation, and consider adding a little extra pampering to your life after the 21st.

ROMANCE AND RELATIONSHIPS
The Full Moon on the 9th emphasizes relationships, or at least your feelings and needs in this realm. An existing relationship benefits from sharing fantasies and allowing extra time for romance. Passions are intense, and the exchange of energy with your lover can solidify your relationship from the 6th–25th. After the 18th you're feeling more sentimental, and will enjoy indulging in your favorite entertainment or a scrumptious dinner.

CAREER AND FINANCE
Very little gets past you on the work front, and your alertness works to your benefit from the 1st–11th, when you're focused on quality. As a result, you may gain recognition for your efforts, and may even get a boost in position or salary after the 20th. The New Moon on the 23rd begins a period in which extra attention to financial details can pay off. Investments fare quite nicely from the 26th–30th.

OPPORTUNITY OF THE MONTH
You're in an excellent position to complete an important project on the 21st or 22nd, when you may also be ready to say good-bye to some old habits or end a situation that is finally over.

AFFIRMATION FOR THE MONTH
"I am confident and courageous."

Rewarding Days: 3, 4, 12, 13, 21, 22, 26, 31
Challenging Days: 8, 9, 15, 16, 28, 29

CANCER/AUGUST

PRIMARY FOCUS

During Mercury's retrograde, which lasts through the 23rd, pay attention to financial details. It's a good idea to balance that checkbook, keep track of your wallet, and be very cautious with contracts.

HEALTH AND FITNESS

Pace yourself, since pushing beyond your limits can wear you out before you know it. During your fitness activities, set goals to increase endurance, but remind yourself that you may not get there tomorrow.

ROMANCE AND RELATIONSHIPS

Love can blossom with Venus and Mars both in your sign, but you have to address old emotional issues during the lunar eclipse on the 7th, or your fears will block your ability to achieve the intimacy you desire. Whether you're in a new relationship or breathing life back into an existing commitment, you can take your love to a higher plane by focusing on your spiritual ideals. An inspiring retreat or travel to a fanciful place can work wonders after the 24th.

CAREER AND FINANCE

Because Mercury's retrograde business will not stop, you do have to be more careful with written documents, contracts, and important presentations. Meetings, conferences, or workshops can be useful, and if you're involved in creative or artistic pursuits, showcasing your talents is advantageous from the 1st–20th. Re-evaluate your finances during the solar eclipse on the 21st, when you need to know where you are before deciding where to go next!

OPPORTUNITY OF THE MONTH

You can't get away with excessive spending or wasting energy from the 13th–25th, so instead of getting frustrated, pull back a little and discover what you can learn in the process.

AFFIRMATION FOR THE MONTH
"My actions and thoughts are filtered through a loving heart."

Rewarding Days: 1, 9, 10, 14, 17, 18, 22, 27, 28
Challenging Days: 4, 5, 11, 12, 24, 25, 26

CANCER/SEPTEMBER

PRIMARY FOCUS

Sharpen your skills, attend a class, and make an effort to learn from someone you admire. Whatever is necessary, this is your time to rise above the ordinary and define your position as exceptional.

HEALTH AND FITNESS

Shaping and toning muscles is easier, so continue to work on endurance. Try a variety of fitness activities to avoid boredom. You might find a completely new approach to staying fit.

ROMANCE AND RELATIONSHIPS

Sometimes love shows up in the most interesting circumstances, like now, when you may look into the eyes of someone totally fascinating while you're studying something you dearly love. The lunar eclipse on the 6th marks a time of serendipity, when you discover magical things about yourself and life by simply opening your mind and heart. You're also building a stronger sense of self-esteem based on renewed honesty and self-acceptance. It feels good!

CAREER AND FINANCE

This is the perfect time to get your ideas out there, to network with others who can appreciate your talents, and to initiate changes. Travel, educational pursuits, and communication all play a significant role in career improvement. Reach out to someone whose influence on your career makes a difference during the New Moon on the 20th. Thinking of buying a new car? You might find just what you're looking for from the 8th–23rd.

OPPORTUNITY OF THE MONTH

Look around; you may find the most amazing opportunities right in your own backyard, just like the old wives' tales say—that's where the gold is buried!

AFFIRMATION FOR THE MONTH
"I am an effective communicator."

Rewarding Days: 5, 6, 9, 10, 13, 14, 15, 23, 24
Challenging Days: 1, 2, 7, 8, 21, 22, 28, 29

CANCER/OCTOBER

PRIMARY FOCUS

Extra attention on the home front can extend from redecorating to dealing with family issues. Your needs and feelings about your place of comfort and family connections are a high priority.

HEALTH AND FITNESS

This is a great time to take walks, jog, or bicycle around your neighborhood or park, since you might want to stay close to home while remaining active. If you're traveling, even on business, try to maintain your fitness schedule in order to keep your energy strong.

ROMANCE AND RELATIONSHIPS

Your needs for emotional honesty may conflict with others' expectations, particularly during the Full Moon on the 5th, when it's difficult to get beyond all those old emotionally charged situations associated with parents and family. Try an approach to family that allows your creativity and tenderness to flow more easily. Romance takes high priority after the New Moon on the 20th, when love blossoms and your heart is ready to sing.

CAREER AND FINANCE

Watch your expenditures this month, since it's easy to start projects, even those at home, which quickly become more costly than you had anticipated. Careful attention to finances is absolutely necessary from the 18th–25th, when speculative ventures should also be curtailed. To further your career, find new ways to use your talents, and look for a creative project to provide a boost of energy after the 25th.

OPPORTUNITY OF THE MONTH

Extra energy applied to communication stirs interest after the 8th, but can also cause trouble if you're not careful with your words or ideas. Watch reactions to help you gauge your progress.

AFFIRMATION FOR THE MONTH
"Change is safe."

Rewarding Days: 3, 4, 7, 11, 12, 16, 20, 21, 22, 31
Challenging Days: 5, 6, 18, 19, 25, 26

CANCER/NOVEMBER

PRIMARY FOCUS

Creativity is the key to your success this month. Although you may have to make a few adjustments in your schedule, allowing ample time to exercise your talents adds a special sparkle to your life.

HEALTH AND FITNESS

Your energy levels remain strong and reliable. However, you may have difficulty relaxing, since there's a lot of nervous energy building. Make sure you're getting ample B-vitamins and minerals, and try a soothing cup of herbal tea to help you relax at the end of the day.

ROMANCE AND RELATIONSHIPS

If you're going to make any progress in your love life, you need to share your feelings and express your desires in a way that leads to closeness. During the Full Moon on the 4th you're feeling quite amorous, and sharing favorite pastimes with your lover can strengthen your bond. Romance fares best through the 18th. If you're ready to begin a relationship, the New Moon on the 18th can provide the right stimulus; just be sure your signals are clear.

CAREER AND FINANCE

Showcase your talents, advertise your services, or make connections that allow others to see your capabilities from the 1st–15th. Concentrate on making improvements in your work situation after the 24th, when cooperation with others is highlighted. Mercury enters its retrograde on the 21st and can be an indicator of troublesome situations at work, particularly if new systems are in place. Just be sure you have a backup plan in case you need to regroup.

OPPORTUNITY OF THE MONTH

In all matters, take the high road. Adhering to your ethical standards places you in an advantageous position, although you do have to make room for diversity from the 4th–12th.

AFFIRMATION FOR THE MONTH
"Love is the light that guides my life."

Rewarding Days: 4, 7, 8, 12, 17, 18, 26, 26
Challenging Days: 1, 2, 5, 14, 15, 22, 23, 29, 30

CANCER/DECEMBER

PRIMARY FOCUS

Dealing with conflicts may seem to require more of your time, although you're quite good at juggling all the situations if you maintain your sense of humor. Try not to take everything personally and strive to remain objective in the face of challenge.

HEALTH AND FITNESS

It's easy to push yourself beyond your physical and emotional limits, but you'll feel much healthier if you can reduce some of the stress. Watch your thoughts and attitudes, since changes in those areas make a huge difference.

ROMANCE AND RELATIONSHIPS

The tense energy from Mars and Saturn to your Sun may leave you feeling unsupported. Although it's important to stand up for yourself, you also need to know when to just step out of the way, and those adjustments can make the difference between peace and warfare in your personal life. Look for the positive things others have to offer. Consider taking time off after the 23rd.

CAREER AND FINANCE

The Full Moon on the 3rd brings frustrations at work out into the open, allowing you to deal with them directly. Since Mercury is retrograding until the 11th, you may encounter problems that have occurred before, but you need a different solution now. Watch out for those who have an ax to grind, and protect yourself by making sure you're meeting your superior's expectations. Don't stir up trouble unless you've already got a battle plan.

OPPORTUNITY OF THE MONTH

By paying attention to your automatic responses and attitudes, you learn something about the ways you either defeat or support yourself. Vote for support and let go of self-defeating attitudes.

AFFIRMATION FOR THE MONTH
"I accept responsibility for my own feelings."

Rewarding Days: 5, 6, 10, 14, 15, 24, 25, 29
Challenging Days: 2, 11, 12, 13, 19, 10, 26, 27

CANCER ♋ ACTION TABLE

These dates reflect the best (but not the only) times for success and ease in these activities, according to your sign.

	Jan.	Feb.	Mar.	Apr.	May	June	July	Aug.	Sept.	Oct.	Nov.	Dec.
Change Residence									24–30	1–11		
Begin a Course of Study		26, 27							20			
Join a Club				26, 27								
Ask for a Raise					24, 25							
Begin a Romance											19	
Visit a Doctor	1–11					1–14					1–30	1–31
Start a Diet	23, 24	19–21	19, 20	15, 16	12, 13	8–10	6, 7	2, 3, 29–31	25, 26	23, 24	19, 20	16–18
Seek Employment	1–11		9–31	1–30	1–15						1–30	1–31
Take a Vacation	2, 3, 29, 30	26, 27	25, 26	22, 23	19, 20	15, 16	12–14	9, 10	5, 6	3, 4, 30, 31	26–28	24, 25
End a Relationship							9, 10					
Change Your Wardrobe									12–31	1, 2		
Seek Professional Advice	25, 26	22, 23	21, 22	17–19	14–16	11, 12	8, 9	4–6	1,2, 28, 29	25–27	22, 23	19, 20
Have a Make-Over					24, 25							
Obtain a Loan	27, 28	24, 25	23, 24	20, 21	17, 18	13, 14	10, 11	7, 8	3, 4, 30	1, 2, 28, 29	24, 25	21, 22

LEO

The Lion
July 22–August 23

Element:	Fire
Quality:	Fixed
Polarity:	Yang/Masculine ·
Ruler:	The Sun
Meditation:	"My energy glows with Light from the Source."
Gemstone:	Ruby
Power Stones:	Sardonyx, Topaz
Key Phrase:	"I will"
Glyph:	Lion's Tail ♌
Anatomy:	Heart, Upper Back
Colors:	Gold, Scarlet
Animals:	Lions, Large Cats
Myths/Legends:	Apollo, Isis, Helius
House Association:	Fifth
Opposite Sign:	Aquarius
Flowers:	Marigold, Sunflower
Key Word:	Magnetic

Positive Expression:		Misuse of Energy:	
Loyal	Self-Confident	Dictatorial	Pompous
Creative	Regal	Domineering	Insolent
Dynamic	Dramatic	Chauvinistic	Dictatorial
Bold	Benevolent	Ostentatious	Selfish

120

LEO

YOUR EGO'S STRENGTHS AND WEAKNESSES

Even though you may not always be in the spotlight, you certainly look good there, and radiate a warm, dramatic vitality that leaves a definite impression. As "The Loyalist" of the zodiac, you have strong confidence in your feelings, opinions, and ideas, and can provide positive encouragement to others who need to focus their own efforts.

Whether regal or garish, your countenance can glow, and you love opportunities to show your generosity and magnanimity. You need plenty of room to exercise your creativity and playfulness, and draw others to you through your benevolent nature. Your luster is brightest when you see evidence of loyalty from those you adore, although you may have a little trouble sharing the limelight when someone else has risen to the top. Much like the Sun, your ruler, you like to be in the middle of the action, and purr with delight when you are the object of adoration. Recognition for your efforts is important, and if you feel unappreciated you can fall into dejected, insolent, or demanding behaviors.

Your courage is unmatched when you take a stand for yourself or someone dear to your heart—and you expect others to honor their convictions as steadfastly as you honor your own. However, your pride can be blinding, and if you're holding a grudge, you can be completely unyielding. By surrendering your ego to the loving guidance of your higher self, you learn the true nature of devotion. Through this love, your life force becomes a brilliant light shining in harmony with the power of Divine Love.

YOUR APPROACH TO ROMANCE

Nothing matches the ardent passion you feel when you're in love, and your lavish affections leave an indelible mark. Romantic surroundings inspire you, and you can become a steadfast partner. You can lash out if you're hurt and once you've removed someone from your list of loyal loves, you may never allow them back into the fold. It takes more than a few faltering steps on the path toward true love to discourage you, though, and once you've found your match, you can create an enduring love. You can continually rekindle the flames of love through your playful, generous nature, and when you know you've made your sweetheart happy, your own heart sings.

Your attraction to your opposite sign, Aquarius, lifts your heart to a new level of freedom, but you each have to learn about true autonomy if the relationship is to last. You may feel most inspired by contact with the other fire signs—Aries, Leo, and Sagittarius. Your instant attraction to Aries can end just as quickly as it began if there is no devotion. With another Leo, you can experience great bursts of creativity, but remember that you each need to shine or ego conflicts will emerge. Sagittarius appeals to your sense of adventure while stimulating an opening of your heart.

You're definitely attracted to Taurus, but may dislike the feeling that you've become a possession. Gemini's intelligence stimulates your imagination, and you may be lifelong friends. Cancer is comfortable, but not always a romantic turn-on. Virgo's attention to perfection is appealing, but you may be better working partners than lovers.

You're romantically enticed by Libra's refined taste and beauty. Although Scorpio's sensuality can be quite breathtaking, you may feel choked by the emotional intensity. For you, Capricorn is better for business than romance. Although you're fascinated by Pisces' mystical qualities, you can feel quite uncomfortable with the sense that you've lost control.

YOUR CAREER DEVELOPMENT

To be dedicated to a career, you need to receive adequate recognition for your efforts, and you may feel most satisfied when you can take a position of authority or leadership. When you reach the top—as a foreman, general, or president—you can excel. You can also be a great promoter, inspiring teacher, or capable supervisor, kindling a positive sense of self-importance in others.

Since you like to be where others are enjoying themselves, you might successfully develop businesses such as amusement centers, theaters, clubs, or restaurants. Politics can be an excellent choice, whether you're running for office or directing a campaign. In the performing arts, you can shine as an actor, musician, model, director, or producer. Whatever your choices, you need to work in a career that inspires your creativity.

YOUR USE OF POWER

When you tap into your true sense of energy that emanates from the power of life, you feel strengthened and inspired. You enjoy the power of authority and influence, and whether you're the head of a company or central force within your family, you know the importance of using that influence. But the effects of power can vary widely, and if your motivations are purely selfish you may be tempted to misuse your power.

You can be a benevolent ruler or dictatorial tyrant: the difference depends on your own sense of self-worth. When you feel good about yourself, it's easy to open your heart and allow others to direct their own lives, but if you're feeling hurt, abused, or uncertain of yourself, you may use your influence to control the lives of others, stealing their power to maintain your own. Remember that you can become self-absorbed to the extent that others' efforts and needs may not be as obvious to you as they need to be.

Even though you may feel that your life path is extremely challenging, if you can maintain a communion with the power emanating from your higher needs, the light of hope and love will shine brightly in your heart.

FAMOUS LEOS

Gillian Anderson, Bill Clinton, Tipper Gore, Iman, Jackee, Bob Keeshan, Stanley Kubrick, Princess Margaret, Michael Richards, Pete Sampras, Wesley Snipes, Billy Taylor, Hunter S. Thompson, Jerry Van Dyke, Esther Williams.

THE YEAR AHEAD FOR LEO

With intensified creative inspiration and a desire to break free and express your individuality you may feel that the sky's the limit this year. This is an excellent time to release the inhibitions standing in your way, but you must also honor your responsibilities and obligations. So, although you may be in the midst of a personal revolution, there may be limitations to incorporate into your life at the same time! By making an effort to integrate personal responsibility with revolutionary change you can alter the course of your life.

Setting reasonable expectations requires several adjustments if you are to be successful in achieving your aims. Jupiter's transit in Pisces this year emphasizes your need to integrate your efforts and resources with others so that the balance of power is evenly distributed. Although you may experience greater opportunities to benefit from the resources of others, you can also end up feeling over-obligated. Be especially careful in money matters, and avoid the temptation to increase your indebtedness beyond your capacity. When you do accept support or resources from others, be aware of what they expect from you in return. Taxes, inheritance, and insurance matters may play a larger role this year. In your personal life, this is an excellent time to get to the core of your psychological and emotional needs and to experience healing at the most profound levels.

Saturn is completing its cycle in the Ninth House of your solar chart this year, challenging you to focus your ideals and philosophies on a path that will allow you to reach your goals. This is an excellent time to complete educational requirements, take certification examinations, and make connections that can boost your career or strengthen your public reputation. During the summer months, when Saturn moves into Taurus for a brief period, you'll also experience a preview of Saturn's focus, which will carry you into the new millennium. Use this time to examine your ambitions, and then fine-tune your goals to reflect your personal needs and aims. Careful reflection on your motivations and a clear understanding of your philosophical and moral leanings will work like a gyroscope to help you pull your life back into balance.

Neptune moves into Aquarius this year, joining Uranus, which has now been transiting in Aquarius since 1996. Although these two energies are not joined in a conjunction aspect, their impact on the collective can be quite powerful. For you, these cycles, which last into the first decade of the next century, mark a time of breaking free. The real freedom arises on a spiritual level — a freedom of consciousness and expansion of your mind are the primary thrust of these cycles. The exact time when Uranus or Neptune will oppose your Sun is determined by your specific birthdate, but you will feel the impact of these cycles for many years.

The solar and lunar eclipses are also powerfully influential in your life, since they move into the Leo-Aquarius axis during 1998. The eclipses in February and March challenge you to examine your values and self-worth, and you may also experience a crisis concerning how you utilize your resources. The influence and impact others have on your life now can be quite profound, particularly those who share an intimate connection. You may also confront your emotional attachments, discovering old issues or hurts from the past that you still hold firmly in the grasp of your emotions. This is an excellent time to release the past and experience healing on many levels. Then, in August, the solar eclipse in Leo draws your attention to your need to confront yourself and your needs honestly and directly. This can be an exceptional period of renewal and empowerment, when you have more latitude to change your life. But if you are in denial about changes that need to be made, then you may also face a crisis that requires you to address important issues in your life.

♌ ♌ ♌

If you were born from July 23rd–27th, you're feeling caught in conflicts between your idealistic dreams and realistic limitations and obligations. With Saturn squaring your Sun while Neptune transits in opposition to your Sun, you're facing two very different challenges at once. Saturn's influence, which is restrictive yet clarifying, can actually work to your benefit if you're paying attention to your priorities.

This is the time to determine what you actually need to do if you are to manifest your hopes. Consider your approach to personal responsibility and self-discipline: If you've been ignoring your obligations, then they may seem excessively heavy now. But if you've been working toward your goals, then you can see the light at the end of the tunnel, although you still have a journey to make before you're free! Neptune's influence works to help you release and let go of what you no longer need, although determining exactly what that may be is more difficult.

Your imagination can work overtime, and it's difficult to define your personal boundaries—knowing where to draw the line in taking care of someone else, for example. It's quite likely that you'll dream about ways to escape the responsibilities you're facing, but if you try to slip away, they may only get heavier. These cycles challenge you to locate the balance within yourself that helps you stay connected to your needs to cultivate your creativity and spirituality while remaining realistic. Your health can become an issue, particularly if you engage in self-destructive or addictive behaviors. Strive to live a more simple life, and approach your health holistically.

ᘯ   ᘯ   ᘯ

If you were born from July 28th–August 2nd, you're experiencing a dynamic period of positive transformational changes while Pluto transits in trine aspect to your Sun this year. You can rise to positions of influence and power now, with the outcome of this cycle depending on how you handle the power you achieve. Your creativity can be strongly enhanced now, and cultivating your special talents works to your best advantage.

Since this cycle can last about two years, there's no rush to change everything in your life. But you may still feel an internal pressure to move beyond your old self and into a more positive self-expression. This is a wonderful time to finally end habits or release attitudes that no longer support your growth, and even though that change may come easily, you may still feel a sense of loss as a result. Yet, you recover quite easily and will love the feeling of strength that results. If you've been blocking your needs for love, then you can more easily open your heart and allow yourself to give and receive loving energy. This is a year of personal healing, rejuvenation, and rebirth on many levels. The extent of the changes depends on what you do with that energy.

$$\mathfrak{d} \quad \mathfrak{d} \quad \mathfrak{d}$$

Expect the unexpected **if you were born from July 30th–August 7th.** You're feeling the impact of Uranus transiting in opposition to your Sun. This can be an exciting year, filled with fast-paced changes and amazing awakening. You may also feel quite rebellious, and your tendency to jump first and look later can be almost overwhelming. The goal of this period is to release the inhibiting circumstances from your life and open to the possibilities you have not yet experienced. You may finally be ready to take a giant leap forward to move beyond your old life and into a new life.

Relationships play a major role, and those relationships that are mutually supportive work quite nicely now. But if you're in a situation that is stale, nonproductive, or unhealthy, then you may finally break away. To own the power of this time, you must be aware of your strengths and use them to promote your growth. Burning bridges too quickly will create unnecessary havoc, so avoid the temptation to wipe out everything. Focus instead on creating a new set of goals, a renewed sense of vision, and revitalized courage to act in accordance with your highest needs.

$$\mathfrak{d} \quad \mathfrak{d} \quad \mathfrak{d}$$

If you were born from August 8th–23rd, you're feeling more stabilized and clear about your priorities. Saturn is transiting in trine aspect to your Sun, providing a positive stimulation for taking responsibility for your life circumstances. By focusing on your responsibilities, plans, and goals you can be quite successful. This is the perfect time to complete unfinished business, honor contracts, make commitments, and build a solid foundation for progress. Educational pursuits fare well, but you can be equally successful in business circumstances. If you put extra effort into meeting your goals, you're likely to gain exceptional recognition and advance more quickly. By setting up a strong structure now, you'll be ready for the challenges that will occur in a couple of years. But if your attitude is too lax, those challenges will be more stressful. The choice is yours.

♋ ♋ ♋

You may be feeling a little confusion about your personal identity **if you were born from August 21st–23rd,** since Neptune is transiting in quincunx aspect to your Sun. You may feel an inner longing to escape from the intensity of life's everyday pressures and just coast for a while, and you can take some time out. But focusing that time out on your inner awareness is the key to truly releasing what you need to release. This cycle, which began last year, can undermine your physical and emotional vitality, particularly if your attitudes or actions tend toward codependency or addictive behaviors.

This is the perfect time to fine-tune your creative or artistic efforts, to work on changing your attitudes toward yourself and others, or to shift your focus to a more positive balance between spirituality and materialism. However, you are easily influenced by others, particularly those you respect or admire, and need to safeguard against falling victim to deceptive or manipulative individuals or circumstances. The fog will eventually lift, and when it does, you'll be in a much better position if you've made the adjustments that allow you to trust your intuitive judgment in coordination with your rational thinking.

TOOLS TO MAKE A DIFFERENCE

Developing your intuitive sensibilities more fully can be beneficial to all areas of your life. Tap into your innate creativity to fine-tune your inner voice—when you're in that creative flow, your senses are heightened on every level. Trusting your creativity is not always easy though, since many things are vying for your attention, like the everyday trials and tribulations of life. But this year, try to allow at least some time every day to do something creative.

To strengthen your physical vitality, give your nervous system some extra nourishment. Make sure you're getting ample minerals like calcium, magnesium, zinc, and phosphorus, and that your diet is rich in foods that contain B-vitamins. To release tension, schedule regular massages or take time for a complete facial every so often—do something that makes you feel pampered. You love the attention, so soak it up! Promise yourself that you'll treat yourself and someone you love to your favorite entertainment this year, since sitting back and enjoying purely pleasurable experiences can be quite fortifying. To bolster your positive qualities of courage, leadership, and generosity, you can benefit from using the flower essence remedies. Those that are particularly helpful to you now are vine, sunflower, nasturtium, and dandelion. When you need an extra sparkle, wear something gold. Let plenty of light into your home and office—the Sun is your special recharge device!

During your periods of meditation, connect to the part of yourself that is the key to your personal artistry. Imagine that you are in a magical forest, where peace and tranquility bring perfect harmony to all creatures and living things. Being there fills your heart with peace and stimulates your mind. As you walk through this place, listen to the sounds, breathe the cool air, and feel the earth's resilience beneath your feet. Winding through the trees, you walk into a clearing. There, a lake sparkles in the sunlight. See yourself reflected in the water, but look carefully at the image. You are dressed as an alchemist, a magician of great power and wisdom. Your scarlet robes glisten with threads of golden and silvery hues. Think about the things you want to change in your life as you know it now, and envision that you can shift the energy and manifest these changes with a wave of your hands. Allow yourself to view these changes in your mind's eye. Feel your laughter and joy, experience a sense of fullness in your heart. When you return to your focus in the present moment, realize that you are capable of changing your life, creating the path you want and need to follow. When you lose faith, remember the magician inside who can alter reality by merely focusing thought and energy.

AFFIRMATION FOR THE YEAR
"True wealth and love exist within my heart."

Leo/January

Primary Focus
Friction with others can try your patience, and your own attitudes and actions can lean more toward belligerence than cooperation. Find healthy outlets for your competitive desires, and try to keep damage to a minimum.

Health and Fitness
It's easy to rush into situations unprepared, so before you take off on the slopes or begin a new fitness class or routine, make a clear assessment of the situation and your abilities. Extra time for rest is important near the Full Moon on the 12th.

Romance and Relationships
If you feel that others are demanding too much of you, you're likely to lash out. Partnerships can be quite difficult, and turmoil in your relationships may seem to be more the norm than peace and support. However, this is an exceptional time to bring issues into the open and focus on your hopes for the future. Conflict can lead to understanding, and a fresh approach to solving problems emerges during the New Moon on the 28th.

Career and Finance
Resolve problems at work by dealing with the issues directly. Clear communication from the 1st–11th solidifies your aims and garners support. Maintain control over your spending after the 16th, since it's easy to get in over your head by allowing costs to exceed your budget, or expecting someone to bail you out if you get into trouble. Your financial life raft may have sprung a severe leak, so pay attention!

Opportunity of the Month
Deciding when to act and when to step aside is not easy, but it is imperative if you are to progress personally or professionally.

Affirmation for the Month
"I am confident and courageous."

Rewarding Days: 4, 5, 9, 13, 14, 18, 23, 24
Challenging Days: 1, 2, 6, 7, 20, 21, 22, 27, 28

LEO/FEBRUARY

PRIMARY FOCUS

Finances require your attention, particularly in situations that involve the actions or resources of others. Examine your long-range financial picture, exploring your options and removing obstacles.

HEALTH AND FITNESS

Investigate your health concerns by contacting a health-care professional who takes a holistic approach. Mental health is an important aspect now, and getting to the core of old emotional issues may actually increase your physical vitality!

ROMANCE AND RELATIONSHIPS

Until after the Full Moon in Leo on the 11th, you may feel emotionally vulnerable, and may not want to share your deepest secrets or concerns with anyone, particularly if you don't trust them. If you discover deception in your relationship, it can be difficult to forgive the transgression, and if you're tempted to deceive your partner, think again. The solar eclipse on the 26th emphasizes trusting your own feelings, so listen to your inner urgings.

CAREER AND FINANCE

Power struggles can emerge from the 1st–7th, and may be the result of undermining or deception from those you least suspect. Avoid any risky financial investments until you're clear about your liability, and if you're thinking of making career changes, get everything on the table so you know what to expect. If you're suspicious or dissatisfied with the answers, walk away.

OPPORTUNITY OF THE MONTH

This is an excellent time for research or investigation, although you may not like everything you uncover. But at least you'll know what you're dealing with.

AFFIRMATION FOR THE MONTH
"I am honest with myself about my feelings and needs."

Rewarding Days: 1, 6, 9, 10, 14, 19, 20, 28
Challenging Days: 3, 4, 17, 18, 24, 25

LEO/MARCH

PRIMARY FOCUS
Making connections with others can be exciting and may lead to advancement and recognition. Travel, education, and publishing are highlighted as excellent avenues for growth.

HEALTH AND FITNESS
An active vacation or taking time to get back to nature can be excellent choices for rejuvenation. If you need motivation to exercise, coordinate with an exercise buddy. Between the two of you, you'll find it easier to stick with your program.

ROMANCE AND RELATIONSHIPS
A renewed commitment or different approach to partnerships adds excitement to your life. Concentrate on options that support mutual growth. A romantic getaway adds sparkle to your love life from the 3rd–19th, and can be the stimulus for positive changes. An intimate relationship is strengthened through sharing your spiritual and philosophical ideas after the New Moon on the 27th.

CAREER AND FINANCE
Reorganizing your finances may be necessary, and you'll make great headway by attending to financial matters during the lunar eclipse on the 12th. Joint financial ventures can prove successful, but avoid anything high-risk from the 1st–14th. Schedule business travel after the 4th. Mercury enters its retrograde cycle on the 27th, so try to complete legal agreements or sign contracts before then.

OPPORTUNITY OF THE MONTH
Dealings with courts or the legal system fare best from the 13th–27th, when you're in an excellent position to present your case or negotiate terms.

AFFIRMATION FOR THE MONTH
"My horizons for growth are unlimited!"

Rewarding Days: 1, 5, 9, 10, 14, 19, 27, 28
Challenging Days: 2, 3, 16, 17, 23, 24, 29, 30

LEO/APRIL

PRIMARY FOCUS

By concentrating on your top priorities, you can make exceptional headway in educational or career pursuits. Whether you're attending business meetings or vacationing, this is a good time to travel, as long as you take ample precautions.

HEALTH AND FITNESS

Overindulgence can be your greatest nemesis after the 6th, particularly if you're trying to control your weight. Tension and stress are potential problems after the 14th, so make time for exercise and take time to relax throughout your day.

ROMANCE AND RELATIONSHIPS

Commitment and intimacy issues are the primary features in your love life, when taking a serious look at your long-term goals and hopes is important. Clear communication leads to agreement during the Full Moon on the 11th. Jealousy raises its head from the 10th–19th, especially if you're feeling competitive. Fascination with someone delectable after the 14th can get you into trouble!

CAREER AND FINANCE

Although Mercury retrogrades through the 20th, you can still be successful in ventures that your innate creativity allows you to share. Pursuits that are a continuation of something already started are more productive. Extracting yourself from long-term contracts can work well, but don't sign any new ones until next month. The New Moon on the 26th stimulates strong ambition and an action plan.

OPPORTUNITY OF THE MONTH

Attending conferences or workshops, completing written projects, and continuing negotiations all work to your benefit. Be aware of the way you handle using another person's ideas, though.

AFFIRMATION FOR THE MONTH
"In all matters I follow the path of Truth and Wisdom."

Rewarding Days: 1, 5, 6, 10, 15, 16, 24, 25, 28
Challenging Days: 12, 13, 14, 20, 21, 26, 27

Leo/May

Primary Focus
Your success in legal matters, academic pursuits, advertising or outreach is supported, although you need to be fully accountable if you are to avoid problems later on. By maintaining the highest ethical standards, your integrity is assured.

Health and Fitness
It's easy to push beyond your limits, particularly if your work demands extra time or effort. Concentrate on increasing your flexibility while you're building strength and endurance. Schedule a massage at least once this month.

Romance and Relationships
Family matters require finesse if you're to avoid getting into hot water over sensitive issues during the Full Moon on the 11th. Love blossoms and sharing your hopes and dreams adds vitality to your relationship. Travel can lead to romance after the 4th. If you're available, the New Moon on the 25th can lead to a new love. Trust a friend's advice, whose objectivity helps you determine the best course of action.

Career and Finance
You're driven to achieve the recognition you feel you deserve, but can easily step on the wrong toes or run into direct opposition to your efforts. The way you handle difficulties or conflict can determine the extent of your success. Financial investments show promise from the 5th–28th, with exceptional options to improve your situation emerging from the 9th–14th. Stability is your primary goal after the 22nd.

Opportunity of the Month
Although you may run into an amazing circumstance from the 13th–23rd, look into the details before you leap. There may be hidden deception or unforeseen problems.

Affirmation for the Month
"My aims for the future are clear."

Rewarding Days: 2, 3, 7, 8, 12, 13, 21, 22, 29, 30, 31
Challenging Days: 10, 11, 17, 18, 23, 24

LEO/JUNE

PRIMARY FOCUS
Political action, involvement in community affairs, or joining forces with those who share your interests provides a platform for your leadership and charisma. Keep your priorities clear, though, because it's easy to become overburdened by the demands of your life.

HEALTH AND FITNESS
Your favorite recreation may be your best resource for fitness, so get involved in the office team, join in your local park department's programs, or encourage a buddy to enroll in a fitness class with you.

ROMANCE AND RELATIONSHIPS
With the Full Moon on the 9th emphasizing love and romance, you're ready to enjoy the most thrilling and satisfying experiences. If you feel like you've stepped into something that's out of your league, you may just be giving in to unfounded fears. But you do have a tendency to over-romanticize, which is quickly brought into the bright light of reality by the New Moon on the 23rd. Trust the message of your heart, but listen to your head, too!

CAREER AND FINANCE
Support from professional allies boosts your career from the 1st–15th. In partnerships, be clear about your responsibilities and be honest with your partner about your individual roles instead of just assuming that everything is being done. Assumptions can be costly. Political action or promotional activities fare best from the 5th–12th. Set new goals, and concentrate on both long- and short-term projects.

OPPORTUNITY OF THE MONTH
Ingratiate yourself with the right people by using your power and influence to help someone other than yourself. Your generosity can be wonderfully inspiring!

AFFIRMATION FOR THE MONTH
"My life is filled with rewards on many levels."

Rewarding Days: 3, 4, 9, 18, 22, 26, 27
Challenging Days: 6, 7, 13, 14, 19, 20

Leo/July

Primary Focus

Connections with others are the key to your advancement, and your outreach and communication can open significant doors. There's a lot to be done behind the scenes, but you must also remain focused on the things that keep you in the public eye.

Health and Fitness

You may need extra rest while Mars transits through the Twelfth House of your solar chart for the next seven weeks. Anxiety and worry can sap your energy. Focus your thoughts on positive options, and release your fears by affirming your strengths.

Romance and Relationships

An unexpected turn of events can change the course of a close relationship from the 1st–11th. Take time for reflection during the Full Moon on the 9th, when your inner voice is your best guide. If you've been having secret fantasies about someone, explore the possibilities of making your dreams real. The New Moon in Leo on the 23rd marks an exceptional time to set your course into motion.

Career and Finance

Communication, short trips, meetings, and presentations work to your advantage. Your confidence about a project or idea generates an enthusiastic response from others from the 4th–12th, and after the 23rd, you may take your ideas onto a different level. Look for situations that allow you to use your creative sensibilities in your work. Invest time or resources in areas that hold your interest.

Opportunity of the Month

Although you may hold great hope for something, avoid rushing in before you're ready. If you've done your preparatory work, you'll enjoy excellent responses on the 24th.

Affirmation for the Month
"My words and actions arise from a pure heart."

Rewarding Days: 1, 6, 15, 19, 23, 24, 25, 28
Challenging Days: 3, 4, 10, 11, 17, 18, 30, 31

LEO/AUGUST

PRIMARY FOCUS

The eclipses this month are exceptionally important, and if a crisis has been brewing, it is likely to reach its climax now. Relationship issues require special attention, and your real feelings and needs must be acknowledged if you are to be satisfied.

HEALTH AND FITNESS

Unresolved health problems can escalate, but you're also in an excellent cycle to get to the core of physical distress. Consult a holistic health practitioner, since looking into a broad range of possibilities will provide the best insights and healing.

ROMANCE AND RELATIONSHIPS

The lunar eclipse on the 7th draws your attention to partnerships and committed relationships. If you've been running away from issues, it's time to deal with them in a straightforward manner. By the time of the Sun's eclipse in Leo on the 21st, you may feel empowered to make necessary changes. This is your time to act on your convictions and allow your most profound needs to emerge.

CAREER AND FINANCE

With Mercury retrograding in Leo from the 1st–23rd, you may feel that everyone is coming to you with their problems. Although you may not have all the answers, you'll be pleased with your resourcefulness. After the 14th, your creative talents shine brilliantly, and you're ready to showcase what you have to offer following the New Moon and the Sun's eclipse on the 21st. Place your bets on yourself!

OPPORTUNITY OF THE MONTH

Conservative factions may seem to block your path from the 13th–23rd, but you can win them over by listening to their concerns and inviting them to be part of the action.

AFFIRMATION FOR THE MONTH
"I trust my intuitive voice to guide me."

Rewarding Days: 2, 3, 11, 12, 16, 20, 21, 25, 30
Challenging Days: 1, 7, 8, 13, 14, 27, 28

LEO/SEPTEMBER

PRIMARY FOCUS

Wise use of your resources pays off, and you attract others whose holdings, time, or energy added to your own create a formidable force of creativity and opportunity. You're the inspiration, though, so keep your mind and heart tuned to that channel of divine power!

HEALTH AND FITNESS

True healing arises when you listen to what physical problems have to say about your deepest needs. Work on your inner health; schedule time with a counselor, therapist, or healer who works on mind, body, and spirit connections during the lunar eclipse on the 6th.

ROMANCE AND RELATIONSHIPS

A solid commitment from you sets the course of your close relationships now. If you're totally invested in the relationship, you'll expect the same from your partner, and will be ready to explore levels of intimacy that allow you to soar to new heights. But if you're uncertain or if your feelings have changed, you can also pull away. Sudden actions from the 3rd–6th can be detrimental, but well-defined actions turn the tide.

CAREER AND FINANCE

Organize your finances after the 7th, when your ideas about how to make the most of what you have can be quite illuminating. You may even want to set up a different budget during the New Moon on the 20th, when you have a clear view of the complete picture. Adjustments in your investment portfolio set you on a positive course after the 23rd, and a partner's innovative ideas can be quite beneficial.

OPPORTUNITY OF THE MONTH

By using your artistic talents and creative ideas you stand head and shoulders above everyone else from the 1st–6th.

AFFIRMATION FOR THE MONTH
"I deserve love, happiness, and abundance in all things."

Rewarding Days: 7, 8, 12, 16, 17, 21, 26, 27
Challenging Days: 3, 4, 9, 10, 23, 24, 25, 30

LEO/OCTOBER

PRIMARY FOCUS

Communication of all types is enhanced now. So whether you're making a business trip, calling a good friend, faxing a resumé, or looking for a new car, you can confidently make excellent choices.

HEALTH AND FITNESS

Staying active can feel great, and setting goals to increase your stamina can improve your health. But weigh your challenges carefully, since you can get into something that is beyond your capacities from the 11th–22nd.

ROMANCE AND RELATIONSHIPS

Send cards, letters, e-mail, flowers—whatever it takes to get your message across to your sweetheart. A romantic getaway can be especially delightful from the 1st–20th, but if you can't take a trip, why not plan something fun near the time of the Full Moon on the 5th? If there's nobody special in your life, someone emerging on the scene is promising during the New Moon on the 20th, when you learn what it means to be in the right place at the right time.

CAREER AND FINANCE

While networking you may discover a new friend who is fascinated with your ideas and talents. Writing projects fare well now, but you can also benefit from business meetings, travel, or conferences that allow you to present your ideas or showcase your talents from the 1st–24th. After the 25th, you may prefer to stay close to home and focus your energy and resources on making improvements there.

OPPORTUNITY OF THE MONTH

Put your resources to work for you now, but avoid the temptation to spend impulsively or waste what you have. Some things are difficult to recover.

AFFIRMATION FOR THE MONTH
"I am an effective communicator."

Rewarding Days: 5, 6, 9, 13, 14, 18, 23, 24
Challenging Days: 1, 2, 7, 8, 20, 21, 22, 28, 29

Leo/November

Primary Focus

Although your creativity gets a boost, you may feel a little reluctant to be the star of the parade. This is the time for disciplined, focused energy that allows you to refine your skills and talents. Selectively share the results in venues you know and trust.

Health and Fitness

You may think you're a magnet for stress and tension, but if you concentrate on letting go of that tension each day, you'll be amazed at the difference in your energy. This is an excellent time to do muscle-building exercises, as long as you remember to stretch!

Romance and Relationships

Family and home require more attention, but you don't have to be in the midst of crisis all the time. Some very enjoyable options arrive now, and they may even entail breaking a few old traditions in favor of innovative change. After the New Moon on the 18th, contact with family is easier, and you may even mend a few fences. Look for areas of shared interest instead of focusing on your differences.

Career and Finance

Defuse a crisis with a superior near the Full Moon on the 4th by keeping your priorities on the job at hand. Writing and communication are favored, even after Mercury turns retrograde on the 21st. Just be attentive to details. Watch your spending, particularly from the 1st–14th, when impulsive expenditures can be too costly. Your resources improve, but only if you avoid waste or mismanagement.

Opportunity of the Month

Innovative ideas and a chance to use your talents put you in the spotlight after the 19th, when you may also meet an influential person whose support is invaluable.

Affirmation for the Month
"My talents are a valuable resource."

Rewarding Days: 1, 2, 6, 9, 10, 19, 20, 29, 30
Challenging Days: 3, 4, 17, 18, 24, 25

LEO/DECEMBER

PRIMARY FOCUS

Your work can be a source of enjoyment, or may provide a chance to experience something unusual. This is also a creatively inspiring time, when reaching into different situations brings a pleasant surprise.

HEALTH AND FITNESS

You're inspired to stay active because you like the benefit of increased energy. This would be a great time to take an adventurous vacation, or to plan a few long weekends that allow you to enjoy your favorite winter sports.

ROMANCE AND RELATIONSHIPS

Children provide an excellent source of joy, and they rekindle your own playfulness during the Full Moon on the 3rd. Watch expectations in matters of the heart, and be sure that you're sending accurate signals to your lover so you're not the one accused of promising what you can't deliver! Special love warms your heart during the New Moon on the 18th, when you're willing to open to deeper feelings.

CAREER AND FINANCE

Until Mercury completes its retrograde cycle on the 11th, you may feel frustrated with negotiations, contracts, or agreements—especially those related to investment or speculation. New ideas emerge after the 10th, when you may also find an excellent technological resource that changes the way you work. Relations with fellow workers or those under your supervision improve after the 20th.

OPPORTUNITY OF THE MONTH

This is a time to open doors by striving for clear communication. Get back in touch or complete unfinished business from the 1st–10th. Then start moving on the 18th.

AFFIRMATION FOR THE MONTH
"My words inspire loving action."

Rewarding Days: 7, 8, 11, 12, 16, 17, 26, 27
Challenging Days: 1, 2, 14, 15, 21, 22, 28, 29

LEO ♌ ACTION TABLE

These dates reflect the best (but not the only) times for success and ease in these activities, according to your sign.

	Jan.	Feb.	Mar.	Apr.	May	June	July	Aug.	Sept.	Oct.	Nov.	Dec.
Change Residence										12–31	1	
Begin a Course of Study			27, 28							20		
Join a Club					25, 26							
Ask for a Raise							23, 24	22				
Begin a Romance												18, 19
Visit a Doctor	12–31	1				15–29						
Start a Diet	25, 26	22, 23	21, 22	17, 18	14–16	11, 12	8, 9	4, 5	1, 2, 28, 29	25, 26	22, 23	19, 20
Seek Employment	12–31	1, 2			15–31							
Take a Vacation	4, 5, 31	1, 2, 28	1, 27, 28	24, 25	21, 22	17, 18	15, 16	11, 12	7, 8	5, 6	1, 2, 29, 30	26, 27
End a Relationship								7, 8				
Change Your Wardrobe	1–11										1–30	1–31
Seek Professional Advice	27, 28	24, 25	23, 24	20, 21	17, 18	13, 14	10, 11	7, 8	3, 4, 30	1, 2, 28, 29	24, 25	21, 22
Have a Make-Over							23–25	22				
Obtain a Loan	2, 3, 29, 30	26, 27	25, 26	22, 23	19, 20	17, 18	12–14	9, 10	5, 6	3, 4, 30, 31	26–28	24, 25

VIRGO

The Virgin
August 23–September 23

Element:	Earth
Quality:	Mutable
Polarity:	Feminine/Yin
Planetary Ruler:	Mercury
Meditation:	"I experience love through service."
Gemstone:	Sapphire
Power Stones:	Rhodochrosite, Peridot, Amazonite
Key Phrase:	"I analyze"
Glyph:	Greek Symbol for "Virgin" ♍
Anatomy:	Abdomen, Intestines, Gall Bladder
Colors:	Taupe, Gray, Navy
Animals:	Domesticated Animals
Myths/Legends:	Demeter, Astraea, Hygeia
House Association:	Sixth
Opposite Sign:	Pisces
Flower:	Pansy
Key Word:	Discriminating

Positive Expression:

Helpful   Efficient
Conscientious   Practical
Humble   Methodical
Meticulous   Precise

Misuse of Energy:

Hypercritical Intolerant
Nervous   Skeptical
Superficial   Tedious
Hypochondriacal

VIRGO

YOUR EGO'S STRENGTHS AND WEAKNESSES

Driven by the desire to learn, your keen observational skills and analytical mind are always working. Through your connection to the energy of Mercury, your planetary ruler, you are readily drawn to intellectual pursuits, intelligent people, and situations that allow you to share what you know. Your approach is that of the perfectionist, and you hold quality in high regard.

Since you're quite the efficiency expert and have a knack for bringing complex information into a practical and workable format, you're probably in high demand, although you may not always feel that you're fully appreciated! Your inclination to feel that almost anything or anyone can benefit from some form of improvement is part of your role as "The Modifier" of the zodiac. Anything you put your energy into will receive your close scrutiny and attention to detail—from a project at home to your closest relationships. This gives you a reputation for nit-picking, and you may have quite a struggle trying to find positive ways to apply your critical analysis to the people and situations around you.

Others may be surprised to discover that you're not really a "neat freak," although you do function best in a well-organized and clean environment. Just don't let strangers open the door to your junk closet! In your quest for excellence and spiritual purity, acceptance is the first bridge you must cross. Once you accept yourself and others and allow ample room for everyone to become proficient in their own way, you'll find that your life journey is more harmonious.

YOUR APPROACH TO ROMANCE

Your dreams of the perfect mate are probably quite detailed, and that long list of qualifications quickly eliminates some of the candidates who cross your path. But when the time, person, and situation are right, your sensuality and romantic dreams awaken. Your loving touch can be magical, and once you make a commitment, your desire to surrender body, mind, and soul to create the perfect relationship provides an excellent opportunity for growth. You'll blossom in an atmosphere of trust and acceptance.

Your attraction to your zodiac opposite, Pisces, can be quite intense, but the relationship will last only if you can integrate your spiritual and practical needs. You're most at home with the comfortable pace and stable energy of the other earth signs—Taurus, Virgo, and Capricorn.

The excitement you feel with Aries is stimulating, but may distract you from your focus. You'll enjoy Taurus' earthy sensuality and conservative practicality. Gemini's intellectual levity is delightful, although you can be confounded by this sign's scattered energy. You may feel both physical attraction and intense friendship with Cancer. Leo's warm embrace may be the stuff dreams are made of, but you may feel most at ease as friends. With another Virgo, you can easily be yourself, but you must agree to keep your grumbling to yourselves some of the time.

You can be objective and open with Libra, but have to clarify where you stand with one another if the relationship is to last. Scorpio can be the ideal lover, with passionate intensity that fills your hunger for complete surrender. It's easy to share private pleasure and favorite pastimes with Sagittarius, even you don't see much of one another. A special playfulness can develop with Capricorn, whose dry wit stimulates your own wry humor. Both fireworks and spiritual strength abound with Aquarius, but you may feel alone when you're ready to settle into a sweet embrace. And you already know about Pisces!

YOUR CAREER DEVELOPMENT

Work that provides a feeling of accomplishment has a value all its own. You need a career that allows you to feel you've produced something, and may enjoy running your own business. A career that challenges your analytical mind and provides options for self-improvement allows you to flourish. Teaching, speaking, or writing can provide outlets for your desire to share knowledge, or you might prosper in service-oriented fields such as the health professions, social services, or counseling. Your planning abilities are in great demand in scientific research, administration, office management, desktop publishing, secretarial services, accounting, or systems analysis.

Occupations requiring manual dexterity can be rewarding. Drafting, design, graphic arts, crafts, or detail work in the building industry can be good choices. You may also be a proficient musician. Over the course of your lifetime, you may develop skills in more than one career, and can probably do more than one job at a time. Whatever your choices, you will do your reliable best.

YOUR USE OF POWER

The possibility of influencing others and changing the course of events is part of your fascination with the broad range of possibilities available to you from a position of power. Since you don't seek power for its own sake, others may be surprised when they realize what you have accomplished. After all, your proficiency sometimes leaves the impression that what you've accomplished was effortless. But when you walk away, there's always a huge gap. As you learn to appreciate your own worth and find ways to accept praise for a job well done, the balance of power emerges in your life.

Since you're frequently drawn into situations that serve the needs of others, you can get caught in the quagmire of co-dependency, which diminishes everyone's power. Sometimes it's just as important to allow someone to fail as it is to show them the best way to do things or to resolve their problems yourself. If you feel compelled to call attention to mankind's inhumanity, you can use your power to speak for those who cannot speak for themselves.

FAMOUS VIRGOS

Leonard Bernstein, Elvira, Gloria Estefan, Paul Harvey, Amy Irving, Jessye Norman, Keanu Reeves, Claudia Schiffer, Gloria Star, Jonathan Taylor-Thomas, Blair Underwood, Hank Williams.

THE YEAR AHEAD FOR VIRGO

This is a year of breakthrough, when your aims can be most easily achieved by focusing on your priorities and letting go of unnecessary details. Although you may be distracted by unusual possibilities or options, you can be most successful when you allow ample room for change while maintaining the basic structure of your life. You may feel that the very foundations of your life are transforming, and you can play a major role in creating that change by releasing your attachments to things that undermine your stability or threaten your sense of security.

Your sense of vision is intensified through Jupiter's transit in Pisces during 1998, which challenges you to expand your horizons and improve your life circumstances. Setting goals that foster growth and opportunity is not only beneficial, but gives you a place to focus your renewed feeling of optimistic self-confidence. You may also benefit from the generosity of others, and this can be an exceptional year for partnerships. The trap of this cycle is a tendency to overindulge in many aspects of your life. Whether you're overeating, overspending, or overextending yourself in other ways, learning to set limits is crucial if you're going to experience the positive benefits of Jupiter's influence. For this reason, maintaining a sense of priorities and concentrating on fulfilling your obligations and responsibilities can actually work like an anchoring device.

Saturn moves into Taurus for a brief period this year—an image of what's ahead from Saturn's influence as you step into the next millennium. But you're still feeling the need to make a few adjustments during 1998, juggling your priorities for a while until you get a clear image of a more singular focus. The cycles of

Uranus, Neptune, and Pluto are also providing their own particular challenges. The intensity of those challenges will depend on your date of birth, which determines the exact degree of your Virgo Sun. But you're experiencing a kind of shakeup due to the influences of the outer planets, and may feel that you're developing a new perspective on life as a result.

The solar and lunar eclipses are also having a strong impact in your life during 1998. The first set of eclipses in February and March are in the Virgo/Pisces axis, with a direct impact on your sense of identity. This influence works like a crisis reaching its climactic point: If there are issues you've been sweeping under the carpet, they're surfacing and in need of your direct attention. By the end of the summer, the eclipse phase enters the Leo/Aquarius axis, drawing your attention to issues related to your past. Learning to let go is the lesson of the cycles for you, but that is not as easy as it sounds. It means you really say good-bye to a detrimental relationship, co-dependent situation, unfulfilling job, or old crutch you no longer need. This requires conscious effort if you are to experience the freedom promised by these eclipse phases.

♍   ♍   ♍

If you were born from August 23rd–28th, you're feeling the supportive energy of Saturn in trine aspect to your Sun. This brings a stability into your life that is centered on adopting a practical philosophy. But you're also feeling some frustration from Neptune in quincunx aspect to your Sun, which generates a kind of inner fog, making it difficult to see yourself or others with clarity.

This does not mean that you're an easy target all of the time, but you need to be on your toes when you're making major decisions, and you must use your ethical and moral values as your guides to reality. Blending your spiritual needs with your practical approach to life may encourage you to incorporate more time into your daily schedule for contemplative thinking. Your career goals may be more carefully geared toward a sense of purpose, and listening to your inner voice, trusting your imaginative creativity, and developing your special talents may be much easier when you allow time for your inner expressiveness to emerge this year.

♍ ♍ ♍

You're feeling a powerful regeneration and personal transformation **if you were born from August 28th–September 2nd.** Pluto is transiting in square aspect to your Sun. This is not an easy cycle, because you may have experiences that leave you feeling that you've lost control of your life. The intensity of the changes you're experiencing can vary, but one thing is certain: You're letting go of the things you've outgrown or that are no longer necessary to your personal growth. You may be challenged to take a stand for yourself instead of accepting that someone else has a right to greater power than you.

Get to the core of any health problems, since your soul and spirit are focused on regeneration, and your body is probably feeling the effects of those inner changes. If you're in a situation that undermines your personal power, find a way to extract yourself from it and allow the restorative energy of this cycle to work. You may feel that you need to move or change your living conditions in some way, and if you do move, it's important to explore your inner motivations. Remember that even when circumstances occur that seem to be beyond your control, you can control your responses to them.

♍ ♍ ♍

If you were born from August 30th–September 6th, you're dealing with some surprises this year while Uranus transits in quincunx aspect to your Sun. The experience of this cycle is something like riding a roller-coaster. There are wild and woolly times, a few smooth sections and it's all pretty fast-paced. Adding innovations, technological advances, or experimental options to your life is part of this cycle; and although those innovations may be quite helpful, your experience with them can be disruptive or unsettling until you get used to them.

New people can be part of this transit, and you may meet a few who streak in and out of your life like comets, rarely to be seen again. If you've thought about striking out on your own or setting a new career path, this is a good time to experiment with possibilities, but avoid the temptation to take the leap unless you have a trustworthy parachute. In matters of physical health, pay attention to your nervous system—get plenty of rest, ample B-vitamins, and relax your mind at least once a day.

♍ ♍ ♍

Reorganizing your priorities is necessary **if you were born from September 7th–23rd.** Saturn is transiting in quincunx aspect to your Sun, helping you determine what you do and do not need in your life. You may feel like you're juggling cinder blocks some of the time, since some of your responsibilities may seem overwhelming. To determine what you need to release, review your obligations and commitments.

If you're carrying burdens for someone else, it may be time to give them back to their original owner! If you need to take more responsibility for developing a particular area of your life that requires you to let go of something, well, this is the time. This is an excellent period to get rid of habits that undermine your health and to let go of attitudes that stand in the way of your success.

♍ ♍ ♍

If you were born from September 7th–10th, you're feeling the confusion wrought by Neptune transiting in sesquiquadrate to your Sun. The effects of this cycle can be almost invisible, but what you feel is a sense of uneasiness that may seem to have no explanation. That unease is stimulated by your inner voice, which is beckoning you to spend a little more time in such "useless" activities as rest and relaxation. But you need to avoid the temptation to escape by unhealthy means. Becoming a couch potato is not the answer, nor is adding a couple of extra cocktails at the end of the day. Try a walk in the park or woods, a relaxing bath or massage, or something that really pampers you. There, that's much better!

♍ ♍ ♍

If you were born from September 11th–23rd, you're experiencing Jupiter's opposition to your Sun throughout most of 1998. The confidence and optimism of this cycle are fabulous, and by utilizing this energy to reach beyond your current situation, you can create opportunities that keep you moving forward for quite some time. Just remember to keep your eye on your limitations,

150

and try not to boast too much when you win the recognition you deserve (maybe a little party, a press release, or new brochure).

♍   ♍   ♍

Make room to exercise your special talents **if you were born from September 17th–21st.** Pluto is transiting in quintile to your Sun, allowing some long-buried talents to finally emerge into the light of day. This is an excellent time to seek out a master teacher, or if you're a teacher, you may also have a prize pupil whose accomplishments make your heart sing.

♍   ♍   ♍

If you were born from September 18th–20th, watch out for red herrings! With Uranus transiting in sesquiquadrate aspect to your Sun, it's easy to be distracted by something or someone that seems completely fascinating, but is totally wrong for you. Although it's good to clear out things that are useless, you need to make sure they're really useless before you get rid of them. Knee-jerk reactions are the most damaging during this cycle, although sometimes you may feel you have very little time to think before you have to react or respond. But if you stay centered, you can actually accomplish some positive and innovative life changes.

♍   ♍   ♍

If you were born from September 21st–23rd, you're more sensitive to your creative, artistic, and spiritual yearnings. With Neptune completing its transit in trine to your Sun, you're experiencing heightened sensibilities on many levels. Take time to pursue the forms of artistry that make your spirit soar and fill your heart. Allow yourself to forgive old hurts and move on with your life. Learn to trust your intuitive and psychic sensibilities. Your consciousness expands and your ability to experience pure joy and inner peace can finally be a reality.

TOOLS TO MAKE A DIFFERENCE

Your foundations may feel a little shaky since you're releasing a lot of old issues, some of which are tied to your early upbringing. Working with a counselor, therapist, or metaphysician, you're ready to uncover some of your past issues. Past-life regression can be especially helpful, but you can also benefit from working in therapeutic techniques like psychosynthesis or gestalt therapy.

Since you're getting rid of things from your past, you might even enjoy weeding through all that stuff you've been storing in your attic, garage, or closets. This period of catharsis can last several years, so you don't have to finish everything now, although you may feel a bit more impatient if you're being directly influenced by the cycles of Uranus or Pluto noted in the previous section by your date of birth. If you're changing locations, some of the sorting will be associated with your move. But you may simply feel that you're ready to clear away the debris from your life.

The cycles this year also point to physical regeneration and healing, and you'll enjoy the benefits of working with alternative therapies. Acupuncture and associated techniques can be especially useful. Try tai chi, hatha yoga, or chi gong to balance your spiritual, emotional, and physical needs. If you wish to work with the flower essence remedies, try crab apple, beech, dill, and corn. Consider wearing natural-fiber clothing, and keep your sleeping quarters as pure and clear as possible

During your periods of contemplation, open to the experience of joy. Imagine that you have just entered the magical kingdom of Shangri-la. It is absolutely beautiful. Everything is serene, the plants are lush, and the air is clear. As you amble through this paradise, butterflies dance around you. You hear birds singing amazing songs and sit for a while to listen. While you are seated, a wise woman walks toward you and asks to join you. The two of you sit in silence for a while and then she speaks. "You deserve this peace and beauty in your life," she tells you. "When you close you eyes, can you feel the perfection that surrounds you?" You smile, nod and think to yourself that life should be this perfect. "I have a gift for you," the woman says. She hands you a small mirror encased in smooth pearl. Looking into the mirror, you see the happiness on your face and the beauty in your eyes. Remember this perfect moment when you feel stressed, distracted, or frustrated. Shangri-la is that perfect place in your consciousness, always there for you.

Affirmation for the Year
"My heart is filled with joy. My life is a reflection of hope."

VIRGO/JANUARY

PRIMARY FOCUS
Frustrations at work can stem from too many things coming due at once. Carefully sorting your priorities defines the line between stress you can handle and crushing tension. Trust your creative instincts.

HEALTH AND FITNESS
If you're having trouble resting, it could be all that unreleased tension. Now is the time to increase your activity level, but take care to follow reasonable guidelines. You're tempted to overdo it or to push beyond your physical limits from the 16th–24th.

ROMANCE AND RELATIONSHIPS
You may have second thoughts about your feelings in a love relationship, especially if your situation falls short of your dreams and ideals. Listen to your heart during the Full Moon on the 12th, and strive to sort through the conflicts you face. Talk to your partner about your needs and hopes, and look for solutions. You can be forgiving now, but you also need to set emotional boundaries and avoid the feeling that someone's taking advantage of you.

CAREER AND FINANCE
The people you've counted on to do their jobs may disappoint you unless you maintain close contact and continually clarify your expectations. Generate enthusiasm in the ranks and work cooperatively with others; but if egos start feuding, the shattered peace can undermine productivity. Seek out a different approach and take action that smooths the way to success after the New Moon on the 28th.

OPPORTUNITY OF THE MONTH
Making repairs, fine-tuning a project, editing, or adding details all work to your advantage from the 15th–29th.

AFFIRMATION FOR THE MONTH
"My words and actions arise from a loving heart."

Rewarding Days: 6, 7, 11, 15, 16, 17, 21, 25, 26
Challenging Days: 2, 3, 8, 9, 10, 23, 24, 29, 30

VIRGO/FEBRUARY

PRIMARY FOCUS

Others' demands can be daunting, especially if you're feeling powerless. Explore your investment in satisfying others; find ways to use conflict to promote growth instead of taking all the wounding shots.

HEALTH AND FITNESS

With Mars in opposition to your Sun, you need to be more active. You may also be more easily angered, particularly if you've been repressing your feelings. Use your exercise periods to release frustration and anger while you get in shape. Now, that's efficiency!

ROMANCE AND RELATIONSHIPS

Power struggles with your partner can be vicious if you've been hiding from the issues. But if you have good communication, this can be the time you finally get to the core of your problems and determine a positive course of action. The solar eclipse on the 26th draws your attention to your honest needs from a relationship, and it's time to end the futility. If there are reasons to stay, make a commitment. If not, find a loving way to say good-bye.

CAREER AND FINANCE

Communication at work improves, and new innovations or technological advancement may make a big difference in your efficiency. Contracts and negotiations need to offer hope for all concerned, but watch a tendency to give in to power pressures from the 2nd until the Full Moon on the 11th. You may benefit financially from your partner's good fortune or an equitable working partnership after the 14th.

OPPORTUNITY OF THE MONTH

The way you handle conflict or turmoil has a strong effect on your self-worth. Seek peaceful solutions from the 26th–28th, when you can turn the tide.

AFFIRMATION FOR THE MONTH
"I respect emotional boundaries—my own and those of others."

Rewarding Days: 3, 4, 7, 12, 13, 17, 22, 23
Challenging Days: 5, 6, 11, 19, 20, 26, 27

VIRGO/MARCH

PRIMARY FOCUS

The lunar eclipse in Virgo adds to your emotional sensitivity, but can enhance your life through increased awareness in regard to your relationships. This is an excellent time to let go of habits and attitudes standing in the way of your happiness.

HEALTH AND FITNESS

Getting to the core of physical complaints or discomfort is easier, and you may uncover an important element that can put you back in the pink. Holistic therapies glean positive results, and counseling can be particularly helpful to release old emotional wounds.

ROMANCE AND RELATIONSHIPS

Your sexual urges are quite strong, but you're not willing to compromise if you feel that everything is not quite right on an emotional level. Illumination about your own emotional blocks occurs during the Virgo lunar eclipse on the 12th, when you can make your needs known to others more easily, too. A unique approach to dealing with intimacy and trust issues succeeds during the New Moon on the 27th.

CAREER AND FINANCE

Joint finances can become rather complex, but once you reach a workable agreement, you'll see immediate results as a clear direction emerges after the 20th. Wrap up negotiations before the 26th, since Mercury's retrograde indicates potential problems with taxes, inheritance, or debt-related issues. If you can't file your taxes before the 26th, consider requesting an extension.

OPPORTUNITY OF THE MONTH

The people who share your life say a lot about how you feel about yourself. Make the choice of sharing your time and energy with those who truly appreciate you and whom you respect.

AFFIRMATION FOR THE MONTH
"I am open to intimacy with someone I trust."

Rewarding Days: 2, 3, 11, 12, 16, 17, 21, 22, 30
Challenging Days: 4, 5, 19, 20, 25, 26, 31

VIRGO/APRIL

PRIMARY FOCUS

Finances take high priority, so pay attention to detail (your special-ty) to avoid costly mistakes. You may also feel pressured by others' problems or oversights, which may affect your own finances.

HEALTH AND FITNESS

Chronic problems can emerge as a result of the stress you're experi-encing, and you must address them to keep your vitality strong. Your energy stabilizes after the 13th, partly as a result of decreased tension.

ROMANCE AND RELATIONSHIPS

Getting to the core of old emotional issues helps you deal with your present situation more adequately. It's easy to fall back into old pat-terns that have very little do with the the here and now, so watch for this tendency near the time of the Full Moon on the 11th. Reaching toward a spiritual focus clears your energy and opens your heart dur-ing the New Moon on the 26th, when a spiritual retreat or inspira-tional travel can lead to romance.

CAREER AND FINANCE

With Mercury in retrograde through the 20th, you may feel like you're stuck in a rut, dealing with delays and problems involved in making the right connections. This is an exceptional time for re-search, when persistence can uncover valuable information. Joint re-sources or financial troubles involving your partner can cause diffi-culty through the 14th. Schedule business travel, conferences, or presentations after the 21st.

OPPORTUNITY OF THE MONTH

From the 1st–12th, you can get the core information that can give you an exceptional platform, but there may be a price to pay. Weigh your options, and go for the key target.

AFFIRMATION FOR THE MONTH
"I release my attachment to the things I no longer need."

Rewarding Days: 3, 7, 8, 9, 12, 17, 18, 26, 27, 30
Challenging Days: 1, 15, 16, 22, 23, 28, 29

VIRGO/MAY

PRIMARY FOCUS
Travel, attending conferences, making presentations, and opening your horizons to new options can be rewarding if you take a practical approach. Combining business with pleasure is an excellent idea!

HEALTH AND FITNESS
Building endurance and strength is much easier now, but take your limitations into account when setting fitness goals. Outdoor activities, adventure-based vacations, or creative gardening can rejuvenate.

ROMANCE AND RELATIONSHIPS
You need to feel a strong spiritual connection with a lover, and may discover that it begins with a meeting of the minds during the Full Moon on the 11th. Recharge your passion by taking time away from everyday pressures and making room for romance from the 14th–24th. An intimate commitment sparks personal growth during the New Moon on the 25th, when you can break away from an old attachment in favor of more rewarding options.

CAREER AND FINANCE
This is an excellent time to show your expertise in an area. Teaching, lecturing, or publishing are excellent options for advancing your career, but this is also a superb time for advertising or promoting your services or talents. Your career may take off in a different direction after the 25th, particularly if you're in the right place to showcase what you have to offer. Keep an open mind and be ready to step into a situation that is ready for change.

OPPORTUNITY OF THE MONTH
Reaching beyond your current limitations may require an attitude adjustment. Search your heart for your fears and methods of self-sabotage, and be ready for them!

AFFIRMATION FOR THE MONTH
"I stand on the threshold of fulfilling my dreams."

Rewarding Days: 4, 5, 6, 11, 14, 15, 16, 23, 24, 28
Challenging Days: 12, 13, 19, 20, 25, 26

Virgo/June

Primary Focus

Contract negotiations, legal matters, and situations that advance your career are a high priority. You may be in a very competitive situation, and handling your challenger requires finesse and confidence.

Health and Fitness

You may find it difficult to rest and relax, with a lot of nervous energy driving you. Make sure you're getting correct nutrition and allow time to burn off your energy through exercise or recreation.

Romance and Relationships

Conflict or crisis within your family requires your attention near the Full Moon on the 9th. Angry words escalate turmoil, but a right-minded attitude, understanding, and tolerance can defuse the situation. Romance fares best after the New Moon on the 23rd, when you're also enjoying the company and support of your good friends. Make sure you're not sending double messages, though, or you could alienate someone you love.

Career and Finance

Watch for potential undermining from someone who sees you as a threat from the 1st–9th. If you try to ignore it, you'll suffer unpleasant consequences. You may simply have to bring the problem into the open. An opportunity to teach may emerge, or you may have a chance to take your career into a more prominent arena after the 22nd. Watch your spending after the 24th, when your impulsiveness may drive you to make unrealistic decisions.

Opportunity of the Month

Taking action to advance your career works to your advantage from the 14th–26th. Engage the support of friends and professional allies if you need a boost.

Affirmation for the Month
"I courageously advance toward my goals."

Rewarding Days: 1, 2, 6, 7, 11, 12, 20, 24 25, 28, 29
Challenging Days: 8, 9, 14, 15, 22, 23

Virgo/July

Primary Focus
Working with others can be stimulating and rewarding. Your success may depend on incorporating unusual ideas or innovative technology, although the importance of human contact, intuitive judgment, and your personal touch cannot be underestimated.

Health and Fitness
You may worry too much, diminishing your energy and undermining your confidence. Find an outside focus for your energy, get involved in community recreation or sports, or join a fitness class with a friend.

Romance and Relationships
Since you may receive some high-profile recognition, you can draw the attention of an admirer. If you're available, consider pursuing the possibilities of that attraction. Romance can be delightful during the Full Moon on the 9th. Friendships flourish, and after the 19th a good friend may play an important role in your love life. Spending time in contemplation during the New Moon on the 23rd prepares you to take an important step after the 25th.

Career and Finance
Political activity, getting involved in important community issues, or interacting with your professional peers enhances your reputation and provides a platform for your advancement. You may gain favorable recognition, and your career actions open the way to dramatically improve your financial picture. Focus on your goals, define new directions, and make the best of your connections.

Opportunity of the Month
Sign important contracts, arrange meetings, or set plans in motion that stimulate growth from the 6th–9th, and then from the 26th–29th.

Affirmation for the Month
"My goals reflect my passions, hopes, and dreams."

Rewarding Days: 3, 4, 8, 9, 17, 18, 21, 22, 26, 27
Challenging Days: 6, 7, 13, 19, 20

VIRGO/AUGUST

PRIMARY FOCUS

You're inspired to use your talents productively, although you might enjoy taking a much-needed vacation now. If you run into resistance or delays in your work, take a deep breath and try not to push. Trust your intuition.

HEALTH AND FITNESS

Work on your inner fitness. Pay attention to your automatic responses and attitudes, and change those that are disturbing, destructive, or self-defeating. Allow yourself to enjoy the things that make your heart sing during the lunar eclipse on the 7th.

ROMANCE AND RELATIONSHIPS

Experience more joy by opening to the flow of giving and receiving love from the 1st–13th. An existing relationship flourishes, and you may also encounter an old love after the 14th. Whether you meet in person or run into old memories, dealing with your feelings is crucial. Maybe it's not over, but you'll never know for sure if you run away. Strive to reach closure in old issues during the solar eclipse on the 21st. It's time to let go of the past.

CAREER AND FINANCE

Let your creativity open new pathways, and refine your skills and abilities. Even though Mercury is retrograding from the 1st–23rd, you can still achieve progress on something already started. It's just that the whole world may not see it! This is a time of preparation and completion. New projects are best postponed until next month.

OPPORTUNITY OF THE MONTH

Weeding through the details of your life can be productive, but only if you don't get caught in unnecessary minutiae. Put your analytical abilities to work solving problems and then move on.

AFFIRMATION FOR THE MONTH
"I embrace all that I am with love!"

Rewarding Days: 1, 4, 5, 13, 14, 18, 22, 23, 27, 28
Challenging Days: 2, 3, 9, 10, 15, 16, 29, 30

VIRGO/SEPTEMBER

PRIMARY FOCUS
The lunar eclipse draws your attention to a need to get your priorities in order. An emerging crisis can trigger positive changes, so try to welcome the possibility of shifting your priorities in order to make room for your higher needs.

HEALTH AND FITNESS
This is the perfect time to make resolutions setting a high priority on your health and fitness. You may need a little extra time for rest and rejuvenation, so try not to fight what your body's telling you!

ROMANCE AND RELATIONSHIPS
Partnerships need special care during the lunar eclipse on the 6th. If you've been sweeping your desires or issues under the carpet, you may feel like you can no longer hold back. It's time to let go of old attitudes and open your heart to new possibilities. You're ready to take a different approach to love during the Virgo New Moon on the 20th, when you may feel much bolder about addressing your needs.

CAREER AND FINANCE
Enhanced communication and an easy flow of your natural creative talents boosts your career after the 7th. Concentrate on getting rid of clutter and eliminating those projects or situations that are simply draining your energy from the 6th–12th. Pay attention to your promises because it's easy to overobligate your time, resources, or energy after the 18th, and end up feeling overwhelmed and ineffective.

OPPORTUNITY OF THE MONTH
This is the perfect time to say good-bye to the old and usher in the new. But you have to be willing to close some doors before you can really move forward. Let go!

AFFIRMATION FOR THE MONTH
"My mind is clear, awake, and open to new possibilities."

Rewarding Days: 1, 2, 9, 10, 14, 18, 19, 20, 23, 24, 28, 29
Challenging Days: 5, 6, 11, 12, 26, 27

VIRGO/OCTOBER

PRIMARY FOCUS
Making the most of your resources produces amazing results, as long as you're using them constructively. If you're wasteful, you'll feel a powerful drain almost immediately. This can be a month of high-level productivity.

HEALTH AND FITNESS
Your vitality improves after the 7th, although it's tempting to burn the candle at both ends. Concentrate on gradually increasing your endurance, and avoid jumping into anything high-risk from the 8th–20th, when your lack of experience can work against you.

ROMANCE AND RELATIONSHIPS
Your fascination with someone reaches a peak, and if you really want to know whether or not to take the risk of becoming more deeply involved, you'll probably have to take the first step and find out. Your intentions are most clearly understood after the 18th, although you may jump in before then, just because you simply can't wait any longer. Love is like that, you know—it has a heart of its own!

CAREER AND FINANCE
Make a careful assessment of your budget during the Full Moon on the 5th, when setting up a plan to decrease your debt and strengthen your investments shows great promise. If you want to completely reorganize your finances, consult a professional or set up a different plan after the New Moon on the 20th. Attend conferences, send important correspondence, or make presentations after the 24th, when your ideas are well-received.

OPPORTUNITY OF THE MONTH
Sometimes finding the right vehicle for your ideas takes some ingenuity, and just such ingenuity emerges after the 12th.

AFFIRMATION FOR THE MONTH
"I show appreciation for the love and support I receive from others."

Rewarding Days: 7, 8, 11, 12, 15, 16, 21, 22, 25, 26
Challenging Days: 3, 4, 9, 10, 23, 24, 30, 31

VIRGO/NOVEMBER

PRIMARY FOCUS
Writing, communication, and travel take top priority. This is an excellent time to pitch your ideas, sell a concept, or share what you know. But you might also enjoy interacting with others and gleaning knowledge while you fine-tune your skills and abilities.

HEALTH AND FITNESS
Your energy stays strong, but your tendency to over-obligate your time and vitality places you in a precarious position. Know your limits, and honor them by building on your strengths. If you exhaust yourself, you'll never get that project finished!

ROMANCE AND RELATIONSHIPS
Contact with your family can take more energy now. Maybe it's time to make things easier and invite more participation and support. Otherwise, you may feel resentful, which can get in the way of enjoying something or someone you really love. Consider a special trip with your sweetheart, or plan to meet at your favorite romantic rendezvous during the New Moon on the 18th.

CAREER AND FINANCE
Attend meetings or conferences during the Full Moon on the 4th, when your special projects shine and gain positive attention. This is also a great time to network, advertise, or promote something important. Watch for problems with contracts or communication once Mercury enters its retrograde cycle on the 21st. This is an excellent time to do research or negotiate, but not good for final commitments.

OPPORTUNITY OF THE MONTH
Your momentum is best from the 1st–4th, although you're still in a good position to move forward until the 15th. After that, concentrate on your existing obligations.

AFFIRMATION FOR THE MONTH
"I am safe, secure, and have a solid foundation for growth."

Rewarding Days: 3, 4, 7, 8, 12, 13, 17, 22, 23
Challenging Days: 5, 6, 19, 20, 21, 26, 26

VIRGO/DECEMBER

PRIMARY FOCUS
How you apply yourself, organize your time, and concentrate on your priorities determines whether or not you feel in control and successful or if you feel like your life has just fallen apart. First things first!

HEALTH AND FITNESS
Consult a holistic health practitioner if you're concerned about your physical needs, since a combination of traditional and alternative techniques may offer the best options for improving your health.

ROMANCE AND RELATIONSHIPS
From the 1st–11th, you're still in the midst of family concerns, although they diminish considerably after the Full Moon on the 3rd if you're willing to get to the core of the issues. Romance is best after the 12th, when you may also enjoy your children more and will feel like letting your own playful energy emerge. The New Moon on the 18th marks a time of fresh beginnings with your family, and you can be the one to initiate the first steps.

CAREER AND FINANCE
Get to the core of dilemmas or negotiations, do your research, and thoroughly consider your options while Mercury is retrograding through the 11th. Before making a final decision, make sure you like the way power is distributed, since there may be at least one hidden agenda. Move toward greater success and recognition by showcasing your talents and abilities after the 20th. Try something new or different after the 24th.

OPPORTUNITY OF THE MONTH
Your most outstanding opportunity arises in the area of your special talents, which emerge clear and strong, and attract the attention of someone influential after the 19th.

AFFIRMATION FOR THE MONTH
"My ambitions are in harmony with my highest needs."

Rewarding Days: 1, 5, 6, 9, 10, 14, 15, 19, 20, 28, 29
Challenging Days: 3, 4, 16, 17, 18, 24, 25, 30, 31

VIRGO ♍ ACTION TABLE

These dates reflect the best (but not the only) times for success and ease in these activities, according to your sign.

	Jan.	Feb.	Mar.	Apr.	May	June	July	Aug.	Sept.	Oct.	Nov.	Dec.
Change Residence	1–12										1–30	1–31
Ask for a Raise								20				
Begin a Course of Study				26, 27							19	
Join a Club						23, 24						
Begin a Romance											19, 20	
Visit a Doctor		2–19					1–31	1–31	1–7			
Start a Diet	27, 28	24, 25	23, 24	20, 21	17, 18	13, 14	10, 11	7, 8	3, 4, 30	1, 2, 28, 29	24, 25	21, 22
Seek Employment		2–20				1–14						
Take a Vacation	6, 7	3, 4	2, 3, 29, 30	26, 27	23, 24	19, 20, 21	17, 18	13, 14	9, 10	7, 8	3, 4	1, 2, 28, 29
End a Relationship									6, 7			
Change Your Wardrobe	12–31	1										
Seek Professional Advice	2, 3, 29, 30	26, 27	25, 26	22, 23	19, 20	15, 16	12–14	9, 10	5, 6	3, 4, 30, 31	26, 27, 28	24, 25
Have a Make-Over									28, 29			
Obtain a Loan	4, 5, 31	1, 28	1, 27, 28	24, 25	21, 22	17, 18	15, 16	11, 12	7, 8	5, 6	1, 2, 28, 29	26, 27

LIBRA

The Scales
September 23–October 23

Element:	Air
Quality:	Cardinal
Polarity:	Yang/Masculine
Planetary Ruler:	Venus
Meditation:	"I am creating beauty and harmony."
Gemstone:	Opal
Power Stones:	Tourmaline, Kunzite, Blue Lace Agate
Key Phrase:	"I balance"
Glyph:	Scales, Setting Sun ♎
Anatomy:	Kidneys, Lower Back, Appendix
Colors:	Blue and Soft Pinks
Animals:	Brightly Plumed Birds
Myths/Legends:	Hera, Venus, Cinderella
House Association:	Seventh
Opposite Sign:	Aries
Flower:	Rose
Key Word:	Harmony

Positive Expression:		**Misuse of Energy:**	
Gracious	Artistic	Conceited	Distant
Diplomatic	Refined	Indecisive	Critical
Placating	Sociable	Logical	Unreliable
Objective	Impartial	Argumentative	

LIBRA

YOUR EGO'S STRENGTHS AND WEAKNESSES

Your attractiveness flows from an innate sense of beauty, charm, and refinement. At ease in social situations, you also have the knack of making others feel comfortable. When diplomacy is required, you're the natural choice, since you can act as an impartial mediator. Your role as "The Judge" of the zodiac arises when logical alternatives, harmony, and symmetry are required.

You love beauty, and prefer to be surrounded by people and environments that appeal to your good taste and artistic nature. Through your connection to the energy of Venus, your planetary ruler, you are continually reminded to be aware of your values, but it's tempting to measure your worth by the wishes or desires of others. Relationships are a high priority, but you'll never feel secure about them until you confidently support your self-worth.

Since everything is relative for you, you exhibit balanced judgment in most situations, but indecisiveness arises when you have lost your sense of relativity. Maintaining a strong sense of yourself in the midst of an ever-changing world is easy when you're centered. Your goals reflect your personal needs from this perspective. By harmonizing with your inner partner, you present an honest affinity with yourself and radiate that same peaceful, loving energy to others.

YOUR APPROACH TO ROMANCE

You may be known as much for your relationships as for your personal accomplishments, and the tales of your broken heart or victorious love conquests may be legendary. Your dreams of the perfect partner may have led you into fascinating situations, but your deep desire to establish a truly harmonious and fair relationship keeps the true nature of love alive. By surrendering to the natural evolutionary changes of relationship, you become more confident asserting your needs and allowing a partner to do the same. Equality is created!

You're most comfortable with the other air signs—Gemini, Libra, and Aquarius—who share your love of socialization, communication, and fascination with the mind. A relationship that does not center on shared ideas has very little chance of surviving in your life.

Your powerful attraction to Aries, your zodiac opposite, is magnetic, but you may feel frustrated by the lack of fairness that emerges. Taurus shares your love for the aesthetic, but you may not like the financial control issues that emerge. Delighted by Gemini's mental acrobatics, you may also enjoy traveling and learning together. Cancer feels nurturing until you feel smothered by all that attention. Leo's passion for life and flair for the dramatic is powerfully attractive and stimulates an opening of your heart.

Virgo is comfortable, and you appreciate that attention to detail, although you may not always feel romantically inclined. With another Libran you share a love for beauty and can develop understanding, but you'll have to work at developing stability in the relationship. Scorpio's tidal wave of energy can overtake you, and you may lose track of your personal boundaries once you're swept off your feet by all that intensity. Sagittarius is exciting, and you'll adore the fun of sharing adventures. Capricorn is strangely attractive and the powerful connection you feel can be amazing, even though control issues are likely to emerge. With Aquarius, your creativity is inspired and you have room to express the art of romance. Pisces can stimulate romantic dreams, although you may feel stifled by all that emotional energy swirling around when you want some personal space.

YOUR CAREER DEVELOPMENT

Hard work is fine with you if you love what you're doing—and that usually means expressing yourself. With your knack for public relations, you might enjoy advertising, retail sales, or personnel management. You also might use your ability to see and enhance the strengths of others in areas like image consulting, counseling, or even in more dramatic arenas such as set design, costuming, or interior decorating.

You can be an effective attorney or judge, or might enjoy diplomatic service. Whether you choose to develop your own artistry or to represent and promote the arts and literature of others through galleries, museums, conservatories, or teaching—the field of the arts is wide open for you. Whatever your choice, you add a touch of class.

YOUR USE OF POWER

Misuse of power is distasteful to you, and you may cringe at the sight of unjust treatment. You can be quite effective from a position of power, particularly once you acknowledge that you can both use it well and that you want some of your own! When you apply your impartial and logical approach to any circumstance and rise above emotions, you can increase your power. However, you can appear cold and uncaring from this position. As always, the key to using the power of objectivity stems from maintaining a balanced perspective.

You may feel driven to seek high ideals for yourself and those around you, and your sense of perfection can bring true refinement into the world. These same tendencies, when underscored by feelings of poor self-esteem, can work against you and undermine your power. By establishing ways to honor your own value as an individual while setting reasonable personal boundaries, you can create life on your own terms, while still sharing your experience with those you love.

Once you accept yourself completely and offer that same acceptance to others, you'll be amazed at what you attract from life! You are challenged to blend the beauty that resides within you with the energy that flows from the Source. From this position, your outer life will reflect a reality joined with the spirit of life.

FAMOUS LIBRANS

Joan Cusack, Michael Douglas, Bryant Gumbel, Phil Hartman, John Lithgow, Marie Osmond, Luke Perry, Anne Rice, Robert Schuller, Cheryl Tiegs, Desmond Tutu, Gore Vidal, Sigourney Weaver.

THE YEAR AHEAD FOR LIBRA

This year represents a period of high creativity coupled with opportunities for new directions in your work and relationships. Although the choices and changes depend on your own actions and reactions, the awakening you feel and desire to reach beyond your limitations can open many doors. You still have to deal with your responsibilities in a clear manner, but you may not feel as limited by your life situation as you've felt for the last few years.

Jupiter moves into Pisces on February 4th, where it will remain throughout 1998. This energy stimulates increased cooperation from others, and you may also find that you're willing to accommodate and tolerate situations that seemed impossible before. These attitude adjustments are partly the result of maturity, but are also a likely reaction to your desire to become more productive and to trust your innate abilities more fully. Your work load can also expand under this influence, and learning to say "No" is an important lesson of this cycle, since you can easily over-obligate your time. But you can also accomplish wonderful changes in your work by finding ways to enhance productivity. This is an excellent time to improve your health by incorporating activities and schedules into your life that support your physical needs. But there is one problem with Jupiter traveling through this segment of your solar chart: it's easy to gain weight, because the temptation to overindulge in those delectables can be overwhelming!

Although Saturn does move out of Aries for a brief period this year, it will spend most of 1998 in this sign, which opposes your own. That means you still have to deal with demands from others and the limitations of reality, but it does not mean that you can't go anywhere with your life. Instead, you may feel more driven to make your life what you want it to be by taking more responsibility for your thoughts, actions, and circumstances.

The transits of Uranus, Neptune, and Pluto all stimulate new directions that will carry you into the next millennium. These planetary energies influence the creative and communicative areas of your solar chart, underscoring your need to trust your personal expression and allow your artistry to emerge. The solar and lunar eclipses of 1998 also stimulate your self-expression, and draw your attention to your need to remain in touch with your inner self. The late winter eclipses in February and March emphasize the body-mind-spirit connection, and provide an excellent stimulus for changing your attitudes toward your health. Then, the Sun's eclipse in August draws your attention to your goals and hopes for the future. The thoughts, attitudes, and responses you develop now will have a significant impact on your immediate life circumstances, but also open the way to your future.

≏　　≏　　≏

If you were born from September 23rd–27th, you're feeling a powerful stimulus of imagination, creativity, and spirituality. Neptune is transiting in trine aspect to your Sun, increasing your sensitivity to the more subtle aspects of life. However, you're also feeling some restraint due to the influence of Saturn transiting in quincunx aspect to your Sun, challenging you to make adjustments to your flights of fancy so that they fit into the reality of your life. These two cycles can actually work to your benefit if you adopt an attitude of developing your spirituality, imagination, and creativity within the realms of possibility. By accepting where you are now and fully embracing all that you have become, you can then create new options for yourself and your life.

This self-confirmation can work in a magical way to strengthen your awareness while you move into more profound levels of self-expression. If you have any artistic leanings, this is the perfect time to develop them, and you may also benefit through studying with a master teacher. If you have an opportunity to teach, you may discover that this experience provides you with a chance to master your own abilities in a special way. Although you might prefer to pretend that you don't really have to be concerned about your physical needs, it is important to pay attention to any health problems that develop. Denying your body's signals can lead to difficulties, when you might instead uncover something that can be immediately resolved.

☷   ☷   ☷

If you were born from September 28th–October 3rd, you're feeling the positive influence of healing and transformational change. Pluto's transit in sextile aspect to your Sun stimulates a positive sense of personal power and strength, but is only useful if you put your energy and effort into making this renewed vitality possible. It's time to release your attachment to the things, people, circumstances, and attitudes that you no longer need.

You can make these changes now without creating a huge disturbance in your life, and may feel that you can walk away from difficult or destructive situations with grace and ease. Become more fully involved in political or community activities, since affiliating with others who share your viewpoints and ideals may provide an excellent forum for creating change. You may also feel inclined to fine-tune your skills or increase your knowledge in a particular field, thereby strengthening your opportunities for personal and professional growth.

☷   ☷   ☷

You're feeling a powerful drive to assert your individuality **if you were born from September 30th–October 7th,** since Uranus is transiting in trine aspect to your Sun. This can be an exciting period of unforgettable changes and emerging new directions. Your love life can soar while your special talents flow easily and magically. If you've been looking for a good time to step out on your own professionally or to make a significant change, it has arrived. New friends, special interests, and unusual circumstances are all part of a year of delightful opportunity. You'll go further and accomplish more if you have a well-defined focus instead of just waiting for a knock on your door. The more effort you put into changing your life now, the faster you will evolve!

If you were born from October 8th–22nd, you're feeling the restraint of Saturn transiting in opposition to your Sun. This can be a cycle filled with challenges and frustration, but it can also be a time to carefully build stability and security. If you've been resisting taking responsibility for yourself and your life, then the effects of this period will be more challenging, since you're likely to have to prove yourself with greater effort. But if you've been developing a life path that suits you, then this may simply be a time to get rid of excess and redefine your goals.

Your objectivity grows stronger, but if you resist being in charge of your own life, then this can be a time when you feel excessively restrained by others and their demands. Deal with your feelings about commitment, too, and you may take a more careful look at your relationships and what they bring to your life. By defining what you want and need from your personal relationships and deciding where you need to place your time and attention, you can actually develop a more positive framework for growth. But if your relationships are based on false pretense or co-dependent interaction, then you may finally decide that it's time to abandon them in favor of a situation that allows you to grow and develop your life according to your higher needs.

You're challenged to move beyond your old attitudes into a new perspective **if you were born from October 14th–19th.** Pluto's transit in semi-square aspect to your Sun can be quite frustrating if you refuse to let go of the past or to release attitudes that inhibit your growth. But you can also experience an amazing series of changes that allow you to spring into an entirely new sense of yourself. For a while during this cycle, you may feel that you have a very shaky foundation beneath your feet, but that's always the case when you're in transition.

This cycle is much like the process of repairing something when it breaks. For a while, there are parts all over the place as you dismantle and tear into the project; then, you find the problems, fix them, and go about putting things together again. That's just what you're doing with your life!

You may feel a little confused about your priorities **if you were born from October 20th–22nd.** Neptune is transiting in square aspect to your Sun, continuing a cycle that began last year. This is a time when dreaming is much easier than doing, but if you can find a way to incorporate your imagination and spirituality into your everyday life, you may actually create something amazing. The trick to making this time work for you centers on how well you assess the reality of things. Fortunately, you have a little help from Saturn's disciplined influence, allowing you to deal with reality more readily while you listen to your inner voice.

But you can feel out of touch or uncertain, and that sense can undermine your effectiveness—particularly if you trust the wrong people or get into vulnerable situations. By avoiding the temptation to just run away from the pressures or to give away your power to someone else who seems to know what's going on, take extra time to center yourself and listen to your inner voice. Your spiritual needs are crying out for more influence in your life—that's where the desire to escape emerges. Making the choices that allow you to develop your creativity and spirituality without losing track of your connection to your responsibilities will bring the most positive results from these influences.

TOOLS TO MAKE A DIFFERENCE

Since this is a period of renewal and revitalization, you have marvelous opportunities to focus those energies into every area of your life. Your mental attitudes are an excellent place to start, and using tools like affirmations, creative visualization, and enhanced mindfulness can be extremely beneficial. You may also be more aware of the subtle energies around you, and can expand that awareness to become a more effective communicator and facilitator for change.

While you're opening your mind, you may also want to explore different options in the world around you. Consider traveling to a place that is inspirational or take an active, nature-oriented vacation. Take time to develop your special talents, and allow the new ideas and unusual directions that are emerging to re-shape your creativity. Use techniques like journal writing to help you stay in touch with your deeper thoughts and feelings, explore symbolic language through art, literature, and metaphysical symbology like astrology or tarot.

If you need to address physical concerns, consider incorporating a holistic approach to your health care, and consult with health-care professionals whose attitudes reflect a broad base of acceptance and understanding of your physical and emotional needs. To balance your energies, enroll in a tai chi, qi gong or aikido class. The flower essence remedies of agrimony, cerato, red clover, sweet pea, and penstemon can help you achieve a strong inner balance. Wear soft blues and pinks when you need to relax, adding translucent colors to your wardrobe to help you feel more invigorated. You also respond quite readily to aromatherapy, and might enjoy the change in energy when you're burning fragrant candles or using an aroma infuser in your personal environment.

During your periods of meditation and contemplation, allow yourself to open to your special artistic gifts. Imagine that you are sitting in a beautiful room, filled with fine furnishings and priceless works of art. There is music playing, and you feel like dancing. A strikingly beautiful person enters the room and invites you to dance. You accept, and swirl through the room with grace and ease, enjoying the uplifting feeling of surrendering to the moment. When the music stops, you realize that the room is filled with interesting people. You walk toward a comfortable chair, sit down, and one by one different individuals stop to chat with you. Each one compliments you, and you return the compliments in kind. The compliments are about things that only you know about yourself—your gifts and talents. Realizing that others notice and appreciate these talents, you vow to develop those that are most precious to you. Remind yourself that you are the one who benefits most from letting these talents emerge, since the experience of exercising these abilities renews your spirit and enriches your life.

AFFIRMATION FOR THE YEAR
"The love I feel in my heart is open, alive, and given freely."

LIBRA/JANUARY

PRIMARY FOCUS
Internal conflicts regarding your personal relationships can stimulate changes. Address unresolved issues before trying something new or different, or the same patterns are likely to repeat themselves.

HEALTH AND FITNESS
Your physical vitality is strong, and you can improve your health by setting new fitness goals and then staying on target with them. Find a fitness routine, class, or sport that you really enjoy.

ROMANCE AND RELATIONSHIPS
Turmoil in your love life can arise, particularly if you've been ignoring underlying problems. Show your affection and take an active role in the things that matter most to you during the Full Moon on the 12th. A different approach to love emerges during the New Moon on the 28th, when romance fares best if you're open to spontaneity. Children may play a significant role in your life, too, and can be a source of inspiration.

CAREER AND FINANCE
Business communications provide new options for growth through the 12th, when making presentations, attending conferences, or networking are to your advantage. Speculative ventures can produce lucrative results from the 13th–24th, although taking unnecessary gambles will work against you. This is a good time to get rid of overstocks, remove the things that drain your resources, or end nonproductive activities.

OPPORTUNITY OF THE MONTH
Let your creativity and artistry work to your advantage after the 22nd, when you're in an excellent position to try an unusual or innovative approach.

AFFIRMATION FOR THE MONTH
"I listen carefully to the yearning of my heart."

Rewarding Days: 1, 8, 9, 14, 18, 19, 27, 28
Challenging Days: 2, 3, 11, 12, 25, 26, 31

LIBRA/FEBRUARY

PRIMARY FOCUS

Pay careful attention to your health and the connection between your emotional and physical wellness. Look carefully at the things that are causing you worry or concern, and take action that will change the situation.

HEALTH AND FITNESS

Several influences draw your attention to physical complaints, and if you feel you've lost control of your body, this is the time to find a way to cooperate more fully with it! Concentrate on getting to the core of problems instead of just treating symptoms.

ROMANCE AND RELATIONSHIPS

Open communication in your love relationships makes a huge difference in your feeling of satisfaction, and if you've felt a block, it opens up during the Full Moon on the 11th. Allow the flowing energy of love—giving and receiving—to work its magic. If you're uncertain about the best way to proceed, talk over your concerns with a good friend. Concentrate on family matters, but stay out of situations that don't concern you.

CAREER AND FINANCE

Power struggles at work can occur, and your position can be undermined if you fail to take notice of them from the 1st–7th. Knowing when to get involved and when to step aside makes the difference between positive change and ego-oriented conflicts. The solar eclipse on the 26th draws your attention to your work situation, and if you're unhappy with it, this is the time to make significant improvements.

OPPORTUNITY OF THE MONTH

Concentrate on ventures that center on cooperation and mutual support, and avoid situations directed toward destructive aims.

AFFIRMATION FOR THE MONTH
"My choices are motivated by a need to be whole."

Rewarding Days: 5, 6, 10, 14, 15, 19, 24, 25
Challenging Days: 1, 2, 7, 8, 12, 22, 23, 28

♎ LIBRA/MARCH

PRIMARY FOCUS
Open conflicts can emerge, particularly in the realm of marriage and partnerships. Creative solutions are possible, but how you handle the issues will determine if you walk away smiling or in tears.

HEALTH AND FITNESS
You're feeling competitive, and need a healthy arena to express your drive. Set new goals for your personal fitness, take time to learn from a reputable instructor or trainer, and concentrate on building strength and endurance.

ROMANCE AND RELATIONSHIPS
Turmoil in your personal relationships can open avenues of communication if you deal with the issues directly instead of trying to be "nice" all the time. Pointing fingers at someone else is rarely effective, but cooperation can make a difference. Try an open, clear approach during the New Moon on the 27th and watch the changes. Love is trying to win, but you have to listen to what it has to say.

CAREER AND FINANCE
The lunar eclipse on the 12th leads to a period of introspection regarding your work situation. If you're unhappy, where are the problems? It's time to deal with your hopes and desires within your career. Your creativity needs a place for expression that is self-confirming. Clarifying contract terms helps define your path more fully from the 8th–21st, when you can use open agreements to reach your aims.

OPPORTUNITY OF THE MONTH
Reaching agreements is one of the keys to your success, and some of those agreements may involve endings instead of beginnings! Determine what you want before you begin negotiating.

AFFIRMATION FOR THE MONTH
"I respect my personal boundaries and honor the feelings and opinions of others."

Rewarding Days: 4, 5, 9, 13,14,15, 19, 23, 24
Challenging Days: 1, 6, 7, 8, 12, 21, 22, 27, 28

LIBRA/APRIL

PRIMARY FOCUS
Continuing to explore options and opportunities presented last month, you can get to the heart of issues more readily now and may feel more clear about your own decisions. Concentrate on finishing what you've started.

HEALTH AND FITNESS
Tension and stress undermine your vitality unless you do something about it. Stay active, remember to stretch after you've warmed up, get at least one massage this month, and take time to play.

ROMANCE AND RELATIONSHIPS
If you've been skirting around commitment issues, you can skirt no longer! Explore your feelings and needs and decide what you want, or you may end up resenting someone else for making all the decisions. Deal with your partnerships honestly and with conviction during the Full Moon in Libra on the 11th. If you want more intimacy, ask for it; and if you want more space, ask for that, too!

CAREER AND FINANCE
With Mercury retrograding until the 20th, you may feel like you're just repeating the same issues over and over. Although this is a good time to clarify details, these things can become tedious if overdone. It's best to avoid signing contracts, although this is a good time to sell, release contractual obligations, and cease your involvement in things that are not productive. Different financial pathways open after the New Moon on the 26th.

OPPORTUNITY OF THE MONTH
Your objectivity can improve now, if you're willing to use it. Look in the mirror and decide what you want to change and what you want to maintain, and go for it!

AFFIRMATION FOR THE MONTH
"I gladly take responsibility for my own happiness."

Rewarding Days: 1, 5, 6, 10, 11, 15, 16, 20, 28
Challenging Days: 2, 3, 17, 18, 19, 24, 25, 30

LIBRA/MAY

PRIMARY FOCUS

Relationships continue to hold your focus. You may have more satisfying results if you're breaking through some barriers that have prevented establishing the understanding and support you desire.

HEALTH AND FITNESS

Getting to the core of physical problems can lead to healing, and you may feel more satisfied if you're taking a holistic approach to your health care. Explore your attitudes, emotional needs, and anxieties, and shift your focus to constructive solutions and away from fear.

ROMANCE AND RELATIONSHIPS

Intimacy and sexuality can be issues now, and you can establish a new bond of trust with your partner if you're willing to explore your deeper needs. If you're uncertain or anxious, talk over your concerns with a counselor to help get things in perspective. The key to growing closer after the New Moon on the 25th rests in developing your spirituality, and if you feel that your partner is supportive in this area, you'll easily trust the relationship.

CAREER AND FINANCE

Money matters can be the bone of contention in your relationships, and joint resources can certainly be problematic during the Full Moon on the 11th, particularly if you do not trust your partner. Determine where your responsibility falls in these matters, and set up a program or budget that gives you more flexibility. Target business meetings, conferences, and important presentations after the 22nd.

OPPORTUNITY OF THE MONTH

Since you do not live alone on an island, you have to deal with others and their demands. The way you handle them paves the way to your success this month.

AFFIRMATION FOR THE MONTH:
"I accept and honor my strengths and my limitations."

Rewarding Days: 2, 3, 7, 8, 12, 13, 17, 18, 25, 26, 30
Challenging Days: 1, 14, 15, 16, 21, 22, 27, 28

LIBRA/JUNE

PRIMARY FOCUS

Educational pursuits, travel, writing, and publishing play a significant role. It's time to broaden your horizons and reach toward a brighter future. Think about long-range results in your planning, but try to keep at least one toe in the here and now.

HEALTH AND FITNESS

Your energy flows more easily now, and you may feel more like staying on track with fitness routines. A more playful attitude and desire to improve your overall vitality are strong, positive drives this month.

ROMANCE AND RELATIONSHIPS

Harmony and ease in your personal relationships are supported by better communication. Your tolerance for the shortcomings of others improves, but you're also more accepting of yourself. Plan a romantic getaway with your sweetheart near the time of the Full Moon on the 9th. If you're looking for love, keep your eyes open and your smile beaming, since you can attract someone fabulous this month.

CAREER AND FINANCE

Talk over contracts and get the momentum going before the 10th. Plan to make important presentations, attend conferences, or launch an important project. Your focus on improving your reputation and advancing your career works nicely now. Seek out better ways to connect to superiors, administrative officials, or other authorities after the New Moon on the 23rd, but watch your expectations (and theirs) when making promises.

OPPORTUNITY OF THE MONTH

Utilizing the resources of others can benefit all concerned if your goals match. Clarify your aims from the 2nd–6th. Then go for it!

AFFIRMATION FOR THE MONTH
"In all things I seek Truth and Wisdom."

Rewarding Days: 3, 4, 8, 9, 13, 14, 22, 26
Challenging Days: 11, 12, 17, 18, 24, 25

LIBRA/JULY

PRIMARY FOCUS
You're in an excellent position to move toward fulfilling some long-held dreams. You'll be most successful with those that satisfy your yearnings for a more purposeful and meaningful life.

HEALTH AND FITNESS
Your workload may increase, adding to your need to make sure that your vitality can support increasing commitments. Chronic problems or physical weaknesses that surface now need to be carefully considered and thoroughly explored.

ROMANCE AND RELATIONSHIPS
Family tension can flare before and during the Full Moon on the 9th, particularly where matters of control are concerned. Instead of trying to keep everybody happy, think about how to facilitate better communication. Romantic travel or getting away from the tension with your sweetheart can provide an excellent opportunity to renew your feelings of love. Friendships shed light on shared values during the New Moon on the 23rd.

CAREER AND FINANCE
Professional associates offer much-needed support and encouragement, and your efforts surrounding special interests, politics, or community activities can open the door to innovation and advancement. It's easy to overextend your time and resources after the 19th, so try to make adjustments for the unexpected before you decide you can make a commitment. Squabbles over joint finances can arise, especially if you feel quality is compromised.

OPPORTUNITY OF THE MONTH
Reconsider your goals after the 23rd, and develop plans to suit your current needs, desires, and abilities.

AFFIRMATION FOR THE MONTH
"My principles and ideals center on Truth and Understanding."

Rewarding Days: 1, 2, 6, 10, 11, 19, 20, 28, 29
Challenging Days: 8, 9, 15, 16, 21, 22

LIBRA/AUGUST

PRIMARY FOCUS
Adjustments may seem to take a lot of your time, but if you make room for interruptions and keep an open mind, you may discover that you like the changes. Experiment before making up your mind.

HEALTH AND FITNESS
Emotional tension and stress from your job can take their toll. You need time to play, enjoy your friends, and let your hair down. Plan to get involved in your favorite pastimes, and remind yourself not to take life too seriously!

ROMANCE AND RELATIONSHIPS
Friends and lovers play a powerful role in your life, and the Moon's eclipse on the 7th opens the way for a more intensive emotional connection with loved ones. The flow of love involves opening your heart to giving and receiving, and the way you show appreciation will tell you a lot about how you feel about yourself! Listen to your intuitive guidance during the solar eclipse on the 21st, particularly regarding love, romance, and long-term commitment.

CAREER AND FINANCE
With Mercury retrograding until the 23rd, you may uncover a number of problems but may not always find the solutions right away. Strive for cooperation at work, and be aware of the way others respond to your ambition and drive for recognition. Investments show promise, but avoid high-stakes speculation from the 14th–22nd, when you can get burned.

OPPORTUNITY OF THE MONTH
Innovative ideas may sound good when you first hear them after the 14th, but you need time to look into them before you make major changes. Explore, consider, and take your time!

AFFIRMATION FOR THE MONTH
"I know what I want from life, and I deserve it!"

Rewarding Days: 2, 3, 7, 8, 15, 16, 20, 24, 25, 30
Challenging Days: 4, 5, 11, 12, 17, 18, 19

LIBRA/SEPTEMBER

PRIMARY FOCUS
Your energy level may be strong, but you may still be worried about some health problems. Concentrate on achieving a balance between emotional, mental, physical, and spiritual energy. Wholeness requires it, and that's your goal now.

HEALTH AND FITNESS
With the lunar eclipse on the 6th increasing awareness of your physical needs, you may get to the core of bothersome problems. Work on total fitness by developing a strong connection to your inner self.

ROMANCE AND RELATIONSHIPS
Time spent with friends is precious and provides special support from the 1st–7th, but after that, you may feel a little more withdrawn. This is a good period to clean house emotionally, getting rid of old habits and attitudes and eliminating attachments to the past that are no longer productive. After the Sun's ingress into Libra on the 23rd, you may feel more alive and open to romance. But until then, you're likely to think twice before saying "Yes."

CAREER AND FINANCE
Innovations and unique concepts offer a professional boost from the 1st–5th, when you may also take the lead in political issues. Working behind the scenes on all the details that lead to the perfect result prepares you for the launch of a special project after the 23rd. Conservative spending works best now, since you're not inclined to take too many chances and may not find exactly what you want, anyway!

OPPORTUNITY OF THE MONTH
You're inspired to move forward with your plans from the 1st–6th, so take a chance and let others see what you have to offer. The friends you make in the process will be invaluable.

AFFIRMATION FOR THE MONTH
"In all matters I listen to the voice of my soul."

Rewarding Days: 3, 4, 11, 12, 16, 17, 21, 22, 30
Challenging Days: 1, 2, 7, 8, 13, 14, 15, 28, 29

LIBRA/OCTOBER

PRIMARY FOCUS

You're feeling romantic, and may also crave more attention from loved ones. Create the right situations for others to enjoy themselves in an atmosphere you treasure, and you'll be amazed at the results.

HEALTH AND FITNESS

Take extra time to relax and rejuvenate. Consider a vacation or at least take a day or two to break up your routine. You need to stop and smell the roses, and if you give yourself that much-needed break, you'll be more productive in the long run.

ROMANCE AND RELATIONSHIPS

With Venus transiting in your sign, it's easier to highlight your best features, adding to your attractiveness. The Full Moon on the 5th emphasizes partnerships, and marks an excellent time to listen to the needs of your partner and to identify what you want from the relationship, too. You'll feel most comfortable in quiet, intimate, and familiar surroundings. Make changes at home that reflect your inner desires during the Libra New Moon on the 20th.

CAREER AND FINANCE

Finances improve, and prudent use of your resources gives you a comfortable edge. Be conservative in your spending from the 12th–18th, when you may be tempted by something unusual, but expensive. If you have a use for it and your budget can accommodate it, go ahead, but any unnecessary risks can compromise your financial integrity. Watch for power plays at work from the 7th–20th, and get involved only if necessary.

OPPORTUNITY OF THE MONTH

Your outstanding talents set you aside from the crowd from the 1st–10th, so use them. Hiding your light rarely works to your benefit!

AFFIRMATION FOR THE MONTH
"My life is overflowing with love and joy!"

Rewarding Days: 1, 2, 9, 10, 13, 14, 18, 19, 23, 28, 29
Challenging Days: 5, 6, 11, 12, 25, 26, 30, 31

LIBRA/NOVEMBER

PRIMARY FOCUS

You're feeling inspired, and this is an excellent time to follow your creative muse. Showcase your talents in venues that allow you to shine. Why settle for second best when you're giving your all?

HEALTH AND FITNESS

You may need extra rest, although you can find it difficult to stop pushing yourself if you've got a lot happening at work. Take frequent breaks during the day, and allow time for reflection or meditation.

ROMANCE AND RELATIONSHIPS

It's easier to communicate with clarity and impact, which can be helpful when you're trying to let someone know how you feel. But if you're dealing with power struggles or the fear that bringing problems into the open will work against you, the right words are difficult to say. Watch for misunderstandings with siblings after the 16th. You may experience a change of heart in a close relationship after the New Moon on the 18th.

CAREER AND FINANCE

Disputes over finances can escalate during the Full Moon on the 4th. Convoluted problems can arise if you're trying to be indirect just to keep things quiet and peaceful. If there's a storm brewing beneath the surface, it can be just as damaging as open hostility. Watch for potential undermining of your position. Pay attention to communication after the 20th, when Mercury enters its retrograde cycle that continues into next month.

OPPORTUNITY OF THE MONTH

Look for ways to eliminate unnecessary or nonproductive situations from your life, and take a well-defined position in ethical matters. Your integrity works to your advantage.

AFFIRMATION FOR THE MONTH
"My words and actions reflect honesty and integrity."

Rewarding Days: 5, 6, 10, 14, 15, 16, 20, 24
Challenging Days: 1, 2, 7, 8, 22, 23, 29, 30

LIBRA/DECEMBER

PRIMARY FOCUS

Travel, writing, and active expression of your interests and talents put you on the fast track to success early in the month. But after the 11th, you may prefer to concentrate on personal matters and focus on issues closer to home.

HEALTH AND FITNESS

With Mars in your sign all month, you feel an extra boost of energy. There's just one problem: It's easy to overdo it and then burn out, unless you pace yourself. This is an excellent time to begin a program to improve your endurance.

ROMANCE AND RELATIONSHIPS

A flirtation during the Full Moon on the 3rd can lead to sudden romance if you're ready. Otherwise, your actions may stimulate gossip that is difficult to control. As long as you maintain your usual graceful demeanor, you'll be OK. After all, you deserve a fabulous romance from time to time. Consider going away with your lover where you can enjoy yourselves without prying eyes or outside interference.

CAREER AND FINANCE

During Mercury's retrograde through the 11th, you may uncover valuable information. This is an excellent time to research a new idea or complete work on something that's been waiting on the back burner. Your concepts, manner of expression, and unique approach work to your advantage, even if Mercury does indicate that you'll have to repeat yourself at least once. Sometimes that's not a bad idea!

OPPORTUNITY OF THE MONTH

Consider starting an important project around the house after the New Moon on the 18th, when your artistic flair can be unleashed.

AFFIRMATION FOR THE MONTH
"Change is safe."

Rewarding Days: 3, 7, 11, 12, 13, 16, 17, 21, 22, 30, 31
Challenging Days: 1, 5, 6, 19, 20, 26, 27

LIBRA
♎
ACTION TABLE

These dates reflect the best (but not the only) times for success and ease in these activities, according to your sign.

	Jan.	Feb.	Mar.	Apr.	May	June	July	Aug.	Sept.	Oct.	Nov.	Dec.
Change Residence	12–31	1, 2										
Ask for a Raise										20		
Begin a Course of Study					25, 26							18
Join a Club							23, 24	22				
Begin a Romance	23, 29											
Visit a Doctor		20–28	1–7									
Start a Diet	2, 3, 29, 30	26, 27	25, 26	22, 23	19, 20	15, 16	12–14	9, 10	5, 6	3, 4, 30, 31	26, 27	24, 25
Seek Employment		20–28	1–8		15–29							
Take a Vacation	8, 9	5, 6	4, 5, 31	1, 28, 29	25, 26	22, 23	19, 20	15, 16	11, 12	9, 10	5, 6	3, 4, 30, 31
End a Relationship										5, 6		
Change your Wardrobe		2–19										
Seek Professional Advice	4, 5, 31	1, 2, 28	1, 27, 28	24, 25	21, 22	17, 18	15, 16	11, 12	7, 8	5, 6	1, 2, 29, 30	26, 27
Have a Make-Over										20		
Obtain a Loan	6, 7	3, 4	2, 3, 29, 30	26, 27	23, 24	19–21	17, 18	13, 14	9, 10	7, 8	3, 4	1, 2, 26, 27

SCORPIO

The Scorpion
October 23–November 22

Element:	Water
Quality:	Fixed
Polarity:	Yin/Feminine
Planetary Ruler:	Pluto (Mars)
Meditation:	"I achieve mastery by transformation."
Gemstone:	Topaz
Power Stones:	Obsidian, Pearl, Citrine, Garnet
Key Phrase:	"I create"
Glyph:	Scorpion's Tail ♏
Anatomy:	Reproductive System
Colors:	Burgundy, Black
Animals:	Reptiles, Scorpions, Birds of Prey
Myths/Legends:	Phoenix, Hades and Persephone, Shiva
House Association:	Eighth
Opposite Sign:	Taurus
Flower:	Chrysanthemum
Key Word:	Intensity

Positive Expression:		Misuse of Energy:	
Incisive	Sensual	Destructive	Violent
Investigative	Transforming	Jealous	Extreme
Passionate	Regenerating	Obsessive	Lascivious
Penetrating	Healing	Overbearing	Caustic

 **SCORPIO**

YOUR EGO'S STRENGTHS AND WEAKNESSES

Your keen perceptive abilities stem from your desire to know what's happening beneath the surface, and you love mystery and intrigue. Your discoveries of the mysteries of life are often the source of your creativity. Since you enjoy the process of bringing things back to life, you play your role as "The Catalyst" in many capacities. Others are fascinated by your charisma, yet mystified by your enigmatic nature, and you like it that way!

Since you have a tendency to keep the volcano of your emotions under control, you may project a cool quality that contrasts sharply with your deeper feelings. You're protective of your needs and rarely expose the details of your own life or your feelings until you've established a bond of trust. You're secretive for a reason: Your sensibilities tell you when someone's hiding something. All this intrigue can weave a tangled web until you bridge the gap created by that hidden agenda.

Your connection to the energy of Pluto, your planetary ruler, confers a profound sense of the deeper qualities of human nature and the inevitable experiences that bring change into each of our lives. Walking the path of the shaman, focused on creating healing, restoration, and regeneration, you may experience all the extremes of life—from joy to despair. As you direct your energy toward higher principles you can rise to heroic action, but if you've been wounded, you can become consumed by vengeful feelings. Your life lesson involves learning to forgive yourself and others by releasing shame and guilt to experience true spiritual and emotional rebirth.

YOUR APPROACH TO ROMANCE

Your deep yearning for a love that will allow you to bond with your soulmate is both intriguing and intense. You may relish sharing sensual moments with a lover, and can be extremely enticing when you're ready for love. Through your erotic sensibilities that drive you to rise beyond the gates of ecstasy into rapture, you may develop love-making into an art form. Unlocking the doors to your heart may not be easy, but once you trust love, your life transforms. If you've been hurt by a lover, you may bolt the doors to your heart forever, which succeeds in protecting your vulnerability, but leaves you longing for the dream you've lost.

A partner who accepts and shares your desires may be most easily found with the water signs — Cancer, Scorpio, and Pisces. However, you're attracted to Taurus, your opposite, whose steadfast sensuality fills many of your needs; but in the face of disagreement, you can both be monumentally stubborn.

Aries can seem too much of a tease. Gemini is entertaining and witty, but you may not reach the deep bond you hope to achieve. Cancer may share your ideals while providing caring and inspiring a sense of security. Leo's magnetism can leave you feeling weak in the knees, but you may tire of this sign's self-absorbed attitude. Developing a relationship with Virgo can, over time, move from friendship to lasting passion.

You're at ease with Libra, although you may resent feeling that you're the one who has to make all the decisions. With another Scorpio you may feel you've found a soulmate, although the relationship can range from extreme passion to volatile power struggles. Sagittarius' independent attitudes can bother you, but you can have fun together. Capricorn can be supportive, helping you achieve worldly success while confirming your security needs. Even though you're intrigued by Aquarius, the emotional distance makes it difficult to achieve the passion you require. Pisces stimulates your romantic and creative side, while providing endless imaginative sensitivity.

YOUR CAREER DEVELOPMENT

Since you're an excellent strategist, you'll feel best in a career that requires probing, renovation, or creative schemes. In the arts, music, painting, or writing can provide outlets that have positive transformational effects. You could become an exceptional performer, producer, or director, and may be fascinated by science fiction or mystery.

Positions of influence and power suit you nicely, and you have a knack of making the most of others' resources. Financial counseling, investment banking, career management, insurance, politics, or corporate law can be fascinating. If you're drawn to the healing arts, including counseling, you can help others restore their lives. Scientific probing, research, studying history, or archaeology can fulfill your needs to look beneath the surface.

YOUR USE OF POWER

Scorpios exude power. You easily identify with true power, and have done so since your youth—when you were fascinated by super-heroes and powerful people. You also know when someone does not possess their own power, and may resent those who misuse their influence. Although you might feel most at ease when the total extent of your power is not open to scrutiny of prying eyes, you can function well when you surrender to the higher nature of power itself. You embrace the whole of life experience, including many "taboos"—from birth to sexuality to death—with an acceptance of the changes that shape reality. Yet your desire to hold onto life's richest treasures may be driven by a feeling that you want to control these natural processes in some way.

By reaching deep within your soul for your true needs, you will experience healing that allows you to step into your full strength. Once you're probed your own inner realm, you'll find a warrior spirit residing at the core of your being that constantly guards you from harm. As you develop compassion for yourself, you'll feel the strength to reach out toward the world and bring about changes that impart hope and growth, now and for the future.

FAMOUS SCORPIOS

Oksana Baiul, Pat Conroy, Richard Dreyfuss, Jodie Foster, Bill Gates, Lee Grant, Mary Hart, Robert Kennedy, Lyle Lovett, Andrea Mitchell, Roseanne, Leon Trotsky, Anne Tyler, Sean Young.

THE YEAR AHEAD FOR SCORPIO

Your experiences this year center on awakened creativity and the development of new foundations. Setting well-defined priorities and focusing on choices that center on growth and personal development, you can make alterations that allow you to cope with the endless shifts and changes in the world around you. There are tests and surprises, opportunities and challenges—all in abundance. One thing is certain: It's not likely that you'll be bored during 1998!

Jupiter's transit in Pisces, which begins on February 4th, will last through the remainder of the year, bringing expansion and growth into the realms of self-expression, artistry, and the expression of love. Children may play a more significant role, and your ability to embrace joy is enhanced. This influence also improves your self-confidence and confers a more optimistic attitude. It's easier to trust the yearnings of your heart and love relationships can blossom, particularly if you share similar philosophies and allow time for the pleasures of life. The downfall of this cycle results from a tendency to take things and people for granted, and to miss opportunities to move beyond your current limitations by adopting a lazy attitude. If you learn to use this energy, it can be an excellent time for promotion, outreach, travel, education and learning. But if you're too self-indulgent, you can also waste your resources and may reach beyond your limits in detrimental ways, like overspending or overeating.

Saturn's cycle challenges you to deal with the demands and expectations of others, and you may also face some personal dilemmas regarding your feelings about age and aging. From June through October, when Saturn moves into Taurus before retrograding back into Aries, you're experiencing a preview of the challenges and tests you're facing as you move into the new millennium. By using this year to assess your life, you can establish a set of priorities that will allow the ultimate growth as you step toward the future. The cycles of Uranus and Neptune can be somewhat disruptive and unsettling over the next several years, particularly in the areas of family, home, and personal environment. However, changes in these areas can bring a sense of relief if you've been holding back or afraid to move out of a rut.

The solar and lunar eclipses draw your attention to the way that you give and receive love, with an emphasis on learning better ways to allow love to flow in and out of your life. Creating a life of abundance and joy requires not only that you give energy, but that you find ways to keep your heart open to receiving support, care, and love. If you're uncertain about the best ways to trust this experience with others, begin by further developing your artistic or creative talents and allow an opening of energy during this experience. From this point, it can be easier to open up to others. The eclipses of late summer can bring a crisis centered on family, but remember that crisis points are not always negative. In order for any change to take place, energy builds to a certain level and is then released. This point of release is crisis.

♏   ♏   ♏

If you were born from October 23rd–28th, you're feeling some restraint due to Saturn's transit in opposition to your Sun. Although this is most marked during the summer and fall months, you'll feel the restrictions building in different ways. This cycle will continue next year, but the first impact of the cycle can seem abruptly challenging if you're unprepared to deal with the increased responsibilities it brings. This is the perfect time to eliminate the things from your life that you've outgrown. Like many life stages, this period marks a time of maturity, particularly in the area of partnerships and relationships. Your approach to commitment says a great deal about your trust of your own feelings. If you're settling for something you don't want just because it seems safe, you'll feel unhappy and unfulfilled now—and it's not your partner's fault! Additionally, you're experiencing some confusion from Neptune's transit in square aspect to your Sun, which makes it difficult to maintain your personal boundaries at times. This cycle will last about two full years, and understanding its influence can make a difference in your sense of fulfillment and happiness.

This is a cycle of spiritual initiation, a period that challenges you to look at reality from a different perspective. You may enjoy some of the effects, like increased artistic sensitivity and a stronger sense of your inner self. But other effects can be difficult, like a desire to escape or a tendency to get into situations that are filled with deception. Any major changes you contemplate now should be carefully considered and accomplished at a reasonable pace. Give yourself time to adjust to the new consciousness that is emerging, and then the confusion will be much less problematic. It is important to pay attention to your physical health during these cycles, since your body is also changing. If you're concerned, see a professional who can help you discover what, if anything, you need to address. Knowledge is power; worry is a waste of energy.

♏ ♏ ♏

You're taking steps to change your life **if you were born from October 28th–November 3rd.** With Pluto transiting in semisextile to your Sun you may find it easier to break away from circumstances that have become intolerable or that you no longer need. Your personal identity shifts during this cycle to allow an easier expression of your power, although you may run into a few power struggles with others as a result. Your subtle approach can be rather effective now; instead of blasting into a situation like a parade, you're more willing to work your way into a different position. Revitalize something that's been waiting for renewal, by bringing your talents to life or breathing new life into a stale relationship. Physically, you may experience new levels of healing and strength emerging, and you can now tap into resources that may have been unreachable before this time.

♏ ♏ ♏

You may be feeling rather rebellious **if you were born from October 30th–November 6th,** since Uranus is transiting in square aspect to your Sun. You're ready to eliminate repressive situations from your life, and may crave freedom at any price if you've been held back too intensely. This is a cycle filled with unexpected changes and challenges, some of them arising from circumstances beyond your control. The old order is falling away, and a new sense of freedom and self-expression is emerging; it's best if you adopt a cooperative attitude and find positive ways to address your needs for change.

If you're resisting moving forward with the times, then this cycle can be exhausting—all that resistance is hard work. But if you're open to experimentation and willing to express yourself, you may find that you actually enjoy this period. Just remember that rebellion for its own sake rarely accomplishes true change, but that a revolution in consciousness provides the backdrop for a renewed life.

♏ ♏ ♏

If you were born from November 7th–22nd, you're feeling the influence of Saturn in quincunx aspect to your Sun. The period of adjustment signified by this cycle can extend into several areas of your life, but may be most marked in your approach to your work and the way you care for your health. If you're experiencing health problems, it's crucial to do whatever is necessary to take responsibility for your health. That may include adjustments in your diet or daily routine, and probably requires adopting a more positive attitude toward yourself and your needs. Since you're also experiencing a transit of Chiron in conjunction to your Sun, the health aspects of this cycle are further emphasized.

However, there are also other effects of the Saturn and Chiron transits that allow you to direct your life and your priorities toward a more profound sense of purpose. Your career and work situations may need to undergo changes, and this is a good time to define what you want and need in these areas. If there are requirements for advancement you've not met, it's time to decide if you're going to fulfill them. Educational pursuits, important projects, and focused energy can make a huge difference in your life work. Take advantage of situations that allow you to either learn or teach, since each experience helps you refine your understanding and skills.

♏︎ ♏︎ ♏︎

Take time to develop your special talents and gifts **if you were born from November 16th–21st.** Since Uranus is transiting in quintile aspect to your Sun, you may experience an awakening of some long-slumbering abilities. This is also a great time to study with a master teacher, or if you're a teacher, you may be working with a very talented student. Listen to your intuitive voice now, because you may hear some promptings that are rather subtle and require careful inner awareness.

♏︎ ♏︎ ♏︎

Your creative sensibilities and spirituality are strong focal points this year **if you were born from November 19th–22nd.** Neptune is transiting in sextile aspect to your Sun, enhancing your psychic abilities and prompting you to be more attentive to the subtle energies of life. However, the effects of this cycle can go almost unnoticed unless you cultivate them. You may feel more inner peace and a sense of contentment, and can be quite effective in your efforts to do something that will make a difference in the quality of life. This is an excellent time to give back, to do something for your community or for humankind. If you're involved in creative expression, this influence adds a wonderful element to your creativity, and your work may also hold appeal for a wider audience. Relationships can also improve now, since it's easier for you to let go of old hurts or to release unresolved feelings. The purity of love itself is both healing and inspiring now. Let yourself surrender to it, and watch your life transcend the ordinary.

TOOLS TO MAKE A DIFFERENCE

Balancing the different elements of your life takes concentrated effort now, and it's easy to give in to feelings of frustration if you focus too much on the externals. By spending some time each day listening to your inner voice or simply experiencing the quiet energy of contemplation, you'll feel much more alive and free. You also require good outlets for your need to expand, and activities like travel, reading, education, or cultural exchanges can help you feel more connected to life in a larger sense.

To strengthen your physical vitality, consider a complete health assessment and then formulate a program that will encourage greater energy and endurance. Alternative healing incorporated with more traditional methods is likely to be most effective, but the centerpiece of your health involves your own attitudes and outlook. Watch your automatic responses, and infiltrate your consciousness with more positive, uplifting messages. To help transform your desire nature and release old emotional issues, work with the flower essence remedies. Those that have the most specific influence for you are rockrose, holly, willow, fuchsia, and trillium. You might also love the feeling of wearing power stones like obsidian, pearl, and smoky quartz. Surround yourself with deep reds and burgundies and soft, luxurious fabrics, both in your dress and personal environment.

This is also an excellent time to take up a hobby, refine your artistic talents, or become involved in the arts in some way. Indulge in your favorite entertainment more often, and allow yourself to play. Choose fitness programs that are fun, not torture. A little pain seems reasonable when you're trying to improve, especially since you're a Scorpio! But too much pain gives you too many reasons to resist working out!

During your periods of meditation or contemplation, concentrate on allowing your heart to open to joy. Imagine that you are a young child, running freely at the seaside on a sunny day. As you run toward the beach area, you kick off your shoes and wade in the shallows of the waves lapping onto the shore. The sound of the surf makes you laugh, and you dance along the edge of the water. Then, you head into the waves and let go, allowing your body to float in the cool water. You swim out a short distance, and a family of dolphins playfully surrounds you. For a while you swim together, feeling their power and gentility. When you tire, a dolphin urges you toward the safety of the shore. The feeling of freedom, letting go, and trust stays with you. Remind yourself of these moments when you need to be lifted up.

AFFIRMATION FOR THE YEAR

"Abundance in all forms comes to me now, in perfect ways."

PRIMARY FOCUS

Although achieving an understanding with others around you is a clear priority, your motives are likely to be centered on getting ahead. It's easy to say or do things that irritate or inflame others. Maybe you should carry a fire extinguisher.

HEALTH AND FITNESS

Staying active serves two major purposes now: generating energy and releasing tension. If you repress your energy, including your emotions, the frustration and tension can drain your vitality and undermine your effectiveness.

ROMANCE AND RELATIONSHIPS

Turmoil at home can be the result of emotional dilemmas, but may also occur if you're changing your environment or if there are extra activities in your household. Open communication during the Full Moon on the 12th offers resolutions, but watch the trap created by expectations and clarify specific objectives to avoid disappointments. Romance is best after the 25th. Make innovative changes at home during the New Moon on the 28th.

CAREER AND FINANCE

Review your finances before the 12th, and outline a plan for any special projects before you begin. Business meetings, presentations, or conferences fare best after the 12th, but you're likely to run into pressure from conservatives from the 21st–24th, so be ready for them. Be aware of your competitive drive, since you may be pushing harder than you think and can alienate the very people you need to impress!

OPPORTUNITY OF THE MONTH

Your artistry draws positive attention from the 9th–17th, when your efforts, ideas, and creativity inspire enthusiastic support.

AFFIRMATION FOR THE MONTH
"My words and actions promote harmony and ease."

Rewarding Days: 2, 3, 11, 12, 16, 20, 21, 22, 30
Challenging Days: 1, 6, 7, 13, 14, 27, 28

SCORPIO/FEBRUARY

PRIMARY FOCUS

Creative projects, activities that center on children, and situations that encourage you to open your heart provide outlets for your self-expression and may even lead the way to prosperity.

HEALTH AND FITNESS

Your physical vitality improves, and you'll be even stronger if you add regular fitness activities or get involved in sports that are both challenging and enjoyable. Play has many benefits. After all, the quality of your life improves when you're smiling!

ROMANCE AND RELATIONSHIPS

Although home and family issues can arise near the time of the Full Moon on the 11th, your focus is more on the pleasurable things life has to offer. This is a wonderful time for love, although you may have to get a few barriers out of the way before everything is to your liking. Your loving expressions encourage the development of a special relationship, when someone new may step into the picture during the solar eclipse on the 26th.

CAREER AND FINANCE

A power play in speculative ventures can escalate from the 1st–6th, when you're in an excellent position to step aside until the dust settles. But if you experience some losses, re-evaluate and then focus in a new direction after the 26th, when you may find something much more lucrative anyway. Showcase your talents after the 11th. Your efforts attract positive attention, and an agent or supporter can be extremely valuable after the 22nd.

OPPORTUNITY OF THE MONTH

If you feel that you're ready, make plans and then launch an important project or idea, or show what you have to offer after the 22nd.

AFFIRMATION FOR THE MONTH
"My thoughts and actions flow from pure love."

Rewarding Days: 7, 8, 12, 13, 17, 18, 22, 23, 26, 27
Challenging Days: 3, 4, 9, 10, 24, 25

SCORPIO/MARCH

PRIMARY FOCUS
Work can be demanding, and if you've fallen behind, you may feel the brunt of the pressure. This is a good time to concentrate on a major project, and if it's something that utilizes your creativity, then you may even enjoy it!

HEALTH AND FITNESS
Pay careful attention to your health, particularly if you're concerned about a loss of energy or recurring condition. Get to the core of physical complaints and seek solutions after the New Moon on the 27th.

ROMANCE AND RELATIONSHIPS
Family gatherings or activities that bring those you love together can be self-confirming and also offer an opportunity to stabilize your life. If you're questioning your love for another during the lunar eclipse on the 12th, examine your heart for conflicting inner turmoil related to the past. Old blocks, fears, or anxieties may be getting in the way of love. Get clear about your own worthiness to be loved.

CAREER AND FINANCE
Convoluted financial situations or losses can occur because the value of something has changed. Be attentive to changing markets, and avoid getting into any investments or spending that compromises your long-term stability from the 2nd–14th. Communication problems may arise after Mercury turns retrograde on the 27th, but try a different approach, since the New Moon on the 27th helps when you're juggling your production schedule.

OPPORTUNITY OF THE MONTH
Speculative ventures or artistically oriented endeavors show promise from the 1st–7th. After that, you're making alterations that lead to greater productivity.

AFFIRMATION FOR THE MONTH
"I appreciate the beauty of life."

Rewarding Days: 6, 7, 11, 12, 16, 17, 21, 22, 26
Challenging Days: 2, 3, 9, 10, 23, 24, 29, 30

SCORPIO/APRIL

PRIMARY FOCUS
Relationships draw your attention and it's time to mend fences or clarify your intentions. At work, your creativity shines, and using your artistry to your advantage leads to advancement.

HEALTH AND FITNESS
Continued attention to bothersome physical complaints produces positive results, particularly if you acknowledge your limitations during the healing process. You move beyond an impasse during the Full Moon on the 11th.

ROMANCE AND RELATIONSHIPS
Love blossoms, and from the 12th–22nd you may feel completely invigorated through the experience of opening your heart. It's easy to fall victim to illusion or to jump into a relationship without considering all your options after the 14th, so try to move carefully and be aware that you may be blinded by infatuation. You can still enjoy the experience without altering your life. Try a different approach to partnership after the New Moon on the 26th.

CAREER AND FINANCE
While Mercury continues its retrograde through the 20th, you may experience several delays at work, and can have problems due to inadequate support from your staff or others who work with you. Finances can improve through the promise of a working partnership, but before you agree, make sure you like the particulars in the contract, and wait until after the 21st to sign long-term agreements.

OPPORTUNITY OF THE MONTH
Your best solace and more fulfilling experiences arise through the things you do as part of your creative expression. Give in to your creative urges after the 6th.

AFFIRMATION FOR THE MONTH
"In all matters I listen to the voice of my heart."

Rewarding Days: 2, 3, 7, 8, 12, 13, 18, 22, 23, 30
Challenging Days: 4, 5, 15, 20, 21, 26, 27

SCORPIO/MAY

PRIMARY FOCUS

You may be feeling a bit competitive, and that energy can emerge in your personal relationships and in your work environment. Seek out healthy ways to express your drive for control.

HEALTH AND FITNESS

Although team sports or fitness classes can be excellent options for increasing your fitness level, you need a challenge. Set goals to boost your endurance while satisfying your need to accomplish something.

ROMANCE AND RELATIONSHIPS

You're increasing the heat in your relationships, and during the Scorpio Full Moon on the 11th may be quite assertive about your needs. This can be a very romantic time, especially if you have a playful way of dealing with your sexual and sensual desires with your partner. If not, it's time to start! A variety of approaches to intimacy can be the key to a more rewarding phase in your love life after the New Moon on the 25th.

CAREER AND FINANCE

Well-defined communication moves your work forward from the 1st–14th, when you may also find better ways of working cooperatively with others. But you can get caught carrying burdens that are not yours, so keep your priorities in order. Joint finances are the primary sources of dispute; if you feel manipulated by someone you're likely to retaliate. Just be sure you don't set a trap that compromises your integrity.

OPPORTUNITY OF THE MONTH

Get clear about your feelings, because any internal conflicts will surge into your work and relationships. It's time to create life on terms that fulfill your deeper needs.

AFFIRMATION FOR THE MONTH
"I listen to my intuitive voice."

Rewarding Days: 1, 5, 10, 11, 14, 15, 19, 20, 28
Challenging Days: 2, 3, 17, 18, 23, 24, 29, 30, 31

Scorpio/June

Primary Focus

A serious commitment with a partner can change your life. Your priorities and needs have changed, and your business and professional relationships should reflect those changes. If not, now's the time to reconsider your agreements.

Health and Fitness

Getting to the core of physical complaints gives you more control over your own health, and you may feel more comfortable working with a health-care professional who respects your knowledge of your own body.

Romance and Relationships

Intimacy issues arise, and you may feel uncomfortable and vulnerable in unusual situations or with requests that are out of the ordinary from the 1st until the Full Moon on the 9th. However, if you trust your partner, a few changes might be just what you need to get out of a rut. Take time to travel, or share a favorite retreat or inspirational event with someone you love after the New Moon on the 23rd.

Career and Finance

Dealing with taxes, insurance, and indebtedness can be frustrating from the 1st–7th, and if you're trying to get ahead of the game, you'll succeed only if you know the rules! Business partnerships can be a positive alternative for growth, but before you agree, make sure you're happy with what you're asked to give in return. Too much control from either side will lead to disaster.

Opportunity of the Month

Schedule conferences, meetings, or special presentations after the 16th, when your ideas are well-received. Watch out for the competition and be ready with counter-proposals.

Affirmation for the Month
"I am comfortable using my power in productive ways."

Rewarding Days: 1, 2, 6, 7, 11, 12, 16, 24, 25, 29
Challenging Days: 13, 14, 19, 20, 21, 26, 27

SCORPIO/JULY

PRIMARY FOCUS
The horizon looks brighter and your reputation improves due to efforts to promote your ideas, talents, or objectives. Even restrictions posed by regulations or competition can be positive challenges.

HEALTH AND FITNESS
Get back to nature for at least some time and connect to your element —water—with a swim or a walk around the lake. Your vitality improves, and that extra energy can boost productivity.

ROMANCE AND RELATIONSHIPS
If you're looking for love, you may find it while traveling or exploring something that enriches your mind and spirit near the time of the Full Moon on the 9th. The spiritual significance of your connection to your partner expands, and you may feel more open to allowing a love that feels like part of your destiny. Something unique is on the horizon during the New Moon on the 23rd, and may alter your sense of reality. Enjoy it!

CAREER AND FINANCE
Educational pursuits, travel, publishing, attending conferences, or advertising—all the things that allow you to expand your career options—can be just the ticket for advancement after the 5th. This is the time to share your ideas and connect with like-minded groups or individuals. It's OK if you don't all think alike, as long as you have a similar focus. If you're thinking of changing your career path, create a solid footing before you take the leap.

OPPORTUNITY OF THE MONTH
You're in the perfect position to reach beyond limiting circumstances from the 18th–31st. Just be attentive to details, since new territory can be confusing.

AFFIRMATION FOR THE MONTH
"My ethics are driven by a philosophy based on truth and integrity."

Rewarding Days: 3, 4, 8, 9, 13, 21, 22, 26, 31
Challenging Days: 10, 11, 17, 18, 23, 24

Scorpio/August

Primary Focus
Mercury's retrograde can play havoc with your work schedule, and you must also be quite careful about your communication, since unsettled misunderstandings can affect your reputation. Try to stay flexible if you want to succeed.

Health and Fitness
Give yourself a vacation from old mental patterns that increase stress. Channel your thinking to positive possibilities and seek out alternatives when confronted with difficulties.

Romance and Relationships
With a focus on reaching a higher plateau in your love relationships, you may awaken to the possibility of long-term fulfillment. But questions can arise during the lunar eclipse on the 7th, particularly if you distrust your own feelings. Talk about your vision for the future, and if your partner cannot share it, reconsider the validity of your commitment. You're feeling rebellious after the solar eclipse on the 21st, when you have no patience for unnecessary restraints.

Career and Finance
Everything intensifies in your career, and until Mercury ends its retrograde on the 23rd you may have difficulty moving forward. Watch out for deception from the 12th–22nd, when you may be presented with something almost too good to ignore. Look into the options, but don't fall for a con job. Check out charities before you offer your resources, since your motives may be pure but the options may not be!

Opportunity of the Month
Allow your consciousness to move into more expansive directions from the 1st–22nd, when you can have fabulous inner experiences and awakened ideas, despite the hassles of life.

Affirmation for the Month
"My ideas are inspired by Divine Truth and Wisdom."

Rewarding Days: 1, 4, 5, 9, 10, 17, 18, 22, 27, 28
Challenging Days: 7, 8, 13, 14, 20, 21

Scorpio/September

Primary Focus
An attitude of unconditional acceptance can alter your self-awareness and may even change the course of your life. Concentrate on setting goals that feed your soul and stimulate your ability to experience life at its fullest.

Health and Fitness
Team sports, fitness classes, or getting together with friends to work out or play can be fun and invigorating. Watch your competitive drive, though, because you don't want to alienate someone just because you're feeling unstoppable!

Romance and Relationships
Last month's complex emotional issues are more easily clarified during the lunar eclipse on the 6th. Open your heart to receiving love and let that flow of love work its magic in all your relationships. Friendships play a significant role, and may be a primary factor in your love life. The New Moon on the 20th stimulates you to re-examine what you thought was just a friendship.

Career and Finance
Make connections with professional peers after the 6th, since their support and influence may help you take those steps to get ahead. You're feeling driven in your career, and it's easy to step on sensitive toes by taking an approach that engenders a defensive response. You can be just as effective by allowing your intensity to cool a bit before pushing toward your goals. Work is more rewarding this month.

Opportunity of the Month
Well-defined plans and goals make all the difference between success and failure. You may set up a difficult situation by ignoring existing structures, so take those into account.

Affirmation for the Month
"I have abundance in every part of my life!"

Rewarding Days: 1, 2, 5, 6, 14, 18, 19, 23, 24, 29
Challenging Days: 3, 4, 9, 10, 16, 17, 30

Scorpio/October

PRIMARY FOCUS

Although you may feel a little withdrawn, contact with others in your field or with good friends can still be of vital importance. Decide to be selective, and honor your needs for privacy when necessary.

HEALTH AND FITNESS

Staying active is crucial if you're to maintain your energy, but you also need ample time for relaxation and rest. Surround yourself with others whose positive attitudes stimulate optimism, since you're sensitive to everyone around you now.

ROMANCE AND RELATIONSHIPS

Spend time alone with your thoughts and reflect on your needs during the Full Moon on the 5th. Then you'll feel much more confident about talking about your wishes and desires after the 13th, when a good friend is an excellent source of support. Once Venus enters Scorpio on the 25th you're feeling quite amorous, when your best features work to your advantage. The forces of attraction are on your side after the New Moon on the 20th.

CAREER AND FINANCE

Do your homework and go over all the details from the 1st–11th, and then schedule important meetings or conferences after the 13th. A power play involving money looms from the 12th–20th, but if you've got the facts, you'll handle it just fine. Finances improve, but remain inconsistent through the rest of the month, so show reasonable caution, particularly in impulsively driven circumstances.

OPPORTUNITY OF THE MONTH

You're in the best position to have things the way you want them after the 25th, but you still have to be personally responsible or you'll lose your position of strength.

AFFIRMATION FOR THE MONTH
"I deserve pure and abiding love."

Rewarding Days: 3, 4, 11, 12, 16, 20, 21, 26, 30, 31
Challenging Days: 1, 2, 7, 8, 13, 14, 28, 29

SCORPIO/NOVEMBER

PRIMARY FOCUS

You're moving ahead, and finances are also improving. There's just one problem: You're likely to spend money faster than you're making it! However, by showing reasonable restraint you can set up a situation for growth.

HEALTH AND FITNESS

Find fitness activities that are fun, since you're not interested in wasting your time on anything that is drudgery. If you look forward to your workouts or recreational time, you'll gain more from them. Plus, you're more likely to show up!

ROMANCE AND RELATIONSHIPS

Your feelings of love grow during the Full Moon on the 4th, especially if a lover shares your enthusiasm for things you enjoy. If you've not yet opened your heart, seek out situations that allow your creativity to flow and then look around and see who else is in the picture. A Scorpio New Moon on the 18th marks a fabulous time for a revolution of the heart, when a new or established love recharges your life.

CAREER AND FINANCE

Investments fare beautifully from the 1st–13th, especially in areas that hold your interest and capture your imagination. Mercury's retrograde from November 21st–December 11th can slow your financial progress, though, since this is a time to reconsider monetary matters. Get all the details of your finances together so you can create a budget that more accurately reflects your current situation.

OPPORTUNITY OF THE MONTH

Get involved in community activities or special interest groups to help further your career from the 1st–18th. Surround yourself with others whose ideals are similar to your own.

AFFIRMATION FOR THE MONTH
"My thoughts and actions reflect compassion."

Rewarding Days: 7, 8, 12, 13, 17, 18, 22, 27
Challenging Days: 3, 4, 9, 10, 24, 25,

Scorpio/December

Primary Focus
With a careful eye on your finances, you need to find ways to strengthen your personal worth. This includes material things, but originates within your own heart and the way you feel about yourself. Let your actions stem from a renewed sense of self-esteem.

Health and Fitness
This is the time to work on inner fitness. Cut through those attitudes that stand in the way of your happiness, and replace them with inner affirmations of strength, hope, and optimism. Break away from the things in your past that you've outgrown.

Romance and Relationships
Personal relationships can be a little rocky due to misunderstandings. If you're unhappy, remember that you can use words like weapons, and before you decide to lash out at someone, make sure you really want to cut them down to size. Make an effort to change what you can control (namely yourself), and set aside time to get away from everyday hassles and enjoy romance after the 23rd.

Career and Finance
Rash actions during the Full Moon on the 3rd will come back to haunt you, especially since Mercury's retrograde until the 11th. So, if you don't want to repeat something, wait before you speak or act. Keep communication simple and to the point. There's time to embellish later. Get that new budget in place following the New Moon on the 18th, and then announce your plans to others after the 28th.

Opportunity of the Month
Reduce the risk of difficult losses by taking your time and watching responses from others. By accurately gauging a situation, you can take action that leads to success after the 23rd.

Affirmation for the Month
"I use all my resources wisely."

Rewarding Days: 5, 9, 10, 14, 15, 19, 24, 25
Challenging Days: 1, 7, 8, 21, 22, 28, 29

SCORPIO ♏ ACTION TABLE

These dates reflect the best (but not the only) times for success and ease in these activities, according to your sign.

	Jan.	Feb.	Mar.	Apr.	May	June	July	Aug.	Sept.	Oct.	Nov.	Dec.
Change Residence		2–19										
Ask for a Raise											19	
Begin a Course of Study						24, 25						
Join a Club									20			
Begin a Romance		26, 27										
Visit a Doctor				8–31	1–30	1–14			24–30	1–11		
Start a Diet	4, 5, 31	1, 2, 28	1, 27, 28	24, 25	21, 22	17, 18	15, 16	11, 12	7, 8	5, 6	11,12 29, 30	26, 27
Seek Employment				8–26	20–30	1–16	1–31	1–31	1–8			
Take a Vacation	11, 12	7, 8	6, 7	2–4, 30	1, 27, 28	24, 25	21, 22	17, 18	13–15	11, 12	7, 8	5, 6
End a Relationship										4, 5		
Change Your Wardrobe		20–28	1–7									
Seek Professional Advice	6, 7	3, 4	2, 3, 29, 30	26, 27	23, 24	19–21	17, 18	13, 14	9, 10	7, 8	3, 4	1, 2, 28, 29
Have a Make-Over										18, 19		
Obtain a Loan	8, 9	5, 6	4, 5, 31	4, 5, 28, 29	1, 25, 26	22, 23	19, 20	15, 16	11, 12	9, 10	5, 6	3, 4, 30, 31

SAGITTARIUS

The Archer
November 22–December 21

Element:	Fire
Quality:	Mutable
Polarity:	Yang/Masculine
Planetary Ruler:	Jupiter
Meditation:	"All things in harmony with Higher Law are possible."
Gemstone:	Turquoise
Power Stones:	Lapis Lazuli, Azurite, Sodalite
Glyph:	Archer's Arrow
Anatomy:	Hips, Thighs, Sciatic Nerve
Colors:	Royal Blue, Purple
Animals:	Fleet-Footed Animals
Myths/Legends:	Athena, Chiron
House Association:	Ninth
Opposite Sign:	Gemini
Flower:	Narcissus
Key Word:	Expansion

Positive Expression:		Misuse of Energy:	
Wise	Understanding	Foolish	Extravagant
Adventurous	Tolerant	Bigoted	Condescending
Jovial	Philanthropic	Opinionated	Gluttonous
Optimistic		Self-Righteous	

 # SAGITTARIUS

YOUR EGO'S STRENGTHS AND WEAKNESSES

Enthusiastically reaching out into the world to discover the grand quest of life, you are "The Adventurer" of the zodiac. Your optimistic attitudes result from your faith in Truth, and provide buoyant inspiration for others who are both charmed by your sincerity and disarmed by your directness.

Limitations rarely stop you from extending your horizons or boosting your attitudes. Your desire to experience as much of life as possible may lead to educational pursuits, travel, foreign language study, or a voracious appetite for reading, as you fill your mind with new ideas and open your life to diverse friendships spanning many cultures. Stimulated by the energy of Jupiter, your planetary ruler, your aims are high, particularly within the context of your spiritual quest to reach higher levels of consciousness and true understanding of universal law.

Sometimes your expectations for yourself and for others can interfere with your personal growth. You can even become too judgmental of others who seem to be ignorant of the profound truths you've uncovered, creating a trap of self-righteousness or fanaticism. As you redirect your zeal and focus on tolerant understanding, the Greater Truth will illustrate that you really do not know everything, and furthermore, that it's not a requirement that you know it all!

YOUR APPROACH TO ROMANCE

For you, love can be the grandest of all adventures and finding a partner who can share your enthusiasm for life is a pure delight.

You can be happy on your own, but the excitement of romantic conquests or flirtatious jousting is truly pleasurable for you. Because you require personal freedom, you're likely to resist becoming tangled in the lair of love until you're ready to surrender some of your independence. Even then, you'll feel more in love when you know your partner gives you room to breathe, and you can then be a steadfast partner. You may leave several old loves behind in the confusing wake of your sudden disappearances!

Although you're attracted to Gemini, your zodiac opposite, you do have a few differences to bridge; but you can have an exciting partnership through open communication and surrender to the magnetic energy that draws you together. You're most comfortable with the other fire signs—Aries, Leo, and Sagittarius, who share your need for illumination and passion for life.

With Aries, love can remain strong and is constantly charged with excitement. Taurus, although comfortable, can seem to slow you down too much. You may adore Cancer's safety net and great cooking, but don't like feeling overprotected. Leo's demonstrative and dramatic manner can transport you into ecstasy. Virgo can be interesting, but may feel too much like your mother with all those directions for doing things the right way.

You're fascinated by Libra's refined grace, good taste, and artistry. Watch out for the allure of Scorpio, because you can be overcome and momentarily lose your sense of independence! Another Sagittarian can be your perfect traveling partner whose ideals and philosophies mesh with your own. Capricorn offers steadfast security, but you may feel uneasy if you sense that you're being controlled. Aquarius' originality and unique way of thinking are wonderful for you, and you can honor your mutual needs for independence. Pisces' imagination can be enticing yet confusing, since you may not easily understand one another.

YOUR CAREER DEVELOPMENT

Your career can offer an opportunity to utilize your enthusiastic optimism and you'll be most productive in a field that offers unlimited potential and lots of freedom. Your ability to influence and inspire others through your ideas or speech can be used in fields like the law, politics, the ministry, promotional activities, advertising, or acting as an agent or representative for the talents of others. Careers in writing, publishing, or journalism offer good outlets for sharing your thoughts while gathering information. A natural salesperson, you can relate to people from diverse backgrounds and may be drawn to diplomatic service or the travel industry.

Speculative investments will always catch your attention — whether in real estate, stocks, sports, racing, banking, or even gambling. Your desire to continue learning may encourage you to seek a profession in academics or education, where you can foster incentive in your students and reach higher levels of personal mastery yourself. Regardless of your choice, you think big!

YOUR USE OF POWER

Freedom is power to you: freedom to think and to act in accordance with higher law is a true expression of the power ordained by a higher source that inspires your quest for Truth and Right. You view power without wisdom as a waste, and abhor the idea of using power to limit the development of human potential. You're willing to apply the necessary effort to get through all the useless double-talk in order to achieve enlightenment, even though you may feel frustrated by the time it takes to get there. Material abundance may appear to symbolize power, but you may not fully appreciate an abundant life until you have harmonized your actions and thoughts with your higher needs.

Although it's easy to fall into the trap of dogmatic beliefs that can, in themselves, become a kind of prison, your search for wisdom and understanding helps you keep your mind open to new paths and a variety of possibilities. The power of Truth overcomes the shackles of narrow-mindedness. As you study, write, travel, and teach, your inspiration will reach toward others, helping you realize that true power lies in shaping the future by improving understanding among all humankind.

FAMOUS SAGITTARIANS

Willa Cather, Walter Cronkite, Tom Hulce, Billy Idol, Don Johnson, Madeleine L'Engle, David Mamet, Brad Pitt, Marisa Tomei, Dick Van Dyke, Gianni Versace, Katarina Witt, Yanni, Neil Young, Kurt Vonnegut, Jr.

The Year Ahead for Sagittarius

Y ou're filled with ideas about new directions and can afford to take a fresh approach to opening your mind and developing innovative concepts of your own. Your creativity flourishes under the influence of this year's cycles, and now you're stimulated to give yourself plenty of room for growth. Your underlying motivations may center on a desire to increase your security base, and as a result, you may make significant changes in your home environment or family structure.

The transit of Jupiter (your planetary ruler) in Pisces challenges you to open to different traditions and to question your needs at the deepest levels. This stimulus changes the way you approach creating stability, although you may have a number of distractions in the way before you feel you've achieved your aims. Sometimes, making changes in your home environment is helpful during the period Jupiter travels through the Fourth House of your solar chart, particularly if those changes give you more room. Moving may be an option, but you may just have to add a room, knock out a wall, or rearrange the furniture to achieve your desired aims. On an emotional level, seek out situations that give you a chance to increase your self-confidence without overstretching yourself. It's tempting to go beyond your limitations in areas like spending, eating, or making promises—propositions that can leave you feeling extremely frustrated. Knowing when to say "No" may actually confer just as much confidence as saying "Yes" when you know it's too costly to do so.

Saturn's transit emphasizes your creative expression, and this is an excellent time to get serious about developing your talents and abilities. You may also have obligations in relationship to children that provide both joy and the challenge of becoming a loving and tolerant guide; many people increase their family size under this cycle. The primary focus of this time centers on developing your ability to love fully, completely, and responsibly.

The cycles of the outer planets—Uranus, Neptune, and Pluto— are all making strong aspects to your Sun. Since Pluto entered Sagittarius in 1996 you've probably felt an increased intensity in everything in your life. That intensity may change your approach to all you're doing, and may also prompt you to dig beneath the surface for answers instead of accepting things without making an effort. Uranus and Neptune are providing stimulation that can alter the way you apply your thinking, communicate your ideas, and develop your mind.

The solar and lunar eclipses draw your attention to two primary areas: intellectual and spiritual merging, and your need to balance career and family. On February 26th, the solar eclipse in Pisces emphasizes your connection to your roots—home, family, and at a deeper level, soul. Any brewing family crises finally reach their peak, giving you an opportunity to let go of the past and move toward a brighter and lighter expression of your deeper needs. You may also feel a pull to spend more time at home or develop a real sense of roots. This can be a nesting cycle, and balancing the demands of your job with your needs for personal comfort and security may require some soul-searching. On August 21st, the solar eclipse in Leo brings a powerful emphasis to your spiritual path and search for Truth. During the Moon's eclipses on August 7th and September 6th, you may find that your viewpoints about your spiritual path need to be more carefully integrated into your daily life. This can be accomplished by developing greater mindfulness and being more attentive to the here and now.

If you were born from November 22nd–27th, you're caught between your dreams and the squeeze of reality. You're experiencing two major cycles: Saturn is transiting in quincunx to your Sun while Neptune sextiles your Sun. Saturn's influence brings pressure to bear that requires you to take a closer look at the way you're handling your responsibilities and to make adjustments that produce greater efficiency and effectiveness. This means that you may have to change your schedule or your habit patterns in order to gain what you want from life, but you can do that if you'll listen to your inner voice. That's what Neptune's influence does for you: It helps you tune in to your inner self and spiritual needs. This cycle of Neptune stimulates your dreams and creative sensibilities. Between these two influences, you may finally take the time to fully develop your talents or to reach out into the world through your creativity and make a difference in the quality of life. It's a good idea to pay attention to any physical conditions that are chronically bothersome, so you can get to the core. You may respond more readily to therapies that target your whole self instead of those that just treat symptoms.

↗ ↗ ↗

You're in a strong position to increase your personal influence through transformational change **if you were born from November 27th–December 2nd.** Pluto is transiting in conjunction to your Sun, a once-in-a-lifetime cycle that can bring far-reaching changes in your sense of personal identity that can alter your life path. You've been feeling this energy for a year or so as it has been approaching the conjunction to your Sun, and may have discovered that you're more in touch with yourself. This can be a period of profound healing and regeneration, and you may experience a miraculous sense of renewal as you release the things you no longer need and move toward embracing your personal power. It's time to get rid of the circumstances, people, and attitudes that are not in harmony with your higher needs.

In most instances, these changes seem to feel like a natural evolution—unless you're resisting the need to grow. Some of the effects of this cycle can be difficult, particularly if you're resistant to change. But if you're willing to cooperate with your needs to review your emotional attachments to the way things have been and strike out on a path that is true to yourself, then it's not so difficult after all. In fact, for once in your life you may discover that true sense of celebration you've been dreaming about all along!

Your unique talents and abilities work to your advantage this year **if you were born from November 29th–December 6th.** You're feeling the influence of Uranus transiting in sextile aspect to your Sun. This is an exciting time, filled with new ideas, powerful inspiration, and fresh opportunities for growth and self-expression. Exercising your independence is a primary part of this cycle, but you will discover that the true independence you seek incorporates a renewed respect for cooperation with others.

Taking a path through your career or within your family that allows you to exercise your needs for personal autonomy can lead to changes like striking out on your own, becoming more comfortable taking the risk of being yourself, and letting others see you for who you are. The awakening you experience now depends a great deal on whether or not you're willing to let go of some of those old crutches so you can finally run freely. Do you remember that scene in *Forrest Gump,* when Forrest is running and drops his braces? Well, that can be you now! Fly like the wind!

It's important to deal with your obligations in a responsible manner **if you were born from November 30th–December 7th.** Saturn's transit in sesquiquadrate to your Sun brings a cycle that feels like one step forward, two steps back. You can make progress, but many of the steps may feel cumbersome, especially if you're carrying unnecessary burdens. So, in your plans for success, decide whom you're trying to please and why you want to get there. It's OK to alter your plans if you discover that your destination is not where you want to go. Just be sure that's the case, since changing horses midstream sometimes leaves you a bit soggy.

If you were born from December 7th–10th, you're experiencing the confusing cycle of Neptune transiting in semi-square to your Sun. The frustrations associated with this period are directly related to your tendency to lose track of your priorities or to be distracted by something that is too unrealistic. You may just want to escape the pressures of life, and that's OK as long as your escapes are healthy ones. If you adopt abusive or addictive behaviors, you'll lose a sense of your personal power and strength of self. Your physical body is more sensitive too, and it's crucial to pay attention to any vague or chronic problems, since denial can be damaging.

If you were born from December 7th–21st, you're feeling the stabilizing influence of Saturn traveling in trine aspect to your Sun. Educational pursuits, well-defined career goals, and commitments all fare nicely during this cycle, particularly if they're on target with your needs for growth. If you're not sure where you're heading, this is the time to make a decision and step on the path. You'll be pleasantly surprised at the doors opening for you if you make the effort. But if you just wait around or continue to be distracted by situations that aren't what you want or need, then you may just spin your wheels. You're always happier with an adventure on the horizon, and this is your time to create the adventures that take you exactly where you want to go.

Your desire to break free from restrictions is stimulated by Uranus in semi-square aspect to your Sun **if you were born from December 14th–19th.** By choosing healthy forms of rebellion, you can accomplish an excellent series of changes. However, if you adopt contentious attitudes, the trouble you cause may result in setbacks or the loss of friends. Choose your words carefully; learn to listen to your inner thoughts and the message of your heart. Your life can undergo revolutionary changes without burning every bridge — especially if you're not yet on the other side!

TOOLS TO MAKE A DIFFERENCE

The challenges of the long outer-planet transits are stimulating your need to become more aware of the power of your thoughts. Mindfulness exercises can be an important part of your personal growth, and becoming more aware of the profound significance of your daily experiences can change your outlook to one of hope, peace, and compassion. Spend time each day in contemplation, making entries in your personal journal, meditating, or getting back to nature. Search for joy and laughter, and smile frequently. You can move toward the wisdom you experience in your dreams.

At home, focus on creating a nesting space—a comfort zone where you can let go of your worries and feel content. Fill your environment with things you love and that remind you of your identity. Celebrate—daily! You say there's nothing to celebrate? Well, look for it: Celebrate the color of the sky, the sound of the birds, the taste of a delicious meal, the smile in the eyes of your lover, the fact that you awoke this morning. Develop your natural jovial attitude and enjoy the fact that you are on the Earth to stimulate mirth, laughter, and provoke contemplation.

To strengthen your physical health, get back to nature. Find a sport you love, promise to take walks. When you drive by the park, stop for a few minutes and stand under a tree. To balance your tendencies to go too far, work with the flower essence remedies. Those that are keyed to Sagittarius are vervain, wild oat, larkspur, and mountain pride. When you're feeling vulnerable, wear beautiful blues and purples, or add these colors to your environment. Dedicate this year as the perfect time to finally let go of habits that undermine your physical health and adopt routines that give you energy and support your body.

During your periods of meditation, concentrate on opening your mind to new thoughts. Imagine that you are sitting in a fabulous library, surrounded by volumes of books. Before you get up to choose your book, you stop, center yourself and concentrate on exactly what it is that you want to know. Think about the questions you've held. Then ask to learn something new. Rise and walk through the rooms and shelves. You feel a powerful warmth and light emanating from one of the books, and it gently slips from the shelf into your open hands. As you open the book, you discover amazing information. Remember what you have learned. When you return to your conscious state, know that in your quest for knowledge, there is always a place to find your answer.

AFFIRMATION FOR THE YEAR

"My mind is open to new ideas.
I am open to pursuing positive new directions!"

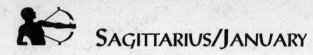

SAGITTARIUS/JANUARY

PRIMARY FOCUS

Networking pays off, with regional travel and correspondence playing a significant role in the way you touch base with important individuals. Pay attention to the way you say what's on your mind.

HEALTH AND FITNESS

Staying physically active increases your ability to focus mentally. Your health can also benefit from adopting a more positive attitude toward yourself, your life, and your needs. Use affirmations and visualization to fine-tune your focus.

ROMANCE AND RELATIONSHIPS

Transformational changes in your relationships begin with the way you present yourself now, since some people may not know how to respond to the new you! Connections to your siblings may require more attention, but you can also forge pathways that are more applicable to your current needs, leaving old issues behind. Adopt an open-minded attitude during the New Moon on the 28th, when fresh directions hold the greatest promise.

CAREER AND FINANCE

With Venus activating your solar Second House for the next two months, it's a good idea to review your finances and get rid of unnecessary expenditures. In business, this is an excellent time to get rid of slow inventory, reduce risk, and consolidate your focus. Financial worries can loom large during the Full Moon on the 12th, but a methodical approach helps resolve them. Send correspondence, or travel for business from the 14th–25th.

OPPORTUNITY OF THE MONTH

Schedule important business meetings from the 1st–12th, emphasizing new directions and plans for growth.

AFFIRMATION FOR THE MONTH
"I am an effective communicator."

Rewarding Days: 1, 4, 5, 13, 14, 18, 23, 24, 28
Challenging Days: 2, 3, 8, 9, 10, 16, 17, 29, 30

Sagittarius/February

Primary Focus
It's easy to get carried away and push too hard or go too far in your efforts or with your ideas. Measure your actions against the circumstances and move carefully when you're in new territory.

Health and Fitness
Avoid high-risk situations from the 1st–7th, since it's easy to get in over your head. Tension runs high this month, and you need to stay active to release pent-up energy. You'll even rest better as a result.

Romance and Relationships
Improvements in communication strengthen your personal and professional relationships from the 2nd–19th. Plan a special retreat or inspiring trip with your sweetheart for the Full Moon on the 11th. Money matters can impede your love life, especially if your self-esteem is on the low side. The solar eclipse on the 26th brings family matters to the forefront, and a crisis can be the perfect launching pad for a new way of creating familial support.

Career and Finance
Plan important business meetings from the 8th–21st, when presenting your ideas is easier, although you may still meet with resistance from those who see you as a threat. If your budget is tight, it's best to work with it and avoid wasting resources, since replenishing them can be too costly. You'll make the best progress by using a conservative approach in your plans, saving those expansive ideas for later.

Opportunity of the Month
It's time to dig deep and determine how you're accomplishing your security needs. If you feel unstable, what can you do to create a platform that works for you?

Affirmation for the Month
"I am safe and secure in the face of change."

Rewarding Days: 1, 9, 10, 14, 15, 19, 20, 24, 25, 28
Challenging Days: 5, 6, 7, 12, 13, 23, 26, 27

SAGITTARIUS/MARCH

PRIMARY FOCUS
The Moon's eclipse on the 12th draws your attention to the balance between your personal needs and career obligations. Determine where you want to go and clarify your ambitions.

HEALTH AND FITNESS
Finding exciting and challenging recreational outlets changes your perspective on life. Direct that enthusiasm into a new class, your favorite sport, or a creative endeavor. The key is to keep moving!

ROMANCE AND RELATIONSHIPS
In hot pursuit of romance, you're eager to make the object of your affections your own. Not only are you willing to take a few more risks, but your open affection and teasing playfulness can be rather engaging. Whether you're breathing life back into a stale relationship or opening your heart to a new love, your approach is more natural and comfortable. If she or he doesn't get the point, try again after the New Moon on the 27th.

CAREER AND FINANCE
Sharpen your creative skills and trust your inventiveness. You're eager to define your unique abilities and showcase your talents, and letting others see what you have to offer can result in advancement in ways you had not anticipated after the 7th. Even though Mercury enters its retrograde on the 27th, you can still make progress. Just try to stay focused on what you already have in the works, particularly in the realm of investments.

OPPORTUNITY OF THE MONTH
Let your inner child emerge, or get involved in situations that serve the needs of children if you're looking for ways to increase your influence. Your enthusiasm works like a magnet.

AFFIRMATION FOR THE MONTH
"Love directs my thoughts and actions."

Rewarding Days: 1, 9, 10, 14, 15, 19, 20, 23, 24, 27, 28
Challenging Days: 4, 5, 11, 12, 16, 25, 26, 31

Look for our complete line of almanacs, date books and calendars.

GET 15% OFF YOUR NEXT PURCHASE!

WE WANT TO KNOW ABOUT YOU! Knowing about our audience helps Llewellyn to keep developing quality products with YOU in mind. Please fill out this survey and send it in to receive a catalog and coupon for 15% off your next purchase of Llewellyn products.

Name: _____

Address: _____

City: _____ State: _____ Zip: _____

Please check the boxes that apply:

Gender: ☐ Male ☐ Female

Age: ☐ Under 18 yrs old ☐ 18-26 ☐ 27-36
☐ 37-54 ☐ 55-65 ☐ 65+

Marital Status: ☐ Single ☐ Married
☐ Divorced ☐ Other

Do you have children? ☐ Yes ☐ No

Income: ☐ less than $15,000 ☐ $15,000-20,000
☐ $20,000-30,000 ☐ $30,000-40,000
☐ $40,000-50,000 ☐ $50,000+

Where did you purchase this product? ☐ Independent bookstore
☐ Chain bookstore ☐ Newsstand
☐ Mail order ☐ Other_____

What attracted you to this product? (choose all that apply):
☐ Interested in subject/content ☐ Artwork
☐ Friend's recommendation ☐ Gift for someone
☐ Received as a gift ☐ Buy it every year
☐ First time purchased ☐ Book review

How many books do you purchase a year? _____

What subject matter would you like to see more of?_____

We welcome your suggestions and content ideas. Write to: Attn: Annuals Editor, Llewellyn Worldwide, P.O. Box 64383, St Paul, MN 55164-0383

SAGITTARIUS/APRIL

PRIMARY FOCUS
If you've never believed in second chances, you may see some proof of them this month. Although you can't take back some things, you can undo problems and rectify mistakes. It's time to set the record straight and move on.

HEALTH AND FITNESS
Sports can still be an excellent outlet, although you may need to pull back a little after the 13th and assess your schedule and capabilities. Avoid risky situations, particularly anything involving machinery.

ROMANCE AND RELATIONSHIPS
If you've been playing the tease and running from commitment, you'll discover the importance of making a choice from the 1st–13th. Issues or problems in your love life need to be directly addressed and finding better ways to give and receive love can strengthen romance during the Full Moon on the 11th. You'll prefer situations with your lover that allow you to feel at home, and quiet evenings together can be just what you need.

CAREER AND FINANCE
Mercury's retrograde through the 20th draws your attention to speculative ventures, and may also emphasize complex problems associated with investments. Negotiate and investigate, but avoid signing long-term contracts until next month. Conflict or turmoil at work can be undermining after the 14th, so try to nip situations in the bud before they escalate into ridiculous battles.

OPPORTUNITY OF THE MONTH
After a few weeks of trouble-shooting, make positive changes in your work environment after the New Moon on the 26th that will allow room for increased productivity and cooperation.

AFFIRMATION FOR THE MONTH
"I seek cooperative solutions that work for the good of all."

Rewarding Days: 5, 6, 10, 11, 15, 16, 20, 24, 25
Challenging Days: 1, 7, 8, 22, 23, 28, 29

SAGITTARIUS/MAY

PRIMARY FOCUS
Nonproductive activities can undermine your effectiveness on the job, although it's difficult to maintain your priorities all the time. Deal with issues as they arise; postponing them will complicate matters.

HEALTH AND FITNESS
It's easier to irritate or hurt your body during this cycle, especially if you're not paying attention to your personal limitations near the Full Moon on the 11th. Double-check all exercise equipment, and set goals that gradually improve your endurance level.

ROMANCE AND RELATIONSHIPS
Although you may want to spend time on a romantic adventure with your sweetie, it may not be a simple proposition to get past all the adjustments in your schedule. A romantic getaway can inspire a loving exchange from the 4th–14th. Examine your needs, feelings and attitudes toward partnership during the New Moon on the 25th, when it's easier to be realistic about the needs of both parties.

CAREER AND FINANCE
Your return on investments can be solid, and seeking out innovative investment options can improve your monetary picture considerably from the 1st–13th. At work, turmoil or conflict can be disruptive during the Full Moon on the 11th, but productivity increases when you use this energy to cut through red tape and get down to business. Others demand a lot, but you also have your expectations; communicate with one another!

OPPORTUNITY OF THE MONTH
Let your ideas and enthusiastic support for the things you hold dear stabilize your position. You're much more influential from the 1st–16th, when your inspiration gives you wings.

AFFIRMATION FOR THE MONTH
"My intuitive voice inspires my creative expression."

Rewarding Days: 2, 3, 7, 12, 13, 17, 18, 21, 22, 30
Challenging Days: 4, 5, 6, 19, 20, 25, 26

SAGITTARIUS/JUNE

PRIMARY FOCUS

Your involvement in relationships and partnerships can dictate your priorities this month. If you want to make changes, it may be up to you to take action instead of waiting for your partner.

HEALTH AND FITNESS

You're feeling a little bit lazy when it comes to exercise and may prefer to be a spectator. Well, that's OK if you're enthusiastic, but it does little for your fitness levels unless you're a cheerleader.

ROMANCE AND RELATIONSHIPS

The Sagittarius Full Moon on the 9th adds to your emotional vulnerability, but also marks an excellent time to clarify what you need from your relationships. You may want to just walk away from a problem, but unless you reach closure, you may just be shooting yourself in the foot while trying to run from the issues. The problem may connect to your fear of intimacy. Take a good look at those feelings during the New Moon on the 23rd.

CAREER AND FINANCE

Situations at work can improve through greater cooperation from others. Social obligations related to your career may be the perfect way to get information and make connections that would otherwise be difficult. Just watch out for your competitors, because they're out there this month. If you stick your head in the sand, they may just cross the finish line before you've stepped onto the track!

OPPORTUNITY OF THE MONTH

You may have some great ideas, but need support to make them happen. Share your ideas with a trustworthy ally from the 1st–14th.

AFFIRMATION FOR THE MONTH
"I achieve harmony by supporting my highest needs."

Rewarding Days: 3, 4, 8, 9, 13, 14, 18, 26, 27
Challenging Days: 1, 2, 15, 16, 22, 23, 28, 29

SAGITTARIUS/JULY

PRIMARY FOCUS
The research and investigation you do now can support your creative ventures, but may also lead to new directions as the summer progresses. It's amazing what you can uncover with a little extra effort!

HEALTH AND FITNESS
The connection between your psychological needs and issues and your physical health is more marked, and this is the perfect time to finally let go of some of those old hurts or to release emotional attachments that stand in the way of your sense of power and wholeness.

ROMANCE AND RELATIONSHIPS
Intimacy issues arise as the Full Moon on the 9th draws closer. You must determine your wants and needs, and then release your inhibitions. If trust is a question, make sure you trust your own feelings before you accuse your partner of anything! Your need to share spiritual goals emerges, and striking out in a direction that supports your spiritual path strengthens your sense of worth during the New Moon on the 23rd.

CAREER AND FINANCE
Conferences or business meetings offer new options, and this is also an excellent time to travel or pursue educational endeavors. If you're promoting your services or ideas, try innovative approaches for the best effect. Contentious issues can arise over joint finances, taxes, or inheritance matters after the 6th, although these problems can be resolved once values are agreed on.

OPPORTUNITY OF THE MONTH
If you're uncertain about the best way to proceed in any matter, take a closer look at your ethics and philosophical attitudes for the answer, and then make your case after the 23rd.

AFFIRMATION FOR THE MONTH
"By releasing pain, I make room for joy and laughter."

Rewarding Days: 1, 6, 7, 10, 11, 15, 23, 24, 28, 29
Challenging Days: 12, 13, 14, 19, 20, 26, 27

SAGITTARIUS/AUGUST

PRIMARY FOCUS

You're thinking big now, with your hopes for the future boosting confidence in your plans and abilities, but a few unexpected delays and obstacles may crop up in your path. See what you can do about incorporating those unexpected elements into your plans!

HEALTH AND FITNESS

Working on your mind-body link, you can uncover the core problems of disease or distress by digging beyond the obvious. Be especially careful in unfamiliar or high-risk surroundings from the 14th–25th.

ROMANCE AND RELATIONSHIPS

If you are to experience the depth of love you crave, you may have to initiate exploring the mystery of your connection with your partner. It's time for the alchemy of love to work its magic during the lunar eclipse on the 7th, when your highest needs will determine if you continue in this situation or move into another. You can discover the uplifting ecstasy of Divine Love by following your bliss at the prompting of the Sun's eclipse on the 21st.

CAREER AND FINANCE

Legal matters, publishing, and foreign travel or diplomacy take you into unusual arenas, and you may not make the progress you hope to achieve during Mercury's retrograde from the 1st–23rd. Be confident in your inspiration if you've left ample room in your plans for delays in funds or excessive costs that can arise from the 14th–26th. If not, re-evaluate, make adjustments, and move forward after the 23rd.

OPPORTUNITY OF THE MONTH

Reach into new territory now, or return to situations or connections that have offered inspiration in the past but you've left unattended. It's time to uncover your own Truth.

AFFIRMATION FOR THE MONTH
"I value the support and understanding of others."

Rewarding Days: 2, 3, 7, 11, 12, 20, 21, 25, 29, 20, 31
Challenging Days: 1, 9, 10, 15, 16, 22, 23

Sagittarius/September

Primary Focus
Your career takes front and center stage, with your energy and enthusiasm sparking renewed optimism for your future as you experience recognition for your efforts. But you can't rest on your laurels, since you're already making plans for your next accomplishments.

Health and Fitness
Your physical vitality improves, and increased activity levels provide just the energy you need to feel awake and alive. Get back to nature and let its perfection and power inspire you.

Romance and Relationships
A romantic getaway from the 1st–6th can give you just the time you need to refine your perspectives. You gain insight into your motivations for success during the lunar eclipse on the 6th, as you break away from doing things that satisfy those old needs to please your parents and focus instead on creating a life that fulfills your dreams. Your friends provide just the encouragement you need after the 23rd.

Career and Finance
Mix a little business with pleasure, and if you have the chance, schedule important meetings or presentations from the 1st–5th or after the 24th. Travel, publishing, and educational pursuits give your career a boost throughout the month, although you have some social obligations to fulfill from the 8th–24th that can affect your success. Watch your spending on large projects after the 19th, when you can easily blow your budget.

Opportunity of the Month
You're ready for a change after the New Moon on the 20th, and have the perfect opportunity to try something completely different from the 26th–30th.

Affirmation for the Month
"I am aware of the effects of my actions on the lives of others."

Rewarding Days: 3, 4, 7, 8, 16, 17, 21, 26, 26, 30
Challenging Days: 5, 6, 11, 12, 13, 18, 19, 20

SAGITTARIUS/OCTOBER

PRIMARY FOCUS
You're redirecting your energy as new goals emerge, but you can be distracted by a red herring. Watch out for temptations that simply cost time, energy, and money and pay attention to the things that fit your true goals.

HEALTH AND FITNESS
Stress at work may lead you to believe that you don't have time to stay in shape, but try making fitness a primary goal. You're ready for challenges, and might enjoy sports or an exciting fitness class.

ROMANCE AND RELATIONSHIPS
Part of loving is knowing how to open your heart, and if you're uncertain, your friends can provide excellent encouragement. Romance is a high priority during the Full Moon on the 5th, when the flow of love can recharge you. If you're seeking love, begin by spending time doing the things you enjoy most. You may meet that special someone enjoying the same interests near the New Moon on the 20th!

CAREER AND FINANCE
Your career is much more rewarding now, and a completely different opportunity or unusual event can be a key ingredient in advancing your position. Watch the way you handle positions of influence or power after the 7th, because it's easy for others to misread your intentions, particularly if they're jealous or perceive you as a threat. Seek out situations that allow the work to shine, but enjoy your time in the spotlight, too.

OPPORTUNITY OF THE MONTH
Improve your life by taking advantage of career changes that give you a chance to show your strengths. Take the initiative, but be wary of loopholes from the 15th–20th.

AFFIRMATION FOR THE MONTH
"I am following a path that fulfills my dreams."

Rewarding Days: 1, 5, 6, 13, 14, 18, 19, 23, 24, 28, 29
Challenging Days: 3, 4, 9, 10, 15, 16, 17, 30, 31

SAGITTARIUS/NOVEMBER

PRIMARY FOCUS
Mercury spends the next two months in Sagittarius, making this an excellent time to concentrate on writing, education, travel, publishing, or cultural exchange. Others may seek your expertise; be confident about sharing it!

HEALTH AND FITNESS
The temptation to burn the candle at both ends can exhaust your energy from the 1st–13th, so set a pace that allows ample time for rejuvenation. Find healthy ways to release stress—try a massage.

ROMANCE AND RELATIONSHIPS
If you're admiring someone from afar from the 1st–16th or involved in a secret romance you'll probably feel more comfortable keeping a low profile. It's quite possible you'll run into someone from your past after the 20th, especially if there's unfinished business. You're definitely ready for love, and your most attractive qualities shine. This time, you're interested in getting to the heart of the matter, so take a deep breath and go for it!

CAREER AND FINANCE
If there are problems at work, they're likely to be most intense during the Full Moon on the 4th, but your cutting-edge communication exposes the truth. The transformations can be difficult at first, but you have an excellent period of adaptation once Mercury enters its retrograde on the 21st. Just don't expect new systems to run smoothly for a while! Financial prospects are promising after the 17th.

OPPORTUNITY OF THE MONTH
A fresh look at an old situation provides hope after the 22nd, when your intelligence and understanding are the key ingredients to changing the shape of your future.

AFFIRMATION FOR THE MONTH
"I am a careful observer and a confident communicator."

Rewarding Days: 1, 2, 9, 10, 14, 19, 20, 24, 25, 29, 30
Challenging Days: 4, 5, 6, 12, 13, 26, 27

SAGITTARIUS/DECEMBER

PRIMARY FOCUS

Your personality shines, and you have a chance to lead the way toward a brighter day when surrounded by friends and allies. Celebrate your triumphs and focus your energy on using your influence to inspire growth.

HEALTH AND FITNESS

If you need inspiration to stay fit, grab an exercise buddy and join a fitness class or get involved in team sports. This is a great time to enjoy the social benefits of staying in (or getting into) shape!

ROMANCE AND RELATIONSHIPS

Plan a party with your friends or at least meet for lunch. You need the contact, and may discover a wonderful source of mutual support. Partnerships play a strong role during the Full Moon on the 3rd, when you're willing to make the effort to revitalize a tired relationship. If it doesn't work, you'll feel more like striking out on a singular path during the Sagittarius New Moon on the 18th.

CAREER AND FINANCE

During Mercury's retrograde from the 1st–11th, you may finally be able to connect with that hard-to-reach person or agency. This is a great time to schedule second interviews, edit manuscripts, negotiate contracts, or review your finances. Watch your spending; it's tempting to go into debt over something you don't really need. Finances improve after the 18th, when you're better organized.

OPPORTUNITY OF THE MONTH

This is your time to go after what you want. Try something different if you're bored or dissatisfied. Just remember your obligations in the process!

AFFIRMATION FOR THE MONTH
"The Universe provides abundance in accordance with
my highest needs."

Rewarding Days: 7, 8, 11, 12, 13, 16, 17, 18, 21, 26, 27
Challenging Days: 2, 3, 4, 9, 10, 24, 25, 30, 31

SAGITTARIUS

ACTION TABLE

These dates reflect the best (but not the only) times for success and ease in these activities, according to your sign.

	Jan.	Feb.	Mar.	Apr.	May	June	July	Aug.	Sept.	Oct.	Nov.	Dec.
Change Residence		20–28	1–7									
Ask for a Raise												18, 19
Begin a Course of Study	28, 29						23, 24	22				
Join a Club										20		
Begin a Romance				28, 29								
Visit a Doctor					15–31					12–31	1	
Start a Diet	6, 7	3, 4	2, 3, 29, 30	26, 27	23, 24	19–21	17, 18	13, 14	9, 10	7, 8	3, 4, 30	1, 2, 28, 29
Seek Employment					15–31				7–23			
Take a Vacation	13, 14	9, 10	9, 10	5, 6	2, 3, 29–31	26, 27	23–25	20, 21	16, 17	13, 14	9, 10	7, 8
End a Relationship												3, 4
Change Your Wardrobe			8–31	1–30	1–14							
Seek Professional Advice	8, 9	5, 6	4, 5, 31	2, 28, 29	25, 26	22, 23	19, 20	15, 16	11, 12	9, 10	5, 6	3, 4, 30, 31
Have a Make-Over												18
Obtain a Loan	1, 12	7, 8	6, 7	2, 3, 30	1, 27, 28	24, 25	21, 22	17, 18	13, 14	1, 12	7, 8	5, 6

CAPRICORN

The Goat
December 21–January 20

Element:	Earth
Quality:	Cardinal
Polarity:	Yin/Feminine
Planetary Ruler:	Saturn
Meditation:	"I master challenges of the physical plane."
Gemstone:	Garnet
Power Stones:	Diamond, Quartz, Onyx, Black Obsidian
Key Phrase:	"I use"
Glyph:	Head of Goat ♑
Anatomy:	Knees, Skin, Skeleton
Color:	Black
Animals:	Goats, Thick-Shelled Animals
Myths/Legends:	Cronus, Pan, Vesta
House Association:	Tenth
Opposite Sign:	Cancer
Flower:	Carnation
Key Word:	Structure

Positive Expression:		Misuse of Energy:	
Sensible	Ambitious	Controlling	Machiavellian
Disciplined	Conscientious	Inhibited	Repressed
Patient	Frugal	Fearful	Miserly
Cautious	Prudent	Rigid	Melancholy

CAPRICORN

YOUR EGO'S STRENGTHS AND WEAKNESSES

Your determination to achieve your aims is unrivaled, and you use your sense of structure to ensure your rise to the top. You function best in situations that allow you to be in charge, and since you're "The Pragmatist" of the zodiac, you're always looking for ways to keep everything running efficiently. Moving forward is important for you—whether you're making your way up the ladder to success in your career or seeking ways to achieve personal mastery over something that holds great importance to you.

Through the energy of Saturn, your planetary ruler, you can develop unrivaled discipline and focus, creating a solid foundation to support your dreams. You don't take "No" for an answer when you want something, a trait that can be irritating to others. You don't particularly like to follow all the arbitrary rules either, unless you've made them yourself! Sometimes others may complain that you're taking unfair advantage of them unless you become more attentive to their needs and concerns. By learning to share responsibilities you may actually reach goals beyond your expectations, and developing your natural ability to teach and guide others can be especially rewarding. To avoid losing your vision of the future to clouds of despair when reality presses too intensely on your dreams, find ways to unite your sense of the spiritual with the tangible physical plane. Give yourself time to get back to basics and connect with the simple pleasures of life. From that perspective, you'll more easily develop a pattern for success that serves you well and that may be eagerly emulated by others.

YOUR APPROACH TO ROMANCE

Since your manner is sometimes reserved and matter-of-fact, others may be under the mistaken impression that you are not sensitive or romantic. You can be guarded until you know it's safe to let someone see your vulnerable side, yet once you open your heart to love, your child-like playfulness can emerge. You need love that can withstand the tests of time and may feel that a brief romance is a waste of your energy. You may even be reluctant to experiment with romance until you feel that you've achieved a measure of material stability. Once you open to love, you can be a sensual and steadfast partner.

You may be strongly attracted to Cancer, your zodiac opposite, and can create a relationship built on strong family values and a mutual desire for security once you learn to value your differences. You're most at ease with the other earth signs—Taurus, Virgo, and Capricorn—who appreciate your down-to-earth ideas. With Aries, you can play delightful teasing games, but you can lock horns with your mutually headstrong attitudes. Taurus is engaging in an earthy, sensual way, and you may feel you've found your ideal lover. Gemini can get on your nerves, especially if you feel he or she is fickle. You may be very attracted to Leo, but to avoid power struggles or regrets, decide who's in charge!

Virgo can be a reassuring companion and you're likely to share values that are mutually supportive. Your attraction to Libra is legendary but you may not find it easy to feel close on an emotional level. Scorpio's sensual passions can fuel a love that leads to magical alchemy. Inspired by Sagittarius' search for the best that life has to offer, you'll have to allow ample freedom if the relationship is to last. It's easy to feel close and comfortable with another Capricorn, but alter stale routines if you want to keep your love alive. Aquarius can be a lifelong friend, and you'll discover a magical escape with Pisces' imaginative and romantic energy.

YOUR CAREER DEVELOPMENT

Career growth is high on your priority list and you'll be most content when your life work affords you an opportunity to improve the quality of your life while promoting your sense of self-respect. The world of business can be appealing, particularly if you're in a position of authority that allows you to delegate tasks or exercise your executive and administrative abilities. Teaching and higher education can be rewarding, particularly in the healing arts, physics, life sciences, geology, or practical hands-on fields.

If you opt for politics or the ministry, your ambition supports your desire to reach the heights. You may be a natural metaphysician, working as a counselor, herbalist, naturopath, chiropractor, or in traditional medicine as a holistic physician. The construction industry can be appealing, and you might excel in design, development, or contracting. Managing a ranch, farm, forest, or zoo can answer your need to stay in touch with nature. Whatever your choices, you're determined to become a success.

YOUR USE OF POWER

You've experimented with power since you were a child, and are happiest when you're in control of something. However, rigidity and control are not necessarily the best methods to gain a real feeling of personal power. Developing flexibility in your attitudes can help you accomplish your aims more readily. Giving yourself ample time to review and evaluate situations and working toward positive changes that will lead to improvements is also an important factor in creating the power you need to feel in your life.

You'll undermine your own power if you try to control the lives and ideas of others too intensely, or if you are stringently holding to traditions or concepts that have long outlived their usefulness. By acknowledging the power of others, you'll become more influential. Since others are likely to look up to you, your sense of responsibility toward them can lead to positive power when you keep honest attitudes about your motivations and desires. Only through support and direction that serves more than your ego can you have the power to help others positively shape their destinies.

FAMOUS CAPRICORNS

Kirstie Alley, Nicolas Cage, Mary Higgins-Clark, Barry Goldwater, Carolyn Bessette Kennedy, Judith Krantz, Frank Langella, Mario Van Peebles, Elvis Presley, Andy Rooney, Tracey Ullman, Loretta Young.

THE YEAR AHEAD FOR CAPRICORN

Progress awaits you during 1998, especially if you've been working to remove blocks from your path toward success. If not, this is still an excellent time to get rid of obstacles standing in your way or to complete the prerequisites necessary to advance toward your goals. Innovative methods of using your resources can lead to exceptional changes in your material picture, and it's time to dust off your talents and put them to work. Making contact with others can also prove to be both rewarding and inspiring, and if you'll take advantage of the possibilities suggested by reaching out to others, you may be pleasantly surprised as new avenues open for you to pursue.

Jupiter's transit in Pisces this year marks an excellent period for learning, travel, and improving your communication skills and abilities. If you've been hoping to find a good time to take an extra course, to get to know your hometown better, or to fine-tune your skills, this is a great time to do just that. You may be making a few more short trips or your work may involve more travel or communication. This is also a good time to advance your technological expertise or to upgrade your personal computer. At the highest level, however, this cycle represents a time of improving your attitudes, opening your mind to more optimistic options and looking at life as an uplifting challenge instead of a series of tests! As your self-confidence improves during this period, take time to express your pleasure with the beauty of life around you, and remember to compliment and thank those whose efforts and support you value.

Saturn is completing its cycle through the Fourth House of your solar chart, marking a period of ending of old family traditions and helping you establish a more solid foundation for your emotional security. However, this cycle does take its toll in the form of stress, especially if you're reluctant to let go of outworn attitudes, useless situations, or unhealthy relationships. You're also seeing ways to leave the past behind, and to use the knowledge from the lessons you've learned as a solid footing for your personal growth. The transits of Uranus, Neptune, and Pluto are also providing strong influences in the form of opportunities to move into different dimensions of life, particularly if you're reaching out to make a difference in the world around you.

The solar and lunar eclipses draw your attention to your state of mind—exactly how hopeful and positive are you about life? This is a wonderful time to listen to your inner dialogue and to let go of those old messages that undermine your optimism and damage your self-esteem. The way you respond to the needs and requests of others will also be tested this year, and you may gain valuable insight into your approach to and needs for intimacy. If you run into financial problems, they may only be a symptom of something that runs much deeper. Treat the cause by reminding yourself that you deserve true prosperity in all things.

♄   ♄   ♄

If you were born from December 22nd–26th, you're experiencing the positive support of Saturn transiting in trine aspect to your Sun. You're also feeling a need to shift your vision since Neptune's cycle is transiting in semisextile aspect to your Sun, opening your consciousness to a different realm of possibilities. By coordinating responsible action with this new insight into your visions and dreams you may be able to accomplish exceptional feats, but you'll have to put some effort into it. These are cycles that require a clear focus on your priorities, but you can also have a bit more fun. If your creative skills have been sitting on a shelf, now's the time to dust them off, polish them, and let your light shine. You may also become more involved in helping others develop their talents, and can become an inspiring mentor or teacher. Emotionally, it's time to embrace the things, people, and situations you truly need while releasing those things you've outgrown.

♄   ♄   ♄

You're eliminating some old emotional barricades **if you were born from December 27th–31st.** Pluto's transit in semisextile aspect to your Sun adds an intensity to your sense of ambition and drive to succeed, but there may be some unfinished business from the past standing in your way. Probing into your psyche to release your old attachments can be rather illuminating, in addition to helping you release the things you no longer need for your growth. You may also feel drawn to work within the collective realm, and can be quite effective in using your influence and power to shape changes in the world around you. In many ways, this cycle is like clearing a path while climbing uphill. There is some effort required to accomplish your aims, but once you can see where you're going, it's much easier to get there!

♄   ♄   ♄

If you were born from December 29th–January 4th, you may feel that you're learning to fly. With Uranus transiting in semisextile to your Sun, you may not be quite used to the experience of being temporarily airborne, so finding workable ways to keep at least one foot on the ground can be rather helpful. This is your year to try something different, to experiment with innovative possibilities, and release some of your old inhibitions. You may also experience a wonderful feeling of relief from the heaviness of life by revamping your value systems and simplifying your financial picture. At the core of your changes is a new view of your own personal worth: It's time to look in the mirror and remind yourself that you deserve a life filled with all the things you need!

♄   ♄   ♄

You're coping with challenges **if you were born from January 5th–20th.** Saturn is transiting in square aspect to your Sun, marking an important cycle of self-awareness. This period can be rather trying, particularly if your burdens are too great. But before you drop everything and attempt to dance away, make sure you've fulfilled your obligations, since your responsibilities will definitely follow you! Your attitude toward your responsibilities may be in need of revision, especially if you've been filled with resentment. Guilt and resentment can be especially crippling to your creativity, and if you find yourself running into those emotions on a regular basis, consider them to be signals that something needs to change. It may be just as simple as shifting your focus, but you may also need to deal with old issues that serve to paralyze your ability to grow and prosper. Think of this as a personal audit—a year when you have a chance to review the past, release what you no longer need, and step forward from a more stable platform.

♄ ♄ ♄

You're experiencing a cycle of transformational change **if you were born from January 11th–16th.** With Pluto's transit in semi-square to your Sun, you may feel that you're faced with a challenge to leave some things behind in the process of becoming whole. Changes can occur that seem to be beyond your control, although you can fine-tune your responses in a way that will allow you to maintain a reasonable sense of self-direction. The healing that emerges during this cycle occurs at a very deep level, and if you're interested in achieving optimum growth, then you'll open to your inner self in more profound ways.

Although there may be external changes that echo your inner process, the real transformation is happening within your attitudes and viewpoints. This is a good time to consider working with a therapist to dig deeply into your psyche, or you might also benefit from becoming more aware of your inner dialogue by learning about your dreams. By taking advantage of this time to heal and let go of ghosts from your past—unresolved issues, old trauma, or buried resentment—you'll feel more free, alive, and complete. But if you try to repress the changes that are prompting your growth, you can actually retard your progress.

♄ ♄ ♄

Let your creativity and imagination soar **if you were born from January 18th–20th.** Neptune's transit in conjunction to your Sun will not occur again in your lifetime! This very special period of time can enhance your artistic sensibilities in a remarkable way, and your vision for the future may seem to be quite pure. Although it's sometimes difficult to distinguish between visionary fantasies and dangerous illusions, you still need to allow your consciousness to open to the wonderful possibilities inherent in this cycle. Allow time to become more introspective without completely withdrawing from the world. You may need to escape, but seek out healthy escapes. Develop your talents, attend more concerts or arts events, surround yourself with others whose artistic sensibilities inspire you, or do something that enhances the quality of life around you. But also be aware that you easily attract others whose character may be questionable, and may even surround yourself with people whose energy drains your own. You're learning about surrendering to the flow of life and can experience a true sense of transcendence. The trick is finding a pathway that yields growth and enhances your evolutionary process.

TOOLS TO MAKE A DIFFERENCE

You're becoming more multidimensional, which means you're ready to open your life to possibilities that may have been unavailable to you in the past. Whether these options involve technologies that are just now accessible or levels of consciousness to which you are now open, the end result is likely to be the same: You're ready to feel more alive and excited about life!

Taking care of your physical health is important and dealing with stress and tension needs to be high on your priority list. You may experience an increase in energy and healing through alternative healing methods, and can benefit from taking a holistic approach to any health issues you're facing. Keep your spine intact by staying flexible: hatha yoga, tai chi, chi gong, swimming or other stretching exercises help you maintain a fully flexible body and consciousness. Herbal medicine can be a beneficial alternative, and you may also respond well to the flower essence remedies of elm, oak, rock water, Scotch broom, and sweet chestnut. To relax, schedule regular massages, or consider taking a massage class. When you need an extra boost of energy, take time to walk in the woods or a park, or hike along a mountain trail. You're invigorated when you're surrounded by the grandeur of natural beauty.

To streamline your finances, consider purchasing an easy-to-use computer program, which might also be helpful when tax time rolls around. It's time to find more efficient ways to deal with daily tasks, including the process of keeping track of your material resources. At work, you might also boost efficiency by sharpening your own skills and finding more effective ways to use the resources available to you, including the talents of others.

During your periods of meditation and contemplation, concentrate on clearing away old issues from your past. Imagine that you are climbing toward a mountain peak. The climb is not especially dangerous, but along the way you feel that you need to lighten your load. As you stop at different points along your upward path, remove the things from your pack that are just weighing you down. You may discover all sorts of things, some you did not even know you packed!

You discover a small cabin by the time you reach the peak. The door is open, and a warm fire is burning in the hearth. It feels right to enter, so you go in, sit down, and rest from your journey. There are ample supplies, and fresh water is nearby. Everything you need is here, as though you were expected. After refreshing yourself, you decide to walk onto the edge of the cliff overlooking the valleys below. It is a beautiful sight, and you feel inspired to change your life once you return. But for a while, enjoy your space in the clouds at the top of the world. When you're back in your everyday existence, remember that there is always a mountain top from which you can see forever.

Affirmation for the Year

"My life is filled with joy. My heart is full of hope and love!"

Capricorn/January

Primary Focus

A little extra effort reaps exceptional rewards, improving your financial picture and expanding avenues for material success. Just avoid the temptation to count your chickens before they hatch!

Health and Fitness

Concentrate on building endurance, but remember to spend time stretching and improving your flexibility, too. Tension works against you, exhausting your vitality unless you find healthy ways to let go and relax; remember to breathe deeply.

Romance and Relationships

If you're having second thoughts about your relationship it could be because someone has been holding back. If it's you, find out why and be honest about what you really want. Relationships take top priority during the Full Moon on the 12th, when you may not like dealing with the demands of others. Give yourself time to indulge your fantasies a bit after the 17th, and plan a romantic getaway after the New Moon on the 28th, when making up can be delightful!

Career and Finance

Get rid of things that aren't working and concentrate on activities that produce worthwhile results. You're vulnerable to deception now, and if you suspect that someone or something is not quite on the level, you'll do yourself a favor by looking into it. A conservative approach is best when making changes, although your frustration with the status quo can tempt you to burn all your bridges and start over.

Opportunity of the Month

Listen to your intuitive voice. Everything may not seem to be logical in the way it works out, but your inner voice can be your best ally to help you stay in the groove.

Affirmation for the Month
"I am honest about my true feelings and needs."

Rewarding Days: 2, 6, 7, 15, 16, 25, 26, 30
Challenging Days: 4, 5, 11, 12, 18, 19, 31

CAPRICORN/FEBRUARY

PRIMARY FOCUS
Make contact with others to strengthen your personal growth and open the way to fresh possibilities in your career. Attending conferences, taking an active part in communication, and launching new ideas all work to your advantage. Reach out and touch someone!

HEALTH AND FITNESS
Your vitality improves, and you may even feel inspired to join in team sports or sign up for a marathon. If you're not quite that inspired, at least apply your increased energy to a challenging fitness routine.

ROMANCE AND RELATIONSHIPS
Let your sweetheart know how you feel. Send flowers, special e-mail greetings, or plan a romantic rendez-vous. Making excuses about time and money will only postpone the opening your heart craves. Romance fares best after the 17th, and near the time of the solar eclipse on the 26th you may finally feel ready to risk taking bolder steps to win the love you need. Maintain a purity of thought, guided by a loving heart and you're assured of positive results.

CAREER AND FINANCE
Writing and communication are significant to your progress, and you may also benefit by striving to improve your skills or increase your knowledge. Attending workshops and meetings and clearly outlining your plans paves the way to your success. Be attentive to finances during the Full Moon on the 11th, when you're ready to expand your territory. Get everything in order, and take bold steps after the 26th.

OPPORTUNITY OF THE MONTH
Keep an open mind, listening to the ideas of others while you fine-tune your own plans and objectives. With an eye on the future, you're ready to incorporate innovative possibilities.

AFFIRMATION FOR THE MONTH
"I am a clear and effective communicator."

Rewarding Days: 3, 4, 12, 13, 17, 18, 22, 23, 26, 27
Challenging Days: 1, 2, 7, 8, 14, 15, 28

CAPRICORN/MARCH

PRIMARY FOCUS
Conflict or tension at home can be time-consuming and distracting. A lot depends on what's creating the turmoil and how you handle the pressure. Remember, some things are beyond your control!

HEALTH AND FITNESS
You need plenty of options for dealing with stress and tension. Schedule a massage, if you can fit it into your busy schedule, or at least promise to exercise and stretch on a regular basis.

ROMANCE AND RELATIONSHIPS
With the lunar eclipse on the 12th drawing your attention to your needs to connect on an intellectual and spiritual level, you may feel more like going out of your way to develop open lines of communication in your close relationships. Because of potential crisis at home, you may be trying to avert conflict. Sometimes conflict leads to healing and progress. Deal with problems as they arise, and try something different during the New Moon on the 27th.

CAREER AND FINANCE
Plan to attend meetings or conferences, and send important communication from the 1st–12th, when sharing ideas can advance your career and your reputation. You may feel stonewalled by someone else whose power issues get in the way of progress from the 13th–31st, although this is a good time to concentrate on finishing a major project. Tension mounts when Mercury turns retrograde on the 27th. You may make better strides by standing still!

OPPORTUNITY OF THE MONTH
Strive to reach important agreements, sign contracts, and complete negotiations from the 2nd–12th. After that, concentrate on projects you already have in motion.

AFFIRMATION FOR THE MONTH
"In all matters I seek truth and honesty."

Rewarding Days: 2, 3, 11, 12, 16, 21, 22, 26, 30
Challenging Days: 1, 6, 7, 13, 14, 15, 27, 28

CAPRICORN/APRIL

PRIMARY FOCUS

You may feel like everything is at a standstill, and you could cause problems if you try to push before a situation is ready to go forward. Patient understanding is crucial to your success. Progress follows before the end of the month.

HEALTH AND FITNESS

If you're feeling inflexible or stiff, take an easy approach to regaining momentum. Listen to your body, and respect your limitations. You can lose strength if you remain inflexible for too long.

ROMANCE AND RELATIONSHIPS

Power struggles at home can be difficult, although this is an excellent time to make repairs in the basic foundations of your life. Open lines of communication with siblings can heal a breech after the 6th. Your love life gets a boost after the 13th, and you may even feel like allowing more love to flow into your life during the New Moon on the 26th, when someone intriguing can enter the picture.

CAREER AND FINANCE

The way you handle problems or crises at work determines the way others see and respect you. Situations escalate through the Full Moon on the 11th, although you may still have some misunderstandings to clarify until after Mercury finally leaves its retrograde cycle on the 20th. After that, you have more room in your life for your creative and artistic endeavors, and may even have some luck in speculative ventures after the 21st.

OPPORTUNITY OF THE MONTH

Applying your imagination and creativity in practical ways works to your advantage after the 22nd, when your efforts and ideas are well-received by even the most conservative individuals.

AFFIRMATION FOR THE MONTH
"My actions are guided by a need for harmony and love."

Rewarding Days: 7, 8, 13, 17, 18, 22, 23, 26, 27
Challenging Days: 2, 3, 10, 11, 24, 25, 30

CAPRICORN/MAY

PRIMARY FOCUS

Your talents shine, and this is an excellent time to trust your creative instincts. But you may still have trouble balancing your personal and professional commitments. Take care of your needs for security first.

HEALTH AND FITNESS

Focus your fitness activities on recreation or sports you enjoy. This is also a good time to take an adventurous or nature-oriented vacation. At the very least, spending time in your garden can ground your energy. Find a way to connect with nature.

ROMANCE AND RELATIONSHIPS

Even though you may feel more confident about asserting yourself in your love relationship, you may still be uncertain about whether or not you're fulfilling your needs. In many ways, this is a nest-building cycle, a time to create a personal space that reflects your needs. You're more romantic during the Full Moon on the 11th, when you feel at home. Watch a tendency to be too critical from the 17th–29th, when you can also be extra-sensitive to criticism.

CAREER AND FINANCE

You may prefer to work in quiet surroundings, particularly if you're facing deadlines or involved in a major project. You're facing a period of testing now, and instead of getting nervous about your performance, concentrate on what you need to know and fine-tune your skills. Then, take a deep breath and go for it! Work conditions improve after the New Moon on the 25th.

OPPORTUNITY OF THE MONTH

Your confidence and optimism are highest from the 1st–11th, but you may struggle with excessive worry or negative thoughts after that.

AFFIRMATION FOR THE MONT
"I gladly surrender control to my higher self."

Rewarding Days: 4, 5, 10, 11, 14, 15, 16, 19, 20, 23, 24
Challenging Days: 1, 7, 8, 21, 22, 27, 28, 29

CAPRICORN/JUNE

PRIMARY FOCUS

Your work brings positive rewards, but you may still run into conflicts with others over the balance of power. If you're in charge, find helpful ways to direct others. If you're following orders, be sure you know what's expected of you if you want to move forward.

HEALTH AND FITNESS

A challenging fitness class or sports provide positive outlets for your competitive drive. Just watch your limits, particularly during the Full Moon on the 9th, since it's easy to push too hard!

ROMANCE AND RELATIONSHIPS

You'll feel better if your love relationship is on solid footing. Otherwise, you're likely to back away from a situation that is not giving you what you need or want. Opening your heart to your lover flows magically after the 15th if you're both in touch with what you need from one another. Initiating a partnership or marriage near and after the New Moon on the 23rd paves the way to success. It's also a good time to reaffirm an existing commitment.

CAREER AND FINANCE

Although you may be somewhat frustrated with the people who work under your supervision, you'll progress further and faster by striving toward cooperation instead of creating divisiveness. Projects that require mutual creative support fare best, especially if you feel confident showcasing your talents. Speculative investments fare best after the 19th, so look for good options.

OPPORTUNITY OF THE MONTH

Instead of resisting the needs and demands of others, try the novel approach of listening and incorporating them into your own actions and plans. Productivity levels rise as a result!

AFFIRMATION FOR THE MONTH
"There is great reward working in harmony with others."

Rewarding Days: 1, 2, 6, 11, 12, 15, 16, 20, 28, 29
Challenging Days: 3, 4, 9, 17, 18, 24, 25

CAPRICORN/JULY

PRIMARY FOCUS
Partnerships and relationships take top priority, and may be a source of dispute. If conflicts arise, use them to create positive new directions. Before burning your bridges, make sure you really need them.

HEALTH AND FITNESS
Even though you need to remain active to keep your energy moving, try to take time to relax each day. Schedule in a period of contemplation or relaxation just to help ease you through the daily grind.

ROMANCE AND RELATIONSHIPS
Since marriage and partnership take center stage, it's time to be clear with yourself about those unfulfilled needs or desires during the Capricorn Full Moon on the 9th. Your confidence about making a commitment to love is strong from the 8th–14th, but then you may begin to have second thoughts. Doubts clear away after the 20th, when intimate encounters allow you to be more expressive.

CAREER AND FINANCE
Joint endeavors need careful consideration if you are to avoid trouble later on. Make sure that you're comfortable with the roles, expenditures of energy, and projected outcome before you sign agreements. Surprising elements can change your career direction or financial picture after the 20th. Get finances in order, especially concerning taxes, after the New Moon on the 23rd. Read the fine print and familiarize yourself with current laws and obligations.

OPPORTUNITY OF THE MONTH
Channel your competitive drives positively by knowing your competition from the 6th–18th. Sometimes it's important to know when to pull back and let a situation reach its own level.

AFFIRMATION FOR THE MONTH
"My relationships reflect my highest needs."

Rewarding Days: 3, 4, 8, 9, 13, 17, 18, 26, 27
Challenging Days: 1, 2, 15, 16, 21, 22, 28, 29

CAPRICORN/AUGUST

PRIMARY FOCUS

Details concerning joint financial matters, taxes, or inheritance are very important now. But you have a little time to sort things, so take it easy and get the facts straight before you panic about the outcome.

HEALTH AND FITNESS

You may prefer spectator sports to situations that force you to push your limits, but you do need some excitement in your life. Choose activities that are fun, and allow some time for pure enjoyment. Laughter is your best medicine, even if you are chuckling at your own jokes!

ROMANCE AND RELATIONSHIPS

Partnership is just what you make it. If you're leaving a relationship behind, beginning a new commitment, or breathing new life into an existing situation, it's crucial to put your best possible energy into the relationship if you are to achieve the results you desire. The eclipses center on your self-worth and the barriers you have concerning intimacy. During the solar eclipse on the 21st you either open the doors or lose a significant opportunity to experience the alchemy of love.

CAREER AND FINANCE

With the lunar eclipse on the 7th emphasizing your values, it's time to take careful stock of your resources and to find ways to use them to the best advantage. Mercury is retrograde through the 23rd, so use this time to dig into details and do important research. Don't sign anything until after the 24th!

OPPORTUNITY OF THE MONTH

This is an excellent time to do some in-depth research, including probing into the mysteries of life. You may also discover fascinating information about your inner drives and motivations.

AFFIRMATION FOR THE MONTH
"I go with the flow!"

Rewarding Days: 4, 5, 9, 10, 13, 14, 22, 23, 27, 28
Challenging Days: 11, 12, 17, 18, 19, 24, 25, 26

Capricorn/September

Primary Focus

Educational pursuits or travel may draw your attention, but you're also coping with a compulsive drive to accomplish your aims. Try to pull back on the intensity a little if you're feeling overwhelmed or if your supporters seem to be dropping like flies.

Health and Fitness

This is an excellent time to uncover deep-seated problems, whether they're physical or emotional in their origins. Heal by focusing on wholeness and learning to give and receive in a balanced measure.

Romance and Relationships

Love can blossom in magnificent ways. Shared spiritual goals and ideals serve to fill your heart and soul during the lunar eclipse on the 6th. The sexual elements of love can also be a key to learning trust and communicating deeper understanding, especially if you're willing to let go of old stereotypes and allow yourself to surrender to the moments you share. Try something different during the New Moon on the 20th.

Career and Finance

Clarify joint financial goals from the 1st–8th and liquidate assets that you need to satisfy debts or clear up financial problems. Attending conferences, workshops, or meetings can lead to career advancement after the 5th, and if you have presentations to make, target the 8th–23rd. Sign contracts after the 8th, and deal with legal matters now if you want to be in the best position later.

Opportunity of the Month

Expand your horizons after the 6th, and if you need time to get your plans in order, then wait until the 20th to launch an important project or idea. The heavens are on your side!

Affirmation for the Month

"My words and actions are supported by Truth and Integrity."

Rewarding Days: 1, 2, 5, 6, 9, 18, 19, 20, 28, 29
Challenging Days: 7, 8, 13, 14, 15, 21, 22

CAPRICORN/OCTOBER

PRIMARY FOCUS

This is a high-profile month for you, and you can be very effective in positions of leadership and authority. Travel, education, publishing, and cultural exchange also play a significant role in your success.

HEALTH AND FITNESS

Your physical energy grows stronger after the 7th, when your improved sense of discipline adds consistency to your fitness and health regimen. Team sports or fitness classes offer excellent avenues.

ROMANCE AND RELATIONSHIPS

Although you're focused on strengthening your reputation, you also need to be attentive to your personal and family needs, particularly near the time of the Full Moon on the 5th. Sharing your successes with loved ones adds special sweetness, so invite your good friends and your intimate others to celebrate the good things in life. Open your heart to receiving support and love from others after the 24th.

CAREER AND FINANCE

Despite a few misunderstandings that can be clarified through open communication, your career is moving along nicely. By forging your efforts through a strong sense of moral and ethical values, you not only improve your reputation, but your spirit soars! Attend conferences, meetings, and make presentations after the 13th. Try something different and exciting after the New Moon on the 20th, when your superiors are more easily impressed.

OPPORTUNITY OF THE MONTH

If you have a chance to teach or train others, take advantage of it after the 8th. Connect with others who share your interests and find ways to be mutually supportive.

AFFIRMATION FOR THE MONTH
"I am clearly focused on my goals."

Rewarding Days: 3, 7, 8, 15, 16, 17, 25, 26, 30, 31
Challenging Days: 1, 5, 6, 11, 12, 13, 18, 19

CAPRICORN/NOVEMBER

PRIMARY FOCUS
Political and community-oriented activities offer your best options for growth and advancement. Your reputation grows stronger if you know how to work within the limitations you're facing. If you fail to set boundaries, you'll get in trouble.

HEALTH AND FITNESS
If you've been putting off that fitness class or other options, maybe you need a buddy to motivate you and share the experience. If so, this is a great time to join forces and improve your health—together!

ROMANCE AND RELATIONSHIPS
It's easier to be open with friends, and if your lover does not have that "friend" quality, then you may feel like something is missing. Developing unconditional love requires that you accept yourself and your needs, and sometimes a friend helps you do that more easily than someone you're trying to please or impress. Romance can blossom during the Full Moon on the 4th if you're open.

CAREER AND FINANCE
Your career path is smoother from the 1st–18th, although your competitive nature can be troublesome if others feel threatened by your attitudes or actions. Reconsider your long-range plans during the New Moon on the 18th. Once Mercury enters its retrograde on the 21st, you may feel trapped in a maze of unpredictable communication, faulty technology, or other problems. Allow ample time for interruptions and keep an eye on your spending.

OPPORTUNITY OF THE MONTH
Get everything in order, schedule important meetings, and sign contracts from the 3rd–14th. Then, promise to concentrate on completing what you've already begun.

AFFIRMATION FOR THE MONTH
"I am an excellent problem-solver."

Rewarding Days: 3, 4, 12, 13, 17, 18, 22, 23, 27
Challenging Days: 1, 2, 7, 8, 14, 15, 29, 20

CAPRICORN/DECEMBER

PRIMARY FOCUS
Spend extra time listening to your inner voice. If you're simply trying to respond to outside influences or direct your life according to an external focus you'll feel rather frustrated. You're better prepared for challenges when you're centered within yourself.

HEALTH AND FITNESS
Stress levels can be very high, especially if work is more challenging or demanding. Avoid wasting your energy worrying about what you can't control and concentrate on taking care of your health during the Full Moon on the 3rd.

ROMANCE AND RELATIONSHIPS
Loving energy flows more readily after the 12th, although you may run into some opposition from family or parents if you're putting your love life ahead of family obligations. If you feel that you're being manipulated, confront the problems directly, but with a loving heart. Anger flares easily, and releasing it in a healthy way can help resolve a crisis. Enjoy a getaway with a loved one after the 23rd.

CAREER AND FINANCE
Until a few days after Mercury leaves its retrograde cycle on the 11th, you may run into conflicts, misunderstandings, and communication breakdowns. You're feeling driven to accomplish your aims, and pushing too hard will only alienate your supporters. After the New Moon on the 18th, you'll find more open avenues. Think of this as a time to get everything organized and ready for next year.

OPPORTUNITY OF THE MONTH
Although you may run into disappointments, your persistence is amazing. Just try to watch where you're going on your climb to the top. That climb gets easier after the 18th.

AFFIRMATION FOR THE MONTH
"Courage inspired by love and Divine Wisdom guides my actions."

Rewarding Days: 1, 9, 10, 14, 15, 19, 20, 28, 29
Challenging Days: 5, 6, 11, 12, 26, 27

CAPRICORN ♑ ACTION TABLE

These dates reflect the best (but not the only) times for success and ease in these activities, according to your sign.

	Jan.	Feb.	Mar.	Apr.	May	June	July	Aug.	Sept.	Oct.	Nov.	Dec.
Change Residence			16–31		5–11							
Ask for a Raise	25, 26											19, 20
Begin a Course of Study		26, 27							20			
Join a Club											19	
Begin a Romance				26, 27								
Visit a Doctor	1–11					1–14					1–30	1–31
Start a Diet	8, 9	5, 6	4, 5, 31	1, 28, 29	25, 26	22, 23	19, 20	15, 16	11, 12	9, 10	5, 6	3, 4, 30, 31
Seek Employment						1–14			24–30	1–11		
Take a Vacation	15, 16	12, 13	11, 12	7, 8	4, 5	1, 2, 28–30	26, 27	22, 23	18, 19	15, 16	12, 13	9, 10
End a Relationship	12											
Change Your Wardrobe					15–31							
Seek Professional Advice	11, 12	7, 8	6, 7	2, 3, 30	1, 27, 28	24, 25	21, 22	17, 18	13–15	11, 12	7, 8	5, 6
Have a Make-Over												19, 20
Obtain a Loan	13, 14	9–11	9, 10	5, 6	2, 3, 30, 31	26, 27	23–25	20, 21	16, 17	13, 14	9, 10	7, 8

AQUARIUS

The Water Bearer
January 20–February 18

Element:	Air
Quality:	Fixed
Polarity:	Masculine/Yang
Planetary Ruler:	Uranus
Meditation:	"I create new paths by focusing my mind."
Gemstone:	Amethyst
Power Stones:	Aquamarine, Black Pearl, Chrysocolla
Key Phrase:	"I know"
Glyph:	Waves of Energy ≈
Anatomy:	Ankles, Circulatory System
Colors:	Iridescent Blues, Violet
Animals:	Talking Birds
Myths/Legends:	Ninkhursag, Deucalion, John the Baptist
House Association:	Eleventh
Opposite Sign:	Leo
Flower:	Orchid
Key Word:	Unconventional

Positive Expression:		Misuse of Energy:	
Friendly	Altruistic	Aloof	Subversive
Unselfish	Humanitarian	Intransigent	Extremist
Independent	Ingenious	Anarchistic	Detached
Progressive	Self-Reliant	Undirected	Thoughtless

Aquarius

Your Ego's Strengths and Weaknesses

Since you're willing to step outside the boundaries of the mainstream, taking the risk of being different is a positive challenge for you. Not only are you unique, but you appreciate the qualities of life and in others that are out of the ordinary. Taking on the role of "The Reformer" of the zodiac, you're capable of creating innovative changes and adding an air of invigorating revision to outworn ideologies or structures. You can be an individualist in the purest sense of the term, fascinated by the unconventional and capable of marching to the beat of your own drum.

Through the influence of the untamed energy of your planetary ruler, Uranus, you're most comfortable when you know you are free. Your ideas, which may at first seem revolutionary, may set a precedent for what later becomes classical style. Since you can be readily connected to the energy of the collective consciousness of humanity, you are capable of piercing the veil of future possibilities. For this reason, you can be just as at home in a high-tech environment as you are when you listen to your powerful intuitive voice. You can also become highly rebellious, especially if you've lost your objectivity because of excessive restraint.

In your attempts to function as a rational and objective person, you can appear aloof or cold. However, in your heart of hearts you need to feel a connection to Universal and Unconditional Love, which will allow you to express your creative genius to its fullest. By filling yourself with this loving energy, your true path is illuminated and you can more readily pour the rays of divine light and wisdom into a world facing a new dawn.

Your Approach to Romance

Friendship commands high value in your life, and before you can allow yourself to develop the love that transcends the ordinary you may first develop a powerful friendship. The ideal of an equal and loyal partner makes sense to you, although you can be more possessive than you realize! Sometimes, when you've felt that you have finally found love, you can actually talk yourself out of it. (After all, love is not logical.) But once you surrender to the urging of your intuitive voice, you'll know when love has opened the door to your heart.

As an air sign, you prefer relationships centered on shared ideas, and will function best with others who are openly communicative. The other air signs—Gemini, Libra, and Aquarius—seem most at ease with you, and vice versa. You're most strongly attracted to your zodiac opposite, Leo, whose magnetic warmth and drama appeal to your playful side. Just watch out for those claws if you become too detached! Aries stimulates passion and fun and keeps you on your toes. With Taurus you may feel that you can't breathe if he or she becomes too possessive. Gemini's intelligence is charming and engaging, and you can open your mind and heart to one another. Cancer's need for constant contact can dampen your need for independence. With Virgo you're inspired to search your soul, but may not always agree on everything.

Libra's refined grace is charming and you'll enjoy sharing beautiful experiences and exploring culturally rich avenues. Scorpio can be too intense and you may feel that you're drowning in a sea of unspoken complexities. Enticed by Sagittarius' adventurous spirit, you're also inspired to enjoy life more fully. Although Capricorn may become a good friend, you may disappear in a puff of smoke if control issues arise! Be careful with another Aquarian, since what seems to be easy at first can fry your circuitry if you're on incompatible wavelengths. Your affinity with Pisces is through similar ideals, although you can get lost in the vapors if you are on different planes of reality.

Your Career Development

Your career is an important reflection of your life path, and you'll be most at ease in fields that are mentally stimulating and allow you to express your originality. You can excel in fields like communication, writing, advertising, public relations, sales, broadcasting or the news media. The scientific fields of electronics, computers, astrology, meteorology, theoretical mathematics, aviation, or the space industry can be productive.

In the fine arts, your talents may range from visionary art to original music. Owning your own business gives you a chance to market your uncommon creations, but you might also enjoy political service or working in humanitarian endeavors. Your trademark uniqueness stands out in any field you choose.

YOUR USE OF POWER

On the deepest level, you may desire to merge your consciousness with that of a higher source to experience the purest form of power. Since the world around you may illustrate the most appalling abuses of power, you may go out of your way to avoid power struggles. But if there is a cause that tugs at your soul, you're capable of harnessing an exceptional level of revolutionary energy and creating a ripe climate for change. Faced with human suffering or abuse, you can be a champion for those who are crushed by power-mongers whose selfish actions threaten to diminish the flame of human integrity. Because you are different, you can become notorious. Representing a common cause or universal ideal appeals to you more than seeking power for the sake of pure personal recognition. Yet you must be aware of your own inner shadow that craves recognition and may emerge in an overwhelming way if your motives are selfish.

Once you've won the trust and respect of others, your energy can generate clear new directions for a company, group, or nation. Through the power of vision of your creations, words, actions, and ideas, you can become the vessel for evolutionary change.

FAMOUS AQUARIANS

Levar Burton, Princess Caroline, Placido Domingo, Bridget Fonda, James Michener, Graham Nash, Aaron Neville, Joe Pesci, Vanessa Redgrave, J. Arlen Specter, John Travolta, Alice Walker, Oprah Winfrey.

THE YEAR AHEAD FOR AQUARIUS

As 1998 unfolds, your inspiration to utilize your creative capacities is strengthened. You're clearly definng your goals and hopes for the future while manifesting some of your most cherished dreams. The restrictions represented by realistic limitations can provide a grounding influence, but you may also find that your attitude toward your responsibilities is changing. All in all, this is a year of opening your consciousness to new possibilities while maintaining your focus. It is definitely a challenge—and one that should keep your creative juices flowing!

Jupiter's transit in Aquarius ends on February 4th, when Jupiter moves into Pisces for the remainder of the year. The increased optimism and confidence you've felt through 1997 can be continued in 1998, but now it's time to find substantial ways to employ your resources and make the most of what you have on hand. By focusing on expanding your self-worth your life can open to a new experience of abundance and prosperity. An abundant life begins spiritually and psychologically, and this year you're applying your ideals and beliefs to changes you're making in your lifestyle. You may feel more generous and can seek out distinctive avenues for sharing your resources with others. Just be sure you're also keeping a reasonable balance and know what you can afford to give. It's also easy to take your resources for granted and not to show the gratitude necessary for them. Whether you're thanking the people around you or showing your gratitude to the Universe for your good fortune, it's important to maintain a reasonable humility for the goodness life has to offer if you expect it to continue.

Throughout most of this year Saturn continues its cycle in Aries, which will end early next year. However, Saturn moves into Taurus at mid-year, providing you with a preview of the areas you'll need to be watching as you create your foothold and step into the new millennium. By concentrating your energy on finding the most effective ways to communicate with the world around you, you'll set the stage for a more solid foundation. Uranus continues its cycle in Aquarius, and Neptune also moves into your sign during 1998. These influences mark a significant period of several years, when you will find it easier to surrender to an evolving consciousness and deepening awareness. Pluto maintains its cycle in your solar Eleventh House, underscoring your need to transform your goals to fit your new sense of Self.

The solar and lunar eclipses draw your attention to the way you are using your resources during the February 26th solar eclipse in Pisces and the lunar eclipse in Virgo on March 12th. You may also discover some hidden elements in your psyche that you're finally ready to release, allowing you to feel more whole and alive. In August, when the eclipses enter the Leo/Aquarius axis, you begin a two-year cycle of intensified awareness of yourself, your relationships, and your place in the world. The Moon's eclipse in Aquarius on August 7th can stimulate exceptional inner awareness. Emotional issues that have been building to a crisis may finally come to the surface. During the Sun's eclipse on August 21st, pay particular attention to your relationships; they will become a powerful mirror that provides an excellent source of feedback concerning what you do and do not own about yourself.

≈≈≈   ≈≈≈   ≈≈≈

If you were born from January 20th–24th, you're feeling an increased sense of creative imagination while Neptune transits in conjunction to your Sun. This once-in-a-lifetime cycle will continue for two years, and marks a significant period of spiritual awakening. You're also experiencing some frustration in making your dreams reality since Saturn is traveling in a tense square aspect to your Sun. To work constructively with both of these cycles, it is imperative to discover the ways you sabotage your own efforts to raise your consciousness to a different level and experience the quality of life you know you deserve. It may be as simple as adopting a new attitude toward your responsibilities, determining that you can still carry those burdens that belong to you, but that you can do it with more flow and flexibility. You may also discover the very tasks you need to accomplish in order to make your dreams come true. If there are necessary requirements, obligations, or prerequisites, this is the time to learn about them and find a way to fulfill them. Spend more time doing things that will advance the quality of your life. Pay special attention to your physical health, and if you have concerns, consult a knowledgeable and trustworthy professional.

≋   ≋   ≋

You're feeling empowered **if you were born from January 25th–30th.** While Pluto is transiting in sextile aspect to your Sun you can completely renovate your life, releasing the things you've outgrown and stepping into a more satisfying expression of your true power as a whole person. This is an excellent year to take a careful look at yourself in the mirror, literally and figuratively. The changes you make to your life now can be revitalizing, but only if you're willing to let go of the things you no longer need, including self-defeating attitudes and destructive habits. Sweeping changes are possible, but you may also find that the changes you're making seem like a natural progression of your personal growth. A connection to special friends deepens, and if you're involved in political or community activities, you may experience positive rewards in these avenues, too. This is the perfect time to do something good for your health and wellness. Maybe you'll finally discover a workable fitness routine and create a lifestyle that supports your true needs.

≋   ≋   ≋

You may feel that you've sprouted wings **if you were born from January 28th–February 2nd.** With Uranus conjuncting your Sun, you're waking up to all sorts of possibilities. This can be an exciting time, when the world seems like a new place and your options are more varied than ever before. It's unlikely that you'll experience this cycle twice in a lifetime and to make the most of this time you need to focus on allowing your uniqueness to emerge. The ideals and principles of freedom and independence are your watchwords during this period, and you're not likely to allow old inhibitions to stand in the way of your progress. You may also be feeling rather rebellious, but have options about the way you stage your revolution. Not only are you changing, but you may discover that some significant people in your life are also changing. If you've been reluctant to make changes, some may come as a surprise from circumstances or events that seem to be beyond your control. Even if you embrace the possibility of change, you're still likely to be surprised by the unexpected at least once this year. Your responses to these ups and downs make the difference between a sense of success or failure. Think of life as a grand experiment and promise yourself that you're open to all sorts of options. It will be more fun that way!

≈   ≈   ≈

Concentrate on developing your special talents **if you were born from January 31st–February 6th.** You're experiencing a positive cycle of support while Saturn transits in quintile aspect to your Sun. This is an excellent time to seek out an inspiring teacher or mentor, or you may attract some very talented individuals if you are teaching or guiding others. Since the effects of this planetary cycle can be subtle, you'll make the best use of it by doing some "inner work" and determining the areas in your life that allow you to utilize your talents and abilities. This is the right time to enroll in that art class, take up an instrument, or try a new approach to your work.

≈   ≈   ≈

If you were born from February 7th–19th, you are experiencing the advantage of clarity and increased personal discipline. With Saturn transiting in sextile aspect to your Sun, you can bring your goals more clearly into focus and will find that it's even easier to keep your priorities in order. This is your time to manifest life as you want it to be, but it will require some effort on your part. Saturn cycles are like that: If you want something, you have to be part of making it happen. The more clear you are about your goals and responsibilities, the more likely you are to manifest them now. Whether you're on a clear path toward success in your job, enrolled in an educational program, or busy with family obligations, your attitudes toward your responsibilities are important. You also need to draw well-defined boundaries between what you will and will not do. Commitments that reflect your true self will work beautifully now. Those that are designed to simply please someone else will only delay your sense of personal gratification and may even stand in your way.

≈   ≈   ≈

If you were born from February 9th–14th, you may uncover some aspects of your life that were previously hidden. Pluto is transiting in quintile aspect to your Sun, a cycle that sometimes functions like finding gold in your own backyard. To uncover that hidden treasure, you may need to concentrate on your relationship with your inner self. This is an excellent time to deepen your understanding of the mysteries of life, but it is also a good period to fine-tune your talents and skills. In many ways, this period is like peeling away the layers of your life and finding the jewel of your spirit at the center.

≈   ≈   ≈

Neptune is transiting in semisextile aspect to your Sun **if you were born from February 18th–19th,** stimulating enhanced imagination and creativity. Because you're also more sensitive now, you might be inclined to engineer better ways to insulate yourself from the harshness of the world. This period completes a period of spiritual initiation that began last year, and incorporating your spirituality into your daily life can provide a new sense of strength and heightened awareness.

TOOLS TO MAKE A DIFFERENCE

Your first priority this year is to learn to trust your intuition more fully. Even if you've been working toward this goal for some time, you'll find it easier to surrender to your intuitive flow now that Neptune is entering your Sun sign. Commit time to regular meditation and contemplation. Reflect on your dreams. Keep a dream diary. Maintain a personal journal. Allow yourself to play music, paint, dance, or create whatever feels like a natural outpouring from your soul. Your intuitive and artistic selves are strongly linked—one nourishes the other.

Developing more profound connections with others who share your beliefs and ideals can have a significant impact on your life this year, and if you have political interests, working as an active part of the body politic can prove to be quite inspirational. As always, friends play a strong role, and their unconditional acceptance can strengthen your ability to open to love.

Boost your physical vitality by working with energy on its purest levels. Listen to your body, and incorporate alternative healing methods that will help your energy flow more fully. Ancient knowledge centering on acupuncture and the flow of *chi* (a Chinese word meaning "life energy") are key elements to enlivening your body and your spirit. You may become overly sensitive to alcohol and heavy medications, particularly those that affect your central nervous system. The subtle healing techniques of the flower essence remedies of vervain, water violet, star of Bethlehem, walnut, self-heal, and chamomile can be very useful.

During your meditations and visualizations, concentrate on opening your imagination to new dimensions. After getting into a comfortable position in a place that feels secure and safe, allow your mind to drift. Imagine that you are walking through a parallel dimension. The world seems to be much like the world you know, but then you realize that the colors are different. The ground beneath your feet is whirled with colors of blues and violet, and the sky is shimmering pink and gold. The sparkling beauty around you awakens your senses, and you hear transcendent music sung by the trees and plants around you. The fragrant air lifts your heart. Creatures emerge showing rare beauty. They approach you with curiosity and dance around you as you continue to walk along the path. The experience you have here awakens new sensibilities, and when you return to the world you know so well, you will see it from a different perspective. Enjoy it!

AFFIRMATION FOR THE YEAR
"My heart is abundant joy!"

AQUARIUS/JANUARY

PRIMARY FOCUS
This high-energy month can be an exceptional time to emphasize an important project, extend your influence, or expand your outreach. Just be sure you're adequately prepared, because mistakes can be rather costly.

HEALTH AND FITNESS
Channel your competitive drive through fitness or sports. Instruction and guidance from a pro can be worth its weight in gold, so ask for assistance or training from someone knowledgeable.

ROMANCE AND RELATIONSHIPS
Your enthusiasm for love may dim somewhat, particularly if you've been disappointed. It's important to consider what you need from your close relationships now, and to work on your own attitudes about being involved. A strong bond forged through shared ideas and similar beliefs sparks the strongest emotion, and you may begin a romance or take a fresh approach to an existing relationship near the New Moon on the 28th.

CAREER AND FINANCE
Although you're ready to forge ahead, there may be a few problems from past situations that still haunt you or get in the way of your progress. Strive to complete unfinished business before the Full Moon on the 12th, then you'll have more time and room for the things you really want to do during the auspicious period from the 14th–29th. Avoid impulsive spending after the 11th, since you can easily pay too much for too little!

OPPORTUNITY OF THE MONTH
Work with others to accomplish your aims from the 1st–10th, and you'll have the stage set for a new area of growth after the 21st.

AFFIRMATION FOR THE MONTH
"My actions and words are inspired by Truth and Love."

Rewarding Days: 1, 4, 5, 8, 9, 10, 18, 23, 27, 28
Challenging Days: 6, 7, 13, 14, 20, 21, 22

Aquarius/February

Primary Focus

You're concentrating on making the most of your resources now, and can see some major changes in your financial picture. Just try to avoid getting carried away with spending, since you can easily spend money faster than you can make it!

Health and Fitness

By concentrating on developing endurance you'll experience long-range health benefits. Strengthening muscles is important now, especially if you're balancing strength with flexibility. Avoid high-risk situations from the 1st–6th.

Romance and Relationships

Your hesitation about opening your heart may be due to a lack of trust, and if that's the case, get to the source. During the Full Moon on the 11th, you need to feel close to someone, and sharing your feelings and needs can work like a magical elixir, but if you don't trust yourself or your partner then it's much more frustrating. This is an excellent month to clear the air and determine what you actually want from a relationship. Be honest about it.

Career and Finance

With Mars and Jupiter stimulating your spending you can be exceptionally generous, but you can also be wasteful. Your judgment is more balanced after the 8th, and you may even feel prompted to establish a new financial plan. Set up a budget or realign your finances after the solar eclipse on the 26th. At work, plan meetings, conferences, or important travel or communication from the 2nd–20th.

Opportunity of the Month

Working in a cooperative or partnership venture can be rewarding from the 2nd–12th, but only if it's an egalitarian situation!

Affirmation for the Month
"Abundance in all forms comes to me now!"

Rewarding Days: 1, 5, 6, 14, 15, 19, 20, 24, 25, 28
Challenging Days: 3, 4, 9, 10, 11, 17, 18

AQUARIUS/MARCH

PRIMARY FOCUS

Your self-esteem can improve, adding a glow of confidence to your personal expression. You'll also feel more comfortable sharing your ideas, and you can build a strong network of support.

HEALTH AND FITNESS

Your physical energy and vitality increase, inspiring you to extend your fitness routine. Set up some new challenges. Consider taking an active vacation, spend time hiking in the woods, or bicycling through your neighborhood. Explore the world around you.

ROMANCE AND RELATIONSHIPS

The lunar eclipse on the 12th draws your attention to your needs for intimacy, and your close relationship can reach new heights if you're willing to surrender some of your old hurts and flow with the tide of possibilities emerging from a love relationship. Communicate your thoughts and feelings if you want to see changes. Send cards, e-mail messages, and small gifts. Plan a weekend away. Use your ingenuity and delight in what blossoms!

CAREER AND FINANCE

Business travel, writing, and communication all fare well, especially if you have something interesting to share. Launch pet projects from the 4th–12th, or after the New Moon on the 27th. Use this time to sharpen your skills, attend workshops, or bone up on important data. Mercury enters its retrograde on the 27th, so be prepared with a back-up plan. You can still make headway; it just gets more complex.

OPPORTUNITY OF THE MONTH

You're in an exceptional position to showcase your talents and ideas after the 3rd, and you're likely to gain recognition for your unique contributions from the 4th–19th.

AFFIRMATION FOR THE MONTH
"I am an effective and competent communicator."

Rewarding Days: 4, 5, 13, 14, 15, 19, 23, 24, 28, 31
Challenging Days: 2, 3, 9, 10, 16, 17, 29, 30

Aquarius/April

Primary Focus

Clarifying communication details is crucial, since if you fail to do so you could end up with a confusing mess. Pay special attention to your finances, and leave room for unanticipated expenditures.

Health and Fitness

Tension builds, and excessive stress begins to take its toll by mid-month. Allow time in your schedule for frequent breaks, and remember to clear your mind. Worry saps your energy, so focus your mind and heart on more positive efforts.

Romance and Relationships

You're ready to clarify your intentions, although it's easier to renew a commitment than it is to step into a new obligation during the Full Moon on the 11th. If there are problems, they may center on differences in value systems, or you may finally admit feeling unappreciated. The roots of your issues reside in the things you've absorbed from your family, and you can break away from these old patterns and create a different foundation during the New Moon on the 26th.

Career and Finance

During Mercury's retrograde through the 20th, you're likely to confront some long-standing problems and finally reach a resolution. But you may also be ending some obligations, and setting the stage for something new and innovative. Deception and undermining are likely, and it's imperative to keep your eye on your competitors. Just as dangerous are those who seem too eager to please.

Opportunity of the Month

Get to the core of misunderstandings and look for practical solutions from the 1st–10th. The rest of the month is a mixture of power struggles and strange dilemmas.

Affirmation for the Month
"I am an attentive and careful listener."

Rewarding Days: 1, 10, 11, 15, 20, 21, 29
Challenging Days: 5, 6, 12, 13, 14, 26, 27

Aquarius/May

Primary Focus
Friction at home can undermine your sense of stability and security. Get to the core of issues, and break away from habitual responses that undermine your effectiveness.

Health and Fitness
Stress continues to play an important role in your sense of well-being, and finding healthy outlets to release tension will actually increase your energy and productivity. Stay active, and spend time talking over your concerns with a compassionate friend.

Romance and Relationships
Tension on the home front is never pleasant, but once you're clear about the issues you can make changes that will allow for healing. Unresolved issues reach a critical point during the Full Moon on the 11th, when listening to your heart is your best resource. However, contact with your siblings is rewarding and may lead to resolutions. Romantic notions occupy your mind and heart after the 22nd, and love flows readily during the New Moon on the 25th.

Career and Finance
Although you may feel driven toward success, make sure the direction you're heading is really where you want to go! Travel and communication play increasingly significant roles in your advancement, and you have a marvelous opening to showcase your talents and ideas after the 21st. Look into speculative investments after the 24th, when you may also see excellent results from your current holdings.

Opportunity of the Month
Your network of contacts and professional allies form an excellent support for your ideas, and your ability to connect others works to your advantage from the 1st–15th.

Affirmation for the Month
"I am clearing the way for a solid foundation in my life."

Rewarding Days: 7, 8, 12, 13, 17, 18, 24, 25
Challenging Days: 2, 3, 10, 11, 23, 24, 30, 31

AQUARIUS/JUNE

PRIMARY FOCUS
Your creativity zooms, and this is a great time to get busy with a project that puts fire in your eyes! You may experience periods of frustration, when your dreams are grounded by practical considerations.

HEALTH AND FITNESS
Mental and physical alertness are important, and if you feel a little hazy, make sure you're getting adequate rest and foods high in B-vitamins. Work on improving your lung capacity during workouts.

ROMANCE AND RELATIONSHIPS
Romantic urges are powerful, and you're ready for a passionate exchange with your sweetheart. Playful and inspirational activities energize you during the Full Moon on the 9th, when a meeting of the minds can lead to a blending of souls. Your generosity of spirit helps attract the love you need, because you're already in the flow. Home and family are more secure, although there's a little wrinkle from the 8th–12th due to your unpredictability.

CAREER AND FINANCE
Let your special genius open the doors to your success, but watch for undermining early in the month from those who are skeptical of your new ideas. You may feel inclined to make changes in your work environment, or may even be working with someone different after the New Moon on the 23rd. Before spending money on home or property, look into all the details and examine the property with great care. Don't rush into anything.

OPPORTUNITY OF THE MONTH
Experimenting with innovative ideas, new technology, or unusual circumstances can be rather advantageous from the 1st–9th. After that, keep an open mind but watch out for traps.

AFFIRMATION FOR THE MONTH
"I trust my creative instincts."

Rewarding Days: 3, 4, 8, 9, 10, 13, 14, 22
Challenging Days: 6, 7, 19, 20, 26, 27

AQUARIUS/JULY

PRIMARY FOCUS

Interactions with others are intensified, and you may feel that you're the one making all the adjustments. Before selling your soul, step back and examine your priorities. Now, start again and see what happens.

HEALTH AND FITNESS

Your body is more sensitive, and over-stressing muscles or weak points can lead to inflammation or injury. Take care in new surroundings and watch your responses to stress and tension. Staying active helps, but try not to think of it as more work.

ROMANCE AND RELATIONSHIPS

Partnerships need extra care and attention, especially if your communication seems to be suffering. Take time out for some pure enjoyment from the 1st–19th, but watch a tendency to overindulge after the 12th. To enliven an existing relationship, try something unusual after the New Moon on the 23rd. If you're seeking a new love, be clear about your signals or you could be trapped in something rather strange.

CAREER AND FINANCE

Legal action and contracts run into snags near the Full Moon on the 9th, but you have time to work out the details. At work, watch for potential conflicts with those who work under your supervision after the 7th and avoid getting pulled into situations that do not involve you. Watch spending or investments after the 14th, when you may be attracted by something that looks much better than it really is.

OPPORTUNITY OF THE MONTH

The good thing about knowing that you're in an area with land mines is that you're forewarned. The problem is finding the darn things! Step carefully, and take it easy.

AFFIRMATION FOR THE MONTH
"I am flexible and cooperative."

Rewarding Days: 2, 6, 10, 11, 19, 20, 28, 29
Challenging Days: 3, 4, 17, 18, 23, 24, 25, 30, 31

AQUARIUS/AUGUST

PRIMARY FOCUS
Partnerships can be trying, especially if you're hoping for a quick fix. It's time to look in the mirror and ask yourself if you're really ready to embrace your own power.

HEALTH AND FITNESS
Your well-being depends on many factors, with your emotional needs playing a stronger role this month. Getting re-acquainted with your inner self can be a positively revealing experience, and may help you get to the core of any physical discomfort.

ROMANCE AND RELATIONSHIPS
The Aquarius lunar eclipse on the 7th signifies a time of increased awareness of your deeper feelings. If you've not taken an inventory for a while, then this is a good time to ask yourself how you feel and what you want. If you're concerned about your love life, open better lines of communication. Then, when the solar eclipse on the 21st arrives, you'll be ready to establish the ground rules for that equitable partnership you've seen in your dreams.

CAREER AND FINANCE
Mercury's retrograde from the 1st–23rd can be frustrating, particularly if you're trying to reach an agreement. Just when you think you have all the details, something new is likely to emerge. Partnerships can be beneficial after the 14th, but only if everything is carefully defined. Conservative attitudes overwhelm innovative thinking, so be prepared. Watch for power struggles and attempts to be in control.

OPPORTUNITY OF THE MONTH
Break habits that are counterproductive to your growth. Why continue with something that steals your energy?

AFFIRMATION FOR THE MONTH
"I am happy to do the work necessary to get the job done!"

Rewarding Days: 2, 7, 8, 11, 15, 16, 24, 25, 30
Challenging Days: 1, 13, 14, 20, 21, 27, 28

Aquarius/September

Primary Focus

Money matters take priority, especially those involving your financial associations with others. Whether it's inheritance, taxes, joint property, or mutual investments, take time to re-evaluate your involvement and make sure you're getting what you deserve.

Health and Fitness

You need a new fitness challenge that will help you reach beyond old limitations without causing problems. Consider working with a personal trainer who can help you achieve your goals.

Romance and Relationships

Barriers to intimacy can be removed if you're willing to release old pain buried deep in your psyche. Keep lines of communication open, and during the lunar eclipse on the 6th, allow some of those old walls to fall away. This is a wonderful time to work with a counselor, since objectifying your needs helps you see yourself more clearly. Adopt a playful attitude with your partner, trying a more fun-loving approach to sexuality during the New Moon on the 20th.

Career and Finance

Unworkable partnerships are likely to collapse early in the month, giving you a chance to consider whether or not you want to rely on someone else for your financial stability. Pay special attention to eliminating debt and resolving complex financial concerns from the 6th–24th. This is an excellent time for research or investigation, and after the 23rd, travel and education provide their own rewards.

Opportunity of the Month

You can clearly see your competition. In fact, it may be another part of yourself! Take a careful look, because you're better prepared when you know what you're up against .

Affirmation for the Month
"My vision penetrates beneath the illusion of the surface."

Rewarding Days: 3, 4, 7, 8, 12, 21, 22, 26, 30
Challenging Days: 6, 9, 10, 16, 17, 23, 24

AQUARIUS/OCTOBER

PRIMARY FOCUS

Extend your influence and strengthen your awareness through cultural exchange, travel, educational pursuits, and other activities that expand your sense of yourself and the universe. Moral, philosophical, and ethical matters play a significant role in your life now.

HEALTH AND FITNESS

A real vacation to a place that inspires your imagination and sparks your faith in the wonder of life can completely revitalize you now. Choose a destination that offers something that pampers you while strengthening your spirit.

ROMANCE AND RELATIONSHIPS

If your love life needs a charge, take your show on the road. Even a romantic weekend with your honey near the Full Moon on the 5th can take you to a new plateau! If you're seeking a new romance, get involved in life. Find a special interest group whose values echo your own and enjoy yourself. While you're laughing, you may just look up and find the perfect eyes staring right back at you! Love is definitely in the air during the New Moon on the 20th.

CAREER AND FINANCE

Writing, publishing, or teaching can all add to your success and may be the best avenues for strengthening your reputation. Advertising and public relations can also give you a boost from the 1st–23rd. Plan meetings, conferences, and presentations from the 1st–12th, and be ready for a few questions from your superiors after that time. You'll shine brilliantly if you're on top of the game.

OPPORTUNITY OF THE MONTH

In all matters, take the high road. Your moral integrity sets you apart and inspires others to reach a new plateau.

AFFIRMATION FOR THE MONTH
"My thoughts and actions are inspired by Truth and Wisdom."

Rewarding Days: 1, 2, 5, 9, 10, 18, 19, 23, 24, 28, 29
Challenging Days: 7, 8, 13, 14, 20, 21

Aquarius/November

Primary Focus

Your reputation can grow due to your expertise and knowledge, but some will not understand your motivations or plans. The way you handle advancement or changes in your prosperity is crucial.

Health and Fitness

It's important to get to the core of physical problems and to consider the emotional and spiritual elements of your life. Probing into the past can uncover significant information that can lead to healing at the deepest levels.

Romance and Relationships

Intimacy needs are powerful and establishing or renewing your trust is crucial during the Full Moon on the 4th. A good friend provides objectivity if you're feeling overwhelmed by personal or family matters, especially if you're trying too hard to please everyone but yourself! Clarify expectations in all your relationships to avoid being crushed by disappointment. You'll feel much freer after the 23rd, but maneuver carefully until then.

Career and Finance

It's easy to overspend from the 1st–10th, and you may not realize how much you've exceeded your budget at first, so beware of getting in over your head. Keeping up with details is likely to be more difficult now, since there's a lot happening. Everything gets more scattered with Mercury retrograding on the 21st. Clarify your career goals during the New Moon on the 18th, and try to stay with your plans!

Opportunity of the Month

Professional associations and special interest groups provide a wonderful avenue for your growth, and after the 17th there's an infusion of fresh energy in this area.

Affirmation for the Month:
"I am hopeful and confident now and for my future."

Rewarding Days: 1, 2, 5, 6, 14, 15, 19, 20, 24, 25
Challenging Days: 3, 4, 9, 10, 11, 17, 18, 27

AQUARIUS/DECEMBER

PRIMARY FOCUS

Think about expanding your horizons and opening to possibilities that you've never before considered. Let yourself feel inspired by others, and listen to your inner yearnings. It's time to fine-tune your life path in harmony with your highest needs.

HEALTH AND FITNESS

Increase your activity levels. Find ways to connect with nature, and feel the rhythm of life that pulsates around and within you. Healing begins with a spiritual spark, and you're the one who ignites it!

ROMANCE AND RELATIONSHIPS

Truly unconditional love is rare, but you're capable of allowing it to permeate your life and flow from the center of yourself. Your friendships glow, and your special intimate relationships can soar if you share similar ideals and values. Make room for beautiful romance during the Full Moon on the 3rd. Do something special. Invite your friends to share joy during the New Moon on the 18th.

CAREER AND FINANCE

Mercury's retrograde through the 11th provides an excellent period to get back in touch with those who understand and support your aims and concepts. Move into a new direction, schedule a significant meeting, or showcase your talents from the 11th–22nd, but watch for some surprising developments! You may be able to use them to your advantage. Take a break from the action after the 23rd.

OPPORTUNITY OF THE MONTH

Contracts, legal proceedings, or publishing can play a significant role in your life from the 1st–18th. Keep an open mind.

AFFIRMATION FOR THE MONTH
"I am confident, courageous, and delighted with my life!"

Rewarding Days: 3, 4, 11, 12, 13, 17, 21, 22, 23, 30, 31
Challenging Days: 1, 2, 7, 8, 14, 15, 28, 29

AQUARIUS ~~~ ACTION TABLE												

These dates reflect the best (but not the only) times for success and ease in these activities, according to your sign.

	Jan.	Feb.	Mar.	Apr.	May	June	July	Aug.	Sept.	Oct.	Nov.	Dec.
Change Residence					15–31							
Ask for a Raise	28, 29											
Begin a Course of Study			28, 29							20		
Join a Club												18
Begin a Romance					25, 26							
Visit a Doctor	12–31	1, 2				15–30						
Start a Diet	11, 12	7, 8	6, 7	2, 3, 30	1, 27, 28	24, 25	21, 22	17, 18	13–15	11, 12	7, 8	5, 6
Seek Employment						15–29				12–31	1	
Take a Vacation	18, 19	14, 15	13–15	10, 11	7, 8	3, 4	1, 2, 28, 29	24, 25	20–22	18, 19	14, 15	11–13
End a Relationship		11										
Change Your Wardrobe						1–14						
Seek Professional Advice	13, 14	9, 10	9, 10	5, 6	2, 3, 29–31	26, 27	23–25	20, 21	16, 17	13, 14	9, 10	7, 8
Have a Make-Over	28, 29											
Obtain a Loan	15, 16	12, 13	11, 12	7, 8	4–6	1, 2, 28–30	26, 27	22, 23	18, 19	15, 16	12, 13	9, 10

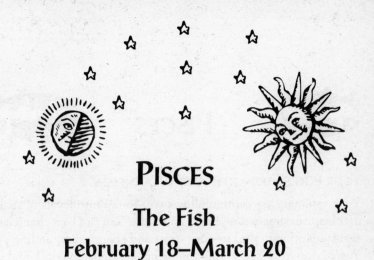

PISCES

The Fish
February 18–March 20

Element:	Water
Quality:	Mutable
Polarity:	Yin/Feminine
Planetary Ruler:	Neptune (Jupiter)
Meditation:	"I surrender to the heart of Divine Compassion."
Gemstone:	Aquamarine
Power Stones:	Amethyst, Bloodstone, Tourmaline
Key Phrase:	"I believe"
Glyph:	Two Fish Swimming ♓
Anatomy:	Feet, Lymphatic System
Colors:	Sea Green, Violet
Animals:	Dolphin, Whale, Fish
Myths/Legends:	Aphrodite, Buddha, Jesus of Nazareth
House Association:	Twelfth
Opposite Sign:	Virgo
Flower:	Water Lily
Key Word:	Transcendence

Positive Expression:		**Misuse of Energy:**	
Quiet	Compassionate	Addictive	Escapist
Idealistic	Impressionable	Self-Deceptive	Victimized
Poetic	Visionary	Susceptible	Confused

PISCES

Your Ego's Strengths and Weaknesses

Your visionary perception allows you to tap into levels of reality that inspire compassion, hope, and faith. You can be a chameleon, easily adapting to the circumstances and energy surrounding you. You're drawn to everything that is imaginative, mystical, and out of this world, and may have a special appreciation for the arts and music since they are linked to your spirituality. It is through this connection that you play "The Illusionist" of the zodiac, which can manifest as a keen talent in artistic expression.

It is the energy of Neptune, your planetary ruler, that serves as your subtle driving force, expanding your awareness of the vibrational plane of reality and forging your strong sense of spirituality. When others are trapped in despair, your faith remains strong and inspires the promise of transcendence. Despite your own occasional feelings of vulnerability, you can always imagine different possibilities, and it is your dreams that fuel your inner power. However, you can fall victim to illusion and deception, and need to allow ample space and time in your life for recharging your energy so you can safely maneuver through the storms of life. Just as important, you need to learn how to create positive personal boundaries to avoid a tendency toward co-dependency or addiction in your relationships.

Your desire to escape emerges when you are out of touch with your inner self. You can fall prey to addictive behaviors, whether they involve substances or other people. By maintaining a strong connection between your inner self and the physical plane that sustains your life you'll have greater opportunities to exercise your magical abilities to alter the world.

Your Approach to Romance

Romance can be your forte and you may have always felt a deep sense of yearning for a soulmate. You can see beauty and potential in almost everyone, but will feel more complete when you find that special glow of love in the eyes of one who stirs your soul. Others may not grasp the depths you seek, but even in the face of disappointment, your dream of the perfect love remains. Once you've found true love, you can experience the pure enchantment of opening your heart, and can create a spell-binding space where the two of you can retreat into ecstasy.

You feel most at ease with the other water signs — Cancer, Scorpio, and Pisces. However, your zodiac opposite, Virgo, can be extremely attractive, and you may be able to manifest a wonderful dream once you find common ground. Aries inspires your spontaneity, but you may feel hurt if the romance dies too quickly. With Taurus' taste for the good things blending with your imaginative ideas, you can sustain your dreams long enough to make them real. Gemini's changeability can throw you off-balance, even though you'll enjoy the thrill. Cancer's nurturing encourages you to fully express love and stimulates your creative potential.

Leo's demands can exhaust your patience and your energy. Although Libra's elegance intrigues you, you may get the impression that you're somehow short of the mark. Scorpio's sensual intensity draws you into the depths of love, launching you into another dimension. You'll have to remain alert if you want to keep up with Sagittarius' pace. As long as you maintain personal boundaries, you can have an exceptional relationship with a calm, safe, and stable Capricorn. With Aquarius, you may have an unequaled friend, but you may not feel quite comfortable as lovers. With another Pisces, you may feel a deep sense of understanding of your hopes, dreams, and desires.

Your Career Development

You may prefer to think of your career as a vehicle for expressing your vision of life, and need an outlet for your imaginative talents. Ambition may not be your incentive as much as your desire to reach beyond the ordinary into the realm of what could lead to your success. You may be artistically talented as an artist, actor, dancer, musician, or photographer; or you might enjoy work in interior design, make-up artistry, fashion design, hairdressing, landscape design, or the floral industry.

Fields that appeal to the collective consciousness like advertising, media, movies, or TV can be appealing, or you might enjoy working in the computer industry or in graphic design. Counseling, social work, medicine, or the ministry can be excellent outlets for your desire to uplift the human spirit, or your special sensitivity to animals may set your sights on a career focusing on their needs. Whatever you choose, happiness is assured when you feel you're in harmony with the natural flow of life.

YOUR USE OF POWER

Your dream is not so much for raw power as it is to feel one with the Source. Your special ability to tap into the energy that allows you to become a radiant vision of faith, hope, and love is the key to your personal power. Once you've mastered the ability to surrender to the flow, your life can become an instrument for the expression of the power of divine compassion. This current of energy will continually recharge your vitality and it is the key to your resilience and creative imagination.

You can lose your power when others lead you astray through their own selfish desires or if you sacrifice yourself unnecessarily to their demands and needs. Your personal salvation rests in uncovering a spiritual path that allows you to surrender to the power of the Absolute, allowing you to discover the perfect teacher residing deep within your own soul. As you align yourself with the Source, you become empowered to return that energy to the physical plane through your creativity. Glowing with the light of love, your radiant joy and light can evoke healing and transcendent peace into the world around you.

FAMOUS PISCEANS

Edward Albee, Drew Barrymore, Michael Bolton, David Geffen, Kelsey Grammer, Peter Graves, Alan Greenspan, Kathy Ireland, Jackie Joyner-Kersee, Yitzhak Rabin, Lynn Redgrave.

THE YEAR AHEAD FOR PISCES

T his is your year to open to more profound levels of self-confidence and hope for your future. You're continuing to eliminate elements from your life that are unnecessary and counterproductive to your growth while focusing on your goals. Your consciousness is changing, and along with this shift you may also be viewing your place in the world differently. With the help of renewed personal values and through developing a more comfortable connection between the spiritual and physical parts of yourself, you may feel that it's finally time to enjoy the simple beauty of life itself.

Jupiter, the energy of abundance and expansive growth, moves into Pisces on February 4th, where it will continue throughout the remainder of 1998. This period represents a time when you can tap into the true nature of abundance and prosperity. To experience an abundant life, you must open the doors to joy and allow yourself to absorb the feeling that you deserve to have all your needs fulfilled. Think back to 1986, because many of the opportunities that are open to you now have their links to that time. You may even reach a new plateau that has its roots in the good fortune of your past. This is a wonderful time to travel, study, write, increase your creative expression, and listen to the voice of your soul. The journey of your life can inspire you to reach beyond your current circumstances into the realm of the place where you manifest your dreams.

For most of this year, Saturn continues its transit through the Second House of your solar chart, indicating that you still need to pay careful attention to your finances. If you're taking a prudent approach to material matters, you may also find that you're more secure and that you can actually feel a more stable foundation in this part of your life. During the summer months, Saturn moves into Taurus before it retrogrades back into Aries to complete the year. This is your "preview" of the influence of Saturn during the last two years of this century. From this time, you will learn where you need to train your focus in order to step onto the platform of the new millennium. Uranus and Neptune are transiting through your solar Twelfth House, stimulating an awakening to your inner self. This period can be filled with amazing dreams that may be prophetic, so pay attention! The energy of Pluto continues its cycle through your solar Tenth House, challenging you to create a life path that fulfills your inner calling.

The solar eclipse on February 26th and the lunar eclipse on September 6th are both in Pisces, marking significant periods of self-awareness and inner change. The Moon's eclipse on March 12th can stimulate a period of crisis in relationships, and then on August 7th, the Moon's eclipse is centered on your inner focus as you are challenged to release the things from you past you no longer need. On August 21st, the Sun's eclipse draws your attention to your work and health, and if you've been ignoring these areas, then it's time to bring them in line with your needs.

♓   ♓   ♓

If you were born from February 19th–23rd, you're experiencing a strong period of stability while Saturn transits in sextile aspect to your Sun. This cycle becomes strongest from summer through the end of autumn, but the effects grow gradually and have long-lasting impact. In addition, Neptune is transiting in semisextile to your Sun, helping you employ your imaginative sensibilities while you're formulating a more workable structure in your life. These two energies provide an important stimulus to incorporate external influences with your dreams and inner needs.

By examining the way you communicate your ideas and creativity, you can alter not only the perception others have of you, but may even change the way you think and feel about yourself. This time period can illustrate the true power of thought, and if you honestly want to create life on your own terms, you will work toward a clear sense of mindfulness and expanded awareness.

You may feel that your life is undergoing a complete transformation **if you were born from February 24th–28th.** Pluto's transit in square aspect to your Sun brings an energy of intensity and change. You may certainly be taking a closer look at your career path, and if you feel that you've fallen into a situation that seems beyond your control, you definitely need some careful evaluation of your responses and choices. Your experience with authority figures in general may also be shifting, especially if you're dealing with power issues.

This can be a period of positive healing, but only if you're willing to release your attachment to the things that are standing in the way of your growth. Whether you're eliminating self-defeating habits and attitudes, changing your career path, taking a stand for your ideals, or altering the way you handle your personal relationships—this is the time for you to allow your real sense of personal power to emerge. Transformation is a multilevel experience, and you're likely to feel that you're peeling through many layers of your life during this process of self-discovery and restoration.

♓ ♓ ♓

If you were born from February 26th–March 4th, you're feeling a bit rebellious this year while Uranus is transiting in semisextile aspect to your Sun. This is an exciting cycle, but not as crazy as those times that have felt like riding a roller-coaster. The freedom you're experiencing is generated from within, and may be strongly centered on letting go of the past and moving into a new dimension of awareness and self-expression. You're less likely to fall into traps of co-dependency and may also view your beliefs and ideals quite differently than you have seen them in the past. Since most true change begins within, the perfect place to start is by listening to your inner voice while freeing your spirit from those old behaviors that have inhibited your self-expression.

♓ ♓ ♓

You're experiencing frustration **if you were born from February 28th–March 12th,** since Saturn is transiting in semisquare aspect to your Sun. During this year you may feel that you're running into the same blocks over and over again, especially if you weren't paying attention the first time! You can make significant progress if you're taking your responsibilities seriously, but if you're not carrying your own burdens, you may discover that you're left behind while your dreams fade in the distance.

This is one of those cycles when applied effort makes a significant difference. You may even feel more motivated, because you'll also experience results, although some levels of gratification may be somewhat delayed. If you need to satisfy requirements, enroll in classes, take certification exams, or complete a major project, this is the time to get busy and finish those obligations. Your efforts can then create building blocks that add to your stability and sense of security, making it easier to enjoy the experience of life.

♓   ♓   ♓

If you were born from March 6th–10th, you need to watch out for confusing circumstances, while Neptune is transiting in semisquare aspect to your Sun this year. Although you may be tempted to escape the pressures of life by hiding from them, you'll undermine your sense of power if you repress your energy by sticking your head in the sand. Addictive behaviors or tendencies can be amplified under the influence of this cycle, so find ways to remain objective. Sometimes it helps to listen to a good friend or counselor if you're uncertain about your own sense of direction.

You may also need more time for inner exploration, and you can achieve new levels of peace by increasing your meditation periods, spending more time developing your creative expression, or simplifying your life by becoming more mindful. But it will require devotion to attain that peace on a consistent basis. Think of this as the year when you peek into new levels of awareness and ultimately bounce high enough to stand on the platform of that awareness and alter your life.

♓   ♓   ♓

Take special care with your responsibilities **if you were born from March 13th–20th.** With Saturn transiting in semisextile to your Sun, you're taking the steps necessary to stabilize your life and to create a solid platform for growth. This is an excellent year to build your career, make commitments in relationships or take on new responsibilities. However, your choices need to be centered on growth-oriented options that will provide opportunity and open doors. Your burdens need not be excessively heavy. In fact, you'll function best if you keep life on the simple side, focusing on your priorities.

♓   ♓   ♓

If you were born from March 13th–18th, you're feeling a bit scattered while Uranus is transiting in semisquare aspect to your Sun. Just when you think you know what to expect, you can be surprised by the unexpected. Others may also be surprised by some of the choices you make, especially if they've always assumed you would stay the same. Well, now, you're opting for being different, and may even be a little rebellious in your attitudes. Just try to maintain your inner "center" in order to avoid burning bridges you may need to cross again. Listen to your intuition.

♓   ♓   ♓

Your creativity and imagination are strengthened **if you were born from March 18th–20th.** You're feeling the influence of Neptune traveling in sextile aspect to your Sun, which can lead to a deepening awareness and more comfortable expression of your talents. Incorporating your spirituality into your everyday life seems the most natural choice. By embracing a deepening inner awareness and taking time to extend your energy into the world in ways that will bring about peace and harmony, you can make a significant difference in the quality of your life.

TOOLS TO MAKE A DIFFERENCE

As you move through the cycles of this year, give yourself ample time to listen to your heart and feed your soul. Your natural sensibilities continually point you in the direction of inner awareness, and this year underscores that tendency. A top priority during 1998 should be recharging your sense of joy. The energy of joy is buoyant and alive, and it is the source of optimism, self-confidence, and generosity. Look for joy in the world around you.

Spend time with others who love to laugh, especially children. Let yourself smile with the changes of season. Feel the joy of all you have accomplished. Celebrate yourself. Celebrate others. Celebrate life!

To heal your body, promise to take better care of it. Eliminate habits that undermine your vitality. Since you're especially sensitive to vibration, use music and sound to alter your energy. You may also respond well to the flower essence remedies, and can benefit specifically from aspen, clematis, lotus, manzanita, and yarrow. Wear the colors that make your eyes sparkle. Bring beautiful sea-greens into your home and work environment. Make or buy something in fabrics that you love to touch, and wear those items frequently.

In order to help you release the past, make an effort to sort through your personal archives. Get rid of the things that you need to eliminate, or give away things that are unused and could benefit someone else. While reviewing your past, spend time assembling a collection of the things that remind you of your accomplishments and that warm your heart. Study old photographs and see the joy in your eyes. Remember, you're building a storehouse of joy in your life now!

During your meditations, learn to listen to your heart. Find a place you love, get comfortable, and allow yourself to drift into the space that surrounds your soul. As you breathe, feel the energy shimmering around you and permeating every cell of your body. Drift back into time and remember a moment when you were completely happy, filled with absolute joy. Let this feeling dance through your heart and warm you completely. Now, think of your life as you know it today, and bring that feeling of joy into your awareness of the present moment. Release your anxiety, anger, fear, or doubt, and simply feel the joy. Be grateful for what you have. Let gratitude work like wings to carry your joy forward. From this moment, you can build your dreams on a solid platform of hope.

AFFIRMATION FOR THE YEAR

"My life is filled with abundance in all forms.
The Universe provides for all my needs."

Pisces/January

Primary Focus

Although your career takes a great deal of time and energy, you also need to allow extra time for rejuvenation and contemplation this month. This period is like the end of a gestation cycle, preparing you for a sense of renewal.

Health and Fitness

Concentrate on your "inner" fitness, releasing anxiety and worry, opening your mind and emotions to the healing that arises from developing a sense of inner peace and calm. Center your activities on increasing your flexibility.

Romance and Relationships

An old relationship from the past resurfaces, although you may not have direct contact. If you do, listen to your feelings very carefully before you make any promises. A friend's advice is golden during the Full Moon on the 12th, when you may also feel especially romantic. Although you may be attracted to someone different during the New Moon on the 28th, impulsive actions may not be appropriate.

Career and Finance

Take a careful look at what you receive for your efforts in your career. If you feel that you deserve more, create a proposal for consideration, but give yourself some time before you take action. Dropping a few hints could give you important clues after the 11th. This is a good month to get rid of assets that are not performing well or to liquidate stock and increase your options. Special interest groups play a significant role after the 12th, so get involved.

Opportunity of the Month

Isolation can be beneficial, but avoid overdoing it. Networking with others can be self-confirming and illuminating from the 12th–27th.

Affirmation for the Month
"My dreams are messages from my inner self."

Rewarding Days: 2, 3, 6, 11, 12, 20, 21, 29, 30
Challenging Days: 1, 8, 9, 10, 15, 16, 17, 23, 24

PISCES/FEBRUARY

PRIMARY FOCUS

If you're feeling anxious about life in general it could be due to a brewing crisis, but the crisis is precipitated by new growth and change. You're changing and the world around you is shifting, too. Be clear about the way you are directing your energy.

HEALTH AND FITNESS

Avoid high-risk situations or dangerous circumstances from the 1st until the Full Moon on the 11th and again after the 21st. These are good times to get to the core of problems, but don't create new ones!

ROMANCE AND RELATIONSHIPS

Since the solar eclipse in Pisces on the 26th is drawing near, you'll be better prepared for it if you take an internal inventory. Exactly what do you want from yourself and your relationships? You may run into power struggles early in the month that amplify deep-seated problems and help you determine a new course of action. Take those steps on the 26th and 27th, when you have the power to reshape your destiny.

CAREER AND FINANCE

If you're dissatisfied with your financial picture, take a look at your values. It's time to focus on what you want from life and to shift your attitudes and actions into arenas that will allow you to expand your options. Be reasonably cautious in investments You have plenty of time to act on a tip and don't want to end up footing the bill for someone else's mistakes. Schedule meetings, presentations, or conferences after the 20th.

OPPORTUNITY OF THE MONTH

The contrasts in your life after the 21st are quite amazing, so get your preparatory work done and be ready to step into high gear and take advantage of something exciting.

AFFIRMATION FOR THE MONTH
"My actions reflect loving generosity and gratitude."

Rewarding Days: 3, 7, 8, 17, 18, 22, 23, 26, 27
Challenging Days: 5, 6, 12, 13, 19, 20

PISCES/MARCH

PRIMARY FOCUS

You're feeling optimistic but reckless, so try to remain realistic in your actions and choices. This is particularly important in the realm of finance, since foolish choices can be more costly than you realize.

HEALTH AND FITNESS

Set positive fitness goals to develop your endurance. The combination of strength and flexibility is always important, and will be especially helpful during the next sixty days. Do yourself a favor and get with the program!

ROMANCE AND RELATIONSHIPS

Sometimes fantasies improve your love life, and you may become wildly infatuated with someone new whose very presence takes your breath away. Before your dreams alter your life, take a closer look at your current situation during the lunar eclipse on the 12th. An existing relationship may end, but you may just need to give it a jump start. Look for new options if it can't be revived, but avoid the danger of running away into something risky.

CAREER AND FINANCE

Your confidence continues to increase, but you may run into an ethical or philosophical dilemma that causes you to reconsider your plans and circumstances. Avoid impulsive expenditures early in the month, since you're likely to have regrets later. By making the best use of your resources you can experience a new level of prosperity, but waste or excess quickly undermines your stability.

OPPORTUNITY OF THE MONTH

Your ideas and creative energy provide excellent avenues for growth from the 1st–12th. Just watch for power plays from the 9th–14th that can unravel the best-laid plans.

AFFIRMATION FOR THE MONTH
"My actions reflect a positive sense of self-worth."

Rewarding Days: 2, 3, 6, 7, 16, 17, 21, 25, 26
Challenging Days: 4, 5, 11, 12, 19, 20, 27, 31

PISCES/APRIL

PRIMARY FOCUS

Mercury's retrograde frustrates your attempts to keep your life on track. Make a special effort in finances and contractual agreements, and take a cautious approach in business endeavors.

HEALTH AND FITNESS

Stress and tension can be big energy drains this month, and if you try to ignore them then you'll just feel tired and depressed. Take charge of the situation by staying active, allowing ample time for rejuvenation, and acknowledging your personal limitations.

ROMANCE AND RELATIONSHIPS

Your feelings about someone are changing, and if you've been fooling yourself or falling into the trap of denial, you're ready to wake up to the truth near the time of the Full Moon on the 11th. Be honest with yourself about your needs, and if you're not experiencing real support, then do something about it. Romance flows more readily after the 17th, and you might even feel like a romantic getaway during the New Moon on the 26th. A change of scenery can be magical.

CAREER AND FINANCE

Although Mercury is in retrograde until the 20th, your greatest frustrations center on the first half of April, when you need to be particularly attentive to financial matters. Double-check your facts, and clarify all documentation on any important paperwork. Communication improves after the 21st, but you may still feel like you're in foreign territory for a while. Schedule important presentations or meetings after the 25th.

OPPORTUNITY OF THE MONTH

Set up a budget and stick with it. Irresponsible attitudes concerning your finances will only lead to disastrous results.

AFFIRMATION FOR THE MONTH
"My actions reflect my values."

Rewarding Days: 3, 4, 13, 18, 22, 23, 26, 27, 30
Challenging Days: 1, 7, 8, 15, 16, 28, 29

PISCES/MAY

PRIMARY FOCUS

You're on the move, and making connections with others proves to be invigorating and inspirational. Listen to your intuitive voice; while logic is helpful, sometimes you just need to follow your hunches.

HEALTH AND FITNESS

Allow plenty of time to connect with nature and feel your own flow with the rhythms of life. Sometimes the simplest things have the best results, so try not to complicate any health issues and take the most direct approach to resolving your problems.

ROMANCE AND RELATIONSHIPS

Personal relationships improve through better communication, including the non-verbal kind. If you're looking for love, you're more likely to discover someone new while you're involved in something that sparks your spiritual yearnings near the Full Moon on the 11th. To resolve family matters or improve a situation at home, take action that leads to open discourse. Tension can mount following the New Moon on the 25th if power plays are involved.

CAREER AND FINANCE

Direct your energy toward improving your skills and increasing your knowledge, since your expertise may be tested and you want to be on top of the game. Professional networking proves exciting and beneficial, although there is a period of confusion from the 15th–18th. You're more competitive than usual after the 24th, and may stir up trouble if you step on the wrong toes, so dance carefully.

OPPORTUNITY OF THE MONTH

Seeking truth and following the path of higher ground takes you out of the way of danger and into the flow of expanding horizons from the 1st–11th.

AFFIRMATION FOR THE MONTH
"My ideals are centered on Truth and Divine Wisdom."

Rewarding Days: 1, 10, 11, 15, 19, 20, 23, 24, 27, 28
Challenging Days: 4, 5, 6, 12, 13, 25, 26

PISCES/JUNE

PRIMARY FOCUS

You may feel strongly driven to push toward your goals but may run into a power struggle that causes you to reconsider your motivations. Determine what you want and why, since discovering your inner drive yields a truer measure of success.

HEALTH AND FITNESS

You may be experiencing high levels of stress. Defuse the tension in your life by placing your physical needs at a priority that equals your other responsibilities.

ROMANCE AND RELATIONSHIPS

Turmoil at home can be the result of something as simple as rearranging the furniture, but there are likely to be underlying problems or unresolved issues that are ready to burst forth by the Full Moon on the 9th. Support from a sibling helps you reach a resolution. Romantic notions are quite favorable after the 22nd, and you may even feel like trying some fresh ideas during the New Moon on the 23rd that can lead to all sorts of delightful possibilities.

CAREER AND FINANCE

Large-scale changes in your career can result from circumstances beyond your control, but you can direct your responses to those changes. If you are in a position to orchestrate a shift in direction, examine your career carefully to be sure you're satisfied with it. You have the power to move into different directions and to break away from unfulfilling situations. Invest your time and resources in something that sparks your imagination after the 16th.

OPPORTUNITY OF THE MONTH

This is no time to hide your talents. Dust off those hidden attributes and let yourself shine. Set your debut after the 23rd.

AFFIRMATION FOR THE MONTH
"A loving heart fuels my drive to succeed."

Rewarding Days: 6, 7, 11, 12, 15, 16, 20, 24, 25
Challenging Days: 1, 2, 8, 9, 10, 22, 23, 28, 29

PISCES/JULY

PRIMARY FOCUS

Light an inspirational fire beneath your dreams to move from reverie to action. Listen to the echo of your heart to decide if you'll pursue your hopes, and get to work creating your life on your terms.

HEALTH AND FITNESS

Staying active can be wonderful, especially if you're enjoying that activity. Go ahead and enroll in that dance class or tai chi workshop, get into a class at your local "Y," or join in team sports.

ROMANCE AND RELATIONSHIPS

Love is in the air and you may be hungry for some wildly wonderful romance by the Full Moon on the 9th. If you're feeling a little more on the quiet side, spend a weekend reading one of those steamy novels or writing out your fantasies in your private journal. It's time to let your imagination stimulate the music of your heart. If you've been hesitating about telling someone how you feel, then do something that shows your feelings from the 9th–23rd.

CAREER AND FINANCE

This is a great time to smooth out rough edges in the work place and to clarify any problems that may have arisen with your co-workers. If you're going to do your best work and have fun with it, then the environment needs to be clear and supportive. Your fanciful creativity is working overtime after the 7th, and you may even be ready for a different job after the New Moon on the 23rd. Sharpen those skills and give yourself room to rumba!

OPPORTUNITY OF THE MONTH

Working cooperatively with others is a plus and you can even change your working conditions so that you're able to do your best work from the 5th–11th and after the 20th.

AFFIRMATION FOR THE MONTH
"My life is filled with love and joy!"

Rewarding Days: 3, 4, 8, 9, 13, 14, 17, 21, 22, 31
Challenging Days: 1, 6, 7, 19, 20, 26, 27

Pisces/August

Primary Focus
Exceptional inspiration energizes your ingenuity, which you'll need to overcome frustrations resulting from Mercury's retrograde. This is a perfect time to concentrate on refining your talents.

Health and Fitness
Recreational activities are a great way to improve your fitness, and you'll benefit from setting new goals or getting involved in a challenging sport or exercise routine. Take it a little easier after the solar eclipse on the 21st, when you need a bit more rest.

Romance and Relationships
Stabilizing your commitment in a love relationship fuels the fire of romance from the 1st–20th, but this is not the best time to exchange marriage vows or to begin a new love affair. Clarifying your feelings and needs in an existing relationship is another story. If you're single, it's safe to indulge in a flirtation after the 15th, but what you see may not be what you get! The fog lifts after the 23rd, so wait until then to determine your course of action.

Career and Finance
Since Mercury is retrograding until the 23rd, you may run into a few snags on the job. Delays caused by mechanical or communication breakdowns can slow you down and it can be difficult to get everything back on track. Try to stay calm during the Moon's eclipse on the 7th, when others' actions may seem out of line with your expectations. Be careful with your money and belongings after the 14th.

Opportunity of the Month
This is a good time to finally finish those projects that have been gathering dust or to clear away the clutter so you have room for something new. This is a time of preparation.

Affirmation for the Month
"I am whole, healthy, and filled with energy."

Rewarding Days: 1, 4, 5, 9, 10, 14, 17, 18, 27, 28
Challenging Days: 2, 3, 15, 16, 22, 23, 29, 30, 31

PISCES/SEPTEMBER

PRIMARY FOCUS
You're especially sensitive and may feel that your emotions are taking charge of your life. But you can direct your emotional responses once you get to the center of yourself. Spend extra time in contemplative activities to tune into your intuitive voice more clearly.

HEALTH AND FITNESS
Allow time in your routine to care for your body, but you need to avoid high-risk activities from the 1st–12th. Watch your driving, too, and pay attention to the other guy.

ROMANCE AND RELATIONSHIPS
The Moon's eclipse in Pisces on the 6th draws your attention to your deeper feelings and needs about marriage and partnership. This energy can stimulate a period of crisis that can be used to clarify your hopes and needs and bring harmony into the relationship. You may finally decide that you're ready to renew vows or make a long-term commitment. Your hopes are high during the New Moon on the 20th.

CAREER AND FINANCE
Legal matters, contractual agreements, and business arrangements that involve the support and energy of others work to your benefit after the 6th. Watch for hidden clauses or power plays from the 9th–12th, when you may end up feeling manipulated if you've missed these details. Take action to improve your working conditions or increase your productivity this month. Your creativity and artistry are powerful resources this month, so put them to good use.

OPPORTUNITY OF THE MONTH
Social events and casual interaction with others can provide excellent options for strengthening your reputation while putting you in touch with good sources of support.

AFFIRMATION FOR THE MONTH
"I project an image that allows my true light to shine brightly."

Rewarding Days: 1, 2, 5, 6, 9, 10, 13, 14, 15, 23, 24
Challenging Days: 11, 12, 18, 19, 26, 27

Pisces/October

Primary Focus

Diving into the deeper levels of your psyche can be a fascinating experience. Metaphysical, spiritual, and psychological studies and practices can be a source of strength.

Health and Fitness

You may be feeling a little more competitive after the 8th, and sometimes fitness and sports are good ways to channel this type of energy. Break destructive habits and eliminate things from your life that undermine your overall sense of well-being.

Romance and Relationships

If you're going to reach the levels of intimacy you crave, you may have to remove some of your own inhibitions and fears. Even if you have a partner who seems to be the source of some of the problems, look first at yourself during the Full Moon on the 5th. Then, strive to open the doors of communication and understanding with your lover. If it's going to work, you'll know. If not, you may part after the New Moon on the 20th.

Career and Finance

Joint finances undergo surprising changes from the 1st–9th and can provide an excellent chance for everyone involved to achieve more autonomy. But if someone is acting selfishly, disputes can arise and you may be involved in a full-blown power struggle by mid-month. Schedule business meetings, conferences, and presentations after the 14th, and consider the benefits of business travel, advertising, or publishing after the 24th.

Opportunity of the Month

Expanding your horizons is easy once the barriers are out of the way. Find ways to remove them from the 3rd–24th.

Affirmation for the Month
"My cooperative spirit attracts cooperation from others."

Rewarding Days: 3, 4, 7, 11, 12, 20, 21, 22, 30, 31
Challenging Days: 1, 9, 10, 15, 16, 17, 23, 24

PISCES/NOVEMBER

PRIMARY FOCUS
You're more high-profile now, so be aware of how others interpret your actions, especially in education and career realms. This is a wonderful time to gain the support of others or to expand your business.

HEALTH AND FITNESS
Before you get started in a new fitness class or sport, make sure you're aware of your body's needs and limitations. If you're uncertain, consult your health-care professional before you begin. Then, set goals that will help you increase your endurance.

ROMANCE AND RELATIONSHIPS
Loving relationships grow through developing a meaningful spiritual connection, and you'll be more open with your partner if you know he or she supports and understands your ideals. A retreat or inspiring experience can lead to romance during the Full Moon on the 4th. In your own search for truth and wisdom, you may also uncover a more profound quality of love during the New Moon on the 18th.

CAREER AND FINANCE
Be clear about what your superiors, co-workers, and partners expect and need from you, and make sure that they also know your plans and capabilities. Your expertise gives your career a boost, but only if you really know what you're doing. Otherwise, you can run into problems if you attempt something beyond your capacity from the 1st–15th. Changes at work can alter your plans once Mercury retrogrades on the 21st, so give yourself some latitude.

OPPORTUNITY OF THE MONTH
Your philosophical ideals are extremely important, and if you're facing a situation that tests your values against something you feel is against Truth, you already know the best option.

AFFIRMATION FOR THE MONTH
"My words and actions are guided by my higher self."

Rewarding Days: 3, 4, 7, 8, 17, 18, 22, 26, 27
Challenging Days: 5, 6, 12, 13, 14, 19, 20

PISCES/DECEMBER

PRIMARY FOCUS
Your life path comes into focus now, and you're ready to move into a direction that brings your higher ideals and needs for creativity into greater harmony. Not only can your career be more rewarding, but you may also be helpful to others who need your support.

HEALTH AND FITNESS
Get to the core of physical discomforts, since ignoring problems can spell trouble. Eliminate the things from your life that work against you. It will be easier now than later, so what are you waiting for?

ROMANCE AND RELATIONSHIPS
Maintaining a balance between personal and professional needs can be rather trying, particularly near the Full Moon on the 3rd, when you may want to be two places at once. Arrange your priorities so that you're satisfying your deeper needs, but make sure you're not caving in to manipulation by someone else. The sexual elements of your intimate relationship can strengthen your bond with your partner, so allow time to enjoy one another more fully.

CAREER AND FINANCE
Although Mercury ends its retrograde cycle on the 11th, you may still be dealing with the fallout from some of the problems until the end of the month. Be very careful with important documents, financial agreements, and anything that is classified, since these areas show particular vulnerability. Wait to sign significant contracts until after the 23rd.

OPPORTUNITY OF THE MONTH
This is an excellent time to do research, investigate hidden problems, or uncover facts. The way you use the information is crucial, so think before you act!

AFFIRMATION FOR THE MONTH
"I freely release the things I no longer need."

Rewarding Days: 1, 5, 6, 14, 15, 24, 25, 28, 29
Challenging Days: 3, 4, 9, 10, 16, 17, 18, 30, 31

PISCES ♓ ACTION TABLE

These dates reflect the best (but not the only) times for success and ease in these activities, according to your sign.

	Jan.	Feb.	Mar.	Apr.	May	June	July	Aug.	Sept.	Oct.	Nov.	Dec.
Change Residence						1–14						
Ask for a Raise		26, 27										
Begin a Course of Study				26, 27							19, 20	
Join a Club												19, 20
Begin a Romance					24, 25							
Visit a Doctor		2–19					1–31	1–31	1–7			
Start a Diet	13, 14	9, 10	9, 10	5, 6	2, 3, 29–31	26, 27	23–25	20, 21	16, 17	13, 14	9–11	7, 8
Seek Employment	1–11						1–31	1–31	1–7		1–30	1–31
Take a Vacation	20–22	17, 18	16, 17	12–14	10, 11	6, 7	3–5, 30, 31	1, 27, 28	23, 24, 25	20, 21, 22	17, 18	14, 15
End a Relationship			13									
Change Your Wardrobe						15–30						
Seek Professional Advice	15–17	12, 13	11, 12	7, 8	4–6	1, 2, 28–30	26, 27	22, 23	18, 19	15, 16	12, 13	9, 10
Have a Make-Over		26, 27										
Obtain a Loan	18, 19	14, 15	13, 14	10, 11	7, 8	3–5	1, 2, 28, 29	24, 25	21, 22	18, 19	14–16	11–13

THE TWELVE HOUSES
OF THE ZODIAC

You may run across mention of the houses of the zodiac while reading certain articles in the *Sun Sign Book*. These houses are the twelve divisions of the horoscope wheel. Each house has a specific meaning assigned to it. Below are the descriptions attributed to each house.

FIRST HOUSE: Self-interest, physical appearance, basic character.

SECOND HOUSE: Personal values, monies earned and spent, moveable possessions, self-worth and esteem, resources for fulfilling security needs.

THIRD HOUSE: Neighborhood, communications, siblings, schooling, buying and selling, busy activities, short trips.

FOURTH HOUSE: Home, family, real estate, parent(s), one's private sector of life, childhood years, and old age.

FIFTH HOUSE: Creative endeavors, hobbies, pleasures, entertainments, children, speculative ventures, loved ones.

SIXTH HOUSE: Health, working environment, co-workers, small pets, service to others, food, armed forces.

SEVENTH HOUSE: One-on-one encounters, business and personal partners, significant others, legal matters.

EIGHTH HOUSE: Values of others, joint finances, other people's money, death and rebirth, surgery, psychotherapy.

NINTH HOUSE: Higher education, religion, long trips, spirituality, languages, publishing.

TENTH HOUSE: Social status, reputation, career, public honors, parents, the limelight.

ELEVENTH HOUSE: Friends, social work, community work, causes, surprises, luck, rewards from career, circumstances beyond your control.

TWELFTH HOUSE: Hidden weaknesses and strengths, behind-the-scenes activities, institutions, confinement, government.

LLEWELLYN'S

1998
SUN SIGN
ARTICLES

CONTRIBUTING WRITERS:

Donna Cunningham,
Estelle Daniels,
Alice A. DeVille,
Ronnie Gale Dreyer,
Ken Johnson,
Barbara A. Koval,
Kim Rogers-Gallagher,
Jeraldine Saunders,
Noel Tyl

ABOUT OUR CONTRIBUTORS

DONNA CUNNINGHAM has written ten books, including *The Moon in Your Life* (Samuel Weiser Inc., 1996) and *Moon Signs* (Ballantine Books, 1988). She writes a column for *Dell Horoscope* magazine.

ESTELLE DANIELS is a professional, part-time astrologer and author of *Astrologickal Magick* (Samuel Weiser Inc., 1995). She also writes for *The Mountain Astrologer* magazine.

ALICE A. DEVILLE has been a professional astrologer for more than twenty years. She is an intuitive consultant, writer, and spiritual teacher specializing in business, career, and personal issues.

RONNIE GALE DREYER is an internationally known astrological consultant, author, lecturer, and teacher. She is the author of *Vedic Astrology: A Guide to the Fundamentals of Jyotish* (Samuel Weiser Inc., 1997) and a contributor to the anthology *Astrology for Women: Roles and Relationships* (Llewellyn, 1997).

KEN JOHNSON is a professional astrologer and author of *North Star Road* (Llewellyn, 1996). He also co-authored *The Silver Wheel* (1996), *The Grail Castle* (1995), and *Mythic Astrology* (1993), all from Llewellyn.

BARBARA A. KOVAL is a professional astrologer who publishes a monthly newsletter on astrology and stock-market trends, *Intelligent Market Insights*. She is the author of *Time and Money: The Astrology of Wealth* (Llewellyn Publications, 1993).

KIM ROGERS-GALLAGHER is a writer, speaker, and editor of *Kosmos* astrology magazine. She writes monthly columns for *Welcome to Planet Earth*, *Dell Horoscope*, and *Aspects* magazines. Her first book is *Astrology for the Light Side of the Brain* (ACS Publications, 1996).

JERALDINE SAUNDERS is a professional astrologer who lectures on astrology, graphology, and numerology. Drawing on her experience as a cruise-ship director, she wrote *The Love Boats*, which inspired the long-running *Love Boat* TV series in the 1970s. She has written eleven books, including *Signs of Love* (Llewellyn, 1990).

NOEL TYL has been a professional astrologer and lecturer for more than twenty years, and has written and edited many astrology textbooks for Llewellyn Publications, including *Predictions for a New Millennium* (1996) and *Synthesis and Counseling in Astrology: The Professional Manual* (1994).

ON THE PATH TO PROSPERITY:
A JOURNEY THROUGH THE SIGNS

BY ALICE A. DEVILLE

F ew of you celebrate the new year without giving some thought to financial goals and your overall state of prosperity. Fresh from the glow of the holiday season, you experience a cycle of renewal that inspires you to share, care, and give thanks for your blessings. You greet the glorious year ahead with a new level of expectancy in terms of growth, accomplishment, and personal satisfaction. To feel in your innermost being that you will achieve what you set out to do puts you at the threshold of prosperity. Now it is up to you to take that leap into the void and make those inner reflections a reality.

What you hold in your heart about prosperity determines how successfully you experience it. Your thought patterns can lead to a world of success or a prison of gloom. Negative thoughts do not bring positive results. Fear can paralyze you into doing nothing when a viable plan would solve your problems. Optimism and a clear idea of what you want to do in the year ahead make a difference in your success cycle.

Prosperity wears many faces. The key is unlocking your potential and understanding the specifications that make you feel wealthy. While most of you equate prosperity with having money, you may not realize that *you* are your own best resource. That's right, and the resulting energy exchange is one that *you* create. So are you choosing from a menu or taking life as it comes? If you're ready for a change, you may find profound insight in an astrological interpretation of your attitude about prosperity.

Each Sun sign embraces prosperity with a unique perspective and desired end result. If things have seemed out of kilter, you may be unaware that you are generating conditions contrary to your hopes and desires. You could be experiencing a transit from one of the planetary visitors known as Saturn, Uranus, Neptune, or Pluto. Their intimate contacts with your natal-chart placements indicate areas where transformation is necessary to the success of your prosperity goals.

Perhaps this is your year to make a career change, expand your business, or learn a new skill. The time may be right to complete the company merger, hire a new team, or expand the operation in a foreign market. You may be contemplating a new car, a trip to an exotic island, or the purchase of a dream house. Maybe this year you want to improve the quality of your relationships or seek avenues of spiritual growth. If you would like a natal chart, see the back of this book for an order form from Llewellyn's Computerized Astrological Services. In any case, consult your astrologer for an up-to-date assessment of your chart. Timing is of the essence in making meaningful changes, and no discipline reveres it more than astrology. Your prosperity cycle depends on being at the right place at the right time. Synchronicity occurs when you exercise options on dates that maximize your effectiveness.

Let's take a look at the Sun signs to see how each embraces prosperity. If you have had an astrology chart constructed based on the time, date, and place of your birth, also read the information that corresponds to the sign on your Ascendant or Moon.

ARIES: EXERCISE YOUR CREATIVITY

You are your own money, Aries, when your creativity quotient gets a workout. To increase your cash flow, you are drawn toward speculative investments and dramatic takeovers or financial coups. Nothing turns you on like competition, the ingredient you need to sustain your interest in a new project or group endeavor. You believe there are golden opportunities everywhere and will act on a hot tip at the drop of a hat, especially if the financial return seems imminent.

Partnerships normally work best for you if your ideas and ingenuity drive the machine and the partner picks up and runs with the pieces that bore you. In other words, you want someone at bat in the cleanup position. Leading becomes you, makes you feel prosperous and in charge of your life. You like to take credit for accomplishments and don't particularly care to share the limelight. If someone has been unusually cooperative on your behalf, you do respond to the effort. Bonuses or pricey lunches are prosperity rewards you are likely to share with those who carry out your wishes or make you look good. Some Aries prefer to give high-tech phones or other leading-edge gadgets to stellar performers. Yes, Aries, the better you look, the more generous you will be to partners, associates, subordinates, or co-workers.

You feel prosperous when someone gives you an exotic gift, and you return the show of generosity with an equally unique offering. Very few Aries would turn down free airline or cruise tickets. In fact, many of you fervently visualize yourself winning contests that offer vacations in far-off lands—and enter often.

True, Aries, you sometimes wind up sitting through lengthy sales pitches in return for all-expenses-paid weekends at ski or beach resorts. Although you may duck out early, this routine charges your batteries and you soak up lots of sun, fun, and adventure anyway. The return on your time investment makes you more creatively productive when you return to the workplace. Since athletic Aries understands the need to regenerate by combining work with sufficient doses of play, a healthy routine is important for you in the years ahead, when Saturn has a transforming effect on your physical body. One of your prized investments may be a new trampoline or treadmill to keep you fit.

Your prosperity attitude has been challenged since April 1996, when Saturn, the planet of responsibility and restriction, entered your sign for a lengthy stay through February 1999. Aries, you have not missed the signs and signals! You are being called on to lead, get along with others, and shape up. Impatience and lack of balance in relationships highlight the need for other options. You are chomping at the bit for new structure that may include a job or career transition, a promising partnership, or an intense fitness routine. Friendships and groups are undergoing transformation and you are most likely building new relationships of a personal and business nature. Since you must derive satisfaction from any work you do, you have probably accepted a new position or are working feverishly behind the scenes on a more prosperous, rewarding endeavor.

Aries, everyone knows you want the self-replenishing pot of gold handy to satisfy your purchasing goals. You usually have plenty of confidence in your earning potential and don't hesitate to spend the money you make. With Saturn pointing out the need for new rewards, you're in gear to make some powerful investments in the year ahead. Your purchasing preferences may include those ultimate status symbols—a sleek, red convertible to whisk you to your next vacation hideaway, a sparkling diamond ring to pamper your "Precious," or enrollment in a fitness club to keep you looking good. May fun, uplifting ideas flow from your consciousness, and may love reshape your life!

TAURUS: PAMPER YOURSELF

Talented Taurus turns out tempting tarts in a tantalizingly decorated kitchen equipped with state-of-the-art appliances and a well-stocked pantry. Anyone who knows you well, Taurus, is aware that your sense of prosperity revolves around your gourmet tastes in food and wine, served with gusto and genuine hospitality to cherished guests and your esteemed family. You usually make the decisions in determining your kitchen palette, and your dining room appropriately reflects a serene environment for enjoying food where decor may include a colonial wall mural, cherished painting, or antique mirror.

Not that you don't enjoy the amenities of dining out—you are likely to be a premier subscriber to popular discount dining clubs, a restaurant reviewer, or contributing editor to your newspaper's weekly food section. Elegant china and table arrangements make you feel pampered. Flowers are another touch that contributes to your sense of enjoyment. You rave over the ambiance long after the meal is over. The host loves you!

One of the ways you express your prosperity, Taurus, is when you artfully rearrange the living-room furniture. Rather than going out and replacing everything when you are bored with a scheme, your knack for making simple adjustments goes a long way toward rejuvenating the look of a room. Many a Taurean partner, protesting what appears to be considerable expense for new furnishings, has been fooled by the magic you create with a bolt of tapestry, brocade, or lace. No wonder Taurus is often found in the interior decorating and design fields. Your talent makes believers out of the unimaginative and adds reserves to your already stable bank account.

"The king was in the counting house counting out his money," appropriately describes Taurus' prosperity mindset. Most of you have a nest egg and like to know where it is. Counting money makes you feel richer. Whether you stash your holdings behind the piano or in the bank vault, you want to visit your cache frequently. Every dime of interest amps up your sense of security. Not an investment risk-taker, Taurus likes to dabble in the super-safe government treasury or bond markets, or real estate. You like slow but steady growth and prefer to live within your means. When you do take a trip to the casinos, you carefully calculate exactly what you are going to bet and quit as soon as you win or break even. You're not fond of debtor's prison and have been known to turn people down for a loan (not from my reserves!), even though you might have come out ahead in the interest game. When you do part with a few shekels in this manner, you charge a fair interest rate and expect payments on time. You truly respect money and usually excel in handling it.

An elegant gift for tactile Taurus is a crushed velvet purse, a hand-tooled leather briefcase, or a monogrammed marble desk set. You have an uncanny knack for knowing exactly what your friends and relatives need and give practical, attractive gifts. A favorite china pattern may be the focal point of your gift-giving for years to come, until you are sure the recipient has a complete set. Your quirky side is that you are a recycler by nature, and if someone gives you something you can't use, you put it on a shelf rather than return it. Many a giver has received their original gift attractively repackaged long after Taurus remembered who gave it to them in the first place.

The prosperity picture for many Taureans is undergoing challenging vibrations from transiting Uranus in Aquarius. You don't like drastic change, yet you have had your fill of certain issues and conditions and are reaching a slow but steady boiling point where you can ignore reality no longer. Likely areas are work, non-rewarding personal relationships, toxic shame, and education. Some of you will walk away from what you no longer desire; those of you who get in touch with your buried tempers may be shown the door. If you have chosen an untrammeled path, you may find personal satisfaction in new areas of study that lead to resourceful career transition. If you're releasing tension and bridging emotional gaps, creativity flows through your healing Taurus hands as a sculptor, artist, tailor, or hands-on healer. As challenges emerge in the years ahead, know that opportunity knocks and invites you to taste a rare vintage. Embrace new prosperity cycles through centered thinking and Divine inner guidance.

GEMINI: PRIME YOUR MONEY-MAKER

Better than any sign in the zodiac, Gemini, you know the importance of having more than one iron in the fire when it comes to amassing funds. You are curiously excited about new money-making prospects and have a knack for making lots of it with seemingly little effort. As a quick learner of any subject that interests you, entrepreneurial magic usually nets you a gold mine in record time. A true surfer of Universal knowledge, you know what's hot and quickly package new information and products before most of us learn the current buzz words. By the time the rest of the world catches on, you have moved on to the next invention. It had better be lucrative! Yes, I'm suggesting you easily get bored with your work and have materialistic interests at heart when juggling your many options. Imagination and variety drive your psyche, so it's no surprise that you sink your clever hands into more than one project at a time. The more seed money you generate, the more you can afford the luxuries in life that keep you happy. You like to spend what you earn and the saying "Money burns a hole in his pocket" easily reflects your Geminian tendency to go overboard in treating yourself to an instant reward for a job well-done. When you receive a bonus or windfall, you already know what new "toys" are languishing on the store shelves waiting for your complete enjoyment. You often buy the same item in two or three different colors or models. After all, duality is one of Gemini's traits. Why have only one of a good thing?

The "multiple thing" expresses Gemini's prosperity style. One of my Gemini clients has a unique collection of telephones. She moved into her newly built home with many more phones than she had rooms. Her solution? She had multiple phone outlets installed in several of the rooms so she could display her instruments. The bedazzled construction crew, who usually referred to the homes by lot number, labeled my client's home "The Gadget Phone Factory." She even arranged for three telephone numbers, to allow even more opportunities to use her multiple phones. If you have the idea that you Geminis spend freely, you are partially right. You don't always consider your checkbook's "big picture" before fulfilling a whim. Not that you don't pay your bills, but it does seem like torture to sit down long enough to study the relationship between your income and your budget. You might miss a sale or the opportunity to play Santa Claus.

Yes, you Geminis enjoy bestowing gifts on your loved ones and are seldom last-minute purchasers—your dilemma is keeping the number of gifts per person to a minimum. Everything looks good, so you buy several gifts for each occasion. You're hooked on flyers or catalogs and read each and every page to make sure you don't miss something that might be just right for your friend or you. Unless you sleep on your selections before sending in an order, you are apt to do some expensive impulse shopping. The advertising media found its best customer in you, one who revels in attractive packaging, the perfect find, and a good sale price.

Your level of expectancy is also high when it comes to receiving gifts. You show enthusiastic gratitude for items that provide intellectual challenge and game skills, concert or theater tickets, unique silver jewelry, or dashing clothing. You feel pampered and prosperous when someone gives you a specially selected, beautifully wrapped gift. In your thank-you note, you are just as apt to describe the elegant packaging as you are the contents. Gourmet food gifts, strikingly wrapped and packaged as a tower, fill the bill. You love surprises, especially if the gift meets your standard of quality. It is difficult for you to fake enjoyment over a present that is an obvious afterthought and does not reflect your taste. You like the unique but not the ridiculous. If disappointed, your well-known Gemini sarcasm is apt to surface in your "thank you" re-marks. "I took one whiff of the peanut butter-scented stationery you sent me and decided to conduct a taste test here at the office to see if employees can tell whether smooth or crunchy went into the paper."

Speaking of food, you love trendy smorgasbords that appeal to your diverse palate. When you entertain, you choose buffets or cocktail parties and offer guests several food varieties—way too many. Anyone expecting just tidbits will regret eating a big meal before one of your parties, and leftovers travel home with grateful guests.

During the next few years, partnerships light up your prosper-ity pathway. You may experience either trips to the altar or emo-tional trainwrecks. Truth sets you free. Face it and move on. True love is in sight. Choose partners who cherish your time together, love you for your fine mind, and give you space to grow. Joy becomes you.

CANCER: HARNESS YOUR CREATIVITY

Cocoon-building Cancers carry on contentedly by turning every corner of the home or office into a work of art or unique conver-sation piece. Your flair for decorating may bring you prosperous amenities as a primary occupation where you receive lavish praise and big bucks for your striking creations in interior decorating and design. If these talents are your sideline, you excel as an arm-chair advisor and consultant, or as a trusted home coordinator for family and friends. One Cancer client's mother asked for her help in selecting everything from custom paints to chandeliers; home-improvement specialists wanted to hire her after visiting her home; and the closets in her bedrooms looked like small finished rooms—beautifully painted, papered, and shelved.

Cancers feel successful in noticing detail and seeing how to make a good thing look better. One Cancer, visiting a new home construction site, wandered dreamily through the model discussing improvement options for every room with her spouse. Her "If I were the designer" comments were overheard by the builder's agent, who discreetly followed the couple on their tour of the home and ultimately passed them on to the architect. The builder seriously applied many of her ideas by redesigning major features of the home, the Cancer bought one of the models, and ultimately received a job offer at the sales site from the builder (another Cancer). If remodeling and redecorating are not enough, you Cancers also enjoy rolling out the red carpet for family and friends. A love affair with your oven inspires you to create silky soufflés, coveted casseroles, and chocolate-coated confections for ravenous guests. Guests have been known to fast all day in order to do justice to your culinary treats. You usually turn down offers of help in preparing your party or dinner feast, but welcome clean-up crews. Cancers love their quiet time and worry that distractions from early visitors could disrupt the final touches of meal preparation. Many a sidetracked Cancer has forgotten a dish or two that is waiting in a spare refrigerator (and probably didn't need anyway, but Cancer equates abundance with a well-stocked pantry and a filled tummy). Guests seldom leave early and you don't chase them out, as you love to hear praise for your gastronomic efforts.

You experience fluctuating prosperity cycles, Cancer, due largely to the emotional state that precedes action. If you are up, you go for the risk; if down, you procrastinate and often lose out on high returns. Your intuition often saves the day in preventing financial disasters or in prodding you to make that necessary decision. Many of you amass quite a fortune in real estate and domestic products, and earn a big windfall under speculative conditions, surprising yourself and others with your ingenious moves.

Over the past several years, opposing Neptune in Capricorn has distracted you from financial plans designed to increase your prosperity. Partners pushed you off-course long enough to see your fiscal solidarity shrink through divorce, zany ventures, delayed sale of stocks, or debt. Shifting career goals and market resources have you starting over or taking a new look at how you make your money. Don't worry, there is more of it in sight. Stay flexible and flowing and everything you touch in 1998 will be a glowing success.

LEO: BASK IN GENEROSITY

Lordly Leo wants dominion over the financial empire and likes to spend, spend, spend. You usually have big plans for future dates and are impressed by any shortcuts that may get you there sooner. Never in a quandary when asked what you would do if you won a million dollars, you have your lists and revised lists ready for the interview. You are generous to a fault and seldom forget charities or special causes. Your private list is likely to include the personal wish of a friend or relative and you bestow financial blessings magnanimously. Being a "secret pal" suits you, especially if you are an early Leo.

You like surprising others with unusual gifts—the more expensive and impressive, the better. The bills may shock you later, but you don't even think about it when you are off on an impulse buying streak. You like high impact, even at bargain prices, and add to the Christmas Eve revenue of many a boutique and specialty shop. If an item looks and feels exclusive, you delight in scooping it up for a cherished friend. Often accessories accompany the gift, as you don't like to leave any stone unturned. Why buy the dress for your fiancée without the matching scarf and perfect earrings? These additions put a serious dent in your finances even if you have, for once, budgeted for the main gift. You feel prosperous when you can present a one-of-a-kind or specially designed treasure to someone you like, and you enjoy receiving such gifts yourself. The bigger and more lavishly wrapped the box, the more you feel you have made a statement. When recipients wear or display your tokens of affection, and lavish praise for your generosity, you positively glow in regal contentment.

If you are a business owner, growth and prosperity depend on having excellent support staff in your corner. You probably need a financial advisor to monitor spending so you can avoid cost overruns. With your desire for impressive presentations, business cards that make a dramatic statement, plush surroundings, and a leading-edge advertising campaign, you easily eat up the profits without another conscience to guide you in your strategic execution of the work. The prospect of a big win appeals to you. You are impressed by others' accomplishments, and often leave a meeting eager to launch a similar effort without paying attention to the losses in time and money that it took your rival to get over the top. When you plunge into the game, you become frustrated by the slow return and may leave projects unfinished. This blind spot costs you dearly in dollars and Leo pride, and you may beat yourself up for a while before you find your next enterprise.

A vacation to a sunny climate is sweet balm for many of you leaping Lions. You like to travel in the fall, when the crowds are gone or in winter, when you can recharge your creative batteries at resplendent resorts that offer indulgent creature comforts. A cruise ship is the royal choice of many a Leo for the fulfillment of fantasy, adventure, and service at a price. Leo often returns from a hiatus with a maxed-out credit card and can't remember the spending details when the statement arrives.

In the next few years, you have an opportunity to add to your personal income by valuing what you do, putting your creative talents to work, and reducing debt. Let the power of Spirit move through you to break new ground and harvest financial blessings.

VIRGO: STRIVE FOR SECURITY

You probably sit up nights thinking about the current state of your prosperity. Security comes first with you and you want a sure thing, so you normally pass up opportunities to invest that you haven't thoroughly researched. Some of you still want to see the paper paycheck rather than evidence of an electronic transfer. You respond to a hot tip by dropping it like a hot potato. Of course, you do kick yourself when it pays off and think of how much richer you could have been if you had listened. Many members of your sign equate security with zero debt and let the grass grow underfoot rather than tempt fate with an unknown revenue risk. One Virgo client refused to shelter some of his government income in a thrift savings plan because he feared that he might need it to pay an unexpected bill, depite the fact that he might have sheltered his income-tax base or borrowed against it if the need did arise!

In 1998, many Virgos will spend more than they would like because their partners are challenging the purse strings. Yes, your partner wants you to part with some of the savings to satisfy pent-up needs like new carpet, appliances, and an outside paint job. Partners may be threatening to leave unless you buy a new wardrobe, spring for a state-of-the-art computer or a week's vacation. Some of them want you to be downright frivolous—twin motor bikes, an espresso machine, or a house addition. If the request is a utilitarian toy, like the new computer, you just might go along with it. Your partner may be able to generate additional income or you can keep better budget records!

Ever the bargain hunter, you may take great pride in telling others how much money you saved on purchases of personal goods or gifts for others. "This is the cheapest I could find" is often echoed by a Virgo who revels in the realized savings over the quality and workmanship of the goods. You tend to do considerable comparison shopping before you make a purchase and will drive miles out of the way to get the best price. Recipients of your gifts benefit from practical items or a safe rather than unusual gift. Knowing your "no frills" reputation, friends are not eager to surprise you with something you may not need. Wise shoppers stick with books, cash, and savings bonds. Besides, detail-eyed Virgo may find a flaw and take it back. Now you know why you receive so many gift certificates (and give them yourself) or donations to your favorite charity. One Virgo gave the same cash gift to the same people for every occasion for a dozen years, then increased the amount by $5 apiece to keep up with inflation.

While not all Virgos are cheapskates, many of you remind gift recipients about how much things cost or how hard it is to sacrifice for your loved ones. You do not realize the impact of your words on others, and how much withholding your heart energy may be cramping emotional growth. Parting with reserves, investing, and sharing with others increases your prosperity potential. Shed fears associated with a poverty consciousness and you will significantly increase your creative development and state of wealth in the new millennium. Be generous to your inner child!

LIBRA: SEARCH FOR BALANCE

Personal areas of creativity mean much more to you than high-risk ventures, so you make money if you find the right combination in career or adventure. You need appreciation for your work contributions to be further inspired to produce your greatest work. Sensitivity and inner awareness drive you to great heights of accomplishment and simultaneously create inner tension, usually because you have to fine-tune the work and don't want to drop any facet of it. You often procrastinate rather than act, adding to the nervous tension that often finds you spending far too much time on one thing or another.

Prosperity means creative, entrepreneurial, and social opportunities to you. You thrive on that combination and need people around you to share ideas and help with the decision-making. You desire harmonious work and home surroundings and add beautiful, personal touches for an inspiring touch. Your work may be highly technical or delightfully aesthetic, but balance is important and that is your greatest challenge. Being presented with more than one option throws you a curve. When you don't like your work, you grumble incessantly and everyone knows you're miserable. A lot of the complaining is just blowing off steam, kind of a coping mechanism, yet you saddle others with your tales of woe. Many of you profess a desire for change, yet remain long-suffering in miserable environments rather than forge a new path. You are your own money when your work offers opportunities to maximize your desire for harmony and recognition.

Few of you pass through life without a benefactor. Libras often receive automobiles from assorted friends and relatives or down payments on their dream homes. Others receive hot financial tips from contacts and profit royally. You may be involved in the world of finance and learn self-sufficiency by graduating from the school of hard knocks. Like Leo, you tend to live for today and crave luxuries now. You don't like to suffer. While there are notable exceptions, your attitude about money is often to spend now and worry later. If you had a fiscally conservative upbringing, you may imitate the family spending patterns and question the need for them much later during a mid-life crisis.

You enjoy giving a loved one the perfect gift and spend hours selecting the right one. Colognes, scented papers, grooming aids or treatments, ornate vases, and conversation pieces, especially antiques with romantic flair, are among your favorite items to give or receive. The gift wrap and card you choose must convey a personal statement for you to feel completely satisfied with your purchase. Unless you are one of those rare raunchy Libras who goes for the gag gift in a paper bag, gift-giving lends an opportunity for you to demonstrate your refined taste.

The year ahead promises opportunities to develop your shining traits of discrimination, diplomacy, and negotiation where you profit both personally and professionally. As you change your approach to work and relationship problems, you experience a new prosperity cycle and possibly acquire a new home. Spiritual growth and a desire to resolve old issues with family and friends awaken your capacity to love.

SCORPIO: FLEX YOUR BRAIN

Persistence, regeneration, and dynamic energy are key ingredients in your success cycle, Scorpio. No one bests you when you are on a determined roll to plan, create, and execute a goal. You innately know that power is your best resource and you use it persuasively and effectively to muster interest in financing and promoting your key projects. Your product or concept may go through many rebirths, since you don't particularly see yourself as innovative and distrust your initial judgment. Some of you become critical of what you create or lend too much weight to others' comments. You often beat yourself up for what you perceive as oversights in product integrity. You brood over possible rejection far too long, and this tendency delays your payment and reward cycle.

While you want to be paid well for the work you perform, you Scorpios are not big financial risk-takers. You want progressive returns on your investments and are leery of big killings. You avoid hustlers and hard sales approaches and warn others for their own good. Many of you are apt to retain a good attorney rather than a financial advisor.

Your complex mental skills are your money-maker, Scorpio. When you unravel mysteries or solve problems that no one else has the patience to tackle, you are at your best. "Thorough" and "troubleshooter" appropriately describe your approach and you earn a well-deserved reputation for accomplishing the impossible. No wonder so many of you are crackerjack detectives, private eyes, forensic experts, or undertakers. The sheer intricacy of these professions should net you a lucrative energy exchange.

Your elusiveness challenges gift-givers who sincerely want to please you, yet have seen your reaction to previous offerings. You want to feel a gift was specifically chosen with your distinct taste in mind. Ho-hum gifts make you cranky and the giver may never receive a thank-you note because you don't appreciate mediocrity. You would much rather receive a bottle of fine wine selected for a memorable meal than a pair of bargain gloves that doesn't match your wardrobe. While you are not particularly known for your generosity, you do indulge your favorite people with dramatic events to celebrate special occasions. Rather than present a gift on the birthday morning, you reserve a favorite table at a classy restaurant, select a memorable wine, and make the gift presentation after the wait staff has indulgently sung "Happy Birthday" to the honored guest. If you're feeling particularly generous, you might even spring for a carriage ride around town, attend the theater or a show, or spend the evening at a four-star hotel complete with champagne service. You prefer romantic settings for vacations as well and enjoy music, dancing, festivals, and international celebrations. A dramatic change of scenery gets you out of the doldrums and lets you relax—something you intense Scorpios rarely do when you're on familiar turf.

Prosperity in 1998 may appear as an investment in a high-tech home or state-of-the-art computer equipment, merging households if you meet your significant other, or the start of a home-based business. Your appreciation of the gifts of the Universe opens new doors. You become a source of inspiration and hope for others who are undergoing personal transformation. The future looks glorious!

SAGITTARIUS: ROLL THE DICE

You love money, Sagittarius, and the more you have, the more you spend. Spending is a status expression that lets you buy, treat, gamble, and feel generally magnanimous toward the world. Intuitively you know that sharing the wealth is virtuous, and you are a generous benefactor to less fortunate beings. Many of you are so conscientious of the deprived that you seldom pass a street beggar without dropping a quarter, dollar, or more into the cup. When warned that you may be donating to a lost cause, you counter with the logic that everyone needs a break and you could be the one giving this poor person a reason to live. You know, Sag, because you have been there yourself—in situations where you don't know where you'll find your next dollar. Gambling and risk-taking appeal to your sense of adventure, and you like to think that fame and fortune are just a few lucky streaks away.

A beleaguered Sagittarius spouse related that one fine day her husband could not get himself to work on public transportation because he did not have the thirty-five-cent fare lying around the house. They dug through sofa linings, raided a depleted piggy bank, and eventually found the necessary change—all in pennies. The Sagittarian luck came through, although addictive card-playing habits were behind this state of impoverishment. That's why so many Sag's like to pad the gambling fund with extra earnings and stashed accounts. You use wise judgment when you have a savings allotment automatically deducted from your paycheck for planned expenses or emergencies. A reformed Sag has financial managers and understanding partners.

Prosperity means doing much more than thinking about tomorrow, Sagittarius—it means putting your plans into action. Inertia freezes your cycle of productivity because unlike other signs, it stays with you for months on end. That's why you need a career that matches your skills. While appreciation and praise are nice, your main perk is money and you are one of those people who complain loudly when the golden handshake replaces the monetary bonus in the workplace. You feel that belt-tightening stifles creativity and destroys incentive.

Giving gifts depends on your personal taste, Sagittarius, and you go all over the map in bestowing gifts you would like to receive on others. You are very generous, yet recipients don't always understand your choices, for you seldom do your homework. On the other hand, you are easy to please because of your diverse interests and friends are seldom stumped when shopping on your behalf. If you are a sports fan, you like just about anything you don't already have. If art and entertainment are of interest, you appreciate gallery passes, tickets, autographed books, compact discs, and dinner certificates. You are mesmerized by statement sweatshirts or imported knits. A consignment shop visit is a hidden treasure hunt where you dig up dapper duds at bargain prices.

With Pluto transiting your Sun sign for the next ten years, you have even greater opportunities to step out in the world and make a statement. Your career and money-making capacity are due for a boost once you define the new structure you seek. You are the spirit, light, and energy of renewed expectation in the new millennium.

CAPRICORN: LIGHTEN UP

Survival is imbedded in your soul, Capricorn, and you are an inspiring role model when it comes to regenerating resources, recycling careers, and recovering lost benefits. You know how to bounce back and win despite devastating setbacks and are eager to test success methods in appealing new ventures. You seldom miss opportunity's knock unless severe over-caution immobilizes your sensing skills.

Feeling good about the whereabouts of your money is essential to your emotional well-being, so leave it in a safe investment house to avoid excess worry. You normally keep close track of your money and have excellent accounting systems to make record-keeping a breeze. Of all the signs, you probably have the first appointment with your tax accountant and file an early return so you can get your refund check in the bank as soon as possible.

Most of you Capricorns fell out of the crib and into the job market. To draw out your creative side, you need to make efficient use of time, money, and other resources. If you feel your proposal is not appreciated, you won't spend much free time in the development arena. Besides, you have been through the mill in terms of financial challenge and don't want to risk depleting the "source" for a chancy enterprise. You get edgy without fund replenishment. Often a workaholic, you find earning two incomes to be routine business. Though you say you want free time to just relax and enjoy life, you will almost always place work at the top of the list and get tasks done before you play. As the zodiac's compulsive list-maker, you audit that list several times a day as you whip through the tasks. Your mental health thrives on positive end-results.

You like assurance that a product will net a profit and want to be paid as quickly as possible for what you do. If you are self-employed, you have the bill in hand and expect payment at the time of service. Likewise, you feel prosperous when you pay your bills on time and see something left over for a rainy day. Getting you to spend it is another matter. Not because you are necessarily thrifty, but because you quickly get caught up in the next job and don't get around to the fun part of your life. "I'll get around to letting go" is your inner echo.

If you can leave your job at home, a pleasure vacation is the most therapeutic personal reward you can experience. Too many of you invariably combine business with pleasure rather than shed the old ball and chain, or you spend that coveted week off completing a home-based project rather than indulging in light-hearted fare. If you do take a break, select off-peak vacation times like mid-fall to avoid the crowds and enjoy sights without long lines. Generally, you prefer elegant lodging and fine food. You don't want to work too hard for your fun or get too messy. One Capricorn male wore dress slacks and shirts to the beach! In reality, your batteries beg for belly laughs and a little bedlam. Give them a break to do wonders for your creative expression and pleasure.

You excel at selecting beautiful, practical, statement-making gifts for the home, office, and library. State-of-the-art shelving and storage devices appeal to your sense of organization. If you are handy around the house or automobile, tools and gadgets are a must. You give them and like to receive them. One Capricorn client gave every male on her holiday list a car vacuum at one time or another. Capricorns cut down on shopping time by buying "hot" items in different colors and designs and giving them to several recipients. It helps if what you buy is on sale, as you are very much aware of the markup on goods and tend to shop carefully, thoughtfully, and economically. Friends enjoy your purchases and often compliment you on taste and ingenuity, usually because your purchase is uniquely practical and something individuals "see" in shops but don't get around to buying for themselves. Avid readers also benefit from your choices, and you enjoy receiving books and audio tapes yourself, especially on self-improvement and money management. Few Capricorns can pass by a bookstore without indulging in a literary treat.

Capricorns have been hanging on by the skin of their teeth in recent years with the transits of outer planets (Uranus, Neptune) through their sign. Lifestyle changes, work reorganization, injuries, and health flare-ups have called attention to old patterns that need rearranging in your life. You currently face decisions about real estate, remodeling, people in your home, and fear-based issues. Some of you could see a nice profit through the sale of your home and find an equally attractive replacement. Others have entrepreneurial goals and may launch lucrative home-based businesses in 1998. Let trust replace fear in your psyche. With your radiant spirit, you can attract anything you want. Be generous with praise and make other people happy. The cornucopia is bursting with Spirit's treasures.

AQUARIUS: SHARE THE WEALTH

Visibility is your rising star in 1998, Aquarius, and you will have lots of it for years to come. After all, you selected this special time to fill the coffers of the Universe with your special wisdom and humanitarian savvy. Timid souls are heading for your doorway, looking for tips on how to be more innovative, something you know a lot about. Be willing to share the wealth of information you possess and inspire others to break out of demoralizing ruts. You've got answers that heal heavy hearts. Gladden them with your optimistic and rational approach to problem-solving. The Midas touch could be dwelling within you right now. Set your price and launch the greatest campaign of your career.

Invention drives your creativity and prosperity cycle. You need intimate involvement with your work to derive great satisfaction from it. When you don't have it, you get cranky and pick apart everything that bothers you about the job and then your life. Either you have a great deal of financial success based on other planets in your natal chart or you invent tools or products that make others rich. You take gift shopping seriously and want to do it in as short a time as possible—often at the last minute, but always ahead of the deadline. Catalog merchants love you. You like the telephone or fax when placing an order and trade with specialty shops, software vendors, or dealers in the electronics field. You like to investigate a product before you buy it or have others do it for you. You feel prosperous giving others big-ticket items that have utility, durability, and pleasing power.

Aquarius feels esteemed when gifts from others reflect a personal touch. An item for a favorite collection makes you happy. Tasteful clothing appeals to your trend-setting nature and you are particular about quality both in fashion and home furnishings. You also appreciate gift certificates for personal services, good books, competitive events, and show tickets. Some Aquarians prefer the pampering gift of a cleaning service, because freedom from drudgery gives you more time for visionary enterprise.

You shine in any creative activity and have no fear of blazing an untried trail. You know you'll produce the results you need to make a difference in the world. Intricate plans often leave you little time to take care of mundane tasks and may interfere with business execution. You are adamant about product integrity and may get bogged down in details. A well-chosen business partner might help you promote your work and take care of administrative issues while you perfect the product. As your creative style requires long incubation blocks, you need a sacred sanctuary where you can work undisturbed until your masterpiece is ready. You go through cycles where you detach from the world for long periods while your agile mental processor creates new product ideas. Frantic friends leave messages begging for the pleasure of your company.

Aquarius, you embrace the planet as a loving home and treat upheavals as opportunities to grow. New challenges come to you in 1998 that allow you to reorder your life and the way you make money. Freedom and transformation are in the air. Each bridge you cross takes you to a higher plane of fulfillment. Use your Uranian wisdom to heal and you will line your pockets with gold. Your energy is vital to the planet.

PISCES: BREAK THE CYCLE

Windows open wide for Pisces this year as new partnering opportunities appear on the horizon or those developed last year solidify. Eclipse energy helps you dissolve old patterns. This could be the year the stranger you meet on the plane turns out to be your loving soulmate or your new boss. Why not break the ice, Pisces, and initiate the opening lines? Your witty chatter could get you out of debt via a well-paying assignment or bring you closer to the altar than you have been in some time. Just leave reticence at home and create the energy exchange you desire. You may land a challenging work detail in a far-off land that puts romance in the air. Take to the skies and give your life the creative lift it deserves.

You need creative enterprise to feel truly prosperous. You're highly emotional about your work and produce your best products under pressure. Once you finish, you experience intense letdown or depression. A change of scenery or a new project prevents physical illness and helps you rebalance your fragile constitution.

No one has to tell you to pack a bag and go on holiday. You know when it's time and escape from boring routines as often as your pocketbook permits. Rarely are you a once-a-year pleasure seeker. You don't wait for companions, either, if you find the right getaway. You invariably meet interesting people along the way and may develop pen-pal relationships after you part. As vacation planners, you opt for magnificence in coordinating every detail and selecting a trip that offers ambiance, variety, and a true sense of the environment. Throw in a lake or an ocean and you are instantly revitalized. You avoid time-share arrangements, preferring new places when you want a respite. You're not frugal about vacation expenses and feel you deserve the pampering for its ultimate effect on your mental and physical health. You expect good service and usually get it. You pack far more clothing, especially shoes, than you actually need and enjoy dressing for dinner in stunning ensembles or suits that give the impression of wealth.

While you have known financial ups and downs, you count your blessings even when your change purse is empty. Your optimism and intuition usually lead to a new revenue source, where bosses are inclined to reward you with a bonus or pay increase for outstanding performance. Job benefits have holding power over your decision to stay or leave a position and you do think about the future and the retirement nest egg. The idea of an emergency fund appeals to you and you exclude the contents from your cache of available funds. You like to remain a bit elusive about your true net worth. You give when others ask you for help; retreat when they ungraciously demand your time and money. Compassion never eludes you but you are no fool.

Pisces, you are truly one of the most thoughtful gift-givers on the planet. You take pleasure in noting what others enjoy and surprise them with special treasures. You don't need a special occasion to give gifts, you just make someone's day with an unexpected token of affection. Most of you shop carefully and seldom buy a present for the sake of showing up with a package. You tend to give romantic gifts of perfume, jewelry, art, ornate cosmetic cases, beaded bags, and crystal to women; artistic silk ties, luggage, fine wine and exotic foods to men. If you know someone is planning a trip, you plan your purchase around their adventure and give travel cases, maps, books, passport folders, and slippers. You like to receive these gifts yourself, especially detailed travel guides, which you read from cover to cover. By the time you reach your destination, you have the scoop on major tourist attractions and your camera is ready to capture scenes that your heart will remember for years to come. An itinerary planner or daybook also makes a great gift for you, as do biographies of entertainers and romantic poetry. You would thoroughly appreciate a carry-on bag that complements your already-vast luggage collection. Anyone who gives you an airline ticket is your friend for life for understanding your need for travel.

Partners need attention from you in the year ahead. Communicate openly with gentleness, kindness, and compassion. Attract business opportunities that provide fulfilling outlets for your creativity and experience. Invest your time, love, and vision in metaphysical pursuits and new health routines. Open the door to revelation and truth, and you will grow spiritually rich in 1998.

ALL IN THE FAMILY:
YOUR BIRTH ORDER AND YOUR HOROSCOPE

BY DONNA CUNNINGHAM, M.S.W.

Y ou are responsible, conscientious, organized, perfectionistic, and highly motivated to succeed. You're a Capricorn, right? Maybe, but you probably are the first-born
in your family. Your mate is too independent for his own good, a
maverick, and rebel who doesn't fit into his family but devotes
much of his energy to his groups or friends. He's an Aquarian,
right? Maybe, but he's probably the middle child. Then there's
your adorable but exasperating little brother—the show-off, the
class clown, with charm out the kazoo, but not someone to rely on
in a crisis. A Gemini-Leo mix? Perhaps, but these traits are also
typical for the youngest of the family.

Psychologists have studied the effects of birth position for
decades, and their results are consistent and fascinating. A very
readable exposition of their findings is Dr. Kevin Leman's entertaining and helpful paperback, *The Birth Order Book* (Dell, 1992).

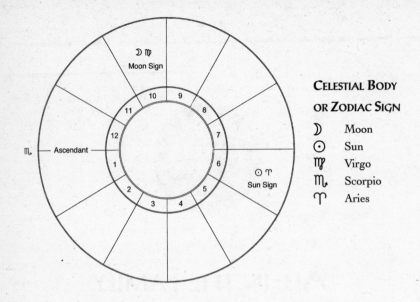

CELESTIAL BODY OR ZODIAC SIGN	
☽	Moon
☉	Sun
♍	Virgo
♏	Scorpio
♈	Aries

Table 1. Sample Natal Chart Showing Placement of Sun Sign, Moon Sign, and Ascendant

Although it pooh-poohed astrology, it moved me to consider how astrology can modify or even increase the effects of birth order. Check out some thoughts on your chart's most important facets—the Sun sign, Moon sign, and rising sign or Ascendant. See Table 1 for an illustration of these placements on a sample natal chart.

ANALYZING YOUR NATAL CHART

The positions of the Sun, Moon, and rising sign (or Ascendant) in your natal chart are important clues to your astrological makeup. To follow these directions, look for the positions of these celestial bodies in your natal chart. Your rising sign was on the eastern horizon when your horoscope was calculated and drawn.

One qualification—you may identify as strongly with the reading for your rising sign as with the one for your Sun sign. The Ascendant and any First-House planets describe the tap dance you learned as a child to get along in your family. Rather than the real you, it represents the role you were assigned by family members. Capricorn rising is often "the responsible one," who had to grow up fast and take on many family responsibilities. Doesn't that echo Leman's description of the first-born? The Moon, which shows a mother's influence, can also be relevant.

Let's take a look, then, at how birth order modifies the nature of the twelve signs. If you don't identify with the description of your Sun, Moon, or Ascendant, perhaps one of the outer planets in the solar system makes an important angle (aspect) to your Sun or sits on your Ascendant. For instance, Neptune aspects give a Piscean flavor, while Pluto imparts a Scorpionic intensity, and a strong Saturn can make you seem like a Capricorn. If you would like to obtain a complete birth chart, see the back of this book for an order form for Llewellyn's Computerized Astrological Services.

As Dr. Leman's book explains, there are many modifications in birth order characteristics, especially with gaps of five years or longer between siblings. The first-born male in a long line of sisters may have a special place. A disabled or otherwise unusual child may make a difference in the lineup, as may step siblings and half siblings. Onlies are a breed of their own, part oldest, part baby. Still, you will undoubtedly see facets of yourself and your siblings in these descriptions.

ARIES SUN, MOON, OR RISING

FIRST-BORN

Except where planetary aspects interfere, the leadership qualities of your sign are enhanced by the steadying effects and strong motivation to succeed of your birth position. An Aries thrives on being first, and you were the ground-breaker for your siblings and now for your set or workplace. Just don't take your followers' compliance for granted, for a good leader is also a good listener.

MIDDLE CHILD

The rebel or maverick side of the middle position would be even stronger in an Aries native, who fumes at criticism or being told what to do. You are ill-suited for mediation, so you are apt to strike out on your own with even more independence than most middle children. Just be sure the groups you so naturally lead don't wind up leading you astray.

LAST-BORN

Aries thrives on attention—indeed, demands it—and so does the youngest of the family. When you don't get your way, temper tantrums are a temptation. Don't indulge in such ploys too often, as they won't make people love you any more than they already do for your freshness, zest for living, and razor-sharp wit.

TAURUS SUN, MOON, OR RISING

FIRST-BORN

Except where planetary aspects interfere, adding the self-discipline and success potential of the first-born to the solid business sense and perseverance of a Taurus can result in a steady climb to the top and a healthy bottom line. As both first-borns and Taureans can be conservative, you are likely to stick to the tried and true path to success.

MIDDLE CHILD

You are the least conservative natives of the sign, for you're enough of a free spirit to stray from the tried and true. The family business is not for you, because you want to make it on your own—and you probably will, but you'll complain that you get no respect or recognition from your loved ones. In your quest to belong somewhere, you may have to learn the lesson of not mixing money and friendship more than once.

LAST-BORN

It's tempting for the Taurean "youngest of the family" to equate money and lavish gifts with the unconditional love your birth position craves. Conspicuous consumption can also be used as an attention-getter, but don't equate possessions with self-worth. You are one of the best-grounded last-borns in the zodiac and thus are likely to do well for yourself.

Gemini Sun, Moon, or Rising

First-Born

More focused and disciplined than the average Gemini, you are likely to excel in scholarly pursuits or communication. Siblings being a major concern, you may well take on more responsibility or worry about them more than is healthy. If there is a family newsletter or round-robin letter, you're doubtlessly the editor.

Middle Child

It's hard enough for Geminis to keep their identities separate from relatives without being caught between elder and younger siblings, so figuring out who you are and where you fit into life is a long-term project. The middle child's propensity for mediation added to that Gemini flair for words could result in professional excellence as a family or marriage counselor, deal negotiator, or mediator of disputes.

Last-Born

The youngest of the family is often the class clown, and who can play that role better than verbal, witty Gemini? You show off, but with such charm and flair! Still, in crisis times when you need to relinquish center stage and get serious, these usually appealing traits can prove disappointing to loved ones who want you to shoulder your share of the burden.

Cancer Sun, Moon, or Rising

First-Born

You were undoubtedly put in the position of being Mommy's little helper—the responsible big sis or big brother—and you may still be playing the indulgent parent to all the waifs and strays you meet. Though you may well have come far professionally, you haven't forgotten your roots and still can be counted on to nurture your loved ones. There's just that distressing tendency to overeat to make up for the energy you burn taking care of others.

MIDDLE CHILD

The middle child's tendency to feel betwixt and between, not fitting anywhere, is so difficult for Cancers, to whom roots are everything. Though family feuds can prove distressing to your sensitive nature, you can provide a nurturing environment for the disputes to be resolved. Where family ties prove too hard to maintain, you are likely to make a second family among friends.

LAST-BORN

Sorry to say it, but you can be the baby of all babies, looking to find mommies and daddies everywhere, and feeling aggrieved and deprived when the T.L.C. you were brought up thinking you had to have isn't forthcoming. Still, you'll do anything to keep the family alive and to make family times a memorable delight.

LEO SUN, MOON, OR RISING

FIRST-BORN

Talk about the heir apparent—you were born to rule and unless other aspects work against you, your birth position makes your ascension virtually a certainty. Coming first in the family, you doubtlessly soaked up tons of attention and came to see it as your due. Still, your sense of responsibility and keen motivation for accomplishment make you anything but a lazy Leo.

MIDDLE CHILD

What a tough thing for a Leo—to always share the spotlight with older and younger sibs, not to mention Dad, when you really wanted the starring role. Still, as family mediator in that pride of lions, you carved out a memorable niche. You may well seek out community groups where you'd shine due to your capacity to create a small universe around you.

LAST-BORN

The Leo's Leo, Lucille Ball, has nothing on you—you were born to perform and hold court. Seriously, you should find some outlet—even a local theater group—for that charm, flair for drama, and star quality. Otherwise, the perpetual propensity for drama can come out in door-slamming domestic tiffs.

VIRGO SUN, MOON, OR RISING

FIRST-BORN

Virgo is known for being reliable, trustworthy, serious, hard-working, perfectionistic, and critical — and so are first-borns! Thus, unless there is serious interference from a planetary aspect, the first-born Virgo is a paragon, the rock for family and employer. However, unlike the usual striving, success-oriented first-born, modest, self-effacing Virgos are worker bees by nature rather than queen bees, uncomfortable at the helm and likely to be the real but unrecognized center of productivity.

MIDDLE CHILD

Rebel? Maverick? Doesn't sound like conservative, careful Virgo at all, does it? Maybe you just every now and then neglect to change your underwear. But independent, for sure. Perhaps you are a natural for the alternative health fields, where non-traditional but sound approaches and attention to detail are an asset.

LAST-BORN

We'd hardly know you were the youngest of the family at all, as those conscientious and hard-working Virgos shun the center stage and feel love has to be earned. Could you be the exception to the birth-order rule? Or do you unconsciously arrange for the attention your birth position craves by suffering from a variety of psychosomatic ailments?

LIBRA SUN, MOON, OR RISING

FIRST-BORN

The first-born seeks to please and thus can be too placating — as can Libras, so be sure you aren't taking on too much responsibility and overdoing in an effort to keep everyone happy all the time. Too much stress comes from the impossible striving to be perfect — looking perfect, always socially correct, considering everyone's needs and point of view. You have more leadership ability and drive for success than the average Libra, but are likely to lead in a gracious, diplomatic manner.

Middle Child

You are sure to seek love outside your family, since it's hard to compete with siblings for the short supply. Middle children are born mediators and so are Librans, so you will doubtlessly find yourself in this position often. You're gifted at reaching compromises between warring parties, so maybe you should do it professionally. Just don't become too committed to peace at any price!

Last-Born

The Libra need for unconditional love can become an obsession for the youngest of the family. "Love me, love me, love me," is your plea to the world, and you can be so delightfully charming, engaging, and winsome, that this demand is almost—but not quite—fulfilled. It's just that people want such tedious and unglamorous things in return for all that love and attention.

SCORPIO SUN, MOON, OR RISING

First-Born

Combine Scorpio's political savvy and understanding of the dynamics of power and wealth with the first-born's dogged determination to suceed, and you have an unstoppable combination, unless there are other planets interfering. It's up to you whether that power to make things happen is self-serving or dedicated to transforming or reforming parts of our world that need to be healed.

Middle Child

The alienation many Scorpios feel in a society that lives on the surface can be intensified by this birth position, where you are betwixt and between and seldom first in your family's considerations. Still, your keen understanding of underlying motivations and dynamics could make you a natural mediator or healer of family or group conflicts, even as a profession.

Last-Born

Last-borns are often manipulative in their quest to get people to take care of them and can be aggrieved if they don't get the attention they feel they are entitled to. Scorpios have a genius for "psyching out" other people and knowing what buttons to push to get the results they want. The combination of last-born and Scorpio could be a bit much, until you learn to appreciate other people's unspoken needs and motivations as only Scorpio can. As last-born, you can be more easy-going, light-hearted, and fun to be around than the intense and murky type of Scorpio.

SAGITTARIUS SUN, MOON, OR RISING

FIRST-BORN

Academia may well be your forte, for you are a scholar at heart. Even if self-educated, you are a serious thinker, a spiritual seeker. More likely than most of your sign to stay focused on a long-term goal, your natural desire for growth and expansion can make you a success.

MIDDLE CHILD

Your roots may not hold you, and you may become the traveling type of Sag. If you're sports-minded, your team commitment and loyalty can make you a valuable player. In scholarly pursuits or your quest to answer the great questions of the ages, you are likely to strike out on your own and take the road less traveled.

LAST-BORN

What enthusiasm, what pizzazz, what *joie de vivre*—no wonder people seek you out! Unless other planets dampen your spark, you're like the Fourth of July every day. The Fourth of July has its place—but every day? When they expect you to pitch in and clean up after the picnic, you can be long gone.

CAPRICORN SUN, MOON, OR RISING

FIRST-BORN

As we noted earlier, traits attributed to Capricorn and to the first-born are virtually identical, so the combination doubles the perfectionism, drive, and success potential. You doubtlessly had heavy family responsibilities growing up, and the result is a highly capable, reliable individual born to be a CEO, unless other planetary aspects undermine you.

MIDDLE CHILD

With Capricorn's innate desire to rise to the top, you are stuck in a position with older siblings always being ahead of you in learning and younger siblings needing more attention and caretaking. You'll probably find your niche in middle management, for you have a sure sense of how to successfully juggle the demands of those above and below you.

LAST-BORN

If you read the description of your position, you probably think it's hogwash, for Capricorns never get to be babies anyway. They emerge from the womb with lunchbox in hand, headed for prep school. If there really are any last-born Capricorns, they were probably born seven years or more after their older siblings, so they're more like only children—that is, like first-borns in spades.

AQUARIUS SUN, MOON, OR RISING

FIRST-BORN

You're more conservative than most Aquarians—based on your experience, you may even be convinced that the old rulership of your sign by Saturn is true. Still, even though you probably organize as well as any Capricorn and are prone to success, your point of view is original and inventive, and you're in the vanguard of your line of work.

MIDDLE CHILD

One of the first observations I made about birth order was how many middle children are Aquarians. Rebel, maverick, and loyal to your homies? Your special destiny—and most Aquarians want to believe they have one—may well rest in your contributions to groups, and that may have been why you chose a birth position that gave you distance from your family.

LAST-BORN

Would the word zany describe you, by any chance? At the very least you march to an entirely different drummer than anyone in your family—part of what gives you that pied-piper charisma.

Just be sure, when you shock for shock's sake, that you're not shooting yourself in the foot at the same time.

PISCES SUN, MOON, OR RISING

FIRST-BORN

Mother Teresa has nothing on you—you probably adopt every stray dog or human that crosses your path and then wonder why you can't keep all your promises. And guilt? You are *not* single-handedly responsible for the burgeoning national debt or the shrinking rainforests, no matter what you think. Work on loving yourself as human and fallible, and you won't be so overwhelmed.

MIDDLE CHILD

You feel for those above you, you feel for those below you. You can identify and empathize with all their woes, but who are you and where do you belong in the universal scheme of things? Sorting out spiritual and ethical questions like these can keep you busy for the next several lifetimes, but at least you'll probably remember enough about the last few to give you a head start.

LAST-BORN

They doubtlessly call you fey, whimsical, and charming. You're a soulful performer even if you never get on stage, with the heart of a poet or musician, but all too many of you are the type mother warned us against. You know, the type portrayed in the song, "Don't Fall in Love with a Dreamer." Ah, well, the rules don't apply to you anyway, because you're not here to run the local savings and loan.

Remember the suggestion that you include your rising sign and your Moon sign, if you know them or that you send for a computer chart if you did not. Which did you relate to the most? My money is on your rising sign!

WHY AM I HERE?
THE SUN AND CAREER CHOICES
BY KIM ROGERS-GALLAGHER

Why am I here? What's my life's purpose? Every astrologer has heard that question a thousand times. It's a good question—one that folks usually ask when they come to see us during a particularly interesting outer planet transit to the Sun. The outer planets of Neptune, Pluto, and Uranus are those on the outer edge of our solar system.

See, the Sun is who we really are, at the very core of our being. Any planet that touches the Sun by transit jostles us a bit by asking us to incorporate its qualities into the very fabric of our being. Transits of the inner planets are manageable, for the most part, since unless they make a station to turn direct or retrograde right on the degree of our Sun, their influence doesn't last for more than a few days at a time. So while a Mars transit to the Sun certainly can indicate a rather testy period of self-assertion, it's not usually indicative of a long-term, ongoing situation. We stand up to whomever we feel is challenging us, put our foot down, and get over it. Mars and the other inner planets are also more familiar to us. They represent issues we deal with on a daily basis, like expressing our emotions, communicating, loving, asserting ourselves, and so forth.

The outer planets, however, are a bit more persistent. They represent such huge issues as freedom and individuality (see Uranus), inspiration and beliefs (see Neptune), and inevitable change, power struggles, and ending, (see Pluto) — all great, big topics we tend not to consider on a daily basis as we go through the business of our daily lives. These three are also more challenging since they camp out around the degree of our Sun for up to three years — which makes them pretty tough to ignore. Needless to say, then, when an outer planet makes an aspect to the Sun, our whole sense of self undergoes an awakening of sorts — one that lasts a good long time and gives us plenty of opportunities to examine ourselves and to make the kinds of major, sweeping changes that allow us to learn, evolve, and grow.

Fortunately for all of us, astrology can help when the outers touch our Sun and set us to wondering what the point of our life really is. Although this wonderful science of ours can be used for any number of things, the real point of individual astrology is to point out our life's goals — to help each of us understand why we're here, what we're supposed to be studying during our current visit to Planet Number Three, and what our own particular magical quest might be.

THE SUN: YOUR ROAD MAP TO LIFE

Think of it like this: Your life is a journey. You've come here to explore and learn. While your birthchart shows what you packed into your tool kit for the trip, the Sun shows what you've chosen to become this time around. Think about how easily we identify with the characteristics of our Sun-sign — and we identify more with it as we grow older. Needless to say, if we want to really make this journey a fulfilling one, it's very important for each of us to get to know our Sun — and to "feed" it by bringing the types of experiences it craves into our lives as much as possible. We need to learn everything we can about the Sun in our charts, and make sure we give ourselves plenty of opportunities to be whatever we want to be.

Now, everyone's Sun wants the same things: to shine, to accomplish something important, and to be recognized for it. It's a perfect description of the Sun—of what it feels like to live life as if it were an ongoing quest, to keep on reaching for your maximum potential. That's what life is all about—reaching and growing, constantly finding our futures—and that's what the Sun in our charts is all about: It's the side of us we came here to specialize in, the inner child that's always hungry for tomorrow. As a result, the Sun is the best indication of career choice in the chart, but often it's also the one spot that's not investigated to any great length.

Think of it this way: Every corporation has many departments, each with its own director. Each of them is equally important, and each of them has very specific jobs to perform so that the entire corporation can be successful. Well, in an astrology chart, the planets symbolically function as directors or heads of departments inside one large corporation: You. You have a Mercury who runs the Communication Department, a Jupiter who runs the Department of Risk-Taking Ventures, a Pluto who decides when things have gone far enough and it's time to just let go, and a Saturn who makes your rules. Each of them needs to do their job well to contribute to the success of You, the corporation.

As with all management groups, however, they each must also answer to an executive director, to a big cheese who gives the final yes or no to all decisions. The Sun is that executive director, the chief in the chart with the final word on every matter. The Sun itself is the center of our universe, the warmth and light around which all the planets dance. Your Sun is your center, the astrological body which, more than any other planet in your chart, describes your mission, your *raison d'être*, your quest. Most importantly, the Sun represents what you enjoy most, and the lifestyle that suits you best. With all that going for it, and taking into consideration that once we do choose a career, it takes up at least a third of our lives, doesn't it make sense to follow the Sun's bliss when deciding what we really ought to be when we grow up?

Well, sure it does. Getting to know the Sun's "specialty" is absolutely necessary if we want to accomplish our life's journey. So finding out what the Sun really needs sure makes the trip easier. It's like this: Pretend you've decided to drive cross-country—regardless of the reason. You have several options. You can put some gas in the tank and wing it, asking directions as you go, trusting that eventually you'll find your destination—through trial and effort. If you'd like to be a little more prepared, but still want some degree of spontaneity, on the other hand, you can get a pile of maps and tourist guides and lay out the trip yourself. You can also go to an agency like AAA to find the fastest or most scenic way to get you where you want to go, and get the latest information on possible delays or detours due to road construction or other inevitables along the way. It's up to you. Regardless of the type of preparation you choose, if you point yoursef in a particular direction, you'll probably get there.

Once you know astrology is out there, and once you know what it can do, you have the same options available for your life's journey. You might decide to wing it, to just go on instinct, trusting that the universe will provide roadsigns and guideposts as you need them. You might opt to get a copy of your chart and learn to do astrology on your own—or you might consult someone who's an expert in the field, and get their help to lay out your trip one step at a time.

Personally, I recommend the last two options for your long-range planning, and the first option at all times. Yes, the Universe will always get you where you're going, and yes, you'll always need to look out for the "directions" it will send along that won't be found on any map—things you wouldn't know any other way than by actually being there. But if you've got a time limit in mind, a particular mode of travel, or if there are certain stops you'd rather not miss, it's a good idea to plan. That's where your natal chart comes in—it's absolutely invaluable. Since the Sun is at the center of each of us, it's best to find out where we're going before we pack the car.

Let's take a look at each of the signs, and try to get a better idea of what the Sun does best when he's wearing them. One way to better understand the astrological signs is to group them by their genders, elements, and qualities, which describe a sign's energy. The genders are masculine and feminine; the elements are fire, earth, and water; the qualities are cardinal, fixed, and mutable.

ARIES: ACTING ON IMPULSE

When you strike a match, it leaps to life immediately. No hesitation. No second thoughts. It's fast fire—pure impulse. That, in a nutshell, is what Aries is all about. Go. Do. Act. Now.

Now, when I say "pure" impulse, I really mean "pure"—Aries is a very "clean" energy, as honest and spontaneous as they come. There's no time to be deceitful, after all—not if you want to be first. Aries lives in the present, right here in this very moment. So Aries Suns really believe in seizing the day, and just doing it— whatever it happens to be. They believe in seizing everything, matter of fact. They want what they want immediately, although yesterday would be preferable. Failing yesterday, they'll settle for now—but it's got to be right now.

See, Aries is the new-born of the zodiac. Sign number one. So, just like infants, it's not known for its ability to wait. Aries is bright red, me-first, start-your-engine energy, equal parts cardinal quality, masculine gender, and fire element, none of which have time for any heel-dragging. Aries Suns arrive equipped with that double-dose of bright-red spontaneity. There are no obstacles in the Aries mind, either—only a straight line, from where they are, at Point A, to what they want, at Point B. Now, Aries is ruled by Mars, the planet that represents energy. Raw energy. He's the planet that's in charge of taking action—a real let's-do-somethin'- even-if-it's-wrong kind of guy. While we're on the subject of wrong-doing—let's talk about the daredevil stuff, shall we? I mean, you guys have got an impetuous streak that's nothing short of amazing—and nothing if not Mars-inspired. You crave adrenaline—you'll do just about anything to get your pulse rate up. Anything. Skydiving. Exploring. Screaming at the car in front of you at the light because they won't just pull out into traffic the way you would.

But it's not just your driving that's, um, forceful. It's everything. Since Mars is the head of the Department of Assertion, Aggression, and Anger, it's natural that you thrive on conflict, on the rush you get from a you-against-them situation. Any battle will do, too—your "job" is simply to do battle and to learn self-assertion. See, fending off the enemy is the specialty you're here to master. It's like training to work the front lines of the war party: You've got to be brave, and you've got to be strong. So there's got to be constant action in your life. You can't learn to assert when you're not being challenged. So if things ever do get boring, you're not above generating some action to liven things up a bit.

Which brings me to a very important point: An Aries who's bored is a very dangerous critter. You need to be "doing" at all times, to keep tapping off that endless fountain of energy you're packing. If you find you're spoiling for a fight, try to identify the enemy. It might be you. Notice that you tend to be especially testy when you haven't allowed yourself time to be yourself. You folks can only take orders for so long, you see. You need to be in charge, up front, and leading the way.

All that said, Aries, it's no secret that you're the fastest-acting, most impulsive sign around and not everyone else is. So, if your job requires you to take orders, wait, or be nice—give yourself a break and start looking for something else. There's a very primitive side to your nature that longs to go back to cave-man days, when things were so much simpler, when there was no such thing as waiting, and all disputes were quickly solved by a swift crack on the head. When that side of you rears its little head at the giver of the orders, it's time to move on.

See, once you do try to tell an Aries what to do, they automatically begin to think of reasons to fight you every step of the way, since their real "job" is to fight. So the first thing all you rams out there should know about your work is that you need to be in charge of it.

Now, that doesn't mean that you need to necessarily be the boss, although that's the ideal situation for all of you. But you absolutely must be able to make your own decisions about what happens during the course of your day, so if you're not a supervisor or a manager of some kind, consider it. You folks are the idea persons of the zodiac, equipped to start all projects off with a bang—and then pass the torch to the fixed signs to finish.

Of course, other signs out there also like to run the show (Capricorn and Aquarius, for example), so if you're not in a job that allows you to be in charge, you might also consider a career in a field that allows you to work with fire, metal, or muscles—all Mars specialties. Now, of all the planet-sign affiliations, the one that works the best is the relationship between Mars and Aries. Mars is energy, remember. So any Mars-like occupation is tailor-made for Aries, especially if tools or weapons are involved. In fact, any manual trade is a good example—anything from construction to floral design, both of which involve the use of metal tools, whether that tool happens to be a hammer or a florist's knife. Folks in the manual trades aren't afraid of hard work, either—in fact, the hard work most folks avoid is fun for them. Welding is an ideal job for Aries, too—it's working with steel and flame, and it's not easy.

Now, Aries of the male and female varieties are also deliriously happy when they're tinkering around, in, or under a car. Chances are, if you're an Aries, you've got at least two or three to "play" with, anyway—you folks share the same "kindred spirit" feeling with automobiles that some of us have with animals. If you're an Aries and you're drawn to cars, if they're "fun" for you, learn more about them—in the only way you can, of course, the "hands-on" way—and make your hobby your profession.

Careers that involve "enforcement" are also appropriate for you feisty fire-folks, since wearing a uniform allows you to be in charge. I can't begin to tell you how many Aries men I've met who've spent time working as police officers, for example. This profession is also appealing since it puts you Aries types directly in touch with the issue of confrontation, and allows you to do the "Mars thing."

Professions involving the muscular system are ideal for you, too—occupational therapy, for example, or work as a sports-trainer. Aries folks are natural athletes. Any job that requires you to be exerting yourself in some way will make you happy, and maybe even keep you out of trouble.

TAURUS: INDULGING THE SENSES

OK, so you're tired of being called "stubborn." You've probably just about had it with that "stable, reliable" stuff you've been lugging around for years, too—it sounds too much like "boring." "Materialistic" doesn't do much for you, either. Well, fine. Stay tuned and we'll talk about the real Taurus, the secret stuff you don't ever reveal and you'd just love somebody to recognize.

Let's start by going back to basics—as basic as it gets, actually. Let's start with your innate ability to enjoy each of the five senses—to the very max. Let's talk about the beauty you find in perfect silence, and the pleasure of a symphony. About the ecstasy that just the right touch can create, and the peace that comes from watching the colors in a perfect sunset dim slowly behind a mountain range. Let's talk about roses, perfume, and the scent of a perfectly prepared, perfectly seasoned meal—not to mention the bliss of the palate that experiences it. That's a little better, isn't it? Well, good, because all these things—all these earthly delights—are all under your jurisdiction. See, you're a sensory specialist, the type of creature who functions mainly on how things feel, physically. Your senses are super-receptors, and pleasure is very important to you. In fact, of all the signs, Taurus, yours is the one that most appreciates and most feels a part of the earth. You're into experiencing things. Touching. Tasting. Listening.

It's natural, then, that you'd want nothing but the very best of everything in your world, since you know exactly what the best is—and what it isn't, too. You're a born connoisseur—which can be a curse and a blessing—because once you've had the best, you'll never be able to settle for less. That's how you folks acquired the "materialistic" label to start with. Why spend a lifetime wishing you'd had what you enjoy? Spend the extra five dollars on the good wine, the extra five thousand on the quality driving machine as opposed to the car, and whatever it takes to get the good seats—so you're close enough to feel the music. Experiencing the senses is your "job." It's not a bad one, either—there's an awful lot of beauty in the world.

Now, to be fair, you do love your things. You're tapped into outlets for good stuff, too. I'm not talking about Wal-Marts, either—yours are exclusive sources for quality merchandise. You probably get about a catalog a day in the mail.

Of course, being this "up" on what the best is, and loving all the senses like you do, audio perfection means a lot to you. Which means you're the first on your block to have the latest in stereo gear, too. You probably had your CD player long before they actually became available in stores. All this love of the physical does not, by any means, make you materialistic. It does, however, make you a truly sensuous creature, in the truest use of the word.

Now, without treading too close to that "practical" stuff I promised to avoid, I must congratulate you folks on your patience and thoroughness. Taurus is fixed, and it's earth. Think about that. Your reputation for "stubbornness" comes from the fact that it's easy to hold on to quality possessions and situations—there's no need to replace what's bought well, and no need to change horses when the one you've got perfectly accommodates your needs. Why leave home when it's a perfect model of comfort? Moving fixed earth takes work, and it takes patience. It also takes time. So it's not that Taurus is immovable—just that you folks always take your time to do anything. Once you get things just exactly the way you like them, you hate to move them around. If it ain't broke, don't fix it—that's your motto.

Of course, if you really want to get a feeling for what Taurus is all about, go outside after a good spring rain, and take a deep breath. That good, fertile, green smell you'll notice is what Taurus is really all about. It's solid, it's clean, and it's real.

In the body, Taurus rules the thyroid gland, which regulates our metabolism. So it's small wonder you're so in love with the comfort of a daily routine. There's tremendous safety in habits, in the familiarity you feel when your finger traces over a groove it already knows. However, realize that you're just enough of a fixed sign to get a little too fond of routine, and that those wonderful, comforting grooves can become ruts without you ever noticing.

All that said, it's easy to see that you Taurus folks are absolutely the hardest workers around—no doubt about it. Although Virgo runs a close second in the "willingness" department, and Aries is known for its love of manual labor, your fixed quality just can't be beat in the category of getting the job done. You'll work from sunrise to sundown, just to finish the job. You also pride yourself on doing it right the first time—on taking your time, and paying attention to every step in the process of a task. So no matter what job you're doing, you're going to be good at it—or you're not going to do it at all.

So much for how you work—now let's talk about what you like to do for work. Since you're ruled by the planet Venus, the lady who loves beauty, you always feel pulled towards situations where your talent for creating beauty can surface. For example, with your flair for colors and impeccable taste, you're a natural at interior design. If you want to assemble those colors on a canvas instead, you'll be drawn to art as a career. In fact, any occupation that allows you to interpret or mold earthly goods into pleasing shapes or sounds will do just fine. That includes everything from pottery—a natural for you, since it's working with earth materials to create beauty—to performing music. Taurus is especially drawn to singing, since yours is the sign that rules the throat. Your fondness for good food makes you a born chef, too. You probably have plenty of practice hours under your belt; you folks are famous for your wonderful dinner parties.

Whatever you do, if you're not absolutely sure that it's profitable right from the start, you won't bother to do it at all. Your sign understands that time certainly does mean money, and you seldom waste either. Your ruling planet, Venus, is in charge of money, so you're born with a knack for creating it. Needless to say, you're probably very, very good at making a profit on all your investments. You may find yourself in a career that calls for daily dealings with money—like accounting, bookkeeping, or banking. You folks are also experts at the stock market—it's almost as if you were born with an understanding of how to make it work for you.

Your connection with the earth will often bring you into dealings with real estate, too. If this is the case, keep your standards high and your morals about you, and you'll be naturally successful. Of course, truth be told, Taurus, no matter what you pour your considerable energy into, you're bound to be successful—you folks are prosperity magnets. Just don't forget to share the wealth with the rest of us.

GEMINI: KEEP ON MOVING

Well, now. Here's the sign of movement. Constant movement. Of tap-tap-tapping, gotta go, and Trivial Pursuit. Life's a game show, isn't it, Gemini? Just full of colors, categories, prizes and endless questions. So here's my first question: Did you know your sign is ruled by Mercury, the dude who heads the Department of Communication and Short Trips? You remember Mercury from high-school mythology, right? The guy with the wings on his head and his heels? His job title at that time was "messenger of the gods," and his job duties involved quite a bit of running around, carrying important news flashes straight from the gods to us down here. Suited him just fine but he never had much in the way of time to spare, and he didn't appreciate being "weighed down" in any way. Sound familiar? It should. Because he passed that love of speed and lightness on to you folks, his very favorite sign of all.

So it's his influence that inspires your world-famous incredible lightness of being, that invaluable way you have of adapting to any situation—immediately.Which sure makes life on this planet a lot easier on you than on the rest of us. You quite literally think on your feet—and you do just about everything else on the run, too. You eat your meals in transit, combine two and three tasks whenever possible, and are perfectly capable of doing at least two things at once—and of doing them right, too. If you don't have a car-phone, you should. If nothing else, it'll save your fingernails when you're stuck in traffic. But be really, really careful when you're flying down the highway, chatting away, all wrapped up in telling a story to your mom across the country. See, you can be very easily distracted from the business at hand—and you just can't drive 55.

You certainly have communication down to a science. In fact, you communicate so well that you can get pretty darned "chatty" on occasion, which can drive the average bear crazy. But, hey— no matter what your subjects, you're not boring. Ever. Your stories are full of data—they're medleys of interesting facts and tid-bits, "greatest hits" you've accumulated over the course of the day. They're full of details, too—because every detail is just as important as the last, in the Gemini mind. So it's natural that you'd tend to go off on a tangent or two, trying to include all the information when you're explaining something.

But that's part of your job, to take just a taste of everything— and then to tell us all about it. See, you're a mutable air sign. Air is intellectual, and mutable energy likes change. So in addition to being interested in everything—for a minute, at least—Gemini has the ability to switch subjects at break-neck speed, to take a right in the middle of a sentence.

Speaking of taking a right, there's just nobody who can learn the short cuts faster than you. That applies to your navigations through town as well as through conversations, by the way. You have no patience for stop signs, red lights, or anything else that makes you pause, including periods at the end of sentences. To avoid all that, you develop a way of negotiating any maze in no time flat. Your brain is your playground, Gemini, and you love to get in there and shake things up.

So it's your brain we need to discuss first in terms of the work you can do to bring you joy and help fulfill your quest. Let's start with storytelling and word-weaving, because that's what you really love best. You certainly do have an active imagination and can be amusing. So whether you write them down, or say them out loud, tell your stories. It's what you're good at, and it brings joy to the rest of us, too. Again, your ruling planet is Mercury, the head of the Cosmic Communication Department—and you're definitely happiest, and most productive in jobs that require you to do the Communication thing—with a capital "C." Although storytelling—literally, to both adults and children—is the very best "job" for you, since you already do it so naturally, if your tastes tend towards something a little more "professional," take advantage of the fact that there's always a pen in your hand, and jot down some of those impressions of the people, and places around you. Become a writer. You have the ability to really see and describe what makes someone or something "tick." That's the stuff good novels are built of.

It's also the stuff good reporters are made of—if you want to write for the *Daily Star*, you've got to be able to move. To get there fast—wherever "there" is—get the gist of the story, write it all out for all of us, get some pictures while you're there, and send it off to the news desk. All in a matter of hours—and maybe even less. Then get ready to do it all again. It's a Gemini dream come true.

So is telemarketing. First of all, it means you've got to be virtually attached to a phone for hours on end—something that might be maddening to some of us. Phones are ruled by Mercury, and you just love them, anyway, so put your skill at chatting to work and describe a product or service so quickly and entertainingly your prospective customer can't wait to get it in the mail. Telemarketing also means you'll never have to talk to the same person more than once or twice—and since variety is the spice of life, that's very tempting, isn't it?

All that mutable air in you is terrified, above all else, at the thought of being bored. Since you're born knowing how to turn a phrase just right, you may also be quite naturally drawn to sales as a profession—especially if a car phone is among the "perks" in the package. Direct sales would be great fun for you, too. It would allow you to do something else you just love—make lots of short trips and have lots of short visits. During those short visits, you'd get to play the word game, your favorite. It's easy. You grab the customer's attention immediately with a clever opening line—which you come up with immediately upon your arrival. You state your purpose quickly—which all business owners appreciate—and have a perfectly logical answer ready for every question, a remedy for every objection. There's no contest. You can talk the socks off the best of 'em, Gemini.

Now, any job that allows you to move around and do various and sundry tasks will keep you temporarily happy—but nothing lasts forever. Remember, you're mutable air, Gemini, and air can't be contained. If you feel it's time to move on, do it.

CANCER: STRIVING TO NURTURE

All you Cancers out there who are sick and tired of being referred to as "moody," raise your hands. OK. Now, tell me you're not. Oh, come on—not even a little? Look, it's nothing to be ashamed of—"moody" just means you actually experience your feelings, instead of shoving them into a closet like the rest of us. You're a water sign, after all, and water is the element that handles feelings. Since water has no walls, water signs are emotionally vulnerable to what's out there on a deeply personal level. So the world can be a pretty scary place—especially in your case, when all you've got to defend your tender little self is your instinct. As a result, you learn early on to depend on that instinct, to use your feelings and memories to navigate.

Yes, somewhere deep inside each of you, there's a little lady with rectangular glasses perched on the tip of her nose who's an expert on how that felt. Everything, that is—everything that ever happened to you, right from childhood on up. She's your historian, your built-in security blanket, and before you do anything, Cancer—anything at all—you check with her. It only takes a few seconds, and it hardly causes a ripple on the surface, but you never, ever make a move without talking to her first to make sure it's safe.

If she says it's a go, your mood is upbeat, cheerful, and chipper, and you'll show up with enough food to feed everyone there—and their families, too. If she votes no, you'll try to hide. But you can't always take her advice. Life here in the real world pushes even the most cautious among us out of our shells occasionally. When you feel forced into being somewhere unsafe, Cancer, you get scared— pure and simple. You react the only way you can—you refuse to participate—emotionally, at least. You may be on the scene physically, but you might just frown a bit while you're there.

The best you can do, since you really are such an emotional beast, is to stay home when you feel like you have to, and let your feelings out whenever you can. Avoid people and circumstances that don't allow you to express, and you won't end up brooding in a corner with your arms crossed.

Speaking of safety, let's talk about your home—or should I say your nest? Because it's here that you feel the safest and the most content. A quick scan of your place, in fact, goes a very long way towards understanding what you're all about. Here's where you keep all the stuff that makes your life more comfortable. Here's where you collect, hoard, store away, and save things for later— all kinds of things—just to be safe and just to be sure there'll always be enough, which is one of your constant concerns.

Cancer's symbol is the crab, and safety is what the shell's all about. It's also very private inside that shell. You can see out, but the world can't see in. That's just the way you like it. You may be so private, in fact, and so good at hiding how private you are, that folks who've known you for years will hardly realize they don't know you at all. You dole out details carefully, Cancer, and pull down your invisible shade when you're done.

Your sign is also traditionally associated with the concept of mother and mothering. Now, that doesn't mean that all of you have wonderful relationships with your mothers. Not at all. Your mother's fingerprint, however, will show up in every corner of your life. Your mom's body, you see, was your original home base, and roots are what you look to most for security, so if your relationship with her isn't good, it will bother you more than you'll ever admit. More often than not, however, you'll have an emotional bond with your mom that will be equally—or more—important to you than any other relationship.

Now, all that said, Cancer, let's talk about your professional life, and about how you conduct yourself when you're at work. First of all, Cancer is a cardinal water sign. Cardinal energy is what we use to begin, create, or start something. Water is emotional. When you combine those two characteristics, you create emotional bonds—and that's what families are made of.

Cancer understands the importance of family, and so you create mini-families wherever you go. Since you spend your days with them, your co-workers quickly become just another family to you. You will be the mommy in the family. You'll bring in the goodies on Fridays, have the whole gang over for holiday parties, and pass the hat when somebody's in the hospital. You'll remember not just everyone's birthday, but their size, their favorite color, and maybe even where they saw that gorgeous sweater they'd just love to have—even if it was only mentioned once, over coffee last February.

You have a magical way of convincing people that you can fix it, too—just by smiling and nodding and saying "Shhhh, it'll be all right." So even the boss secretly wants to climb on your lap when he or she has a bad day. You always assume a position of quiet authority and respect in the company, whether or not you have a title on paper. As a result, you don't change jobs much—that would be too much like leaving your family. You won't like traveling for work either, because that means spending time away from your real family and that's out of the question.

Since your caretaking instinct is so strong, when it come to job selection, you'll often find yourself in the company of children. Whether you're a third-grade teacher or a child-care professional, you're doing what comes naturally. Kids don't fight caretaking like adults, so when you tie their mittens to their sleeves and wipe their noses, they just stand there and enjoy it. Kids are also little bundles of emotion, and whether they're giggling and bubbling over with joy or stomping their feet because they can't have what they want right now, you know how to handle it. You're a regular specialist in the field of feelings.

Cooking is another profession that appeals to the talents you were born wearing. So you may find yourself working as a chef, in a school kitchen, or for a catering service. The care-taking professions will appeal to you as well—nursing, for example, or counseling. No matter what you do, Cancer, make sure it allows your Sun to shine by giving you the chance to nurture.

LEO: SHOW IT OFF!

All right, all you Leos out there—it's show time. Yes, it's your turn—finally, so you can get down off that table now. But before you start thinking I'm about to call you egotistical for getting up there in the first place, or shake my finger at you and tell you to put a lid on the theatrics because it's not nice to show off, let me just assure you I won't. I'm on your side. It is nice to show off. Very nice. Everybody ought to. There's nothing like a little applause to make a body feel special—and no one will ever clap if you don't show 'em what you can do.

Of course, that's not news to you—you're an expert at keeping the attention of the crowd. You have to be. It's your job to perform for us, to delight, amuse, and entertain. Sure, you demand our attention—you're fixed fire. That's the astrological equivalent of a bonfire, and anybody who's ever been to a bonfire knows how hard it is to look away. A little encouragement fans those flames even higher, so you'll perform until the lights go up for the right audience. In return, you ask only our appreciation and our love. Oh, and maybe just a little parade—nothing extravagant. A very small price to pay for the show.

Speaking of fire and parades, Leo, never let it be said that you don't know the art of the grand entrance. You roar into the room, dazzle us with a star-quality smile, make a few sweeping gestures, and immediately have us eating right out of your hand. We're in the presence of royalty, and we know it. We respond accordingly, with attention, affection, praise, and a touch of hero-worship.

Leo is the sign of the hero and heroine, after all, and if you want to be one when you grow up, you've got to be brave, strong, and just about fearless—first. You've got to have an attitude of leadership, too, an ability to pull the mantle of authority over your shoulders at a moment's notice and start giving out orders. And you'd better have lots of personal charisma so others will follow your lead. Leo arrives confident enough to do all that and more—if anybody can. You're a born leader. Your symbol, remember, is the lion—the king of the beasts.

Of course, being royalty means treating yourself like royalty, and you absolutely insist on quality. Fine food, gracious surroundings, and well-made, fashionable clothing. And your vacations? You do everything possible to make them play out like episodes of *Lifestyles of the Rich and Famous*. Nothing but the best will do. Being dressed well and being seen in all the right places is good publicity, after all, and you take tremendous pride in yourself and in those you associate with. Pride and presentation are a big part of what motivates you. You know how quickly others make judgments based on what they see—so appearances are understandably very important to you.

Now, all royalty have a bit of a flair for the dramatic, and you're no exception. You have a very strong predisposition to drama, a wonderful gift for turning the ordinary into the entertaining. A trip to the grocery store becomes an exciting event. See, you really are just a great big pussycat. So next time you start feeling abused by an ungrateful public, remember that every audience needs a commercial break now and then. If we do turn away for a moment, it doesn't mean we don't still love you. So don't pout, and pull that lower lip in before you trip on it. We'll be right back, after this message.

Now, speaking of center stage—if the world really is a stage, Leo, the spotlight belongs to you. So does the star on the dressing-room door. Leos make the best entertainers around because you folks will stop at nothing for applause. If you're not into acting or performance of some kind—well, you ought to be. If you're not, if you're one of that rare breed of shy Leo types, keep in mind that you can perform anywhere, for anyone, so if you don't have a job in the entertainment field, don't panic. You carry your tools with you wherever you go—all you need is a stage and an audience, both of which you can create anywhere. The audience is easy. You automatically attract attention wherever you are—sometimes even when you don't want it. But the stage isn't a problem, either. Ever watch a hotel staff set up a dance floor? They wheel in a cart with twenty or thirty squares on it, start snapping those tiles into place, and in no time flat—ta-daaa—a dance floor is born. Well, that's how you operate, Leo. You walk in, scan the room for the most visible spot, and quickly assemble the imaginary tiles into your stage. Before long, you've got the perimeter mapped out, your boundaries drawn, and all the best spots memorized. Of course, the size and shape of your stage varies, too. Bartenders, teachers, aerobic instructors, and writers have a "stage." Everybody does. You, however, can turn any ordinary space into living theater. As a professional, then, try to become involved in something that will allow you to use your natural gift for drama. It's what will really bring your Sun joy.

Now, Leo also loves to be in love—so working with couples, or helping to get folks together, is also a key part of your mission in life. You're also the sign that most loves to play. So many Leos find themselves working in the company of kids—who are also the best audience around, by the way.

Although performing on a real stage is what you'd really, really love to do, whether or not you'll admit it, no matter where you are or where you work, there'll always be a star on your office door, and co-workers will usually adore you properly, too. You're the entertainment committee, equal parts stand-up comic and storyteller. Of course, you're also willing to help, by going out of your way and performing well above and beyond the call of duty at all times. You don't mind, either—as long as they appreciate you, as long as they say "thanks"—and mean it—once in a while. No matter what you do, make sure it's at a job and in a place where you'll receive the love, appreciation, and pats on the back you need to stay happy.

VIRGO: CHECK OUT THE DETAILS

I know most of you Virgos probably refuse to read descriptions of your Sun sign any more because you're tired of reading about how "picky" and "critical" you are—not to mention "petty." Well, sit down and have a nice cup of herb tea, and we'll make a deal. I promise not to use those words here—not once—if you agree to examine where they came from. Sound like a plan?

All right. First of all, about the neatness thing. What a tremendous reponsibility that must be—hearing all about how organized you are, your whole life, and then trying to live up to it. Well, I'm here to tell you that it ain't necessarily so. You can, in fact, be a Virgo and be sloppy. Some Virgos are really good at it, too. This is for all of you out there who've suspected for years that you must have been adopted, because obviously this can't be your birth date when your living room looks the way it does. Well, you can all rest assured, your parents are your parents, after all, and you won't need to alphabetize your CDs to prove it. You will, however, have to admit that you'd much prefer things to be perfectly neat and tidy, and that if you thought for one minute that you could organize your home, you would. Neatness and organization are important to you—that's inarguable. But whether or not you feel like you're capable of accomplishing that task is another story.

See, Virgo is mutable earth, so it's willing to fix things. Anything that needs it. Only thing is, in order to fix things, you've got to be able to see what's wrong with them—you've got to pay careful attention to details. To the fine print, the lint on his suit, and the run in her stocking. Problem is, you're soooo good at spotting the problem via the details that you get hopelessly hung up on those details, and you aren't able to see the rest of the bedroom past the dresser drawer you've cleaned and rearranged three times. Then you tell yourself that if you can't be as attentive to all the details as you'd like to be, the project will never be truly perfect anyway, and if you can't do something flawlessly, you'd just as soon blow off the whole project. After all, why start a project if you're not going to do it perfectly, right?

It's this attitude that gets you guys into trouble. See, the rest of us are not famous for cheerfully owning up to our flaws. Lots of us don't like to see them at all. But your "job," the mission you've been equipped to execute here on Planet Earth, is to find what's wrong with this picture. To see the flaws, point them out, and suggest alternatives. Now, it's not an easy job, I know—but it's your job. See, all flaws aren't huge, glaring ones. Lots of times it's the small ones that are the worst. So to do the job right, you need a built-in microscope, one that allows you to spot even the tiniest of defects. You've got the technology, Virgo, and the best thing you can do with it is to bring it into your career choice, and put your Automatic Virgo Fault-Finder to work.

So what types of jobs involve details? Well, there's always mathematics and accounting, fields that definitely require attention to detail. The field of medicine is also quite detail-oriented and very help-oriented, which brings in another side of your nature — the pleasure you get from simply doing for others. See, no other sign gets quite so much satisfaction from simply helping out, and health-care fields are areas where your sincere desire to help, to fix, and to mend can be put to good, constructive use. (Besides, you'll just love the uniforms — they're clean, white, and perfect — and the hospital environment is equally meticulous and clean.) Truth be told, you're a natural nurse, doctor, and fitness consultant rolled into one. You can spot the problem with your patient a mile away, and you know what to prescribe, too. If you are in a health-related field, don't resist being drawn to more holistic methods. "Traditional" medicine is undergoing big changes, and so is your attitude about what's "healthy."

You may also be drawn to other helping professions, like restaurant work, cleaning, or being a personal care attendant. Your natural humility makes you a most accommodating worker. You're also capable of getting at least three times more work done in an afternoon than most of us can get done in a day. Your secret? It's the details thing — you know how to prioritize your tasks, trouble-shoot, and spend your time wisely.

You're also wonderful at crafts, since you have such an exacting eye. Many of you are also drawn to writing, since your traditional ruling planet is Mercury, the whiz-kid, the head of the Communication Department. Regardless of what you do, you'll do it well or you won't do it at all.

LIBRA: SEEKING A BALANCE

All right, all you Libras out there — it's your turn to reveal yourselves. Raise your hands, please. Keep them up for a second, too, OK? Now, everybody else — pay attention to these folks — because they're the balance experts of the zodiac. They're very, very good at knowing just what to do to make each and every one of us happy. They're very polite, and they'd keep their hands up all afternoon if asked, because they'd rather die than hurt my feelings. OK, put 'em down—and we'll talk about Librans, those smiling representatives of the Lady Venus, the most social planet around. Now, Venus is in charge of love, beauty, and behavior that is pleasing to others. She's a lovely, graceful, sweet-smelling goddess who'd never, ever say or do anything that others wouldn't like. Being her agent means that same charm and a good dose of compromise are standard equipment in a Libran machine.

Of course, mentioning compromise leads us straight to Libra's favorite key words: "balance" and "harmony"—two very difficult states to achieve. Balance means that two sides of an issue must both give and take just enough so that neither is heavier or lighter than the other. Harmony means that all the components of a group, whether it's an orchestra or a committee, need to participate equally—no more and no less than any other factor. Now, this is no easy task—but Libra's definitely the sign for the job. Contrary to popular opinion, you Librans do not drift peacefully from one balanced situation to the next. See, Libra isn't born balanced, it's born with a knack for fixing the scales when they're out of balance—so you'll most often find yourself in unbalanced situations. Your job is to use your special charm to restore balance, to be our peacemaker, mediator, and our go-between. Somebody's got to tap the scales down when one side grows heavier than the other, and nobody knows how to keep things equal more than you fair-minded folk.

Now, Libra is cardinal, and it's air. So Libra wants to start something, preferably intellectual in nature. Which sounds like a conversation, doesn't it? Well, that's another of Libra's specialties—small talk. However, being so good at charm and manners makes it tough to think of yourself. So, every once in a while, even though you majored in relationships, make sure you see to your own needs. Remember, the idea isn't to lose yourself entirely, it's to balance your needs with others' needs.

When it comes to career, realize that your natural gift for soothing warring factions is your natural choice. Manners, politeness, compromise, and peacemaking are your forte. Now, keeping the peace at all times is impossible, although you'll never stop trying, because that's your business. No matter how exhausting, you'll always like intervening in difficult situations—when it works. Nothing pleases you more than witnessing a compromise you engineered, because that means you managed to please everyone—this time. So when you're thinking about what you ought to be when you grow up, consider mediation, negotiation, or marriage counseling, where folks with your talents are sorely needed. You're a born judge, too, by the way. Remember that your symbol portrays the scales of justice, and that the point of being a judge is to render a fair and impartial decision with regard to all parties involved. In the business world, bring your balancing skills into play by working as an arbitrator or go-between. Librans who prefer a more aesthetic career would do well to pursue careers in the fields of interior design or decorating—where you'd still be restoring balance to "unbalanced" environments. No matter what you do, for your own mental and physical health, make sure to allow time for yourself.

SCORPIO: PURSUING POWER

Pluto is a lot like Darth Vader of *Star Wars* fame: dark, mysterious, controlling—the kind of guy who lures you to peek through your fingers at the good parts in movies even if you really don't want to see what's happening. He's the dude who's got the technology to handle wicked smiles, sly glances, and inevitable change. Definitely not for the faint of heart, this planet.

So when I tell you Pluto is your ruling planet, that he favors your sign more than any other, don't you even try to look surprised, Scorpio. You know why you're his favorite. You've got what it takes to handle intensity, and in Pluto's mind, that's the only way to be. You're very, very fond of power and powerful people, and you meet all new situations with a passion that comes from a place so deep within, you're not even fully aware of it yourself. As one of the zodiac's three water signs, you function on an emotional level, operating on what you sense from your environment rather than what you learn intellectually. No sign is more perceptive—you're equal parts detective, analyst, and researcher.

You often sit up long into the night, mentally reviewing the day, sifting through the details for the subtle clues that most of us miss. Of course, you're equally skilled at sending those signals back out into the world, at imperceptibly altering or transforming circumstances around you with just the right phrase or gesture. In a nutshell, Scorpio, you know how to work the crowd.

Your ability to persuade is the stuff that legends are made of. When you really want something, it's as good as yours. Desire is your middle name, and you're an expert at the delicate art of strategy, which makes for a lethal combination. By the time you actually put your plan into action, ninety percent of the work on your project has already been "done." You're a planner and a plotter. Waiting is no problem. You'll wait forever for what you want. You never, ever quit until you've won—no matter what it takes, no matter how long. For this reason, others may see you as manipulative or controlling. But then, it's easy to become jealous of someone so quietly, patiently powerful.

When it comes to career, then, Scorpio, you're equally focused. Have you ever watched a spider build a web? That's what you're like when you've got a project. You set yourself up in a corner, size up what's needed, and start spinning. If the web gets knocked down, you start again. You fixate on all undertakings in this same relentless way. Once you're involved in a project, as with all else, you can't stop. Not until there's absolutely no stone left unturned.

Speaking of turning over stones, you just love to dig, Scorpio. Probably because there's no telling what you'll find when you uncover treasure or secrets. Anything that no one else has ever seen is irrestible to you, Scorpio.

Does that extend into fields of research? You betcha. You can sit in a corner and work, literally, for hours without realizing it. Naturally, the "hidden professions" appeal to you, those vocations that require operating behind the scenes, in a spider-like corner. Scorpio makes the perfect surgeon, therapist, or analyst. Some Scorpios love to dig in the dirt, ending up in archaeology or excavation. Regardless of what field you choose to pursue, you're always best when you're working alone. Oh, and you absolutely must be the boss, or there'll be hell to pay.

Your affiliation with Pluto and the Eighth House also produces an amazing sixth sense when it comes to making deals with other people's money. Scorpio is born with business sense, knowing what to invest and when to sell. You have a knack for making money, and spotting a good deal when it arrives. For that reason, stockbroking is another good career choice. The pursuit of power may also lead you to a career in politics—as with all else, it's all or nothing with you, Scorpio.

Since your specialty is urgent situations, you often find yourself at the heart of emergencies and crises—which means more than a few of your kind work in emergency rooms. Whether or not you actually experience them, you'll certainly hear all the details—no one is more likely to get a midnight call from a friend, and with good reason. You're a natural psychologist, a good listener, and a shrewd advisor. Your natural intensity makes it easy for friends to tell you anything—and I do mean anything. Bringing that same capacity to understand the deepest, darkest, most secret sides of human nature into your career choice is an absolute necessity.

SAGITTARIUS: ON THE MOVE

Well, first off, Sag, do you realize you're the only sign out there that's got a nickname? I mean, nobody ever calls Scorpio "Scorp," do they? (Not for long, anyway...) And it certainly wouldn't be cool to refer to formal Capricorn as "Cap." You, however, adore nicknames, and that tells us a lot about you. You're an expert at being very, um, casual. You're good at making everyone around you feel comfortable because, for once, they can be exactly what they are—no pretenses required. Sag, you see, has everything to do with letting it all hang out—and that includes your shirttail.

OK, so you're not notorious for your neatness. More than one Sag has driven out a roommate after one too many piles of dirty dishes were left until the next party. But, hey—who's more fun to be around? You're a live-in comedian, cracking jokes right from the moment your eyes open in the morning. Of course, that can be tough to take—especially if your roommate happens to be a Virgo who'd rather discuss the dish situation than hear your Richard Pryor impersonation.

You live in blue jeans, love to cruise around in your pick-up truck, and take weekend hikes regularly with the dogs. You love others because of their faults, not in spite of them. Others love you for your laughter. You do so love to laugh. One of your most-used keywords, in fact, is "jovial," which came from your ruling planet,

Jupiter, who was once known as "Jove." Jupiter has a well-deserved reputation for being a lot like Santa Claus, the ho-ho-ho guy himself. Now, strong Saturn types may scowl at you disapprovingly at times, when that laugh comes out a bit too loud. But life's too short to ever stop seeing the lighter side of it. So laugh on and let them scowl.

All that said, let's not forget about your more serious side, the philosopher that was born to ask "why" and to try to figure out how the answers to those questions fit in with everything else you've stashed in your warehouse of knowledge. You're constantly networking, trying to plug both information and people into their perfect spot in the big picture. As a result, in one way or another, you're a lifelong student, wanting to know everything, never satisfied with what you've already experienced, always game to leap on a plane to see if the grass really is greener over there.

Now, Sag also has a strong tendency to tell the truth, regardless of the consequences—just because it's true, that's why. So you often amaze your friends and astound your enemies with what spills out of the tactless side of your mouth. Now, this is where your reputation for being a bit too "blunt" comes from. In fact, in your relentless quest to speak the whole truth and nothing but the truth, you often say or do things—albeit unintentionally—that bruise the feelings of the average bear. Like when you compliment Aunt Sarah on how good she looks in that dress, and then add, "even though it is a size too small." Fortunately, Aunt Sarah and all the other victims you've left speechless seem to understand it's your intentions that count, not your method. Your genuine warmth makes you absolutely worth the trouble your mouth gets you into. That's lucky for you!

Now, career choice is often a difficult topic for Sagittarians. It's tough for you to stay at any job for very long, first of all, and if your job doesn't allow you plenty of personal freedom, you won't be there on the second day. You have an instinct for sniffing out potentially restrictive situations, and you split if you can't move. Sag is mutable fire, you see, and mutable means "changeable," so your energy level and your attention tend to flare up and die down, more like a series of little bonfires than one roaring blaze. Consequently, you'll need an occupation that will fan your scattered but nonetheless illuminating flames into consistent activity by keeping you interested—which is no easy task.

As a rule, occupations that place you outdoors or constantly on the move will hold your attention longer than others, as will people-oriented jobs. Sales in particular seems to be a Sagittarian niche, since it often means travel and always means change. A Sag is often drawn to journalism, which allows you to "preach" via describing the big picture to the masses.

Your built-in love of far-away places may also prompt you to become a travel agent, an ideal Sag vocation. What's more perfect for Sag energy? This career gives you a chance to use all of your natural talents—dealing one-on-one with a variety of people, networking via telephone and computer to find the ideal arrangements to suit your client's needs, and learning all about the world. Not to mention the travel deals!

Of course, if the philosopher side of you is strong, you may be drawn to a career in the metaphysical or religious fields, choosing to inspire others with your sparkling enthusiasm for life. Regardless of which occupation you choose, expect to wind up teaching others. Your natural sense of humor and wit, along with your ability to draw pictures that illustrate intellectual concepts, make you the ideal teacher—and it also gives you a chance to proselytize, to go on at length about what you believe.

No matter what career draws you, don't kid yourself about what you're capable of committing to. You've got to have enough personal space and time off to keep you coming back. Above all, don't try to stay in a job if you're unhappy there. Remember your innate philosophy—that work involves trading hours of your life for money. Make sure it's a trade you can live with.

CAPRICORN: STAYING IN CHARGE

Before we go anywhere at all, Capricorn, we need to clear up some major misconceptions, to relieve you of the burden of at least some of those depressing keywords you've got to be sick of dragging around. "Serious" and "somber," for example. Not to mention "Melancholy." Please! Anybody who accuses you of being any of those things obviously hasn't ever had a conversation with you. If they had, they'd know that you, Capricorn, are one of the funniest, wittiest signs around. Granted, your wit is dry and, yes, folks really do have to pay attention to catch the punch lines, but that's what makes your humor so great—the sarcastic edge you were born with. So the next time someone groans when you say you're a Capricorn, tell 'em to stick around and pay attention—and maybe they'll learn something.

Oh, and there's another quality you've been saddled with for far too long: the "cheapness" thing. Well, here it is: you're not cheap. You're not. Of course, that's not to say that you don't love bagging a deal, hitting a sale you didn't expect, or rescuing an antique chair at a yard sale from the clutches of some ignoramus who was just using it to prop open the garage door. Still, "cheap" isn't the word I'd use to describe you. Maybe "thrifty," "frugal," or a real bargain hunter." But definitely not "cheap."

In fact, your taste is far from inexpensive, and you have a rather unique eye for the best of everything. You firmly believe that you get what you pay for, and you don't mind paying—it just better be worth it, of course. "Quality doesn't cost—it pays"—that's your motto.

Know what else you're not? You're not dull, boring, lackluster individuals who wander around mumbling statistics all day, who never, ever leave the house without their plastic pocket-protectors. However, you respect experience, especially the experience of your elders. You are even more humble around your own grandparents, since they're elders you're related to, and family is another institution you're deeply attached to. You understand that history is more reliable than theory, you appreciate tradition, and you know there's a lot more to the phrase "It's the right thing to do" than oatmeal. You're solid. You're into integrity. You believe in getting things the old-fashioned way—earning them, that is.

Now, on the job, you're the best—regardless of the type of work you choose. One of the things your superiors love best about you is that you have no problem separating your private life from your job—an admirable trait. No matter what's happening at home, you arrive at the usual time in the usual mood—it seems. You may calmly discuss the problem on a daily basis, or you may not mention that you're divorced until it's completely over—but it doesn't matter. You won't cry when you're telling folks about it, and you'll never, ever allow a customer to see any change in your manner. All in all, you're an ideal employee. The customer is always right, and work should always be separate from other things.

You arrived on the planet with qualities like "self-discipline" and "executive ability" as standard equipment right from Day One, a regular boss-in-training, no matter how old you are. So you guys are born being very, very good at taking charge. Just go ahead and admit it. It's OK—somebody's got to drive. You can sense the natural order of things, have a keen talent for organizing people, and you automatically size up all situations realistically—in one glance. Your only problem in working with others is that you're usually right—OK, you're always right—and people just hate that. Since you're right so much, somebody up in the office is bound to notice you eventually. You do things the way they're supposed to be done, and everybody knows it. You always perform above and beyond the call of duty, and you're good at following the rules. All of which makes you a shoe-in to be drafted into positions of authority at work. Needless to say, your talents are tailor-made for management and big business, where a clear, realistic mind, unaffected by emotions, is the best asset.

Now, since structure-loving Capricorns often arrive on this planet as members of families of military folks, they often are drawn into the armed services as a career choice, especially since following in the family's footsteps is so appealing to tradition-oriented folk. Any vocation that involves wearing a uniform is right at the top on your list, matter of fact. Of course, dark blue pinstriped suits are a uniform of sorts, so if you're not wearing one to work in a business office, you may be drawn to politics, another occupation that requires a strictly neat appearance, and a "just the facts" style of communicating. No matter what you do, Capricorn, remember that you'll do it best if you're allowed to be in charge.

AQUARIUS: YOU'RE UNIQUE, ALL RIGHT

OK, Aquarius, we'll start off by telling you what you really want to hear: You're one of a kind, kid. Absolutely unique. In fact, in all the world, there's no one quite like you. Not even close. You're the last true individual—and everybody knows it. Got it? Good.

Now, can we talk about the purple hair and the safety pin through your nose? I mean, you can be different from everyone else without scaring people, can't you? As for all you Aquarians out there who are shaking your heads like crazy about the hair and the safety pin, saying that's not like you at all? Well, okay, then, let's talk about the fact that although your own technique may be a little less drastic than others of your kind, you still absolutely refuse to do anything that everybody else does. No way. If it's a tradition, it's history in your book. I mean, didn't you quit participating in Christmas six years ago for just that reason? Because you resented being told when to shop?

In a nutshell, Aquarius, you just can't stand anybody telling you what to do, in any department, on any subject. It interferes with your individuality, and we certainly can't have that. Because that's your point, isn't it—your *raison d'être*—to be different.

Of course, all Aquarians don't have purple hair—that was a slight exaggeration. However, you probably do dress like a member of an English rock band or you may have the John Denver look—the granola thing, complete with round wire-framed specs. Now, that doesn't mean you look just like everybody else, so don't get excited, and put down the dye. It just means that you've adopted the androgynous approach in the appearance department. See, you Aquarians have an amazing gift for seeing people as they really are—around the labels. That means that labels like male and female don't matter, either. We're all just people in your mind—the uniqueness has to come from within—but you certainly believe in demonstrating what's going on inside by the way you decorate the outside.

Changeable? Oh, yeah. You betcha. You adore change. Bring it on. See, your ruling planet is Uranus, and you know how he gets. Uranus is the guy who's in charge of lightning, winning the lottery, tornadoes, and sudden reversals, the head of the Department of One Never Knows.

When it comes to work, you'll need as much, if not more, freedom as a Sagittarius. You'll need to be free to be you while you're there, too. Which means you may have more than one co-worker at your desk during lunch, asking to have their astrology charts done, or their cards read—even though they really don't believe in all this stuff, of course. Your sign is the one most often connected to astrology, which means this may be your ideal vocation.

Oh, and even if you're not drawn to metaphysics, let's not forget about a career that involves working with your cause—because whether or not your job involves actually being on the payroll of your favorite environmental organization, you'll definitely put in full-time hours. So what is your cause? Is it Greenpeace, an anti-nuke group, or Amnesty International? Doesn't matter—whatever it is, you'll put it first, before love, marriage, family, money, before anything. Bumper stickers plastered all over your car prove it. It's common knowledge that when you're taken by an idea, that idea becomes All. Everything else pales in comparison. If you're going to be involved in something this deeply, then, why not make it your life's work?

Aquarius also has a built-in affinity for science, a field that may also appeal to the more technical among you. You probably also have a love affair going with computers, the Web and the Internet. Consider working in a lab or for Microsoft, where you can play on your computer all day—and get paid for it, to boot.

Being self-employed is always best for you, but finding a job that allows personal freedom at all times will also do just fine. Regardless of what you do for work, Aquarius, don't lock yourself into situations that rob you of your space.

PISCES: SOAKING UP VIBES

It's not easy being a Pisces. You're mutable and you're water, so you don't have emotional boundaries to separate you from us. You walk around feeling everything everybody feels. Everything. Which can be simultaneously good and bad. When you're with kindred spirits, it's a big plus. Nobody can merge, blend, and fit right in like you can, kid. And nothin' could be finer than sitting in a room full of friends, soaking up the good vibes. It's a gift to be able to take it all in, unobstructed—to let yourself go.

Being this sensitive isn't so great when there's tension in the air, however. Makes you feel like you're walking across battlefields without a shield, dodging hidden landmines and ducking the invisible slings and arrows the rest of us can't even see. It's draining and downright exhausting when there's an argument in the vicinity. It doesn't matter whether you're involved, or whether the anger is spoken or unspoken. You're born with very sensitive antennae, so you can feel what's "generated" on all levels.

I hate to use the word "psychic" to describe you. It sounds so bogus, but there's no other way to say it. You can be really, truly psychic—when your channels are clear. It's neat, for example, when those antennae pick up "friend on phone" and you grab it just as it rings—and even neater when you can do it in front of company. But it comes easily to you. Without any walls or boundaries to separate you from whatever's out there, you "just know" an awful lot.

So sometimes you've got to get away from it all, from reality, because nobody feels the harshness of the world like you do. When you've just about had it with the real world, when you've absorbed one too many negative vibes, then it's time to draw back and regroup. You need to disappear and recharge. Don't be afraid to spend time alone. You really need it—it's the best way for you to really feel whole again.

However, choose your method of retreat carefully. Keep in mind that although alcohol or drugs are a quick escape hatch, their effects are only temporary, and they'll only make the world even harder on you in the long run. It's easier for you to become addicted to anything than for any other sign. Now, I know there are times you'd rather be anywhere but on this planet, chock-full of selfish, heartless fools. I know you spend a lot of time with your eyes closed and your fingers crossed, tapping your heels together, chanting, "There's no place like home" and I'm sure that one day your people will return on the starship and pick you up. But in the meantime, remember that this planet is full of other water signs just like yourself who've already thought of all kinds of constructive ways to get out of here. So go to a movie and get lost in the darkness. Meditate. Go to church, temple, or ashram. You can go save something little, too—an animal from the pound, or a plant from the "reduced" rack at the grocery store. Doesn't matter. What really helps, Pisces, is when you "adopt" someone or something that's as vulnerable as you are. That's when the strength in your sign comes out. After all, your reputation for being the compassion expert is well-deserved. You know how to take care of strays because there's a side of you that will always feel like a pound puppy.

Now, since we spend more time working than we do sleeping, it's important for each of us to find the right occupation. Try to "follow our bliss," as the late mythologist Joseph Campbell used to say, which means, "Don't spend your days doing something you hate." This is especially true for you, Pisces. You can only trudge off to a job you don't believe in for so long. Then you get depressed. Then you get sick.

It's not necessary. You've got several attractive options. First of all, you really do have a strong urge to shelter the homeless, and it's definitely going to come out, one way or the other. So the perfect way to feed this side of you—and keep yourself feeling good about yourself—is by really helping to shelter the homeless or fund-raising for the local animal shelter, or hiring on to the League of Conservation Voters. Whatever it takes, you need to help.

Of course, you can also give that part of yourself away through volunteer efforts, and take up a job that allows the "play pretend" side of you a chance to fantasize all day. There's a special place in your heart for disguises and costumes. Pulling a veil over someone's eyes is your specialty, so the fields of cosmetics and beauty are pretty appealing, too. It's just modern-day spell-casting, and it isn't anything you don't already do, anyway.

You can nurture your spiritual side by taking on a religious or spiritual vocation or counseling others on their own spirituality. Pisces' connection to Neptune, which rules music, makes you a shoe-in for a career in that field.

Speaking of casting spells, consider putting your talent for fiction to work. Tell us a novel or write us a short story. Make it romantic or fantastic. Make it wistful and dreamy. Regardless of what you choose to do, share yourself with us whenever you can. You're a strange and wonderful beast—and we've all got a lot to learn from you.

Navigate The Starry Path of Love

By Jeraldine Saunders

The candle draws the moth to its flame
Some get singed, others win enlightenment and fame.
If you come, do your best to obtain your dreams
But beware of the scam artists and their schemes.
If your horoscope points to this stop
Utilize the stars' timing and you may end up on top.

—Jeraldine Saunders

Hollywood and astrology have long been related. The livelihood of the stars depends on timing. Decisions about when to sign a contract, or when to refuse or accept an offer can make or break an aspiring actor's dreams of stardom.

ASTROLOGY CASTS ITS SPELL

Hollywood and astrology have always had a very exciting, intimate, and prosperous relationship. When a person is signing a contract that may add up to double-digit millions, the alarm clock and the wrist watch won't do for a complete look at the timing. Only the solar system will do. All of our concepts of time are based on the Earth's movement around the Sun. Human relationships are based on how our charts and our planets intermingle, and whether they are in opposition, in squares, trines, or sextiles.

Of course, those who use astrology in Hollywood aren't just actors. Some are among the 25,000 skilled craftspeople affiliated with more than sixty guilds, unions, and associations who combine their talents to make theatrical films or TV shows. They include accountants, zookeepers, carpenters, stunt people, electricians, laborers, sound people, and the list goes on and on. They have all found their niche. Some work with their heads, some with their hands, and above all, with their hearts.

The city of Los Angeles is ruled by the zodiacal sign Virgo and Hollywood is ruled by the zodiacal sign Leo. The hard-working, down-to-Earth, Virgo influence conjoined with the dramatic magnetism of Leo creates a nice dichotomy that has gained worldwide attention.

In show business, people need more than just a wrist watch for timing. Astrology is just timing based on the solar system. It was only natural that these creative and open-minded people would have the intellectual curiosity to turn to astrology, back to the times when Mae West (born August 17th) and Mary Pickford (born April 9th) were interested in this subject. Astrology is now out in the open among the brightest people in Hollywood, including producers, directors or actors, but it wasn't always this way.

Merv Griffin (born July 6th), who loves astrology, creator of the TV game show *Jeopardy*, has astrology enthusiast Alex Trebek (born July 22nd) as his host. Merv had a nightly show in the 1960s on which he would occasionally feature astrology as the theme. I was backstage with Merv's resident astrologer Sydney Omarr, who was waiting to go on stage. Merv's producer came in and I actually heard him say, "Now, Sydney, you mustn't be so accurate this time or you will get us into trouble with the NAB code." Yes, there was a National Association of Broadcasters code, which stated that astrology could not be shown to foster interest or a belief in the subject. The NAB code is no longer officially in existence, but its shadow remains.

Former President Ronald Reagan used astrology long before he met his wife Nancy. He utilized astrology when he was a Hollywood actor and used this knowledge to choose the fortuitous moment, at one minute after midnight, to be sworn in as governor of California in the 1960s. You can use the signs that the Universal Intelligence has given us to help tap into the power, talent, and abundance that is waiting for us. Reaching out from the known to the unknown can be fascinatingly thrilling and your unique horoscope awaits your discovery. Who knows what riches it can uncover, perhaps even your soulmate?

Comparing horoscopes is a must when romance is the question. Isabel Perón (born February 4th) was discovered when she was a cabaret dancer by an astrologer named José Lopez-Rega, who modestly called himself the world's greatest astrologer. Isabel was her stage name, while her real name was Maria Estala. The astrologer promised her that under his astrological guidance she could marry President Juan Perón. She did, and she ran Argentina from 1973–1975 with behind-the-scenes help from the astrologer, who was dubbed *El Brujo* (the Spanish word for "witch").

Actress Faye Dunaway (born January 14th) makes it crystal clear, "I would never think of having a serious relationship unless I checked the man's horoscope," she says. "I would want to find out if his planets are harmonious with my chart." Generally speaking, Capricorns are attracted to individuals born in the signs of Taurus, Virgo, Scorpio, and Pisces.

The famous cinematographer James Wong Howe was an astrologer and made no secret of it. The late and talented actor John Barrymore used planetary hours to choose the best times for shooting movie scenes. For example, if he were to do a scene that required action, he would pick a Mars hour. If it was a love scene, he would pick a Venus hour. Mars rules action; Venus rules love.

Sylvester Stallone (born July 6th), Cancer-born movie star, never tires of reminding people of the role that astrology plays in his life. He says, "My mother is an astrologer, my brother Frankie and sister Louann are amateur astrologers. When I was down and out, I knew I would make it big and I did, just as my horoscope indicated." Stallone says anyone who laughs at astrology will have to face an angry "Rocky."

Actress Meryl Streep (born June 22nd) says very frankly that "if it hadn't been for my Moon in Taurus, I don't think that I would have had this determination to survive such a tough field." The lovely Angie Dickinson (Libra, born September 30th) is an avid supporter of astrology. She says she doesn't know how she could have succeeded without it. Virgo Regis Philbin is also an avid follower of astrology and has dedicated a full chapter to it in his autobiography entitled *I'm Only One Man*. Gifted actor Dick Van Patten and his wife Pat are astrology buffs and she is also very proficient in numerology.

ASTROLOGY LAUNCHES THE LOVE BOAT

After writing my autobiography *The Love Boats* (Pinnacle Books, 1974), I created the TV series and sold the TV rights for the long-running series. Luckily, I retained the feature film rights, which I have just sold to Aaron Spelling and Disney Films for *Love Boat: The Movie* for the big screen. The movie is scheduled for a summer 1998 release.

Astrology helped to launch my career. When I was a cruise director on the world's poshest cruise ships, I would submit my book chapters to an agent only when my ephemeris listing locations of the planets indicated it was a good time to send out mail. This didn't always coincide with the times my ship docked in port, but I stuck with my faith and waited for the astrologically correct time, even though I was eager to get the chapter in the mail. Astrology helped me find out where the luck was in my horoscope, where my talents lie, when to prepare, and when to push ahead.

My interest in love and romance has always made me a natural matchmaker. When I arranged a party for those passengers who were traveling alone, I would have the fire and air signs sit together, and the earth and water signs do the same. That was a lot of help as a conversation ice-breaker and conducive to a friendly party mixer. When on board, I lectured on astrology. Some of the passengers were surprised to discover that the topic is taboo in some circles. I explained to them that it is just a study of time.

If you took a photograph of the heavens at the very spot when and where you were born, that would be your horoscope. No two people can be born on the same spot at the same moment. That is why your horoscope is so unique. The arrangement of the planets, at that moment in time, is the hand of cards you are dealt at birth. If this sounds as though everything is fated, that's not so, because how you play that hand of cards is where the free will comes into play. Now you can understand that one can certainly play a better game of life if one knows which cards they are holding.

Now that I am a landlubber and working "in the business" in Hollywood, it is most delightful to find so much interest in the subjects I lectured on while sailing and entertaining my passengers on some of the poshest cruise ships. No wonder I liked cruising, lecturing, and writing with my Sun in Virgo, Moon in Gemini, and Sagittarius rising.

CHART YOUR LIFE COURSE

With the knowledge of your horoscope, you will find something in life that you can do better than anyone else on Earth. There is a vocation of some sort, somewhere, in which you can excel. Everyone has some special ability and those who become successful in life are those who have found a vocation on which they can capitalize. The horoscope shows clearly where our power and joy lie.

In my book *Signs of Love* (Llewellyn Publications, 1990), I include a simple chart that will enable you to find your rising sign or Ascendant if you know your time of birth. You can find a similar chart on pages 14–15 of this *Sun Sign Book*. You will find your birth time on your official birth certificate. With this information, you can find which zodiacal sign is in your First House and the other eleven houses. Then you will be able to know in which houses your planets are located. You will be able to understand the influence your planets have in every department of your life.

Each of the twelve houses represents a different department in your life including love, money, psychological drives, and which signs harmonize with your own. See Figure 1 to discover the influence of the astrological houses in your natal chart. If you can't find your birth time, use the location of the Sun at birth as your First House or Ascendant.

Success in life will not depend on developing your weakest assets, but in capitalizing on your strengths. How important this is

HOUSE	DEPARTMENTS OF LIFE
First	Personality, appearance
Second	Material goods, money, collecting
Third	Short journeys, siblings, ideas, communication
Fourth	Home, mother
Fifth	Romance, speculation, social life, children
Sixth	Health, jobs, dependents, work, service
Seventh	Marriage, contracts, partnerships, public relations
Eighth	Hidden matters, taxes, inheritance
Ninth	Religion, long journeys, law, publishing, philosophy
Tenth	Profession, public opinion, status
Eleventh	Friends, hopes, wishes, dreams
Twelfth	Secret fears, mystical inspiration

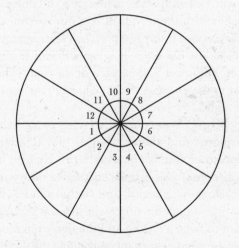

*Figure 1. The Astrological Houses
and Their Influences*

when deciding on a career or even a hobby! Recognizing your uniqueness from your horoscope will point to the path that is easiest for your climb to the top. Achievements in life are accomplished through the application of life's tremendous force. This inner urge typifies energy. Finding where one's energy lies is the secret we can learn from the horoscope.

The key to attaining success in life is to find one's particular sphere. The secret of happiness is work; the secret of successful work is to find, in the horoscope, the thing for which you are best fitted. Don't work to live. If you are working at what you enjoy, you live to work and the harder you work the luckier you become. Everyone can do something or other a little better than anyone else on Earth; consequently everyone has an interest—an objective of some sort—somewhere. If one hopes to succeed in life, one must identify with that objective and direct efforts towards this "something" that can be found in the horoscope. You cannot hope to master your environment, including your love life, unless you can find a sphere where the daily efforts will align with our inner trends. Knowledge of one's horoscope highlights the real part of you. You will know the real from the unreal.

What people call willpower is merely a directing of one's energy in alignment with the trends of one's unique inner urge. After a thorough horoscope interpretation, and learning for certain what you want out of life, use your imaging skills for fast results. Imaging wins over willpower 100 percent of the time! That is why it is so important to never image fears. Change fear thoughts to positive wish thoughts!

Astrology helps prevent chaos by giving us a greater perception of time, harmony, and the rhythm of life. Realize that taking charge of your own fate is not a matter of chance, but of choice. Once you raise your self-esteem to realize that you are special, unique, marvelous, wonderful, and that absolutely no one in the world is just like you, you won't want to leave your life to chance. You will want to have a choice and the determination to use your ability to image what you want and what the Universal Intelligence wants for your good, which is shown in the horoscope.

Whether you are a Hollywood star
Or otherwise want to make the course in par,
Follow the rules of the road above
To find enhanced happiness, health, and love.
Thus you can chart your way through the shoals of strife
Reaching your chosen shore for the best of life.
>   —Jeraldine Saunders

THE AGE OF AQUARIUS

BY ESTELLE DANIELS

Remember when the Moon moved into the Seventh House? That was supposed to be the beginning of the Age of Aquarius. "Aquarius" was the theme song of the 1960s, when peace, love, and bell-bottoms would reign over the dawning of the new age.

When exactly does the Age of Aquarius begin, anyhow? Will it be a date indicated on your calendar, like Columbus' Day, Easter Sunday 2000, or your kid brother's birthday? Sorry, it won't happen that way. You do not wake up one morning to discover it's the Age of Aquarius and everything has changed for the better.

The Age of Aquarius is an astrological thing; all astrologers agree on that. They even agree about what causes it, but they cannot agree on when it begins. In fact, that's a dandy way to start a fistfight among astrologers. Go to an astrological convention, wait until the cocktail hour is underway and loudly proclaim, "The Age of Aquarius began on February 3rd, 1962, and that's that." Then quietly melt into the crowd and watch the fireworks begin.

The traditional (classical) astrologers will probably say the Age of Aquarius won't begin until 2300 or so, when the vernal equinox reaches the last star in the constellation Aquarius. Other astrologers will say the Age of Aquarius will begin anywhere from 1960 to 2410, depending on when the vernal equinox point hits the place one second more than thirty degrees behind Aries. Eventually shouting will begin and maybe violence will even break out.

IS THE AGE OF AQUARIUS HERE YET?

The point of all of this: If astrologers can't agree among themselves (no, it isn't the sort of thing that can be put to a vote), how can the average person expect to know?

The beginning of the Age of Aquarius is more a transition than an actual start date. So when did the transition begin? Opinions vary, but here's a list of some options:

- Industrial Revolution in the 1790s.
- Beginning of the Electrical Age in the 1890.
- First airplane flight in 1906.
- Invention of the zipper in 1913.
- First automobile assembly line in 1914 (the beginning of the Automobile Age).
- World War I (1914–1918).
- First sustained nuclear reaction on December 2, 1942.
- First atomic bomb, Trinity, was exploded on July 16, 1945.
- New-fangled TVs invade American living rooms in 1947–48. Some say it isn't until Uncle Miltie (Milton Berle) came to rule Tuesdays (autumn 1948).
- Beginning of the fast-food age with the first carry-out McDonald's in 1948.
- Invention of Velcro in 1948.
- Beginning of the Space Age, with the Sputnik launch in 1958.
- Song "Aquarius" became a hit in 1967.
- Man landed on the Moon July 20, 1969, and became an interplanetary species. (Others say it doesn't count until an astronaut walked on the Moon on July 21, 1969.)

- Release of the first *Star Wars* movie on May 19, 1977.
- Release of the first *Star Trek* movie on December 6, 1979.
- *Star Trek* premiered September 8, 1966.
- When the Star Wars and Star Trek empires finally merge.
- Premiere of *Star Trek: The Next Generation* in October 1987. Then one cannot ignore the premiere of *Star Trek: Deep Space Nine* in January 1993, or the premiere of *Star Trek Voyager* on January 16, 1995. (These are variations on the Trek Classic vs. New Trek arguments.)
- Ill-fated launch of New Coke on April 23, 1985.
- The Harmonic Convergence on August 16, 1987.
- Start of the Millennium on January 1, 2001.
- End of the Mayan calendar in 2012, when the Earth is synchronized with the rest of the galaxy.
- When human beings finally achieve a stable world government and global peace.

Maybe it will be when a human being finally walks on Mars or when earthlings finally establish a permanent colony on another planet. Some argue it will only come about when a majority of the population can successfully program their VCRs. Some say it won't happen until humankind achieves interstellar space travel, or the aliens land on Earth, whichever comes (or came) first.

Again, there is little consensus. One theme runs through all of these accomplishments. This theme is compatible with the nature of the sign of Aquarius, which is humanitarian, democratic, scientific, technological, future-looking, optimistic, concerned with the betterment of all humanity, and the celebration of each individual to the utmost of their abilities, though in a politically correct manner, of course. Aquarius strives for the eradication of social ills like poverty, ignorance, bigotry, illiteracy, war, disease, monarchies, Swiss bank accounts, The Gnomes of Zurich, and other secret conspiracy groups running the world.

The New Age, whatever that may be (that's a whole other fistfight in itself) is certainly an Age of Aquarius thing. So are video games, VCRs, CDs, the Walkman, PCs, and the Internet.

The Age of Aquarius does not suddenly begin, but sort of oozes in and takes over gradually until most of the old Age of Pisces stuff is history. Most people agree the oozing has already begun. When it began is still a matter for argument, as well as which events signal the Age of Aquarius. Is fast food an innovation or a setback in humanity's evolution? Are you a *Star Wars* fan or a *Star Trek* fan? And do you like Trek Classic or New Trek?

WHAT'S AN "AGE," ANYWAY?

By now, you might be wondering just what the fuss is all about anyhow. What is an "Age,"anyway?

Astrology was invented way back in time, about 5000 BC. or so, give or take a century or two. It did not spring fully formed with transits, computer charts, midpoints, and rectifications, but started with the codification of the phases of the Moon and the naming of the planets in the sky and records of their movements. There were seven planets in all (Sun, Moon, Mercury, Venus, Mars, Jupiter, and Saturn). At the dawn of civilization, it was decided to create standard units to measure time. The first unit of time was the month, from one New Moon to the next. Then that unit was roughly divided into fourths, and seven days became a week, and each day was named for one of those planets in the sky. The seven-day week still exists today.

The ancient astrologers had several things going for them:

1. They could see the sky and stars much better than we can. Modern civilization lights the night and most of the stars are washed out.

2. They lived in the "fertile crescent" in Mesopotamia between the Tigris and Euphrates rivers, in what is now modern Iraq and Iran. This area has a semi-arid climate, so there were relatively few cloudy nights and viewing conditions were very good, which made it easier to track the stars and planets.

3. The priestly class of astrologers had time on their hands. They lived off of offerings from the people, an agricultural society that produced enough surplus to allow for a class that could devote time to the study of such things and not have to raise their own crops.

4. They were believed to interpret the messages of the gods, so their work was given high priority and funded well by the rulers. (Ask any modern research scientist about how vital this one is.)

5. With a stable civilization, storage of records became possible. A body of knowledge accumulated about these stars and planets and their movements through the years and centuries. Once the longer cycles had been observed and codified, then the art of prediction became possible.

(This is the basis for astrological prediction—if a planetary movement caused this result in the past, then the same movement will probably produce the same result in the future. That's all. Really. Now lest you all think that's all there is to being an astrologer, think about how you have to blend the transits of ten planets and take into account the signs those planets are in, and the relationship those planets are making to each other, and you see astrology isn't all that simple after all. This is why computers can only go so far in interpretation. You can program in all the individual definitions for the placements and aspects and transits, but only a human mind is, at present, sophisticated enough to blend it all together into a coherent whole.)

Astrologers also discovered that the stars themselves also move. Not as individuals (even though that does happen, that movement is too slow and subtle even for those ancient astrologers to notice), but the sky itself appears to move slowly backward. What we call the vernal equinox, the point where the Sun's path (ecliptic) crosses from south to north on the celestial equator, or where the Sun is located on the first day of spring changes over the decades and centuries. That point moves backward along the zodiac at a rate of about one astrological sign in 2,160 years. It takes about seventy-two years to move one degree. (A sign has 30 degrees in it—twelve signs times 30 degrees each equals 360 degrees, a full circle.) The duration of the full cycle, about 25,900 years, was calculated accurately around 300 B.C., but many good guesses, based on measurements of increasingly sophisticated accuracy were made from about 2000 B.C. onward. This long cycle is called the Great Year and is divided into twelve

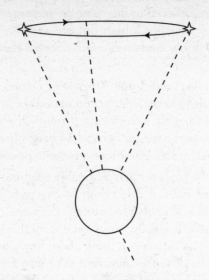

Figure 1. Precession of the Equinoxes

world ages, each named for a sign of the zodiac. We are now in the Age of Pisces, and are moving into the Age of Aquarius.

The Earth rotates on its axis each day, creating day and night. That axis is tilted 23½ degrees to the plane of its movement around the Sun; see Figure 1. This tilt accounts for the seasons and variations in the length of the days and nights as the seasons progress. That axis also rotates slowly. Think of a toy top that "wobbles" at one end as it turns in a circle, as the top spins around the axis. The Earth has a similar motion, its axis turning as the Earth spins from day to day. This wobble is caused by the Moon's gravity pulling on the Earth.

Currently the northern end of the Earth's axis is pointed toward Polaris, the pole star. It was not always pointed there, and it will not always be pointed there. Vega will be the pole star in about 12,000 years, Menkar will be the pole star in about 5,000 years, while Thuban was the pole star about 5,000 years ago. As pole stars go, Polaris is fairly dim and puny. The rotation or wobble of the Earth on its axis is slow. It takes 25,900 years (or thereabouts)

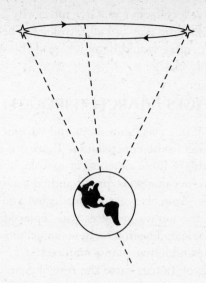

Figure 2. Orientation of the North Star

for the Earth to rotate in a complete circle. As it does so, the vernal equinox point precesses or moves backward through the zodiac, and the pole star also changes; see Figure 2.

The late astronomer Carl Sagan and others who avidly seek to debunk astrology go on about how astrologers are so uninformed they don't even know that when they say the Sun is in Aries, it really is in the constellation Pisces. Astrologers figured all this out before astronomy even existed (starting in 5000 B.C.—if you've been paying attention). Astrology discovered the world ages, and we know we are at the end of the Age of Pisces and moving (backward) into the Age of Aquarius. Maybe if Carl Sagan really had done some proper research, he would have discovered all of this. Or maybe he did, but he would rather ignore it, as he got lots of attention by "debunking" astrology. Only after the invention of the telescope in the 1700s was astronomy divorced from astrology, and astronomy has tried really hard to make the world forget where it came from. Astronomers act as if their mother (astrology) is an uncouth hick who picks her teeth with a knife, belches out loud, and doesn't use underarm deodorant. The way I see it, astronomers have a collective massive inferiority complex, which manifests as picking on any and all astrologers, because we came first. Without us, they would be nowhere. (This snide tirade included at no extra charge.)

THE AGES MARCH THROUGH TIME

By the time all of this was figured out and written up, that vernal equinox point was in the constellation Taurus; it was the Age of Taurus. See Table 1 for a timeline of astrological ages. At that time, agriculture became widespread and civilization settled into towns and cities. Animals were domesticated and used for food, and the role of the hunter-gatherer was replaced by the farmer. Before that, people had been mostly nomadic, moving from place to place as game and native plants matured

After the Age of Taurus came the Age of Aries. This time was characterized by many successive invasions of Europe by nomadic tribes that arrived, conquered, and settled down to rule. During the Age of Taurus, worship was mainly centered on an Earth Mother Goddess type of fertility worship. There were male deities, but they were either equal to or subordinate to the Great Mother Goddess. Property and inheritance was matrilineal, people inherited from their mothers and the women supposedly owned the land and the wealth. The men were companions of the women, helped work the land, fathered children, and helped defend the women, their land, and other property in case of attack. Men also hunted and fought. Some scholars think this was a peaceful time with no wars or large-scale conflict. I won't even go into that fistfight.

With the Age of Aries, invading tribes superimposed their gods onto the old systems. Their male gods were supreme, and the Goddess was equal or subordinate to the supreme sky god. This was a big change, and many cultures had to be "forcibly" converted to these beliefs. Goddess worship still held on into historical times with the Eleusinian Mysteries and other goddess-centered rites and traditions. The Old Testament of the Bible records the change from the worship of the golden calf (Taurus—the bull) and the Goddess Ashteroth to the God-centered worship of Jehovah and the sacrifice of the ram (Aries). Inheritance changed to that of the

ASTROLOGICAL AGES	APPROXIMATE DATES
Virgo	13,060 B.C.–10,900 B.C.
Leo	10,900 B.C.–8740 B.C.
Cancer	8740 B.C.–6580 B.C.
Gemini	6580 B.C.–4420 B.C.
Taurus	4420 B.C.–2260 B.C.
Aries	2260 B.C.–100 B.C.
Pisces	100 B.C.–2060 A.D.
Aquarius	2060 A.D.–4420 A.D.

Table 1. Timeline of Astrological Ages

male lineage, and women were disenfranchised, becoming merely wives of the men who owned the land, and mothers of the sons who would inherit that property. The men still did the hunting and fighting, however.

The civilizations of ancient Greece, Rome, and Persia as well as Alexander the Great and other military empires were manifestations of the Age of Aries. It was an active, bloody time of conflict and warfare between tribes and peoples.

Then came the Age of Pisces. All agree that Jesus and Christianity, as well as Mohammad and Islam, are major legacies of the Age of Pisces. The astrologers of ancient Rome and the rest of the ancient world were acutely aware of the age change that happened around the birth of Jesus. Even then, they could not all agree about when the new age began and the old age ended. Because the shift was from Aries (the first sign of the zodiac) to Pisces (the last sign of the zodiac), they all agreed it was the beginning of a whole new 25,900-year cycle. This change from Aries to Pisces was even more momentous than the previous world age changes.

The New Testament of the Bible tells of Jesus as the herald of the new age, the imminent end of the world, and how the old world will be destroyed and a new world will emerge. Most of these predictions are based on the astrological observations and their interpretation prevalent at the time the New Testament was written (from about 40–250 A.D.) The population in general might not have known about astrology, but a general air of great world changes was in the mass consciousness.

Exactly when the Age of Pisces started is in hot dispute. Speculation ranges from about 200 B.C. (the rise of Rome) to as late as 480 A.D. (the fall of Rome). Common start dates range from about 100 B.C. to about 3 B.C. (The height of power of the Roman Senate in Republican Rome was about 100 B.C.; Jesus is said to have been born in 3 or 4 B.C.) But if each age is 2,160 years long, then precisely marking the start of the Age of Pisces will tell us just when the Age of Aquarius begins. If it started in 200 B.C., then the Age of Aquarius started in 1960. If it didn't start until the birth of Jesus, then the Age of Aquarius will have to wait until 2157 or 2156. If you date it from the fall of Rome, we have to wait until 2640—even after *Star Trek*'s time frame, which takes place in the twenty-fourth century. Now you see why modern astrologers prefer the "oozing into the next age" theory. You avoid the hard-and-fast dates. You can talk about the Age of Aquarius and still be in the Age of Pisces. It's like having your cake and eating it too, and avoiding the fistfight.

Each age vibrates to the influences of the sign of the age and the opposite sign, so the Age of Pisces is like Pisces and Virgo. The Age of Aquarius (as celebrated in the song) will be like Aquarius and Leo. The times of changing influences are "interesting times," like that Chinese blessing/curse "May you live in interesting times." There may be changes in the Earth's climate and topology, the pace of life will accelerate, and important things will happen. People are also more crazy, crackpots abound, new religions, fads, and cults arise, and life is just plain more chaotic.

Does this sound eerily familiar at the cusp of the twenty-first century—*hmmm*? Whether or not you believe we are living in that sort of time probably depends on your age, your socio-economic status, and how fervently you believe whatever it is you believe. And whether it tastes great, or is less filling.

MAYAN ASTROLOGY

BY KEN JOHNSON

During the great days of ancient Mexico, when the pyramids and temples that amaze present-day tourists were first constructed by Native empires, the Mayans and other peoples of that region practiced a unique form of astrology. The system was based on twenty sacred days that repeated endlessly in a great cosmic cycle. Are they connected with the stars and planetary cycles? Are they part of some unique biorhythm that underlies human nature? No one knows for sure. Their origins are lost in time. Some of them, as with Chinese astrology signs, are symbolized by animals; others are symbolized by forces of nature. All we know for certain is that a Mayan day sign is something like a western Sun sign—an essential "signature" of the personality.

Here are the Mayan day-signs, along with basic meanings as given by some contemporary Mayan shamans:

 CROCODILE: Primal and deep, their visionary inner world may sometimes lead them into major trouble, but may also endow them with a talent for creative fantasy.

WIND: The wind blows wildly, and so does the temperament of those born on a wind day. If these people can harness their own ferocity, they can accomplish great things.

 NIGHT: Smooth and clever, these natives can be too slippery for their own good; but when their finely tuned sensibilities turn to good purposes, they can be brilliant.

 LIZARD: Sensual and strong, Lizard people have a number of worldly talents, but need to discipline themselves in order to stay on course—and out of trouble!

 SERPENT: Sly and slow, serious and sexy, the natives of this day-sign can be your most loyal friends or your worst enemies, so treat them with the respect they demand.

 DEATH: This should be called "Transformation!" To the Maya, this is a lucky day-sign; its natives have an ability to gain wisdom while gliding through life's changes.

 DEER: These are the power people, both in worldly and magical terms. At their worst, they're overbearing and domineering; at their best, they can move the world.

 RABBIT: This day-sign is a symbol of abundance and prosperity; lucky for you if this is your birthday. At its worst, it can mean "too much of a good thing"; abundance can become excess.

 WATER: Highly creative and artistic, these natives are very sensitive. In fact, they may well be over-sensitive, with a tendency to fuss and complain.

 DOG: These folks tend to be a bit over-sexed. They need to keep a leash on it (pun intended). At best, they are deeply loyal and eternally good-natured friends.

 MONKEY: These people are very clever, very smart, and very skilled! These are the craftsmen and miracle-workers of the Mayan calendar. At times they can be a bit arrogant.

ROAD: Sometimes known as "Grass," this sign symbolizes the road of life. If this is your birthday, your road will be a good one, with a strong sense of destiny.

 CORN: Also known as "Reed," this sign produces natives who are true "pillars of society," serving as a source of strength and inspiration to those around them.

 JAGUAR: These people are skillful and slick, with a taste for the dark side that is usually redeemed by simple good luck. Jaguar people often become wealthy.

 EAGLE: Like the eagle itself, these people "cry out" for what they want in life—and usually get it. Like the Jaguars, they are likely to become wealthy.

 VULTURE: Slow, good-natured, and easy-going, Vulture people enjoy their lives, their children, and a good time. Karma slides right off them; all is forgiven in the end.

 INCENSE: Also known as "Earthquake," this sign produces the thinkers and philosophers of the Mayan calendar. The lesson is: Learn to control your thoughts!

 FLINT: This is the knife that wounds or heals. Fighters and physicians are both born under this sign—as are a number of remarkably beautiful women.

 STORM: These people are creative, artistic, sensitive, and powerful. This difficult or "stormy" temperament usually comes from a turbulent family history.

 ANCESTORS: The Aztecs knew this sign as "Flower." The soul "flowers" here, for these natives are remarkably close to their families and extremely psychic as well.

Although no easy conversion formula can be given, it's still not that difficult to find your Mayan day sign. You will simply need an almanac or set of tables that convert our western dates to Mayan dates. You can find such tables and an introduction to Mayan spiritual teachings and practices in *Jaguar Wisdom: Mayan Calendar Magic* (Llewellyn Publications, 1997) by Ken Johnson.

THE FINANCIAL
SOLAR FORECAST FOR 1998

BY BARBARA KOVAL, D.F. ASTROL. S.

The millennium is just around the corner and with it comes "end of the world" mania. Not only are we turning into a new century, but we are crossing a new thousand-year mark. Those are merely the numbers. The astrological symbols tell us we are heading for the last earth mutation before we swing into the mini-Age of Aquarius in 2020.

Mutation cycles are conjunctions of Jupiter and Saturn that describe the complexity of supply and demand and long-term economic style.

Capitalism and materialism are about to make one last great thrust before they dissolve into an increasingly humanistic, technocratic, and communal world. Expect to be catalogued, itemized, classified, and crammed into a data bank the size of a pin. The cashless society is coming.

THE YEAR OF THE SUN

For now, there will still be stock markets, numbered bank accounts, and gold as part of the scramble to create and maintain wealth. The Sun is the center of our universe, the source of our power. Its earthly counterpart, gold, is the standard against which we measure our material wealth. In August, we see the first North Node eclipse in Leo. It starts a series of ever-rising tops for the yellow stuff, which should peak in 2000. A node is where the orbits of two planets cross. In the 2020 Aquarius air mutation, the detriment of the Sun, gold may have little beyond ornamental or industrial value. A planet is in its detriment when placed in the sign opposite the sign it rules. For now, the Leo/Aquarius eclipses combined with the strong critical degree/nodal passages of Uranus and Neptune could give us gold's "last hurrah."

Even though gold has appeared insignificant in the last decade or so because of floating exchange rates, it has reflected the slow and low rate of inflationary growth in the United States. The stable trading range of gold in U.S. dollar terms supported the huge price rises in U.S. stocks. Gold is to true wealth what the Sun is to life.

All stock market activity is ultimately driven by the synodic cycles of the Sun. The synodic cycle is the period from a planet's conjunction with the Sun to its next conjunction. In between, the planet makes an opposition. In the simplest terms, the conjunction is the low point and the opposition is the high point. Prices rise to the opposition and fall to the conjunction. For Mercury and Venus, the true conjunction occurs when Mercury and Venus are retrograde and between the Earth and Sun. The true opposition is the conjunction that occurs on the far side of the Sun, when they are direct. The signs in which these phenomena occur mark significant prices in the markets they represent. When the Sun in its own sign forms eclipses, we are seeing super Sun conjunctions and oppositions, and therefore, extremely significant price levels for the stock market as well as gold.

PLUTO IN SAGITTARIUS

Pluto rules debt. Pluto pulls everything beyond its reasonable and equitable limits. It equates to hostile takeovers, raids on pension and trust funds, and debts that cannot be paid off. In Sagittarius it means debt on all levels will continue to expand. Despite reductions in budget deficits, the federal debt is still growing. Consumer debt reached an all-time high as this was being written in December 1996; so are bankruptcies. Transiting in a trine relationship to Aries and Leo, signs of the Sun's strength, indebtedness will continue to promote growth in the speculative markets.

Pluto's continuing inconjunct to the United States' wealth planets, Jupiter and Venus, confirms that money is being sucked into the big black hole of debt and interest rates. This is the year that margin trading could turn a silk purse into a sow's ear.

The greatest rise in indebtedness occurs from the beginning of the year to May 28th; it will ease by November 30th.

NEPTUNE IN AQUARIUS

Neptune rules inflation and influences from afar: international trade, cutting-edge research, spiritual movements, and mass hysteria. For the last fifteen years, Neptune has been bound by the strait jacket of Capricorn. The stock market soaked up all the excess cash that creeping inflation produced. In Aquarius the excess cash may soak the consumer. Neptune in the Third House of the U.S. chart presages a rising tide of exports, but true to the tricky nature of Neptune, imports will rise even higher. U.S. consumers will be competing with foreigners for domestically produced goods, and with the world for goods that are essentially produced by slave labor. (Don't forget that Neptune rules prisons.) Export-import trade is the business to be in. The tourist trade is equally prosperous. Everybody will be traveling all over.

URANUS IN AQUARIUS

Uranus is high technology, the new, the unusual, the unexpected. When Uranus transited Aquarius toward the turn of this century, we went from the horse and buggy, telegrams, and trains to cars, telephones, and planes. Computers and satellites will be your interactive window on the world. People without faces will interact with other people without faces over the Internet. Increasingly, people will remove themselves from a central workplace to do business by computer. Big Brother may not be peering at you from the other side of your four-foot screen, but he will be recording everyone and everything you touch on the World Wide Web. Invest in global technology and the parallel research and development of global privacy.

Uranus in mundane conjunction with Neptune is wonderful for an ever-increasing acceptance of astrology, psychic phenomena, and long-derided intuition. It also bestows crazy fads, hysteria, and floods. Corporations will continue to expand globally. By the air mutation in 2020, only small companies will have a national identity. The big guys will be bound by no nation and no turf. We could also see a renewed interest in outer space, space travel, and communication with extraterrestrials. Everything important will be "outta' sight, far out," and invisible except for the magic of keyboard and screen.

SATURN IN ARIES (UNTIL JUNE)

Not only is Neptune out of the bag, but the bag is full of holes. Minimum discipline, declining order, weak governance, and a decline in civility could ultimately drive us to censorship, but not just yet. Each individual is still responsible mainly to him or herself. Nobody wants to be controlled by anybody else. While the World Wide Web has put us in touch with people all over the world, it also exposes the belly of the beast. The year 1997 will be the best of years and the worst of years. Freedom will ring loud enough to burst your eardrums. Freedom without order creates fear and panic. The universal mantra will be about how bad things are getting and have got.

JUPITER IN PISCES

As if we didn't have enough expansion already, Jupiter enters Pisces in February. Pisces is another inflation symbol. It also rules oil. Money and trade are expanding, like gigantic soufflés. The world is awash in oil, and while this should mean falling oil prices, don't bet on it. In the 1970s, Jupiter hit Pisces just before oil went crazy, and everybody started crying crocodile tears about oil shortages as they waited in line to pump gas. When the price of a commodity gets too low, people stop producing it. When they stop producing it, the price rises. All products of the land, relative to the United States (Jupiter in the U.S. Fourth House) will be abundant. Abundance usually means falling prices. But if the dollar falls in value and we continue to import the bulk of our energy from abroad, oil will rise here while global prices fall because domestic producers will sell their product overseas to people willing to pay higher dollar prices because the dollar is cheap abroad. Watch the exchange value of the dollar and the balance of trade to determine which way Jupiter in Pisces will pump over here.

SATURN IN TAURUS (IN JUNE)

Land may not shrink, but available land becomes scarce or expensive with Saturn, the squeezer, in Taurus, especially if Jupiter in Pisces drove the price sky-high. Saturn in Taurus shrinks capital available for investment and puts tighter restrictions on mortgages and loans. Unload your banking sector holdings and funds. Pluto in Sagittarius means bankruptcies. Saturn in Taurus tightens real estate. The people who have loans don't pay them. The people who don't have them don't want them or do not qualify.

THE TRACKS OF THE SUN 1998

The entrance of the Sun into the four cardinal signs of the zodiac, the ingresses, marks the dominant activity of the social, economic, and political inclinations of each quarter of the year. The forecasts will be divided into analyses of the ingresses, followed by the impact the major solar activity of each month is likely to have on the stock market or relevant sector of the financial markets. It is best to look at the months as blocks of time when the market will rise or fall, not as indicative of a price level relative to one another. For instance, if the market is forecast to rise on May 15th, rise again on May 31st, and rise a third time on June 15th, each top may or may not be higher than the one before. The forecast means only that the price will drop in between.

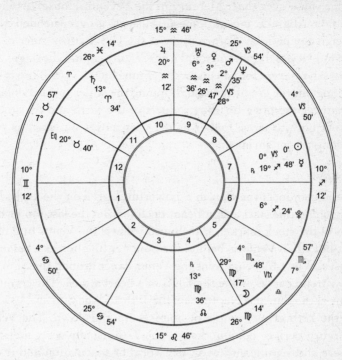

Capricorn Ingress
December 21, 1997, New York, N.Y., 3:07:00 PM EST

FIRST QUARTER:
SUN IN CAPRICORN

The Sun enters the sign of Capricorn on December 21, 1997; this
ingress sets the tone for the first quarter of 1998. The year is off to
a good start with Jupiter on the Midheaven. Hope and confidence
return as Pluto moves off the descendant and Mars and Venus
move away from their conjunction, a low price indicator to bigger
and better numbers when they join with Uranus and Jupiter. The
Sun in the Seventh House, just short of the Eighth House, shines
brightly on debt instruments and bonds. The Ninth House stelli-
um suggests heavy foreign investment, especially in bonds, because of rising interest rates. Remember that a declining dollar
forces high interest rates to compensate for the potential loss of

dollar value over time. Mercury in the Seventh House, debilitated and retrograde, means domestic business is overwhelmed by its foreign competition. Saturn opposes the U.S. Saturn, ruler of the Second House, regulating banks or creating capital shortages and low cash reserves for consumers. Neptune on the U.S. Pluto is still maxing out the credit cards and tipping the scales toward default. Whatever the price for the products of the earth and for stocks, expect both to move higher as the year moves on, even as purchasing power shrinks.

January

Venus conjuncts the Sun in a powerful degree on the 16th. Not only could this start a significant decline from the last top or bottom in the stock market, it technically starts the Venus bull market, but when Venus is behind the Sun, her function as a balancer ceases. When Mercury joins the Venus dance around the Sun, the Dow trend can look like the EKG of a heart attack. The conjunctions of the Sun and Neptune on the 19th and the Sun and Uranus on the 28th give a couple of bounces up and down. The Venus Mercury perigee conjunction on the 27th usually correlates to a severe and significant low in the world of speculation and trade. It is difficult to say whether the perigee conjunction will produce its knockout punch before or after the 28th. Stay alert. Most likely the market will stumble and rise all month. It will either bottom out or take a good-sized hit on or about the 28th.

February

The stock market hits its monthly high around the 23rd as Mercury, Jupiter, and the Sun join forces. Don't expect too much as the normal correction of Venus retrograde is unlikely to unravel fully before March 1st. The eclipse on February 26th is square the U.S. Uranus, bringing some shocking news, maybe very bad weather in the east. It, too, is likely to mark a market low.

March

The eclipse on the 12th marks an important mid-range price for silver. It also presages price reversals and general difficulties in all speculative markets. Prices fall as Mercury takes some bad hits the final ten days.

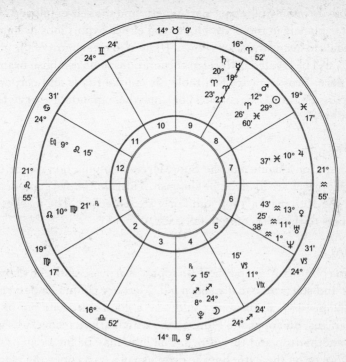

Aries Ingress
March 20, 1998, New York, N.Y., 2:54:00 PM EST

SECOND QUARTER 1998:
ARIES INGRESS

The second quarter looks calmer. The planets are all on the west side of the chart, putting the U.S. at the mercy of the global economy. Saturn in the Ninth House means imports slack off or come under increasing restriction. It also means more government regulation generally. Mercury, ruler of the Second House, placed in the Ninth House, makes our own money our biggest import. Look for an increase in the money supply as foreigners buy up our goods with the dollars we once used to buy theirs.

Venus, Uranus, and Neptune in the Sixth House create a very volatile job market. The government may give us rosy employment statistics, but the jobs gained are either fewer than the jobs lost or made up mainly of temps, part-timers, and the self-employed. The outer planets in the Sixth House can either export jobs or import illegals to keep labor costs down. It can also mean most of the good jobs will be created by foreign corporations, who establish branches here. Prospects are favorable for mutual funds and corporate expansion, but U.S. corporations may be expanding everywhere but here.

APRIL

Except for a bounce at the Sun/Mercury conjunction on the 6th, stock prices are likely to be sluggish. The Sun/Saturn conjunction on the 13th marks a top and fairly steep decline. The market recovers to the 18th, only to fall back.

MAY

Sun conjunct Mars on the 12th tops a sharp rise in the stock market and starts an equally sharp fall. Mercury conjuncts Saturn simultaneously, so this one could take a good-sized bite out of the averages. Sun opposite Pluto on the 28th marks a recovery as well as another top and turn down. The high may be hit a day or two before or on the 29th, but the drop usually starts once the planets are out of orb.

JUNE

Prices continue to decline to the Mercury/Mars conjunction on the 5th, then struggles up to Mercury's superior conjunction on the 10th. Mercury is invisible to the 18th, with little ability to sustain a rise if May took a bad hit. Look for nervous jumps through the first half of the month, even though June usually sets a semi-annual high on or near the ingress, described below.

THIRD QUARTER: CANCER INGRESS

The third quarter looks strong with Venus and the Moon in the Tenth House showering prosperity on the markets. They also make for a hot real-estate market, especially for higher-priced homes. Jupiter in the Eighth House is positive for bonds, as it increases indebtedness, investment capital, and margin buying. The

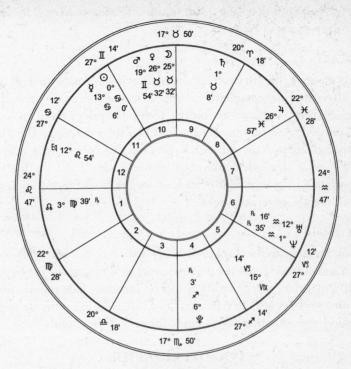

Cancer Ingress
June 21, 1998, New York, N.Y., 10:03:00 AM EST

stock market is likely to hit the year's top now, just before Saturn in Taurus douses the flames.

Saturn in the Sixth House of the U.S. chart is very negative for jobs. Poor job prospects are reinforced by Uranus and Neptune, still in the Sixth House. Temporary and part-time employment is part of the never-ending search for cheaper labor costs, here and elsewhere. The best jobs will be found in small domestic companies that serve fundamental needs: clothing, home, and food. Food prices could rise because of crop damage with Pluto in the Fourth House. The latter bodes ill for the dollar, too.

JULY

Late June and early July find Jupiter in critical market degrees, which correlate with rising stock and bond prices. The Sun opposes Neptune on the 23rd, to top off rising indices. The serious drop starts in August.

AUGUST

This month's Mercury retrograde market decline may hold off until after the Sun completes its opposition of Uranus on the 3rd. Sun-Mercury conjunction on the 13th pulls prices back up for a couple of days as we move to the first Leo solar eclipse on the 21st. Although eclipses are difficult to predict, this North Node eclipse in a sign of strength could mark either a significant top for the month or a long-term mid-price level for the stock market and precious metals, especially gold.

SEPTEMBER

Look for a rise to the Jupiter-Sun opposition on the 15th, followed by a sometimes severe drop. Any planet in Virgo marks important shifts in price, often timing a top or bottom. This month Sun, Venus, and eventually Mercury join forces in the ultimate turnaround sign. Another top is likely the end of the month.

FOURTH QUARTER:
LIBRA INGRESS

Saturn sits right on top of this chart, not very favorable for demand or for prices overall. The more disturbing configuration on this chart is Uranus and Neptune in the Seventh House of enemies, competitors, and trading partners. Either Uncle Sam is being taken advantage of or the world has its hand out for aid. On the side of self-interest, we may "just say no" to some of our more self-sacrificing obligations. Whatever the decision, the people won't like it. It is quite possible the U.S. will make a treaty or reach an agreement with a country, resulting in casualties in 1999. Mars retrograde in Scorpio, Pluto opposite Uranus, and an eclipse on the U.S. Moon in 1999 could push us to the brink of battle, if not over the line.

Imports grow like gangbusters with Jupiter in the Ninth House. The consumer price index grabs the popular attention. Though retail sales look good, everybody's budget is strained with Mars in the Second House. The Moon in the Fourth House

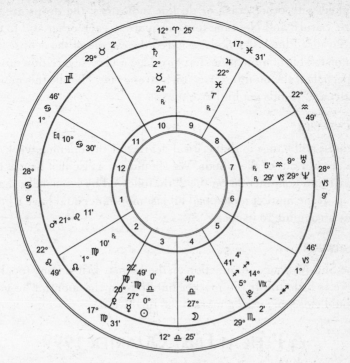

Libra Ingress
September 23, 1998, New York, N.Y., 1:38:00 AM EDT

square Neptune should just about end the boom in real estate. Sell now. Buy later.

OCTOBER

The Libra ingress marks the most difficult time of the year for the stock market. At the Sun/Saturn opposition on the 23rd, we should see a tepid rise and a sharp fall. Venus makes her superior Sun conjunction on the 29th to start the technical bear market. Venus is dark from October 7th–19th, which means all the controls are off. The worrisome condition this month is the station of Uranus in 8 degrees of Aquarius. While not a strong aspect to the great mutation 8 degrees of Capricorn, it does represent its natural Second House of money. Uranus is one of several crash indicators. By itself it breaks through price barriers, upside or down.

Linked with other crash or decline indicators, the drops are severe. Saturn and Neptune form a square to each other and to the U.S. radix Pluto. The nodes entered the degree of the eclipse last August. This combination may produce a very severe downturn, especially if the month started on a strong rise. Handle this month with care. Bonds get hit hard, too.

NOVEMBER

Uranus still hangs in that critical degree for the opening week, so we are not out of the woods. We should see a rise just before the Sun-Pluto conjunction on the 29th, followed by its usually sharp drop. If the market took a bad hit last month, it could have a hard time struggling to its feet.

DECEMBER

The Sun-Mercury conjunction on the 1st may bring a tiny top, but there is little to lift the market until late in the month. The year should close on a rising market the final week.

A PEEK AT FIRST QUARTER 1999

The Capricorn ingress emphasizes the Fifth House of children, speculation, and the energy that drives production. Government will attempt stricter control over energy usage, hiring practices, and worker safety. Look for major changes in trade policy, along with attempts to curtail imports, migrant workers, and illegals. Jupiter in the Eighth House expands debt and taxes. Mercury, ruler of the Second House, conjunct Pluto dittos increasing indebtedness on the consumer side. Investment money flows into bonds rather than stocks. Rising interests rates guarantee a long-term profit without the short-term anxieties of a stock market whose day-to-day direction is uncertain.

A BRIDGE TO THE TWENTY-FIRST CENTURY

The years just before the lesser mutation bring with them financial and economic distress. The economic decline ends at the Jupiter/Saturn conjunction in the year 2000. If the decade of the nineties is as successful as the decade of the fifties, we should see mainly a slowing down, as the stock market catches its breath before making another stab at Dow 10,000, assuming it is still in the running. On the other hand, if the market has seriously declined or crashed, it will take many years to retrieve the loss.

The action of the government is extremely crucial. Attempts will be made to curb imports and to protect the dollar. This means rising interest rates and higher prices across the board. Remember that American workers are competing in a free market, particularly for unskilled and semi-skilled work, with the lowest-paid workers in the world. The globalization of corporations takes advantage of the protection of the U.S. government by its nominal allegiance to the country of its origin, but maintains no loyalty to the prosperity of the citizens who not only are their biggest markets but on whose back these same corporations were built. Perhaps the government will find some middle ground between freedom and regulation that supports both the corporation and the millions of people who must pay for food and shelter despite policies that price them out of the job market. The constant patterns in these ingress charts are burgeoning debt and shaky jobs. The country and its people can afford neither.

Whatever the economic conditions, prudence, hard assets, and freedom from debt carry us through. If you own the roof over your head and the mortgage is paid off, you have eliminated one of the biggest living expenses. The anticipated rises in precious metals, energy, and land do not mean they are increasing in value, but that inflation is filtering back to us from overseas because of a dollar decline. Protect your assets. If you want the generosity of your heart to spill out to others, you must have something to give. Give time or give money. Time is limited. Money expands indefinitely.

YOUR TRAVEL OUTLOOK
FOR 1998

BY GLORIA STAR

Y ou travel for many reasons. Regardless of your motivation, while expanding your sense of the world, travel can be inspiring. Travel provides adventurous exploration, and it affords the chance to learn, to open your mind to new possibilities and to extend your view of the world and her people.

The planetary energies most strongly related to travel are those of Mercury and Jupiter. Through the energy of Mercury, you gather information and link your ideas with those of others. Mercurial travel is shorter in duration and distance, including traveling about town. Jupiter's energy is expansive, stimulating travel of longer distances, including foreign travel. Through Jupiter, you broaden your understanding and experience inspiration. Although other planetary energies may be connected to travel, the cycles from these energies usually stimulate your opportunity to be on the go.

With the advent of computer technology and the Internet, the people of the world are connecting without having to go anywhere. You can see new places, view the arts, hear the music, and converse with people halfway around the world from the comfort of your living room! For centuries, books have helped to bridge this gap, and then radio and TV effectively brought the world's inhabitants closer together. Although these experiences can lead you to a better understanding, when you want to truly immerse yourself in a different place, it's more effective to be there. When you're physically in a different environment, your senses take in the experience, and your psyche assimilates a more comprehensive understanding of the place, its essence, and culture. If you're hoping to take a trip this year or to spend more time away from home exploring the world, different planetary cycles can add to or detract from the experience. These cycles also pinpoint the kind of experience you are likely to have through travel.

The influence of Mercury on travel emergees in all the details —the background reading, booking the trip, making the lists of everything you need, determining the schedule that will suit your needs. Strong aspects from Mercury help to assure that you'll be more mentally alert, and that you'll be able to make the connections necessary to have a successful trip.

You've probably heard that it's not a good idea to travel when Mercury is retrograde. Although travel may be more complicated during these periods, it is not necessarily more dangerous. In fact, if you are traveling during a Mercury retrograde cycle, there's a good chance you'll end up returning to that place, because these can be very good periods for stimulating a deeper interest in the place or its people. For smoother traveling, you'll be most satisfied if you avoid traveling when Mercury is at a stationary point, listed in Table 1. These are the days when Mercury is moving from direct to retrograde motion or from retrograde to direct motion. At these times, Mercury appears to be just sitting there and sometimes you end up doing the same thing! More than once I've sat in an airplane stuck on the tarmac for hours when Mercury was stationary. Check your calendar and try to avoid initiating a trip or returning home on the days when Mercury is stationary.

Table 1. Mercury Stationary Days in 1998

Jupiter's cycles provide a good indicator of the kinds of travel that can be most appealing on a more universal level. In January, Jupiter spends its final month in Aquarius and it is accompanied by the fiery energy of Mars. Although this is likely to be a powerful time for international relations and politics, it is also an excellent time to plan travel that could result in some type of breakthrough or innovation. Travel to unusual places, areas with current global interest, or large cities has wide appeal during January. This is especially true for the air and fire signs—Aries, Gemini, Leo, Libra, Sagittarius, and Aquarius. Once Jupiter moves into Pisces in February, where it will remain through the rest of 1998, travel to places that are more serene. Locales that are surrounded by water (island or coastal vacations) or retreat-oriented may be appealing.

For each Sun sign, there are periods that mark better times to travel, that experiences will be most profitable or enjoyable and when travel should be avoided. In addition to Mercury and Jupiter, it's important to underscore the other long-term transit cycles to your Sun that can indicate factors that could limit or extend your need and opportunity to travel.

ARIES

If you're an Aries, you may indeed have significant travel periods. January is especially notable for travel that will inspire your plans for the future. Because Saturn is in Aries this year, many of your travel plans may be work-related, but you can still enjoy yourself when you're on the road or in the air. Since Jupiter transits through the Twelfth House of your solar chart this year, you'll profit from travel that allows you to let go and relax, taking time out from your high-pressure routine. This would be an excellent year to plan a spiritual retreat. From March 8th–May 14th, Mercury is in Aries, marking a significant time of making contact through travel. However, you may also be busy dealing with details of business and may have better luck with shorter travel periods and distances. For that extended length vacation you'll enjoy the period from August 14th–September 23rd. Travel in November and December can be enjoyable, with your best time for pleasure from November 18th–30th. But since Mercury is retrograde, double-check all your arrangements, and allow a little extra time for delays or interruptions in your plans.

TAURUS

If you're a Taurus, you may be too busy dealing with family or work demands to go anywhere in January, unless you're in and out very quickly. However in February, when Mars and Jupiter are both in Pisces, you may find strong success traveling in association with your work or sharing experiences like conferences with your colleagues. Throughout the year, Jupiter's transit influences the Eleventh House of your solar chart emphasizing opportunities to expand your outreach on a regional level, but can also mark a good year for travel that builds professional connections. Travel from March 1st–21st can be filled with pressing demands or issues that may make it difficult to enjoy. There's an excellent period from April 20th–May 17th for pleasurable travel, but watch out for surprises from April 27th–30th that can throw your plans into a tailspin. Business travel fares nicely from May 15th–31st, but may not be especially enjoyable in July. If you want to travel in August, target August 1st–12th, although you might prefer to be at home. September 8th–30th marks a positive time for travel that caters to your special indulgences. Staying close to home during the fall months is likely to feel better, but if you must travel allow ample time for distractions from November 1st–13th. December 12th–31st can bring an excellent time for travel that frees you from the pressures of the daily grind.

GEMINI

Since you like to be on the go much of the time (and probably arrange your life around the times when you can do just that) you'll appreciate the fact that there are ample opportunities to travel this year. In January, you're ready to go at a moment's notice, but need to scale back on your plans after the 26th to be sure you're not overlooking something important at home. When Jupiter enters Pisces in February, you'll feel a strong wanderlust brewing and can benefit from foreign interaction or travel that takes you to an exotic locale. Since Jupiter is influencing the Tenth House of your solar chart this year, travel can very likely be the result of career growth. March is an excellent month to travel professionally and to also squeeze in a little recreational enjoyment in the process, but April brings your travel time into professional focus. May is a good time to do your homework and networking. Exciting and recreational travel are the highlights in June and July, with July 1st–18th providing your best options for a real vacation. August and September bring your focus closer to home, so ask people to travel to see you! Consider travel for pleasure from October 1st–18th. November and December are your negotiating months and you may be sending a lot of messages in November, but making more successful trips in early December.

CANCER

As a Cancer, you love to travel to places that feel like home and reflect your personal values, but you can also enjoy the diversity stimulated by travel as long as you feel safe. Jupiter moves into the Ninth House of your solar chart in February, where it remains through the rest of the year. This energy marks a significant period for foreign or long-distance travel. Your best periods for pleasurable travel occur from April 6th–May 4th, June 15th–30th, July 19th–August 12th and October 12th–November 14th. Business and professional travel can be profitable from February 20th–March 3rd. But it's a good idea to avoid travel from March 26th–April 11th unless it is work related, since you may not feel like painting the town red. You may be on the go a lot in September and late November, probably running lots of errands and taking care of business! December travels are best limited to your favorite local haunts.

LEO

Leos like to travel for pleasure, and you like going to places that cater to your special needs and desires. This is a great year for business travel, and with Saturn transiting through the Ninth House of your solar chart, you may also have a chance to do some foreign travel, although you'll enjoy it more if you can be away long enough to get into the culture. Jupiter transits through the Eighth House of your solar chart starting in February, indicating that your travel could be the result of good fortune from others. January and February can be good months for shorter trips, but you may not have as much fun from January 29th–February 8th. Your best period for pleasurable extended travel is from March 9th–April 6th. For less extensive journeys, plan to travel from July 4th–18th, September 25th–October 9th, and November 18th–December 11th for business or pleasure. You may not enjoy travel from June 6th–29th because of pressing obligations that require your time and energy, and you can also be very frustrated with travel in August for the same reasons.

VIRGO

Virgos like to travel if the creature comforts are amenable. Since Jupiter is transiting in opposition to your Sun this year, you'll feel restless and in need of a few diversions. Travel can be the perfect option, especially if it challenges your mind or sparks new ideas. The best periods for pleasurable travel are from April 17th–27th, May 15th–24th, July 19th–August 13th (despite the Mercury retrograde cycle!), and the very best from September 6th–30th or from October 13th–November 7th—especially if you can really escape for a while. Business travel can be profitable from January 13th–30th, May 16th–29th, and June 20th–30th. However, you may not enjoy travel from June 20th–July 6th unless it's close to home, since unusual or extremely competitive circumstances may feel too disconcerting.

LIBRA

Librans truly enjoy travel, especially if you can go in style! The exciting energy stimulated by Mars and Jupiter in January can spark a fun-filled travel cycle, although you may spend too much money! In February, when Jupiter enters Pisces, its energy highlights the Sixth House of your solar chart for the remainder of the year, indicating a rewarding period for business travel. You may even travel for health benefits, and this could be an excellent year to plan a spa or fitness-oriented getaway. From February 4th–25th, you'll enjoy travel that provides unusual and innovative experiences for your diversion, and you could be very successful blending business with pleasure. March and April are OK for short business trips, but you may feel too constrained to enjoy fun-oriented trips. From May 24th–July 7th plan foreign travel or a journey that expands your cultural awareness. Business travel is highlighted from July 19th–September 6th, although you'll prefer to stay close to home from August 1st–24th. After making careful plans in September, you're in a perfect position to enjoy a getaway from October 1st–23rd. Your energy is best for holiday travel from December 13th–31st.

SCORPIO

Scorpios prefer to travel with a sense of purpose. You'll enjoy travel most when you can take your time exploring an area or if you're surrounded by people or circumstances that stir your imagination. Jupiter's transit highlights your solar Fifth House, marking a wonderful year for entertaining travel. This is a good year for taking long weekends with your lover and indulging in your most pleasurable pastimes. Too much is happening on the home front to travel far in January and most of February, but from February 21st–March 8th you might enjoy a pleasurable retreat. Short, goal-oriented business trips are OK in March, but you might be more successful directing business in familiar surroundings from March 10th–April 20th. For the rest of the year, the best time to take that perfect vacation is from October 12th–November 16th. Business trips can be successful from August 1st–20th if you're well-prepared, and then from September 8th–24th.

SAGITTARIUS

Since you're a grand adventurer, you love to travel, but only when everything goes smoothly and you don't have to wait around or deal with delays. January is an excellent month for travel, whether for business or pleasure, especially from the 1st–13th, when you could combine both. After that, business travel is most prominent. Once Jupiter enters Pisces on February 4th, it will transit through the Fourth House of your solar chart for the rest of the year, indicating that you can gain from travel close to home, or that you may be moving to a larger home, expending much of your "travel" energy on this very personal level. Shorter business trips are workable from February 2nd–19th. If you want to take a vacation, you'll enjoy the energy from March 9th–April 5th, although you can be distracted by business after March 28th. Foreign travel is highlighted from July 1st–18th and August 14th–September 8th. Your best time to travel for business or pleasure is from November 2nd–December 31st, with pleasure taking top billing from November 17th–December 11th.

CAPRICORN

As a Capricorn, you enjoy the outreach travel provides and use travel as an inspiration for your personal and professional growth. With Jupiter's energy supporting the Third House of your solar chart after February 4th, you'll probably be on the go a lot during 1998. Keep your bags packed for those short, frequent journeys. Your most outstanding periods for profitable business travel are January 13th–February 2nd, February 21st–March 8th, May 15th–June 1st, and October 13th–November 1st. For personal pleasure, consider traveling from June 16th–25th, September 8th–30th and December 12th–31st. Travel from March 25th–April 14th is not a good idea, since there are too many frustrations, delays, obligations, and interruptions.

AQUARIUS

Since you enjoy unusual experiences, travel is always a grand opportunity for discovery. Although January is the most energetic month for you to travel, there are other good travel cycles for you during 1998. Jupiter transits through the Second House of your solar chart from February through the end of the year, marking an excellent period for business travel or travel that profits you and expands your personal resources. You do need to make sure that your expenses do not exceed your capabilities to pay for them, however! Business-oriented travel can be most profitable from February 2nd–20th, March 9th–25th, July 1st–17th, September 25th–October 12th, and November 18th–December 10th. For vacation or pleasure travel, you'll enjoy the energy from March 4th–27th, June 2nd–21st, and December 12th–31st.

PISCES

You're in for a travel treat this year, since Jupiter is transiting over your Sun. Whether your journeys are long or short, you may feel more open to the adventure and opportunity afforded by travel. January is a good month to stay close to home and get everything in order. Avoid travel from February 1st–7th, since you could get caught in circumstances beyond your control that put a big dent in your plans. For business or pleasure, you'll enjoy travel from February 27th–March 8th. The best times to travel for business are from May 16th–31st and October 13th–30th. For pleasurable or vacation-oriented travel, look into these dates: June 16th–30th, July 20th–31st, or October 25th–30th. Consider taking a journey to a place that will lift your spirits and spark your imagination! Travel from November 14th–December 7th can be totally frustrating, so you might prefer to stay close to home. Holiday travel from December 19th–30th could be a nice break, though.

THE WONDERS
OF VEDIC ASTROLOGY

BY RONNIE DREYER

Editor's Note: Used for centuries in India, vedic (Hindu) astrology is based on the sidereal, or fixed, zodiac. The sidereal system uses 0 degrees of the actual constellation Aries as its starting point, while the tropical system (used throughout this book) uses the spring equinox (0 degrees of the sign of Aries). There is about 23 degrees of difference between the two systems.

Based on the position of the planets as they travel through the sidereal or fixed zodiac, vedic (Hindu) astrology, known in India as *jyotish* (Sanskrit for "study of the *jyotis*, or heavenly lights") is an ancient system of astrology whose interpretive and predictive techniques are still used today with amazing accuracy.

In fact, most remarkable about the current renaissance of this age-old tradition is that the heavenly bodies were used as forecasting tools as early as the Vedic Era (1500–1000 B.C.). At that time, noteworthy events and sacred rituals were marked by the positions of the planets in their Moon mansions, or fixed star constellations. Placing the luminaries in their signs and houses didn't come until the Fifth Century A.D., when the rules of jyotish were methodically recorded in a series of classic texts. Given the fact that the scriptures were written hundreds of years ago, it is quite remarkable to think that these descriptions can still apply to contemporary horoscopes. After all, if certain planetary configurations gave way to particular events thousands of years ago, it is just as likely that similar events will occur under the influence of those very same planetary patterns.

Using the "Whole Sign" House System

Table 1 is an illustration of Queen Elizabeth's chart using what is termed a "whole sign" house system. This means that the exact sign and degree of the sidereal Ascendant, or *Lagna*, will determine which sign comprises the entire First House. Since her sidereal ascending or rising degree falls at 28° (degrees) Sagittarius 44' (minutes), the first house contains the entire 30 degrees of Sagittarius; the Second House contains the entire sign of Capricorn; the Third House is Aquarius; the Fourth House is Pisces, etc. Each house is then marked by the number of the corresponding sign. The signs and their corresponding numbers are: Aries, 1; Taurus, 2; Gemini, 3; Cancer, 4; Leo, 5; Virgo, 6; Libra, 7; Scorpio, 8; Sagittarius, 9; Capricorn, 10; Aquarius, 11; and Pisces, 12. You will notice that the signs are in the same order used in tropical astrology.

Instead of using astrological glyphs, we insert the number of the corresponding sign of the Ascendant in the upper central box. In the case of Queen Elizabeth, the number "9" corresponds to the sidereal Sagittarius Ascendant. The subsequent numbers then follow counter-clockwise around the chart to show the sequential houses, beginning with the Second House (number 10, Capricorn, in Queen Elizabeth's chart) and ending with the Twelfth House. Since Queen Elizabeth's vedic Ascendant is in Sagittarius and the number for Sagittarius is 9, the number 9 is placed in the First House in her vedic chart.

We then place the planets in their proper signs or houses as indicated. Since it is positioned in the first sign of Aries, the Sun is

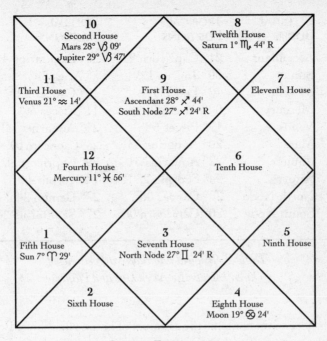

QUEEN ELIZABETH
April 21, 1926, 1:40 AM GMT, London, England
51° N 30' Latitude, 00° W 06' Longitude

Table 1. Queen Elizabeth's Vedic Horoscope

placed in the Fifth House. The Moon is in the fourth sign of Cancer in the Eighth House. Mercury is in the twelfth sign of Pisces in the Fourth House. Venus is in the eleventh sign of Aquarius in the Third House. Mars is in the tenth sign of Capricorn in the Second House. Jupiter is in the tenth sign of Capricorn in the Second House. Saturn is in the eighth sign of Scorpio in the Twelfth House. The North Node is in the third sign of Gemini in the Seventh House, and the South Node is in the ninth sign of Sagittarius in the First House.

The Ascendant, or *Lagna,* is one of the most important elements of vedic astrology, with natives identifying themselves by their rising signs, in much the same way that we tend to identify ourselves by our Sun signs. Because an equal house system is employed, there is only one set of houses for each Ascendant and, therefore,

CELESTIAL BODIES	TROPICAL POSITIONS	SIDEREAL POSITIONS
Ascendant	21° Capricorn 21'	28° Sagittarius 44'
Sun	00° Taurus 12'	7° Aries 29'
Moon	12° Leo 07'	19° Cancer 24'
Mercury	04° Aries 40'	11° Pisces 56'
Venus	13° Pisces 58'	21° Aquarius 14'
Mars	20° Aquarius 53'	28° Capricorn 09'
Jupiter	22° Aquarius 31'	29° Capricorn 47'
Saturn	24° Scorpio 27'R	1° Scorpio 44'
North Node	20° Cancer 06'	27° Gemini 24'
South Node	20° Capricorn 06'	27° Sagittarius 24'

*Table 2. Tropical and Sidereal Positions of
Queen Elizabeth's Ascendant and Planets*

each Ascendant contains the same set of house rulerships. For example, everyone with a Sagittarius Ascendant (in the vedic system) like Queen Elizabeth's will have Saturn as the ruler of the Second Aquarius House, Jupiter as the ruler of the Third Pisces House, and Mars as the ruler of the Fourth Aries House.

FINDING QUEEN ELIZABETH'S HOROSCOPE

Using the horoscope of Great Britain's Queen Elizabeth II, let's illustrate how some of these ancient principles still work. But first we must convert her planets from their tropical to their sidereal positions and place them within the Indian chart. Her birth data is April 21, 1926, 2:40 AM BDT, London, England, 51° N 30' Latitude, 0° W 06' Longitude. Table 2 lists the corresponding tropical and sidereal positions of Queen Elizabeth's Ascendant and planets. Note that Uranus, Neptune, and Pluto are not listed because they are not used in vedic astrology.

Let's see how we can utilize some of these age-old delineations. In *Brihat Jataka*, India's sixth-century classic, its author, Vara-hamihira, lists hundreds of *raj yogas* (royal unions), or planetary

PLANETS	RULERSHIP	EXALTATION	FALL
Sun	Leo	Aries	Libra
Moon	Cancer	Taurus	Scorpio
Mars	Aries Scorpio	Capricorn	Cancer
Mercury	Gemini Virgo	Virgo	Pisces
Jupiter	Sagittarius Pisces	Cancer	Capricorn
Venus	Taurus Libra	Pisces	Virgo
Saturn	Capricorn Aquarius	Libra	Aries

Table 3. Planetary Rulerships, Exaltations, and Falls

combinations that promise to bring luck, prosperity, and success if they are so placed in the chart. One such yoga states that when three or more planets occupy their exaltation or rulership signs, the person for whom the chart was constructed will become a king if he belongs to a king's family. When five or more planets are placed in their exaltation or rulership signs, the person becomes a king even if he is born into a lowly family. However, if the number of powerful planets totals less than three or five, respectively, the native will be rich but not a king.

The modern concept of "kingship" can simply mean being in charge, in the sense of holding a powerful corporate or political position, or owning a successful business. Belonging to a "king's family" means that you may inherit either wealth or opportunities that only your family can provide, while coming from a "lowly family" implies that you may rise above modest circumstances.

These planetary yogas, or combinations, are just a few among hundreds that are easy to compute and provide easy-to-use keys to personal happiness and success. Table 3 lists the exaltation, rulership, and fall signs of the planets used in vedic astrology. These concepts are also used in tropical (Western) astrology.

The sign a planet rules is where that planet operates most comfortably and whose attributes are shared by both the zodiacal sign and its ruling planet. For example, both Cancer and its planetary ruler, the Moon, are concerned with maternal instincts, home, and the family. Whereas the planet's sign of rulership is one that shares common traits with the planets, the sign of exaltation is where the planet truly "shines" most brightly. The planet's fallen sign, opposite of its place of exaltation, is where the planet is exceptionally weak and can never "be itself."

With Sun in Aries (exaltation), Moon in Cancer (rulership), and Mars in Capricorn (exaltation), Queen Elizabeth II is a perfect example of how this raj yoga helped her to achieve the promise of her birth chart. Despite the fact that she was not really in line for the throne, she possessed three planets in their rulership and exaltation signs and was indeed born into a royal family. Elizabeth became queen after the death of her father, who by a twist of fate inherited the throne from his brother, King Edward VIII, who abdicated to marry the woman he loved. Under normal circumstances, Edward would have been expected to provide his own heirs to the throne, but because he chose to marry a commoner, the American-born Wallis Simpson, Elizabeth's father was crowned King George VI in 1937. Of course, this immediately placed Elizabeth next in line to the monarchy. When King George VI died unexpectedly in 1952, his daughter not only became Queen of England at the age of twenty-one, but has maintained her position and popularity among the British people for over forty-five years.

Although her chart does indeed display other successful aspects, it was this particular *yoga* that played itself out rather dramatically and allowed her to become queen. If she had been born into a family of commoners, she may have been quite successful but would never have achieved this type of greatness. These yogas, therefore, will only allow you to achieve what is actually plausible within the circumstances of your birth.

FINDING SHIRLEY MACLAINE'S HOROSCOPE

Table 4 illustrates the horoscope of Shirley MacLaine, the highly successful actress. She was born on April 24, 1934, 3:57 PM EST,

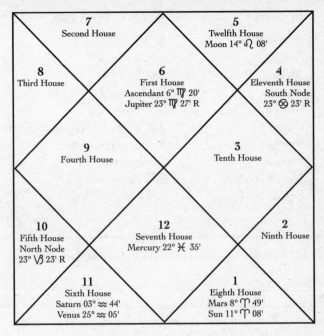

7 Second House		**5** Twelfth House Moon 14° ♌ 08'	
8 Third House	**6** First House Ascendant 6° ♍ 20' Jupiter 23° ♍ 27' R		**4** Eleventh House South Node 23° ♋ 23' R
	9 Fourth House	**3** Tenth House	
10 Fifth House North Node 23° ♑ 23' R	**12** Seventh House Mercury 22° ♓ 35'		**2** Ninth House
11 Sixth House Saturn 03° ♒ 44' Venus 25° ♒ 05'		**1** Eighth House Mars 8° ♈ 49' Sun 11° ♈ 08'	

SHIRLEY MACLAINE
April 24, 1934, 3:57 PM EST, Richmond, Virginia
37° N 33' Latitude, 77° W 27' Longitude

Table 4. Shirley MacLaine's Vedic Horoscope

Richmond, Virginia, 37° N 33' Latitude, 77° W 27' Longitude. Her sidereal Ascendant and planets are listed in Table 5.

With the Sun in Aries (exaltation), Mars in Aries (rulership), and Saturn in Aquarius (rulership), Shirley MacLaine also has this raj yoga, which states that if you have three or more planets in their exaltation and rulership signs, you will become a king if you are born into a royal family. Although her background was middle class, she had creative and financial opportunities that helped her when she first started out in life. Her mother encouraged MacLaine to take acting and dancing lessons in which the actress and author excelled. She became successful beyond her wildest dreams due to the nature of this yoga, which seems to provide extremely "lucky" circumstances. This is illustrated by the "coinci-

PLANETS	SIDEREAL POSITIONS
Ascendant	6° Virgo 20'
Sun	11° Aries 08'
Moon	14° Leo 14'
Mars	8° Aries 49'
Mercury	22° Pisces 35'
Jupiter	23° Virgo 27' (Retrograde)
Venus	25° Aquarius 06'
Saturn	3° Aquarius 44'
North Node	23° Capricorn 23'
South Node	23° Cancer 23'

Table 5. Shirley MacLaine's Vedic Ascendant and Planets

dence" that catapulted MacLaine to instant stardom. While understudying the lead in a Broadway show, the star suddenly became ill and MacLaine took over the role. On that particular night, a movie producer happened to be in the audience and the rest is history.

As you can see from these examples, this raj yoga provides auspicious circumstances that can start you out in life. While you may be blessed with this special gift, it is still up to you to muster the determination and perseverance that allows this yoga to endure throughout your life.

FINDING YOUR AYANAMSA

If you do not know your sidereal positions, you can deduct the *ayanamsa,* or difference between the two zodiacs, of your birth year according to Table 6.

Briefly stated, the ayanamsa represents the difference between the tropical 0 degrees Aries (vernal equinox) and the sidereal/vedic or "actual" 0 degrees Aries, which is related to the fixed stars rather than the equinoxes. Because the vernal point travels slightly backward through the sidereal zodiac, the ayanamsa increases only 50.23 seconds each year. When the ayanamsa

Birth Year	Ayanamsa	Birth Year	Ayanamsa
1900	22°22'	1960	23°12'
1910	22°31'	1970	23°20'
1920	22°39'	1980	23°29'
1930	22°47'	1990	23°37'
1940	22°54'	2000	23°46'
1950	23°04'		

Table 6. Ayanamsas

reaches 30 degrees of its current cycle, it will have reached 0 degrees Pisces. As it begins its retrograde journey through Aquarius, the true Age of Aquarius will have officially begun.

You can calculate the sidereal position of a planet like the Moon by subtracting the ayanamsa for your birth year from your tropical Moon (the degree of your Moon in a regular tropical astrological birthchart). Let's use President Bill Clinton as an example. According to the tropical zodiac, Clinton's Moon is located at 20 degrees 18 minutes Taurus. If we subtract the ayanamsa of 23 degrees (22 degrees 54 minutes, rounded off) for his birth year of 1946, we arrive at a sidereal Moon position of 27 degrees 18 minutes of Aries.

FURTHER READING

Braha, James. *Ancient Hindu Astrology for the Modern Western Astrologer.* Hollywood: Hermetician Press, 1986.

Braha, James. *How to Predict Your Future.* Hollywood: Hermetician Press, 1994.

DeFouw, Hart. *Light on Life: An Introduction to the Astrology of India.* London: Arkana Books, 1996.

Dreyer, Ronnie Gale. *Vedic Astrology: A Guide to the Fundamentals of Jyotish.* York Beach: Samuel Weiser Inc., 1997.

Frawley, David. *The Astrology of the Seers.* Salt Lake City: Passage Press, 1990.

Psychic and Spiritual Planets in Astrology

By Estelle Daniels

In astrology, most everyone is familiar with their Sun sign. "What's your sign?" means what is your Sun sign. It's easy to figure because it just depends on your birthdate, and there you have it. But what about people whose personalities seem to contradict their Sun-sign description? For example, what about an Aries who feels he or she is more shy, mystical, and psychic than the usual description of that sign? The stereotypical Aries is aggressive, active, a warrior who acts or speaks before thinking.

In determining psychic and spiritual potentials in a birth chart, an astrologer can look at many factors. In my research, I have discovered several reliable indicators of psychic potential that I will share with you here. Surprisingly, none are based on the Sun sign.

Certain astrological influences carry specific psychic abilities. These are very broad areas, but they can give you an idea in which direction your talents may lie. A main way to classify astrological signs is the elements—fire, earth, air, and water. All three signs of each element share common qualities. Aries, Leo, and Sagittarius are fire signs; Taurus, Virgo, and Capricorn are earth signs; Gemini, Libra, and Aquarius are air signs; Cancer, Scorpio, and Pisces are water signs.

Each element has a specific method of psychic and spiritual energy expression. Look for the element that appears most often in your chart, and you will discover the easiest way for you to handle spiritual energies. If your Moon, Ascendant, and Mercury are all in different elements, you have a broad range of psychic expressions to draw on. If they concentrate in two elements or just one element, you have fewer modes of expression, but you have more power in the mode with two or more factors represented.

Well, a full astrological chart has a lot more than just a Sun sign. The standard astrological chart has ten planets (Sun, Moon, Mercury, Venus, Mars, Jupiter, Saturn, Uranus, Neptune, and Pluto) as well as all twelve signs and twelve sections of a circle, called houses. This makes for many more factors in a full astrological chart than just one of the twelve Sun signs.

To get a full astrological chart you need the date, year, exact time, and city of your birth. If you do not know the exact time, approximations may work. If you would like to order a natal chart, see the back of this book for an order form from Llewellyn Computerized Astrological Services. You can also consult an astrologer, who can construct and interpret your chart.

The first planet that can indicate psychic potential is the Moon. Whole books have been written about the Moon and its influences in the birthchart. When I look at a chart, I look to the Moon for spiritual needs. The sign the Moon occupies can indicate your psychic potential, while the house the Moon occupies can highlight the areas you can express your psychic abilities. More broadly, the Moon symbolizes your emotional needs and their mode of expression. It can also indicate where you hides when you feel threatened or want to get away from it all. For example, a person with their Moon in Gemini might retreat into books, while someone with Moon in Cancer might cook or hide out at home. The Moon describes instinctual habits and patterns of behavior that are comfortable and non-threatening.

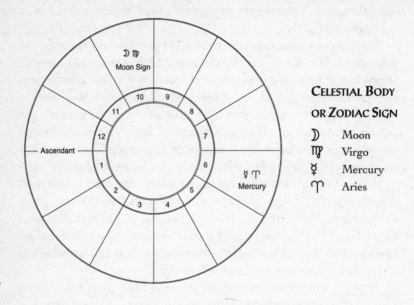

Celestial Body
or Zodiac Sign

☽	Moon
♍	Virgo
☿	Mercury
♈	Aries

Table 1. Sample Natal Chart Showing Placement of Ascendant, Moon Sign, and Mercury

Another big influence is the Ascendant or rising sign. This is the sign located on the horizon at birth and determines the mask you wear as you go out into the world and encounter others. It defines the person's style of relating to the world. This sign can also signal psychic potential, sometimes more than the Sun sign. If there are planets in the Ascendant (also known as the First House), these can also modify a person's psychic abilities and expressions. As the Ascendant is the mask a person wears out in the world, that then becomes the expression most people know the individual for. This can be one factor in determining the "shy" Aries. If a person's Ascendant is in a sign that complements their Sun sign, they will have a mask similar to their "inner nature." If the Ascendant is in a sign at cross-purposes to the Sun sign, they will present a face that can be at odds with their "inner nature." That explains the "shy Aries" or the quiet, gentle Pisces who hides behind a mask of aggression, loud talk, and bluster. Fire and air signs are complementary; so are earth and water signs. Fire and water are not complementary, and neither are combinations of earth and air, fire and earth, nor water and air.

Think of the distinction between the Sun sign and Ascendant or rising sign this way: When you are at a party and everyone is presenting their public face and company manners, you are meeting their Ascendants. They are out in public, they may be a little on their guard and perhaps not totally at ease, so they retreat behind their Ascendant or public persona. If you get to know one of those people well, and form a friendship with them, then you gradually get to know the Sun sign, the true inner expression of the person. How accurately that public persona reflects the inner person depends on how complementary the Sun sign and rising signs are. Only about one-twelfth of the population has the same Sun sign and rising sign (people born around sunrise), so most people have Ascendants that are different from their Sun signs.

The third factor I look at is the placement of Mercury, by sign and house. Mercury is never more than 28 degrees from the Sun, but it is very important, as it is the planet that processes information and gives us our conscious interface with the world. Mercury is also the planet of the mage or magician and its location in a person's chart is another indicator of psychic and spiritual abilities. If it is in the same sign as the Sun, it makes it easier for a person to communicate their basic inner self. Their mind is more subjective and experiences are evaluated more by how it affects the individual personally. If Mercury is in a different sign from the Sun, it gives a mind that is more detached and objective, but the person may be less able to effectively communicate their basic inner nature. They are better able to objectify experiences and see the wider implications beyond just how the individual may be affected.

Mercury is the planet of communication, everyday life, and interaction. How you speak and communicate ties directly to your Mercury. How you go about your daily routine also ties into Mercury. How you think and how your mind works are also Mercury expressions. Because so much psychic and spiritual work is mental, and has to do with mind-sets and inner visualization, Mercury becomes a vital factor in how a person manifests psychic talent or goes about satisfying their spiritual yearnings. If Mercury is located in the same sign as their Sun, they may find their spiritual expressions easier to manifest than if Mercury is placed in a different sign from their Sun.

Let the Elements Be Your Guide

None of the elements or signs are inherently better or worse than any other. Each shows a distinct way of expressing life force. Each is better at some things and worse at others. You are what you are, and you can either drift along and take the world as it comes and react in a knee-jerk fashion, or you can be as pro-active as possible, choosing your reactions according to the situation and making the most of your strengths and weaknesses. Ultimately, astrology is a tool to help a person see just where their strengths and weaknesses lie, and how to best take advantage of the good points and minimize the bad points. Astrology can also pinpoint the times to let the good shine through or tough it out and use some of those rough edges to ride through a bad patch. Theoretically, we all have what we need to be able to cope with life as it comes to us.

Fire Signs

Aries, Leo, and Sagittarius are energy workers. They can manipulate energy for use in healing. They like fire and can use flames as a focus for divination. They have much enthusiasm but can get disenchanted or bored if things don't move along. They like to feel the energies as they work, and one good energy rush will keep them going for a long time. They can give energy to others, but need to be sure that the energy is wanted, and that they don't give away so much of it that they starve their own flames. Active psychic work like martial arts or dance attracts fire people, as they like to keep moving.

Earth Signs

Taurus, Virgo, and Capricorn are creators on the material plane. They are least effective in the ethereal realms, as they need to be able to tangibly measure their results. They judge actions by their results, so purely spiritual workings hold little fascination for them. They work best with tried-and-true formulas and tools that have proven useful in the past. They will work hard if they understand what they will get out of the effort. They will stick to projects to the bitter end. Working with rocks and crystals is effective for earth people. They can also be wonderful gardeners, builders, and creators on the material plane. It may take quite a bit to get these people moving, as they are more inclined to be still and remain in one place, but once they start they can become perpetual motion with enough incentive.

AIR SIGNS

Gemini, Libra, and Aquarius are mental and verbal acrobats. They like the idea of telepathy, mind-to-mind communication, clairvoyance, and all the mental disciplines of psychic advancement. They also can write well and may write chants, meditations, and the like. They get good results with mantras. They like the mental challenge of psychic development and things have to be kept interesting for them to pay attention. Keep their mind busy and they will accomplish much. If they get bored, they are off to the next project. Movement can be beneficial for these people, but just talk is also effective. These people are good communicators and networkers, either in person through travel or on the Internet via computer. These people are natural teachers who can impart information to others.

WATER SIGNS

Cancer, Scorpio, and Pisces are the natural psychics of the zodiac. They work well in the ethereal realms, and if they can "feel" it, they can work with it. They make good psychic barometers and psychic sponges. These people need to be careful to shield themselves from unwanted influences. They work well with clairvoyance and all forms of divination. Because their mood can affect their effectiveness, learning meditation and emotional calming techniques will increase their accuracy and abilities to work for longer periods without tiring. They must be careful not to overtax their abilities, and can burn out if overworked. They have great empathy and may be tempted to help others, even to their own detriment. Water signs can tire easily, but if they do get moving they can enjoy dance and other active psychic techniques.

Psych Out Your Psychic Abilities

Study your birthchart for the location of Moon, rising sign, and Mercury. What signs are represented? How are they different from your Sun sign? How well do these energies blend with your Sun sign? How well do they blend with each other? What houses of your birthchart are occupied by your Moon and Mercury? Are they the same or different from the house your Sun is in?

Generally the Moon will show innate psychic talent, stuff you do unconsciously and naturally. Mercury will show what talents you can work with and develop, things you might be able to teach yourself or learn from others. The rising sign shows your style of dealing with the world and those psychic talents you might use in creating your defenses and in reaching out to others.

Realize that signs and houses have similar influences, but they are not the same. I have combined them here for simplicity and ease of interpretation. Blend the keywords for the placements and see what you can come up with. Aries, Capricorn, and Sagittarius blend into a warrior hermit philosopher or a daredevil prime-minister gypsy. Some combinations may seem silly or absurd, but one will probably stick out as strangely apt for your mode of spiritual expression. Blending keywords for your Sun sign, Moon sign, and rising sign can give you a catch phrase for your basic life expression. This may change with time and circumstances. Give it a try, and discover how you might be able to work with the psychic and spiritual energies.

The Aries or First-House Psychic

Aries or First-House psychics are pioneers and innovators who like to be first. They are good at energy work. They start lots of projects but aren't too good at carrying through and finishing those projects. They can be psychic warriors, preferring action to diplomacy and negotiation. They may prefer to work solo, or want to lead a group. They can get bored quickly and need encouragement in their workings. Feed their egos and they will do most anything for you. They don't like doing anything that has nothing in it for them. They like to wear red and may play with fire, literally and figuratively. These people are quick to anger, but just as quick to forgive and move on. Impatience may be a problem and they may neglect precautions or even court danger. They can be effective in emergency situations, but can become belligerent if they are challenged. They have enormous courage. They also have a tendency to act first and think later. Even in established groups, they often come up with innovations or new techniques, which can be highly effective. Keywords are pioneer, daredevil, warrior, and survivor.

THE TAURUS OR SECOND-HOUSE PSYCHIC

Taurus or Second-House psychics are sensualists and Earth worshippers. They can be into music and dance. They have enormous patience and appreciate beauty and harmony. Sometimes they may be indolent, impossible to get going, but if they are motivated to action, they become an irresistible force. They work well with talismans, tools, and other objects to focus their psychic powers. Tasty food and drink are important to satisfy their appetites. They like flowers and plants, pretty but preferably also edible or usable as herbs or perfumes. They have a green thumb, if they put their hands to Earth. They like routine and stability and tend to stay with one style of psychic work. Ethics are important and they spend time formulating their own ethical codes, which can become rigid if they are pushed too far. They prefer to stay near home, with their creature comforts and familiar surroundings; roughing it is not their style. Anger comes slowly and after much provocation, but when they blow, beware of being in the way, for they don't slow down until all their anger is spent. They do well with money meditations. They love sensual things that make them feel good both inside and out. Keywords are musician, Earth spirit, silent one, and solid citizen.

THE GEMINI OR THIRD-HOUSE PSYCHIC

Gemini or Third-House psychics are jacks-of-all-trades and trivia experts who keep an amazing amount of information on the strangest things in their brains, which seemingly have no storage capacity limit. They are wonderful with words. They are the true eclectics, only stealing from the very best. They go with the flow and adapt to the prevailing style. These people like to be members of several groups, so they have a variety of psychic expressions. They are the networkers in their communities and possibly the worst gossips. Telepathy comes easily. They like to write and communicate about their own and others' psychic experiences. They like to travel to different areas to experience other styles. They read voraciously and probably have a library envied by many. They don't like to stay still, and they cannot talk if their hands are tied behind their back. They often practice their spirituality in group settings, rather than alone. They are lost without a telephone, mail service, or an Internet link. Keywords are teacher, journalist, storyteller, networker, and witness.

THE CANCER OR FOURTH-HOUSE PSYCHIC

Cancer or Fourth-House psychics are empathic, sensitive souls who are able to divine the motives of others. They can be mother hens, worrying about people who may be hurting or in trouble. They like to cook and probably practice a wonderful brand of kitchen magic. They revere the past and traditions and can be the historians of their communities. Mediumistic abilities can be pronounced, and they are good with divination and scrying. They prefer to use their psychic abilities to protect their homes. They can be shy and retiring, but they also make effective leaders who can organize activities. They need time alone to recharge and can become psychic chameleons, soaking up the vibes of any gathering they attend. They need to learn detachment to shield themselves from unwanted psychic energy, or they can become psychic victims, mirroring the feelings and attitudes of their group and may make the psychic community their family. They can be simultaneously extremely effective in some areas and helpless in others. They need hugs and cuddles. They are good at spotting someone who is acting out of character. They have a superior capacity for intimacy, which can scare off many people. They are so sensitive that they can develop a hard shell to protect them from the hurts and injustices of life. Keywords are sensitive, mother, invisible person, and healer.

The Leo or Fifth-House Psychic

Leo or Fifth-House psychics are show-offs who revel in being the center of attention. They are happiest when others acknowledge their accomplishments and abilities. They like parties and fun. They can be artistic and dramatic and need to be able to express themselves in their own unique creative ways. They like children and relate well to them, but do not always become parents because they are really just big children themselves. They have a talent for theatrical ceremonies and circles. They can work well with children. They have a talent for love spells. They are the showpeople and clowns of the psychic community, and can become disruptive and petty if they feel their contributions don't get proper recognition. They can be generous to a fault, and really enjoy the grand gesture. They have strong willpower. They can use fine arts in magic, expressing themselves through ritual painting or sculpture. They are honest and loyal, though if you hurt their pride, they will never fully trust you ever again. Keywords are monarch, child, clown, movie star, aristocrat, and performer.

The Virgo or Sixth-House Psychic

Virgo or Sixth-House psychics are craftspeople who like working with their hands. They are good at gardening, growing herbs and medicinal plants. They like making tools and other objects they may or may not sell. They want things to be perfect and may criticize their own work, pointing out miniscule flaws and imperfections. They are good with details and numbers and are micro-managers. They need to keep busy or they can decide that *you* will be their next project. They have a reputation for being nit-picky and drive people crazy, pointing out reasons why things cannot be done or are impractical. They are shamans, relating well to animals, and they probably have spirit guides. They are into health and diet and may be vegetarians. They like the idea of ritual purification and may fast to cleanse the body and achieve spiritual enlightenment. They are happiest when they feel useful or have accomplished something. Keywords are critic, analyst, servant, martyr, and perfectionist.

THE LIBRA OR SEVENTH-HOUSE PSYCHIC

Libra or Seventh-House psychics are peacemakers and diplomats. They like working with a partner and do not like being alone. They love weddings. They like truth and beauty and other pleasant abstracts. Balance and harmony are important and they dislike discord. They are the quintessential devil's advocates and will take the other side in an argument, just to ensure that all sides will be represented. They can be the advocate for those who are unwilling or unable to speak. Their rituals include both women and men, because they believe that each needs the other. They tend to believe in good, and can become sweetness and light. They like music and dance, with a partner or as part of a group. They like to wear pretty things, ritual garb, or jewelry. They have trouble making up their minds and may delay initiations or commitments because they feel irrevocable steps cut them off from their options. They like to give and receive hugs and cuddles. They like things to be elegant, charming, and classy. They will try to make their corner of the world as easy on the eyes as possible. Keywords are diplomat, host, peacemaker, artist, lover.

THE SCORPIO OR EIGHTH-HOUSE PSYCHIC

Scorpio or Eighth-House psychics like to delve in the depths. They are intensely interested in matters concerning sex, death, and transformation. They like to explore Tantra. They may have very intense and interesting initiatory experiences, and may have nifty collections of New Age "toys." They can be good with money and prosperity meditations, and may be able to successfully do these types of affirmations for others. They are fascinated by the dark side of human nature and seek to embrace the depths in themselves and encourage others to do the same. They are more interested in the villains than heroes because the villains are more complex, driven characters. They have enormous courage and willpower and these are the people who are most likely to try and "conjure Chthulu," just to see if it can be done. They can be psychic warriors, guarding their friends from real and perceived threats. They have many secrets they will never reveal, but will try to uncover others' secrets, because they want to know. They can in extreme cases become paranoid. Research is a hobby. They tell it like it is, in as blunt and forceful a manner as possible. They don't believe in sugar-coating the truth. They are natural detectives, picking out the details and inconsistencies others miss. Keywords are detective, hypnotist, and sorcerer.

THE SAGITTARIUS OR NINTH-HOUSE PSYCHIC

Sagittarius or Ninth-House psychics like to do things in grand style, with all the bells and whistles. They are philosophers and get into comparative studies and obscure disciplines. They can be good at astral travel, dreamwork, predicting the future, and divination in general. They are good with languages and enjoy rituals with non-English words or from other cultures or traditions. They are most likely to become accredited ministers. They like to travel and love to learn and can become eternal students, learning one discipline after another or studying one subject for years to become expert in all its phases. They can become pompous and overbearing, and in extreme cases act like misplaced old-time preachers. They think of life as an adventure. They like physical disciplines like martial arts, which hone the body as well as the mind. They can suffer from foot-in-mouth disease, and are unintentionally adept at back-handed compliments. They mean no malice or harm, it just comes out that way. Keywords are gypsy, explorer, anthropologist, student, and philosopher.

THE CAPRICORN OR TENTH-HOUSE PSYCHIC

Capricorn or Tenth-House psychics are the archetypal elders who have wisdom beyond their years. They are good at organization and pay close attention to the mundane running of any group and are best at dealing with real world concerns. Recognition of achievement is important, so they may collect degrees to validate their knowledge and training. The more mature ones know that experience and wisdom are the only degrees needed for success in life. They like structured spirituality, the stuff that has to be done according to precise formula. They like to be the spiritual leaders of their groups. They may become hermits for a time, as solitude can be healing for these people. They like the mountains and enjoy working with rocks and crystals. They believe in working at spiritual projects; an honest, properly done effort generates an appropriate return. They may tend to allow the end to justify the means. They are result-oriented, and do not believe in well-meaning but ineffectual efforts. They can be the "wise ones" in their circle of friends. They can have a dry, spare wit. They tend to say little, but people listen when they speak, as they use the voice of authority. Keywords are hermit, father, prime minister, power behind the throne, authority, and strategist.

THE AQUARIUS OR ELEVENTH-HOUSE PSYCHIC

Aquarius or Eleventh-House psychics are the tricksters of the zodiac. They like to stir things up, create change, make chaos, upset the hierarchy, lead a revolution. They have incredible flashes of insight, but if they don't write these wonderful ideas down, can lose them as quickly as they came. They are very concerned for the group as a whole, and can forget the needs of individuals if they aren't careful. They prefer to work in groups. They like new, far-out ideas, rituals, and techniques. They may use astrology. They have a talent for spotting truths, although they may not communicate them in a comfortable or fashionable way. They can be the voice in the wilderness, preaching truths or ideas way ahead of their time. They may be more appreciated by later generations than their peers. Some can be rigid and traditionalist, but eventually they loosen up and become as weird and far-out as they once were Establishment. They like things they can prove, although their idea of proof is not always something that can be replicated in a laboratory. They like to make up the rules as they go along. They demand freedom for themselves and can rebel against dogmatic traditions that limit freedom of action and speech. Keywords are genius, scientist, revolutionary, truth-sayer, exile, and voice in the wilderness.

THE PISCES OR TWELFTH-HOUSE PSYCHIC

Pisces or Twelfth-House psychics are, in a sense, a combination of all the other types. Their personal belief system is what powers their workings. They can be mediums, psychics, exhibiting any or all of the psychic talents of the rest of the signs. They have a tendency to lose themselves in the ethereal realms. The best method for Pisces is pure meditation or other mind-altering techniques that do not rely on outside catalysts like drugs. They can make and use oils, incense, and perfumes. Because they aren't known for their grounding and centering abilities, they may want to have someone watching over them when doing their thing to help bring them back to the here and now, if needed. They are most likely to want to live entirely in ethereal realms and just leave the real world entirely. They can write beautiful poetry and excel at dance and song. They are able to see through the material into the ethereal. They can develop the talent to be able to "go between the worlds" at will. They can be effective psychic barometers. Some are incessant chatterboxes, talking about really nothing at all. Some are just quiet and dreamy, and may be daydreaming and not paying attention at all. Their imaginations are fantastic and they can notice things others overlook. Keywords are mystic, face dancer, poet, dreamer, seer, and romantic.

IT'S TIME TO WIND
THE PREDICTION CLOCK

BY NOEL TYL

T
imes to come are times that were. The world-change observations that follow for 1998 are based on real-time happenings in the past! That's the causal nature of progressive history and the challenge for astrological prediction.

We can make predictions that lead us forward in our fascinated study of astrology and our search to understand time. The right data increase the accuracy of our astrological predictions. So, here goes: views of the time far ahead, based on times yet to come, which in turn, are based on events that happened in the past. Let's hope our astrological clock is wound well!

THE UNITED STATES:
CLINTON UNDER SIEGE

There is very serious threat to President Bill Clinton's presidency. The first period of crisis is between October 1997 and July

1998. Several very clear astrological measurements lead to this conclusion. First, Clinton was inaugurated at a terribly negative time, as negative as were the inauguration times of Franklin D. Roosevelt for his last term, John F. Kennedy for his term, and Richard Nixon for his second term. The Clinton inauguration horoscope speaks of violent public attack from an international covert source. Yes, this means terrorist, subterfugal attack.

There can be another meaning for the symbols: a legal attack for misbehavior in office or international intrigue.

This potential also shows strongly in the horoscope of the United States (a horoscope that includes Gemini rising): A tremendous change of perspective is promised at the turn-of-the-year period into 1998. If this horoscope is accurate, we have corroboration of Clinton's difficulties.

There will have been a Congressional investigation of campaign fund-raising practices through the White House, which include influence-peddling by foreign governments. First Lady Hillary Clinton's involvement will have been highest between May and June 1997, and astrological signs point to trouble for her at year's end. Vice President Al Gore's horoscope erupts powerfully in terms of his career between January 30 and April 10, 1998.

President Clinton faces enormous legal attacks threatening to undermine his position throughout early 1997, peaking conspicuously in July, especially around July 5 and 29. He appears in a positive light with these issues at Christmastime 1997, but then another onslaught of jeopardy builds against him, another financial brouhaha emerges, and the threat to his personal safety escalates, maximally in the spring of 1998.

The interrelationship among these measurements heightens the probability of the forecast. Additionally, the public will demand a change of presidential image and national focus, away from political business and international outreach to health, education, and welfare issues here at home. It will be for the next president of the United States to attend to this shift of focus and mend America's education profile and life-value spectrum.

MIDDLE EAST:
PEACE TALKS THREATENED

Beginning in March 1998, the progress of Oslo II negotiations will achieve another milestone for the Palestinians and Palestine Liberation Organization Chairman Yasser Arafat. The talks will revive and escalate public fear and violent response in Israel, focused continuously on the fractured popularity and suspect incompetence of Israel's leader, Benjamin Netanyahu. The threat to Netanyahu's government is extreme between March and April 1998 and again in October 1998, to the point of a "vote of no-confidence," tantamount to impeachment. While the peace process itself will appear to be threatened once again, the negotiations will prevail throughout the harshest of uproars, en route to meeting the deadline of May 4, 1999.

The probability is high that the United States will be called into Israel to establish a dramatic presence and control the peace process in late March or early April 1998. U.S. intervention in Israel may indeed invite the problems Clinton faces personally in spring 1998.

IRAQ:
REBUILDING A NATION

The plot and maneuvers to overthrow Saddam Hussein in Iraq were predicted to come to light in August 1996; Saddam detected the CIA-backed mission and annihilated it. The continued effort to unseat Hussein surely continued and instigated an uprising of the people in the late summer and early fall of 1997.

Between January and February 1998, Iraq should begin its era of new freedom and alliances in the world. Plans will be made for the United States to extend enormous aid and reconstruction energy into Iraq. This gives the Americans strategic presence throughout the Middle East, controlling military staging areas and oil reserves.

In Jordan, King Hussein will have gained world recognition for successful trade and investment development for his country. The probability is high that he will be taken seriously ill in the fall of

1997, lasting until February 1998. King Hussein will be planning seriously to step aside in favor of his younger brother, Crown Prince Hassan. Watch for these developments to emerge beginning in August 1998.

SPAIN AND ENGLAND: FOCUS ON ROYALTY

These two countries are linked in the news because of the focus of attention on King Juan Carlos and Prince Charles at the same time in the spring of 1997. The personal danger to the king at the beginning of May 1997 will have brought to world view the extreme disorder in Spain linked to the "people's revolt," the demands made by the Basques for a separate nation within Spain. This will increase throughout 1998.

The critical personal danger to the Prince of Wales in the spring of 1997 will have called attention once again to his inability to succeed to the throne. The probability is high that he will ask permission to remarry from Queen Elizabeth and the Church of England and have that plea granted at the end of 1998. This will bring the rite of succession to the English throne to the foreground once again. Elizabeth will announce a change in succession to herald the Millennium, probably in spring 2000, naming Prince William of Wales as her heir, the next King of England.

THE PHILIPPINES AND CUBA: PASSING THE TORCH OF LEADERSHIP

Public dissent will rise in the Philippines in October 1997 and between May and November 1998, concurrent with national elections. General Fidel Ramos, who was elected by a million-vote margin in 1992, faces the high probability that he will not be re-elected. The nation is seeking freedom from long-time occupation, first by the Japanese, then by the Americans. The probable defeat of Ramos signals an end to the transition period to international autonomy.

In Cuba, Fidel Castro is facing the end-period of his life and the pressure to fulfill his rule with a decision to bring Cuba back into the free-world scheme of diplomacy and business. The U.S. embargo has been an enormous block for him. Around the turn of the year into 1998, it is highly probable that the United States will lift that embargo under pressure of business expansionism from the sugar, tourism, and oil lobbies in the United States and Canada. Diplomatic relations and trade with Cuba will be resumed.

JAPAN:
THE ECONOMY SLIDES

Japan is in chaos, politically and economically. The stock market is dropping drastically and continually. The system of financial business is in extreme disarray; hundreds of billions of dollars in bad loans, triggered by the collapse of the real-estate market, are plaguing all efforts to stabilize. Taxes have been boosted. The growth rate of the economy is at its lowest since the 1940s.

In the spring of 1998, more chaos will erupt in Japan: yet again, another government will be catapulted into power. The country is lurching toward social revolution and a new constitution beginning in spring 1999.

AUSTRALIA:
FINDING A NATIONAL VOICE

This geographically enormous nation is becoming world-significant with every step it takes toward independence from British dominion. Australia will finally achieve independent status in November and December 2001. While this process will have gained great support in the spring of 1997, there will be a significant setback in the spring of 1998, possibly a political scandal suspending debate until after elections in spring 1999.

SWITZERLAND:
BANKING SCANDAL ESCALATES

The national "neutral" image of Switzerland in this century of two world wars contrasts powerfully with its historical image throughout earlier centuries. In the past, Switzerland was a hotbed of war behavior. Foreign powers (especially the French) hired mercenaries from Switzerland not only because of their great fighting skill but also in exchange for monies to pay international debts. The Swiss fighters were even commandeered by Pope Julius II (in 1505) to serve as the Pope's personal guard force. It took the Treaty of Paris in 1815 and a constitutional prohibition set in 1874 to proclaim an eternal national neutrality and prohibit conscription of Swiss into foreign military service (except for the Papal Guard, which exists as Swiss today).

But the crystalline image of neutrality began to crack throughout the twentieth century, when the Swiss began stockpiling nuclear weapons, trading within the European Economic Community structures, and joined the International Monetary Fund. Finally, in 1995, the cracks appeared, and Swiss innocence collapsed with the revelation of the tens of billions of dollars worth of gold taken from Jews just before and during World War II that was never returned to the depositors. All of these developments are delineated in the national horoscope of Switzerland.

Disclosure of the "Holocaust funds" crisis, which began in the fall of 1995, will have peaked in disclosure by September and October 1997. The shame for the banking institutions of this banking nation is enormous.

Between April and June and in November 1998, an edict of worldwide reparations will be announced for the descendants of the Jewish depositors. The cash burden, even for the cash-rich Swiss National Bank, will be devastating and will affect the standard of living throughout the nation. New laws will jar the world of international commerce. The secrecy and protectionism of strategic Swiss bank accounts will be thoroughly revised, and the world of monetary transaction will be deeply, revolutionarily affected. In the process, anti-Semitism will grow rampant in Switzerland, and will become overt among the young. It will be many years before Switzerland will be able to eradicate the years of deception and duplicity from its national image.

CENTRAL AFRICA:
REVOLT FERMENTS IN ZAIRE, ANGOLA

The principal countries of Central Africa operate like alternating pistons, driving the troubled history of the area and the entire continent. One country drives the rebellion power line while another takes a hiatus; and then the resting nation drives ahead and the aggressive one is toppled. This is the situation once again in 1997 and 1998 in Zaire and Angola.

Zaire is under siege by covert forces outside the country. Formerly the Belgian Congo, the third-largest country in Africa, Zaire gained its independence and new name in 1976 and since then has been a mineral-rich but economically unstable nation under its long-time dictator Mobutu Sese Seko. Throughout 1997, the country will have been under siege, an echo of a mutiny in the country that was squashed late in 1991. The government of Zaire will have been defeated; Mobutu will be ousted from power between January and mid-April 1997, but he remains poised on the sidelines through the spring of 1998. The settling-in process for the new regime will not be peaceful; strife bordering on street enforcement of justice will threaten stability through spring 1998.

Angola is a country of intrigue, through the Marxist phases and revolution earlier with Zaire to its present-day, ostensibly supportive relationship with the United States. But it is Angola that will work successfully to topple Mobutu in Zaire.

This strife is vitally important in the overall scheme of African development, involving Uganda, Rwanda, Burundi, Tanzania to the east, and South Africa to the south.

CENTRAL AMERICA:
BORDER TENSION BUILDS

More trouble is due in Nicaragua. The United States occupied the country from 1912–1933. The powerful Somoza family ruled the country from 1937–1979; Sandinista guerrillas took over. Daniel Ortega was elected president of the Marxist-oriented government. Until 1990, the Sandinistas and the "contras" (those "against" the regime and aided by the United States) fought a civil war.

The present leader of a fourteen-party coalition is Violeta Barrios de Chamorro, but not for long. We can look for extreme, militaristic upheaval of the government in power beginning in February 1998 and peaking between May and July 1998.

The chief issue may well be land dispositions inherited from the Sandinistas. Tensions could spill over into Costa Rica, historically peaceful, proud not to have any military force, and touted as "extremely stable." Nicaragua and Costa Rica share a tense border. If our astrology is accurate for Costa Rica, we can expect the peace to be disturbed in January and between May and June 1998. Should this unrest infect Costa Rica, we can expect an attenuated debilitation and government overhaul into the spring of 1999.

THE VATICAN:
EXPECT A NEW POPE

Pope John Paul II has defied the astrological lay-of-the-heavens that has been highly reliable in Vatican affairs for almost seventy years. A major transition has been imminent for two years, with a new pope at the helm. The probability is still high that the change will have begun around July 1997. Indeed, the change has begun with regard to policy: a thrust for ecumenism pointed up dramatically in the Pope's plea to bring East and West together within the church, presented in his undoubtedly final Encyclical, on May 30, 1995. But the change of the pope himself is imminent, overdue, and vital to the turns of events due for the Vatican.

A major event in church history may well occur between October 15 and November 22, 1997. The point is that a new era is already beginning, begun by Pope John XXIII and brought along into maturation by popes Paul VI and John Paul II.

The leadership vector of the papacy is changing: perhaps two more popes are to come before we see the Vatican changed completely away from a political and missionary cutting force to a softer, ecumenical outreach of health, education, and welfare. The pope is scheduled to visit Cuba early in 1998 and to visit Israel shortly thereafter. The question is: Which pope? An African pope? For what reasons? The end of 1997 and the beginning of 1998 should give us answers.

Planetary Associations

Sun: Authority figures, favors, health, success, display, drama, promotion, fun, and matters related to Leo and the Fifth House.

Moon: Short trips, women, children, the public, domestic concerns, emotions, fluids, and matters related to Cancer and the Fourth House.

Mercury: Communications, correspondence, phone calls, computers, messages, education, students, travel, merchants, editing, writing, advertising, siblings, neighbors, kin, matters related to Gemini, Virgo, and the Third and Sixth houses.

Venus: Affection, relationships, partnerships, alliances, grace, beauty, harmony, luxury, love, art, music, social activity, marriage, decorating, cosmetics, gifts, income, matters related to Taurus, Libra, and the Second and Seventh houses.

Mars: Strife, aggression, sex, physical energy, muscular activity, guns, tools, metals, cutting, surgery, police, soldiers, matters related to Aries, Scorpio, and the First and Eighth houses.

Jupiter: Publishing, college education, long-distance travel, foreign interests, religion, philosophy, forecasting, broadcasting, publicity, expansion, luck, growth, sports, horses, the law, matters related to Sagittarius, Pisces, and Ninth and Twelfth house issues.

Saturn: Structure, reality, the laws of society, limits, obstacles, tests, hard work, endurance, real estate, dentists, bones, matters related to Capricorn, Aquarius, and the Tenth and Eleventh houses.

Uranus: Astrology, the New Age, technology, computers, modern gadgets, lecturing, advising, counseling, inventions, reforms, electricity, new methods, originality, sudden events, and matters related to Aquarius and the Eleventh House.

Neptune: Mysticism, music, imagination, dance, illusion, sacrifice, service oil, chemicals, paint, drugs, anesthesia, sleep, religious experience, matters related to Pisces and the Twelfth House.

Pluto: Probing, penetration, goods of the dead, investigation, insurance, taxes, other people's money, loans, the masses, the underworld, transformation, death, matters related to Scorpio and the Eighth House.

LLEWELLYN'S

DIRECTORY
OF PRODUCTS
AND SERVICES

RESOURCES FOR
THE NEW AGE:

- Astrological Readings
  and Counseling
- Llewellyn Books,
  Calendars, and
  Personal Services
- Astrological
  Computer Software
- New Age Bookstores
  and Gift Shops
- Metaphysical Schools
- Psychic Advice Lines

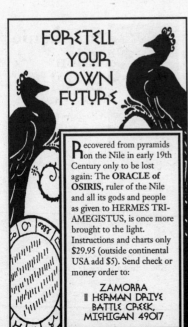

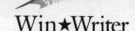
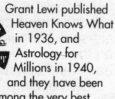

Gloria Star

Personal, professional
Astrological services
(by appointment only)

(860) 664-3590
e-mail: Glostar@aol.com

9AM-5PM Eastern Time
Tuesday - Saturday

P.O. Box 311
Clinton, CT 06413

Also available for classes, lectures and workshops.

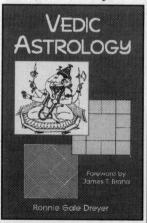

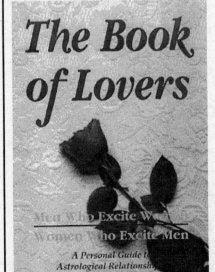

Celebrate the Craft Every Day

JANUARY: House & home by Edain McCoy

FEBRUARY: Celebration of Imbolc by Raymond Buckland

MARCH: Celebration of Ostara by Raven Grimassi

APRIL: Planting magical gardens by Patricia Monaghan

MAY: Celebration of Beltane by Silver RavenWolf and Bried Foxsong

JUNE: Celebration of Midsummer by Ed Fitch

JULY: The herb harvest by David Harrington

AUGUST: Celebration of Lammas by Pauline Campanelli

SEPTEMBER: Celebration of Mabon by Raven Grimassi

OCTOBER: Celebration of Samhain by Silver RavenWolf

NOVEMBER: Divination by D. J. Conway

DECEMBER: Celebration of Yule by Timothy Roderick

Celebrate! This new, all-Witches calendar was designed especially for you, whether you're a solitary Witch, a coven member, a Witch new to the Wiccan path, or one who has journeyed far along that road. Every Witch looking for new ways to keep the Old Ways alive will find them in the *Witches' Calendar*.

Every month, you'll find articles by the most respected writers in Wiccadom on everything from celebrating the Sabbats and planting a pentacle garden to blessing your home. To give your year an extra shine, each page offers invocations and recipes that tie in with each month's theme. But that's only the beginning ... each page of the *Witches' Calendar* is loaded with vital information: herb lore, planting dates, placement of the Moon and planets, color correspondences for each day, Wiccan holidays, spells, important dates in Wiccan history—plus 8 pages of "fundamentals" and tips for beginning Witches.

LLEWELLYN'S 1998 WITCHES CALENDAR
36 pp. • full-color • 13" x 10" • Order # K-938 • $12.00
To order call 1-800-THE-MOON

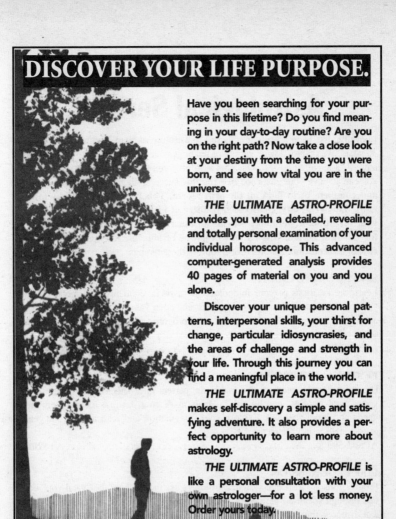

Llewellyn's Computerized Astrological Services

Llewellyn has been a leading authority in astrological chart readings for more than 30 years. We feature a wide variety of readings with the intent to satisfy the needs of any astrological enthusiast. Our goal is to give you the best possible service so that you can achieve your goals and live your life successfully. **Be sure to give accurate and complete birth data on the order form. This includes exact time (A.M. or P.M.), date, year, city, county and country of birth. Note: Noon will be used as your birthtime if you don't provide an exact time. Check your birth certificate for this information! Llewellyn will not be responsible for mistakes from inaccurate information.** An order form follows these listings.

SIMPLE NATAL CHART
Learn the locations of your midpoints and aspects, elements, and more. Discover your planets and house cusps, retrogrades, and other valuable data necessary to make a complete interpretation. Matrix Software programs and designs The Simple Natal Chart printout.
APS03-119 . . . .$5.00

PERSONALITY PROFILE
Our most popular reading also makes the perfect gift! This 10-part profile depicts your "natal imprint" and how the planets mark your destiny. Examine emotional needs and inner feelings. Explore your imagination and read about your general characteristics and life patterns.
APS03-503 . . . .$20.00

LIFE PROGRESSION
Progressions are a special system astrologers use to map how the "natal you" develops through specified periods of your present and future life. With this report you can discover the "now you!" This incredible reading covers a year's time and is designed to complement the Personality Profile Reading. **Specify present residence.**
APS03-507 . . . .$20.00

COMPATIBILITY PROFILE
Are you compatible with your lover, spouse, friend, or business partner? Find out with this in-depth look at each person's approach to the relationship. Evaluate goals, values, potential conflicts. This service includes planetary placements for both individuals, so send birth data for both. **Indicate each person's gender and the type of relationship involved** (romance, business, etc.).
APS03-504 . . . .$30.00

PERSONAL RELATIONSHIP INTERPRETATION

If you've just called it quits on one relationship and know you need to understand more about yourself before testing the waters again, then this is the report for you! This reading will tell you how you approach relationships in general, what kind of people you look for and what kind of people might rub you the wrong way. Important for anyone!

APS03-506 ....$20.00

TRANSIT REPORT

Keep abreast of positive trends and challenging periods in your life. Transits are the relationships between the planets today and their positions at your birth. They are an invaluable timing and decision-making aid. This report starts on the first day of the month, devotes a paragraph to each of your transit aspects and their effective dates. *Be sure to specify your present residence.*

APS03-500 – 3-month report $12.00
APS03-501 – 6-month report $20.00
APS03-502 – 1-year report $30.00

BIORHYTHM REPORT

Some days you have unlimited energy, then the next day you feel sluggish and awkward. These cycles are called biorhythms. This individual report accurately maps your daily biorhythms and thoroughly discusses each day. Now you can plan your days to the fullest!

APS03-515 – 3-month report $12.00
APS03-516 – 6-month report $18.00
APS03-517 – 1-year report $25.00

TAROT READING

Find out what the cards have in store for you with this 12-page report that features a 10-card "Celtic Cross" spread shuffled and selected especially for you. For every card that turns up there is a detailed corresponding explanation of what each means for you. Order this tarot reading today! *Indicate the number of shuffles you want.*

APS03-120 ....$10.00

LUCKY LOTTO REPORT (State Lottery Report)

Do you play the state lotteries? This report will determine your luckiest sequence of numbers for each day based on specific planets, degrees, and other indicators in your own chart. Give your full birth data and middle name. *Tell us how many numbers your state lottery requires in sequence, and the highest possible numeral. Indicate the month you want to start.*

APS03-512 – 3-month report $10.00
APS03-513 – 6-month report $15.00
APS03-514 – 1-year report $25.00

NUMEROLOGY REPORT

Find out which numbers are right for you with this insightful report. This report uses an ancient form of numerology invented by Pythagoras to determine the significant numbers in your life. Using both your name and date of birth, this report will calculate those numbers that stand out as yours. With these numbers, you can tell when the important periods of your life will occur. ***Please indicate your full birth name.***

APS03-508 – 3-month report $12.00
APS03-509 – 6-month report $18.00
APS03-510 – 1-year report $25.00

ULTIMATE ASTRO-PROFILE

More than 40 pages of insightful descriptions of your qualities and talents. Read about your burn rate (thirst for change). Explore your personal patterns (inside and outside). The Astro-Profile doesn't repeat what you've already learned from other personality profiles, but considers the natal influence of the lunar nodes, plus much more.

APS03-505 .... $40.00

ASTROLOGICAL SERVICES ORDER FORM

SERVICE NAME & NUMBER_____

_____

Provide the following data on all persons receiving a service:

1ST PERSON'S FULL NAME, including current middle & last name(s)

_____

Birthplace (city, county, state, country) _____

_____

Birthtime _____ ☐ A.M. ☐ P.M. Month _____ Day _____ Year _____

2ND PERSON'S FULL NAME (if ordering for more than one person)

_____

Birthplace (city, county, state, country) _____

_____

Birthtime _____ ☐ A.M. ☐ P.M. Month _____ Day _____ Year _____

BILLING INFORMATION

Name _____

Address _____

_____

City _____ State _____ Zip _____

Country _____ Day phone: _____

Make check or money order payable to Llewellyn Publications, or charge it!
Check one: ☐ Visa ☐ MasterCard ☐ American Express

Acct. No. _____ Exp. Date _____

Cardholder Signature _____

Mail this form and payment to:

LLEWELLYN'S PERSONAL SERVICES
P.O. BOX 64383, DEPT. K932-6 • ST. PAUL, MN 55164-0383

Allow 4-6 weeks for delivery.